WILDMAN!

The Monstrous and Mysterious Saga of the 'British Bigfoot'

NICK REDFERN

Edited by Corinna Downes/Jonathan Downes
Typeset by Jessica Heard
Cover and Internal Layout by Jon Downes for CFZ Communications
Using Microsoft Word 2000, Microsoft Publisher 2000, Adobe Photoshop.

First edition published 2012 by CFZ Publications

FORTEAN WORDS
Myrtle Cottage
Woolfardisworthy
Bideford
North Devon
EX39 5QR

ISBN: 978-1-909488-04-5

Dedication

For Neil Arnold: a good friend, and fine researcher of, and writer on, monsters, mysteries and all-things macabre. Keep on doing what you are doing, mate!

CONTENTS

Introduction

THE CASE FILES

Chapter 1: Woodwose and Wild Men

Chapter 2: Tales of the Green Man

Chapter 3: The Apes of Shugborough

Chapter 4: Nightmare in 1971

Chapter 5: The Cursed Canal

Chapter 6: Welsh Wild Men

Chapter 7: The Creature of the Lake

Chapter 8: Dartmoor's Hairy Hands

Chapter 9: London's Underground Monstrosities

Chapter 10: The Tragic Tale of Patient X

Chapter 11: Shug Monkeys on the Loose

Chapter 12: A Bridge to Weird

Chapter 13: Slitting Mill's Hairy Trolls

Chapter 14: 'The silence was strange, the landscape unfamiliar...'

Chapter 15: The Cleadon Creature

Chapter 16: A Monstrous Castle

Chapter 17: Go Wild in the Country

Chapter 18: Monsters of the Magic Ring

Chapter 19: The Beasts of Derbyshire

Chapter 20: A Cackling Creature in an Irish Castle

Chapter 21: Sasquatch on the Chase

Chapter 22: A Real Life Stig of the Dump

Chapter 23: Southern Archives

Chapter 24: The Big Grey Man of the Mountains

Chapter 25: Bigfoot in Scotland

Chapter 26: The Littlefoot Phenomenon

Chapter 27: The Baboons of Britain

Chapter 28: Old Ned's Devil and More

THE THEORIES

Chapter 29: A Flesh and Blood Animal?

Chapter 30: Fakery in the U.K.

Chapter 31: The Myth of Menageries and Missing Animals

Chapter 32: Welcome to the Ghost Apes

Chapter 33: From Man to Beast

Chapter 34: UFOs: Connections and Controversies

Chapter 35: Beasts of the Mind

Chapter 36: Mutilations and Anomalous Animals

Chapter 37: Of Hairy Men, Beastly Bridges, and Water-Horses

Chapter 38: From Neolithic to Neanderthal

Chapter 39: Panic on the Mountains

Chapter 40: Rebooting to the Realm of Monsters

Conclusions

About Nick Redfern

Acknowledgments

Sources

INTRODUCTION

O n far more than a few occasions, people have asked me what it was that prompted me to immerse myself so deeply in the dark and disturbing worlds of flying saucers, the Loch Ness Monster, Roswell, Area 51, Mothman, the Men in Black and, of course, the subject of this very book: Bigfoot in Britain. Actually, there was not one reason at all, but a significant handful of them. They were all linked to matters of a definitive supernatural, conspiratorial, or just plain weird, nature but in vastly different ways. And here they are...

Number One, UFOs:

During the early 1950s my dad, Frank Redfern, like all young men of his age at that time, had to serve three years of National Service. And, having a passion for aircraft, he chose to join the Royal Air Force. During his three years in the RAF, and before returning to his regular job as a carpenter, which he held until his retirement at the age of sixty-five, he was trained in the field of, and worked on, radar.

It was towards the end of his service that my dad was involved in several radar-based UFO encounters, all of which occurred at the height of a September 1952 NATO operation, called Exercise Mainbrace. On each occasion, fast moving objects of unknown origin were tracked on the radar-screens, fighter planes were scrambled, and the ominous and official stamp of secrecy came firmly down on just about everyone and everything.

Certainly, my dad didn't tell me about this most weird affair until I was in my early teens, around 1978 or 1979, if memory serves me correct. It was an event that got me deeply interested in UFOs, and set me on a path to seek out the truth concerning all things saucer-shaped and flying. And it's a strange and conspiracy-filled path that I'm still on today. And, arguably, those September 1952 events left a deep and lasting impression on my dad, too, since – if asked - he is still willing to talk about them to this very day.

Number Two, Cryptozoology:

When I was barely four or five years old, my parents took me on a week's holiday to Scotland. And, if you're going to go to Scotland, well, you just have to visit Loch Ness, which is precisely what we did. Although I have now been to the loch on many occasions, the first time is the one I have never forgotten.

Granted, and hardly surprisingly given my young age at the time, my memories of that long-gone day are very brief and deeply fragmentary, but I do recall standing on the shore and staring out, wondering if there really was a monster - or monsters - in those dark waters. I may not have really known it back then, but that holiday got me hooked on, and captivated by, the strange realm of sinister beasts.

Number Three, Animal Mutilations:

I grew up in a small village in central England called Pelsall, which is a very old village, to say the least: Its origins date back to 994 A.D. But, far more important and relevant than that, Pelsall is located only about a five minute drive from the site of what, ultimately, became one of the most controversial, weird, and - some even said - paranormal-themed events of the early 20th Century. And it all focused upon a man named George Edalji.

Edalji, who was the son of a priest, lived in the very nearby, old town of Great Wyrley, and was thrust into the limelight in 1903 when he was convicted, sentenced and imprisoned for maiming and mutilating horses in the area - reportedly in the dead of night, and, some believed, for reasons related to nothing less than full blown occult rite and ritual. Collectively, the horse slashing and deaths generated not only a great deal of concern at a local level, but also anger, fear, and a distinct trust of the Edalji family, who the locals had consistently frowned deeply upon ever since they moved to the area years earlier.

Notably, however, such was the publicity given to the case of George Edalji, and his subsequent lengthy prison sentence, that even none other than the creator of Sherlock Holmes - Sir Arthur Conan Doyle himself - sat up and took careful notice of the case, its developments, and the outcome for Edalji. Actually, Conan Doyle did far more than just that. Fully believing that there had been a huge miscarriage of justice in the Edalji affair, he highlighted it, wrote about it, and even loudly complained to the government of the day about it - events that, combined with the work of others, ultimately led to Edalji's early release from prison.

But, for me, growing up practically on the doorstep of where all of the old bloodthirsty carnage occurred decades earlier, what I found fascinating - even as a kid - were the weirder aspects of the matter. And, I hasten to add, there were a great deal of them, too. Stories did the rounds locally for years suggesting that not only was Edalji not the culprit, but that the attacker wasn't even human! A giant, monstrous bird; a large ape trained via hypnosis, no less; and an equally-well-trained group of wild boar were all suggested as being viable candidates for the attacks.

Needless to say, however, just like the matter of what happened at Roswell, New Mexico in the summer of 1947, who killed JFK, and the identity of Jack the Ripper, so the mysterious saga of George Edalji and the mutilated horses remains exactly that: a mystery. And, in a roundabout way, had I not stumbled upon the story in my early teens, then I almost certainly would not be writing these very words right now.

But, there was one other reason, too, for my fascination with Forteana. It's one that gets to the very heart of this book, and revolves around a vile, nightmarish creature that, many, many years ago became known as the Man-Monkey. And with very good reason, too…

Number Four, The Beast of the Bridge:

From the summer of 1982 - when I left Pelsall's distinctly Grange Hill-like comprehensive school with barely an academic qualification to my name, a couple of meagre CSE Grade 4's aside - to the summer of 1985, along with three of my mates (Dave, another Dave, and a friend named Ian) I rented a large caravan in the Devonshire town of Brixham; one that was a true home from home, and where we had a lot of chaotic and uproarious fun. It was during this particular time period that I undertook a year-long stint as a writer working on a music, fashion and entertainment magazine that went by the moniker of *Zero*, and which was truly one of the happiest times in my life. I most certainly can't say that it was exactly akin to Hunter S. Thompson's classic tale *The Rum Diary*, but I do like to think that it was pretty close.

By the end of 1985, however, the job with *Zero* was gone, and it had become graphically and depressingly clear to me that I was now in dire need of money. The real world was unfortunately beckoning and I was very nearly skint. I really was at the point of checking down the sides of the settee and under the car seats in search of pennies. And so, I was soon back in the Midlands and working full-time as a van-driver and forklift driver for a company that sold paint and wallpaper. Of the very few 9-to-5 jobs I have ever had in my life, I didn't really mind this one too much, as I was out of the boss's hair, driving around, making deliveries to the painters and decorators of Staffordshire and the West Midlands, and all to the hallowed soundtrack of Radio 1 that would relentlessly blare out of the van's speakers throughout the entire day. Aside, that is, from whenever Simon Bates insisted on utterly torturing the airwaves, if not the entire British nation, with the utterly sickening and always doom-laden Our Tune, during which I would regularly and quickly hit the 'Off' button.

Practically every day, my long and winding route took me to the large and sprawling Staffordshre woodland known as the Cannock Chase. While out driving across the Chase, and soaking in the glorious majesty of those huge and mighty trees, my mind often wandered back with much affection to those long gone days and nights as a monster-obsessed child; and, perhaps inevitably, to those exciting stories of the strange creatures that were said to inhabit the thick woods of the Cannock Chase. Indeed, even way back in the mid-1970s, as I very well knew, seemingly magical tales were quietly told by the local folk of the area of sightings of big-cats, of wild boar, and even of the occasional wallaby or several on the loose deep within the dense, expansive woods.

It was around this particular time that my interest in all things weird slowly started to expand even more. And as a direct result, I duly began to subscribe to some of the self-published newsletters on UFOs and paranormal phenomena that existed at the time – including the then-photocopied, fanzine-style periodical of Graham and Mark Birdsall's Yorkshire UFO Society, which proved to be a very early precursor to their glossy, newsstand *UFO Magazine* of the 1990s and early 2000s. I also succeeded in finding a great little bookshop tucked away in a Birmingham side-street called Reader's World that was a veritable treasure trove for out of print and hard to find titles on just about all aspects of the paranormal, the mysterious, and the conspiratorial. I even well remember picking up at Reader's World a copy of Andy Collins' very rare title, *The Brentford Griffin*, for the amazingly cheap sum of just fifty pence! But, I digress!

It was not too long afterwards that my path first crossed with that of a certain beast, which - without doubt - ultimately led me to write the very book that you are holding in your hands right now. And it is a day that I will always remember, for one, central reason. Although somewhat appropriately for what was most certainly such a diabolical beast, it was not a good reason in the slightest.

From a bookseller whose name and location have now well and truly been long lost to the inevitable fog of time, I had ordered a cheap, used, hardback copy of Janet and Colin Bord's book *Alien Animals* - a classic and essential title that dug deep into the many worldwide legends and tales of ghostly black dogs, mysterious big cats, hairy man-beasts, winged monstrosities, and those unknown denizens of the deep, such as the Loch Ness Monster, Ogopogo, as well as a multitude of sea-serpents.

It was in January 1986, I still very well recall, when *Alien Animals* finally arrived in the mail. I eagerly sat down to read it and was completely amazed to find mention of the infamous Man-Monkey; a bizarre, shining-eyed Bigfoot-type creature that I had never previously come across, but that the Bords said haunted Bridge 39 on the Shropshire Union Canal. This was of particular interest to me because the area, it so transpired, was actually very close to that of my daily van-driving route. My first exposure to the Man-Monkey was, however, firmly overshadowed by a far more ominous event that had occurred on the very same day that I began to read the book; namely, the tragic and fatal explosion in the United States of the NASA Space Shuttle, Challenger.

I continued to heartily devour the packed pages of *Alien Animals* and made a careful, mental note to soon make the drive out to the infamous bridge where the Man-Monkey was said to have its lair. Lager, girls and work - in varying degrees of interchangeable order - were very much the collective order of the day, however. And even though my interest in the world of the unexplained had undeniably increased, and certainly to levels that easily exceeded those of my earlier, childhood years, I simply forgot about the Man-Monkey and its crazed and beastly actions, and I began to focus my attention far more on unidentified flying objects - that is, until the latter part of 1987.

Hell in Harlow

During this specific period of time, I was now working down in the Essex town of Harlow. The company that was then employing me was also paying for a very nice hotel room (for nigh-on a year, too), and I most certainly had no complaints at all. There was a wealth of fine and delicious food, the plentiful supply of booze ran flowingly, and there was a much more than adequate nightlife in town, and one that was replete with a regular supply of white stiletto-wearing Essex Girls.

One evening, in October 1987, I was sprawled out on the hotel-room bed, triple whisky and coke in hand (or some such similar potent concoction, at least), and once again casually thumbing through the pages of *Alien Animals* – probably, I'm pretty sure, for the very first time since that fateful day back in January 1986. Very oddly, this second occasion, too, was one destined to be hit by deep tragedy: namely, the devastating hurricane that decimated whole swathes of England, after BBC weather-man Michael Fish had earnestly assured the good folk of Britain that any talk of a coming hurricane was nothing but complete and utter nonsense. Fish was wrong, of course; memorably and infamously so, in fact, as the country and its people found out to their considerable cost and dismay the very next morning, when they arose to what can only be described as an apocalyptic scene of complete and utter carnage.

I actually recall waking up in the early hours of the morning, with macabre images of the Man-Monkey fixed firmly in my mind, as well as hearing the driving deluge, and the wild storm whipping up a veritable frenzy outside of the rain-beaten hotel-room windows. Later, like so many locals, I most strongly suspect, I drove around much of Essex, utterly amazed and appalled, yet also spell-bound and transfixed at the scene of overwhelming destruction and carnage that the mighty storm had wrought, overnight, upon Britain's much beloved countryside. It may have been nothing but mere coincidence and imagination, of course, yet it seemed to me in those slightly paranoid and dark moments which occasionally surfaced, that whenever I chose to delve into the macabre world of the Man-Monkey, disaster seemed to quickly and inevitably follow ominously close behind.

It was from pretty much that very moment onwards that I began to take a far greater note of not only the Man-Monkey legend, but also of just about any, and all reports of a British Bigfoot variety on which I could lay my eager hands. As time progressed, and as the days, the months, the years, and ultimately, the decades, went by, I collected more and more accounts, undertook numerous on-site investigations, discovered a wealth of witness testimony, and developed a startling realisation that far from being the rarity I and many others had assumed it to be, the British Bigfoot phenomenon was actually one of near-epic, nationwide proportions.

The problem, as I saw it, however, was that while many researchers possessed a report or two, there had been no real attempt on the part of the Fortean community of the day to share, collate and assimilate all of the available data – which, had such an action been undertaken way back when, might very well have led to a deep understanding of the sheer, nationwide scale of the phenomenon. In other words, this wasn't just a mystery of not fully understood proportions. It was also an issue that was very much one of not fully appreciated or recognised proportions.

The Quest Develops
Nevertheless, however, from all across the country's forests, woods, hills, mountains and even fairly built-up areas, reports most assuredly did exist. And, unlike my own, personal investigations, those reports spanned not just the years or the decades, but the centuries even. Thus, it very soon became evident to me that this was a phenomenon, which - to a highly significant degree - and aside from only the occasional comment, was pretty much ignored, derided, laughed at – or all three. But, the undeniable fact was that there were dozens – maybe even hundreds – of people all across the nation who had encountered beasts that, if we were talking about the Pacific northwest woods or the Himalayas, we would, without any degree of doubt or hesitation at all, be calling Bigfoot or the Abominable Snowman.

On the Trail of the British Bigfoot
So, I made it my time (well, a small portion of it – a normal life is essential in this field, too!) to dig as deeply as I was able into the puzzle of the Sasquatch of these isles, always intending to write a full-length book on the phenomenon. But always getting sidetracked by something else; until now, finally, just over a quarter or a century or so after my path first crossed with that of the Man-Monkey.

And, with that all now said by way of an introduction, in the pages that follow you will find the cases, the witness reports, my findings and conclusions, and the thoughts and opinions of other friends, colleagues and luminaries within the domains of Forteana and cryptozoology. Collectively they tell a bizarre and beastly tale of Bigfoot-style monstrosities, of wild men, of mysterious apes, and of creatures that should not exist, that logic tells us cannot exist, but that, in some most odd and ethereal fashion, clearly do exist. But there's more. And it's a word of some significant warning for those who may have preconceived notions and ideas about what might conceivably pass for the large and hairy chap in Britain.

Many of the cases, and certainly the vast majority of the available testimony, on record from the British Isles clearly demonstrate that the British Bigfoot most assuredly is not a flesh and blood beast; or, at least, it's not of a flesh and blood nature in the way that most of us generally accept, or understand, the term. There are numerous reports of the British creatures vanishing in the blink of an eye. Such entities are seen time and again in the vicinity of ancient stone circles, prehistoric hill-forts, and areas of historical and archaic significance. They appear to have the unfathomable ability to significantly affect electrical equipment and even people's perception and state of mind - and seldom, if ever, in a particularly positive fashion, either. For the most part, the sightings are always of solitary beasts – hardly ever with others of their kind or with juvenile offspring. And, they are seemingly utterly content to go on about their enigmatic activities quite successfully without the need for even a modicum of food, water or shelter. Such, then, is the strange and monstrous 'existence' and 'life' of the British wild man.

So much for the cases and the phenomenon, but now a bit about the book itself. The beasts themselves, as you will very soon come to see, manifest in all manner of sizes, and the geographic locations in which they lurk vary just about as widely as they do wildly. Thus, and somewhat appropriately for such an undeniably unpredictable phenomenon, the chapters of *Wild Man!* vary in size; chiefly as a result of the amount of data available, or sometimes, and unfortunately, not available, on each of the cases placed under the microscope. And, exactly like the enigmatic Sasquatch of this green and pleasant land itself, those same chapters move around from village to village, from county to county, and from England to Ireland, and from Scotland to Wales, in no particular order and without the benefit of rhyme or reason. And, I'm absolutely sure, the British Bigfoot, given its odd, mystifying and near-anarchic nature, would have it no other way. One final word, before I let you move on to the meat of the matter. During the course of writing this book, a number of people asked me if I intended including, in its pages, entire sections on other undeniably mystifying British man-beasts, including Cornwall's notorious and infamous Owlman (surely, the closest thing in these parts to the Mothman of the United States), and British werewolves. Well, the answer to that question, aside from a very few passing comments and asides where I feel that such matters may be both relevant and integral to the particular story being told, is a definitive 'No.'

Jon Downes' *The Owlman and Others* is, beyond any shadow of a doubt, the essential study of the former mystery, so why would I even attempt to go over ground already so expertly and completely covered by Jon? And, as for the British lycanthropes, well, there's absolutely no doubt in my mind that this is a subject that could – and, indeed, should – very easily, and most justifiably, lend itself to a brand new, full length treatment and study from someone in the British cryptozoological community. But that person is not going to be me.

Many of my personal views on the British Bigfoot and wild men phenomena, I can say for sure, very closely parallel those theories I hold with respect to the true nature of British werewolves. Thus, chiefly, I prefer to focus on Bigfoot alone in this book, rather than crisscross from creature to creature and back again. And, even if I was to follow this book up with one on British monsters allegedly born of a full moon, and possessed of terrible shape-shifting tendencies, well, it would - to a very significant degree - tread extremely similar, and at times, identical, ground to that covered in the title you are now reading, and particularly so when it comes to the theories that have been advanced to explain them and their presence. So, rather than spread myself too far and wide, and be accused of repeating myself big-time, I leave the werewolves of Britain in the hands of someone else – maybe, even in the hands of you!

With that all now said, let me finally introduce you to a truly bizarre cast of monstrous characters and creatures that have absolutely no business, whatsoever, roaming the wilds of Britain, but that in some curious and hard to define fashion, seem to be doing precisely that. Their many and varied names include the Shug Monkey, the Beast of Bolam, the Woodwose, the Big Grey Man of Ben Macdhui, the Man-Monkey, the Green-Faced Monkey of Churston Woods, the Beast of Brassknocker Hill, Martyn's Ape, and numerous others. In their own unique ways, they all add to the mystery and magic of the phenomenon of what, in somewhat generic terms, is defined as the British Bigfoot.

And, when we are done with the case files, we will then turn our attentions to the theories that exist to explain how, why, and under what peculiar - and possibly even paranormal - circumstances the British Isles are host to a beast that people should simply not be seeing…but clearly are. In many ways, the explanations are as jaw-dropping as are the sightings, incidents and events themselves.

Come with me now, then, as we discover that, yes, there really is something in the woods. But, it may not be what you think it is…

Nick Redfern, November 2012

THE CASE
FILES

CHAPTER 1
WOODWOSE AND WILDMEN
'...the woods could conceal a lot...'

A specifically English term that dates back hundreds of years, the Woodwose or Wodewose - possibly derived from a combination of wudu, which means forest, and wasa, that translates in today's language as being – was, essentially, a hairy wild man of the woods, whose rampaging form can be graphically seen to this very day in countless pieces of priceless medieval European artwork from countries including Germany, Italy and, yes, Britain…

A Beast is Born

Tabitca Cope, author of the excellent cryptozoological novel, *Dark Ness*, says of the Woodwose that it

> '...is a savage, naked man decked out in leaves and boughs or moss and ivy, carrying a huge club. He has been reportedly seen in England since 14th Century and up to the 16th Century and has been described as a large bearded man whose entire body was covered in curly hair. Historians theorised that the wodewose may have been some ancestor of man, and during the periods of its existence, had learned to fashion tools from wood. Similar stories of large hairy ape-men are found in the Pacific Northwest, Europe, Canada, Mexico, Belize, Guiana, Ecuador, Brazil, Malaysia, Indonesia, parts of Africa, and of course the Himalayas.'

Of what is probably its initial appearance, in recorded form, at least, Tabitca adds:

> 'The first "Wild Man" appearing in the world's literature was Enkidu in the ancient Sumerian Epic of Gilgamesh. Created by the goddess Aruru (also known as Anu) to appease the prayers of the subjects of Gilgamesh who tired of his iron hand rule, Enkidu was made to match the strength of Gilgamesh and to do battle with him although he actually became Gilgamesh's closest ally. Historian Fred Gladstone Skinner wrote that Enkidu was "a valiant god of battle, whose entire body was covered with hair, shaggy as a woman's head. His clothes were of animal skins and, like an animal, he grazed in the fields and fought with the wild beasts for a place at the water holes."'

Unlike the classic Bigfoot of the Pacific northwest regions of the United States, or the Abominable

OPPOSITE: Welcome to the weird world of the Wild Man. Copyright: Hans Holbein the Younger, circa 1525-1528.

Snowman of the frozen Himalayas, the Woodwose was – despite its oft-reported abundance of body hair - far more human-like in its appearance and nature; something that has led to deep speculation that the legends of such creatures might very well have had their origins in sightings of so-called feral people: human-beings who, either by choice or unfortunate circumstances, lived solitary lives, deep in the heart of the woods and, as a by-product, descended into states of definitive savagery. Then there is the astounding theory that, possibly, the tales of the Woodwose were born out of occasional sightings of pockets of ancient humans, such as Neanderthals, or people of the Neolithic era, who, rather incredibly, may have survived long after conventional wisdom and science tells us they became utterly extinct or absorbed. Added to that, there was a widespread belief across much of Europe centuries ago that if a man or a woman decided to live among the beasts in dense and foreboding forests and woodland, he or she would inevitably become more and more animalistic as time passed by. Eventually, it was accepted, they would become wild people in the literal sense of the term: Nothing less than fully-fledged, hair-covered beasts of the trees.

The well-known Cornwall-based anomalies researcher, writer, and blogger, Kithra, has spent many a moon seeking out the truth behind the Woodwose legends and says of the creature that it

> '...is usually shown as a complete, part human, figure carrying a club with the limbs being leafy. It also often shows a thick beard and wears a cap. The Woodwose may also be shown holding the club in different positions. Sometimes this is on its side and sometimes it is raised. There is a theory that a raised club depicts the figure before it was converted to Christianity, but it's probably more correct to believe that it was raised to ward off evil spirits'.

A memorable description of a Woodwose can be found within the pages of *Konungs skuggsjá* (or *The King's Mirror*), which was written in Norway at some point around 1250:

> 'It once happened in that country (and this seems indeed strange) that a living creature was caught in the forest as to which no one could say definitely whether it was a man or some other animal; for no one could get a word from it or be sure that it understood human speech. It had the human shape, however, in every detail, both as to hands and face and feet; but the entire body was covered with hair as the beasts are, and down the back it had a long coarse mane like that of a horse, which fell to both sides and trailed along the ground when the creature stooped in walking.'

Returning to Kithra, she also notes that it wasn't until the early medieval period that wild men were thought of as being truly human beings, but ones that had been driven wild due to madness. At this particular same time, she comments,

> '...Celtic tales attribute poetic, or prophetic, powers to wild men. In Welsh tradition, especially, such powers are given to Myrddi, (a.k.a. Merlin), who at one point becomes mad and goes into a forest where he finds himself able to write prophetic poetry. Mediaeval literature, and art, is full of wild men stories and icons and, whilst mostly portrayed as being mainly human, they are sometimes shown as crawling on all fours and attacking dogs. Rather than being the true Wild Man of the Woods, who lives a feral life, it is possible that the Woodwose falls into the category of a strange being that manifests itself into reality from time to time. If that is true then it may account for the occasional reports that still surface today.'

A Wild Inn

In 2011, author and creature-seeker Neil Arnold noted: 'Many years ago when I first began writing for *Animals & Men* magazine [the Centre for Fortean Zoology's in-house magazine] I mentioned to Jon Downes something regarding cryptozoological pub signs. There are many *St. George and the Dragon* signs, and I know a few which also mention unicorns. However, one particular pub sign, which is of great interest to me is that which belongs to the *Wild Man* at 29 Bedford Street in Norwich. Now, most pub signs have a meaning, but the legend which pertains to the Wild Man is extremely intriguing.

> 'So the folklore states, many, many years ago a six year old boy named Peter became lost in a wood in Germany. Around six years later the boy had grown wild, and in naked form would prowl the woods, living alongside the resident animals. Eventually he was found and picked up by a travelling showman who exhibited throughout Europe.'

As Neil also said:

> 'St. Mary's Northchurch adds more to the legend, for within its walls there is an inscription which reads: "To the memory of Peter, known as the Wild Boy, having been found wild in the forest of Hertswold near Hanover in the year 1725. He

The wildest pub in the land? Copyright: Neil Arnold.

then appeared to be about 12 years old. In the following year he was brought to England by the order of the late Queen Caroline, and the ablest masters were provided for him. But proving himself incapable of speaking, or of receiving any instruction, a comfortable provision was made for him at a farm in this parish, where he continued to the end of his inoffensive life. He died on the 22nd of February, 1785, supposed to be aged 72."'

And there the inscription ends.

But why was there an association between wild Peter and the Norwich-based pub itself that led the owner to even name the inn after the slightly tragic soul? Neil provides the answer:

'Around 1751 Peter was housed at the public house. In the past the sign would depict the unfortunate chap as a demonic character amid flickering flames. Now the pub sign shows him frequenting the forest alongside bears.'

And still on the subject of pubs and primitive people…

An Even Wilder Inn!

As far as the British Isles are concerned, Richard Holland – formerly the editor of *Paranormal* magazine and the author of *Haunted Wales: A Survey of Welsh Ghostlore and Haunted Clwyd* - offers his own particular thoughts on the nature of the legendary beast under scrutiny in this chapter:

'It has been suggested that the Woodwose is a folk memory of some species of early hominid, a pre-*Homo sapiens* ape man...Perhaps a few remnants of these "wild men" still lingered in inaccessible places when prehistoric man first hacked their way through Europe's primeval forest. They might have been glimpsed by Neolithic settlers in the hearts of what remained of their woodland habitat...'

Richard also notes that:

'In Sproughton, in Suffolk, according to John Michell and Bob Rickard, the Wild Man Inn was so named after a terrifying entity that attacked its builders in the 16th Century. They also cite a police report of a "horrible uncouth creature" which had been living in woods near Salisbury in Wiltshire and attempted to carry off a farmer's wife: this was recorded as late as 1877. I have also spoken to witnesses who may have encountered a similar man-beast in North-East Wales.'

Although some of the stories of the wild man of Sproughton portray him as having been nothing more mysterious than a mad, homeless vagrant who dwelled in the woods and lived a distinctly lawless life, there is a possibility that he may have been something else entirely. On the north side of the River Gipping, which runs from Stowmarket to Ipswich, is a place that just happens to be called – and has been called, for as long as people have inhabited those ancient parts – Devil's Wood, where significant archaeological finds from both Neolithic and Paleolithic times have been made.

That Sproughton is only twelve miles from Stowmarket, and just three and a half miles from Ipswich, that ancient man dwelled in this very area, and that the place itself became associated with the Devil, collectively suggests a distinct possibility that the wild man of Sproughton may have been far more than a mere eccentric vagabond or hermit type, after all. Maybe, incredibly, he was one of the very last of his kind, perhaps even a Neolithic survivor, one who made his lair in old woods that, not surprisingly – given the man's wild appearance and mysterious presence - became so linked with matters so dark and devilish.

A Gang Green

Still on the matter of strange-looking people living wild in Suffolk and, in the process, provoking myths and tales of enigmatic feral-style entities, I feel duty bound to reference the famous story of the green children of Woolpit (which is also associated with the even more renowned tale of the Babes in the Wood), a village situated between the towns of Bury St. Edmunds and Stowmarket. So the tale goes, back in the 12th Century, a young girl and boy, of strangely green-hued skin, appeared in Woolpit one day, claiming to have come from a magical place called St. Martin's Land, which existed in an atmosphere of permanent twilight, and where the people lived underground, on nothing but green beans. While the story has been relegated by many to the realms of mere myth and folklore, it may not be just that. It might, actually, be much more.

According to the old legend, the two children remained in Woolpit and were ultimately baptised by the villagers, who accepted them as their very own. And although the boy ultimately grew sickly and eventually died, the girl did not. She thrived and finally lost her green-tinged skin to normal coloured skin of healthy appearance. She also, somewhat in defiance of the disapproving attitudes of certain members of the village, became, as it was amusingly termed back then, according to the legend, 'rather loose and wanton in her conduct'.

That both wild children were reportedly green-skinned and lived underground in a mysterious locale, has led many to disregard the tale out of hand as one of fairy-based, mythological proportions and nothing else whatsoever.

That may not actually have been the case, however. The pair may have been suffering from a condition called Hypochromic Anaemia, in which the sufferer – as a result of a very poor diet that, in part, affects the colour of the red blood-cells – can develop skin of a noticeably green shade. In support of this scenario, Hypochromic Anaemia was once known as Chlorosis, a word formulated in the early 1600s by a Montpellier professor of medicine named Jean Varandal. And why did Varandal choose such a name? Simple: it came from the Greek word Chloris, meaning greenish-yellow or pale green.

Therefore, we might very well, and quite justifiably even, conclude that the strange children of Woolpit were definitively wild in nature. And given their state of poor health, they may certainly have lived poor and strange lives, very possibly deep underground – or, perhaps, permanently under a thick canopy of dense forest of the type that dominated England at that time - with others of their kind, in and around Suffolk, just as they had claimed to the villagers of Woolpit; and, all the while struggling to survive on the meagre supplies of food available to them that were ultimately responsible for their green / yellow hue.

One final point: The distance from Woolpit to Sproughton, where a wild man reportedly wreaked untold havoc at the local inn at some point during the 16th Century, is less than nineteen miles. Perhaps, then, there really were wild, feral humans on the loose in Eastern England, and possibly as late as only five hundred years ago. Someone else who suggests just such a possibility is Jon Downes, the acclaimed monster hunter, the director of the Devonshire-based Centre for Fortean Zoology, and the editor and publisher of this very book.

Babes in the woods. Copyright: Randolph Caldecott, 1879.

'...the people of their village were in fear of them...'

Jon began as follows when I interviewed him in March 2012:

> 'One of the things that interest me – and I'm going out on a limb with this; it's not something most cryptozoologists agree with – is that the veneer of civilisation of man is very, very thin. Just look at the ways in which otherwise perfectly normal men will behave when they go to war. Look at the way mobs behave.
>
> I believe that all over the world, at various times – including Britain - there have been people that have regressed back through the layers of society and civilisation. In some cases of so-called "feral children", they have been found with a fine down of hair all over their bodies. This is something that is quite well known, and is something that can appear in conditions like Anorexia, or where, for whatever reason, a person is very malnourished. They start to develop fine hair on their bodies, under certain circumstances.'

Jon is correct in his words. The hair in question is known as lanugo hair. On occasion, when anorexics descend into true starvation mode, they may start to develop fine, white hair – typically on their face, back, chest and legs. Notably, and of relevance to the subject of this very chapter, the hair is sometimes even described as being somewhat furry. The reason why it develops is actually quite simple: As starvation increases, and as the body starts to lose its precious and much needed supplies of fat, which help insulate the body from the cold, it reacts by provoking the production of lanugo hair, as a means to try and compensate and offer the body some degree of warmth. You can, I am quite sure, see where all of this is leading to. Back to Jon:

> 'I think it is quite possible that you may have had situations where individuals - in earlier centuries and in Britain and elsewhere - may have been cast out of their village. Maybe they were just mentally ill, but the people of their village were in fear of them, so they were banished to the woods or whatever. They may have lived in the wild from then on, eking out primitive existences, and who being malnourished, may have developed fine hair over their bodies that then gets coated and matted with mud and leaves, and suddenly you have legends of wild men. They may have even bred if there were groups of them. And it wouldn't surprise me at all if, maybe, this led to at least some of the legends of wild men in Britain, but not all of them. They may well have been people who went wild, but who were not primitive people, as such.'

Dorset's Beastly Babies

Robert Newland and Mark North (right) say that Dorset legends tell of Woodwoses inhabiting the woods of Yellowham Hill, which is located near to the town of Dorchester. The creatures had the regular habit of abducting young girls from the nearby villages, many of whom supposedly ended up pregnant during their time spent in the company of the Woodwose. One such incident befell a particular young girl, who, when questioned by magistrates about the nature and name of the father of her impending child, replied: 'Please your worshipfuls, 'twere the Wild Man of Yal'ham.'

No-one should doubt the possibility – perhaps even the probability - that this may simply have been an ingenious ploy on the part of the girl to try and protect her unknown, very human lover from the scalding wrath of her irate father! Or, perhaps, on the other hand, Woodwose really did once inhabit the thick woods of Dorset. And, in view of the many and varied hairy man-beast encounters that have been reported from all across the British Isles for centuries, we might well ask this important question: Are the woods of Dorset still, to this very day, the domain of the Woodwose?

There is one other matter worth noting in relation to the words of Mark North and Robert Newland. It's one that is supportive of the aforementioned theories of Jon Downes. If the Woodwose were truly Big-foot-style entities, then they surely would not have been able to successfully mate with *Homo sapiens*. However, if they were merely human beings who, having reverted to wild lives and states, subsequently developed excessive amounts of body hair as a result of near-starvation, then getting the girls of the local villages pregnant would not have posed much of a problem at all. While the wild men may have looked somewhat unusual, their genetic make-up would have been perfectly compatible with the girls, because for all intents and purposes, they were of one and the same, precise type.

Before we leave Dorset, let's take note of a final few words on the nature of the county from Mark North:

> 'Dorset is a strange place, and you can go into some of the old woods and it's like being
> In a different world, where anything might happen.'

And, just maybe, that even includes encountering a wild man.

The Somerset Wild Men

I cannot resist noting that Dorset borders the county of Somerset, which has also been the location of wild man-type reports that – in view of the very close proximity to Dorset – may have some degree of bearing on the Woodwose legends that have for so long populated the area. The Somerset reports come from Jon Downes, who states that: 'Many years ago, the area around what is now an abandoned mine at Smitham Hill, in Somerset, was linked to tales of strange beasts seen watching the miners. Sometimes on returning to work in the morning, the men would find that carts and equipment had been pushed over and thrown around during the night.'

Jon elaborates further, but on matters of a far more modern day nature:

> 'These things, whatever they were, are still seen in that area today; or, at least, as late as November 1993. This is an exact quote taken from a witness whose case is in my files:
>
>> "I was on a walk through the woods, when I heard a twig snap. I thought nothing of it and continued on. Suddenly the dogs became very agitated and ran off home. At this point I became aware of a foul smell, like a wet dog and a soft breathing sound. I started to run, but after only a few feet, I tripped and fell. I decided to turn and meet my pursuer only to see a large, about seven feet tall, dark brown, hairy, ape-like man. It just stood, about ten feet away, staring at me. It had intelligent looking eyes and occasionally tilted its head as if to find out what I was. After about twenty seconds it moved off into the forest."'

Perhaps, somewhere deep within the wilder parts of southern England, the Woodwose still lives on, totally oblivious to what such an extraordinary revelation, if proved, would provoke in the scientific and zoological communities. Now, with that astonishing thought firmly in mind, let us move on from wild men to green ones.

CHAPTER 2
TALES OF THE GREEN MAN
'...Wild men could still exist in our time...'

Kithra says of the Green Man – a wild character linked with places perceived as magical, such as woods, glades, and streams, and whose very image provokes thoughts of ancient, proto-humans roaming the land - that:

> 'Usually these figures are male, although there are a very few Green Women, together with green cats, green demons, and green lions. The Green Man can appear in different forms, although there are three types that are normally represented.
>
> - These are the Disgorging Head, which emits foliage from the mouth;
> - the Foliate Head: which is entirely covered in green leaves;
> - [and] the Bloodsucker Head, which has foliage emerging from all the facial outlets.'

'The motif can be found right across the world'

As for the point of origin for the phenomenon, Kithra suggests that the Green Man quite possibly surfaced out of the mythology of fantastic deities and mighty gods in very early times. Perhaps, in the British Isles, she muses, the Green Man arose from the Celtic god of light, Lud (also referred to as Lug or Lyg).

On a similar track, in 1942, at West Row, Suffolk, a silver salver which dated from the 4th Century was found and, today, comprises an integral and important part of what has become known as the so-called Mildenhall Treasure. The salver in question, which was uncovered at the site of an old Roman villa, and that is now on display at the British Museum, contains an intriguing image. It resembles a partly leafy mask thought to represent Neptune – the Roman god of the sea and the water - with the foliage being seaweed. But, pretty much for all intents and purposes, it is definitely Green Man-like in its appearance.

Kithra has far more to say, too, of a nature that provides us with a solid body of data and history on the mysterious figure:

> 'Carved depictions of the Green Man can be found not

Green Man and Wild Man researcher, Kithra.
Copyright: Kithra.

only in churches but also in secular buildings. Plus, it is a common name for a public house, where it would appear on inn signs that, occasionally, show a full figure instead of simply a head. The motif can be found right across the world and is, more often than not, related to natural vegetative divinities from throughout the ages. It is first and foremost a symbol of rebirth that represents the spring cycle of growth. From Asia to Europe there are representations of the image. From the 2nd Century to the modern day the Green Man can be associated with similar beliefs.'

Past and Present

It may surprise some to learn that while the Green Man – as a specific entity of traditional British folklore, at least - certainly has ancient origins, the usage of those two combined words (Green and Man, in the particular context they appear in this book to explain the nature of the phenomenon), is most certainly not old in the slightest, as Kithra clearly demonstrates:

> 'The first person to use the term 'Green Man' was Lady Raglan, wife of Major FitzRoy Richard Somerset, 4th Baron Raglan. At one time he was the President of the Folklore Society. And, in 1939 his wife, Lady Raglan, created the phrase Green Man in her one and only article that appeared in the Folklore journal. She invented the term to define the leaf-decorated heads seen in English churches, and to this day her theory concerning where they come from is still discussed.'

So, yes, the name most certainly is recent. But the motif is far, far less so. Kithra shows that, the name issue aside, its origins are just about as long as they are winding and open to question and debate: 'On the surface it seems these images are pagan, but they can often be found in ecclesiastical buildings from the 11th Century onwards. Many look either unsettling or mystical, which is sometimes thought to show the vitality of the Green Man in that it was capable of enduring as a character from pre-Christian traditions. This was probably due to the fact that in early Christianity old symbols were often incorporated into the newer religion. And, from around the 14th Century on they were also included simply as decoration in things such as manuscripts, stained glass, and other items.'

Kithra also notes that in Britain, at least, the Green Man icon became very fashionable again during the 19th Century, when it was used in architecture and arts and crafts. Moreover, to this day, the image is still used as decoration in many parts of the world by artists using many different types of media, including literature.

There is another aspect to the mystery, too, as Kithra also makes clear:

> 'The expression shown on the faces of many Green Men found in churches seems to suggest some form of torture. It may be that such expressions were to remind people of sin and that their souls would burn in hell if they committed such transgressions. As the image also represents renewal and rebirth, in a church the image might be a sign of resurrection where it appears, especially when found on tombs. It might also be a sign of creation. Or, it may just be a sign of nature and fertility.'

Kithra also has much to say on the connections between the Green Man and churches:

> 'It is thought that the Celts adorned their victim's head with leaves, which might lead us to speculate that the Green Man has Celtic origins; however the first depictions of Green Men come from Classical Roman times. But, if it is Celtic, then - where it is shown next to, or above, doors - it might be to protect the building from evil spirits.

Robin Hood: A definitive man in green. Copyright: Louis Rhead, 1912.

However, the problem remains that in the very early years of the Church, and when it took over in Britain, all pagan images were destroyed and banned. So it's hard to see how the Green Man should then have been included in church architecture. And yet, there are no accounts from Mediaeval Times that tell us how the image of the Green Man came to be included in churches. Regardless of what the Green Man was intended to represent in church architecture current congregants see him as the archetype of our oneness with the earth. And, for Wiccans and Neo-pagans he portrays an earth-centred idea of male divinity.'

She adds:

'Today, the symbolism of the Green Man has come to mean the relationship between man and nature. It reveals an essential basic pattern deep in the human mind. It has become an archetype that is common to all and represents a profoundly sympathetic feeling for, and with, nature. This has probably arisen from our current concerns about the ecology, and environment, of Planet Earth.'

Robin Hood: Not Just a Man of Green?

Researcher Luke Mastin notes that the Green Man phenomenon has been linked to some famous and infamous characters over the years, including a particularly acclaimed one that everyone will instantly recognise.

'Although best known as the heroic, bow-wielding outlaw of English folklore since the 14th Century, along with his green-garbed band of Merry Men and the beautiful and virtuous Maid Marian, Robin Hood (originally a contraction of Robin of the Wood) was also traditionally seen as a protector of the old ways and of the woods and forests.'

Interestingly, it transpires that, for a number of years, sightings have been made of a creature sounding suspiciously like Bigfoot from within what is left of none other than Sherwood Forest. A Royal Forest located in Nottinghamshire, it was - a curious and swirling mix of history and mythology tells us - the home of the famous and heroic Robin of Loxley, far better known as the aforementioned Robin Hood.

Chris Mullins, who has investigated many reports of Bigfoot in Britain, said of the Sherwood Forest controversy that:

'While having some reservations myself, I believe it's feasible. Wild men could still exist in our time. Notts [Nottinghamshire] and Derbyshire are known for their underground caves and catacombs, explored and unexplored, and the woods could conceal a lot.'

Not everyone is quite so open to such possibilities. In 2002, Izi Banton, the manager of the Sherwood Forest Visitor Centre, said of the rumoured man-beast:

'I think its existence is highly unlikely. We have one eccentric who wanders around wearing part of a tree on his head, so they might have spotted him.'

Sherwood Forest, then, might – or, conversely, might not - be home to far stranger puzzles than merely the man who supposedly stole from the rich and gave to the poor.

CHAPTER 3
THE APES OF SHUGBOROUGH
'...the borough of the demon...'

Situated near to the picturesque, ancient hamlet of Milford, Staffordshire, Shugborough Hall is both a large and renowned country house that serves as the ancestral home of the Earls of the city of Lichfield. And its spacious grounds are connected to the nearby village of Great Haywood by the Essex Bridge, which was built during the Middle-Ages. Around 1750, the hall was greatly enlarged, and then yet again at the beginning of the 1800s. Today, Shugborough Hall is open to the general public and boasts a working farm museum that dates back to 1805, and which is complete with a watermill, kitchens and a dairy. Interestingly, the grounds of Shugborough Hall are also home to something known as the Shepherd's

The mysteries of Shugborough Hall. Copyright: Nick Redfern.

Monument, upon which can be found a very strange and baffling inscription, and one which, many students of the puzzle believe, contains a secret code that identifies the alleged resting place of none other than the legendary Holy Grail. The Shepherd's Monument is not the only such construction of note on the grounds of the sprawling old hall: The Tower of Winds, the Cat's Monument, and the Doric Temple also have pride of place. But, get this: The thick and mysterious woods that surround Shugborough Hall are said to be the domain of nothing less than a diabolical, hairy wild man, or perhaps even several…

The Beast of the Hall

So the controversial story goes, at some point in the early to mid-part of 1981, distinctly strange events took place late at night in the finely landscaped grounds of ye olde Shugborough Hall. On no less than five occasions – and specifically between February and June of that year – an undisclosed number of the many geese and ducks that frequented the pleasant waters that surround the hall were found brutally decapitated, and with their lifeless bodies laid out in what one employee of the Shugborough estate described concisely and notably as resembling 'a witchcraft ceremony'. Precisely how the man knew what 'a witchcraft ceremony' involving decapitated water-fowl might look like, however, is pretty much anybody's guess.

And far more was to come. All of it was much, much worse.

On at least two occasions strange, loud, guttural noises were heard coming from one particular tree-shrouded area of the spacious grounds, and a large, hairy, man-like thing was observed by a shocked employee bounding at very high speed across the lawns long after the sun had gone down - and specifically heading in the direction of the winding waters that continue to run throughout the Shugborough Hall estate to this very day. Somewhat significantly, the very same employee recalled hearing a loud splashing noise in the immediate aftermath of the sighting, which suggested strongly that the creature had actually propelled itself deep into the heart of those very same, darkened waters.

One of those willing to discuss certain, salient aspects of the above – albeit from the promised safety and camouflage of a thick veil of secrecy and anonymity – is a now-elderly man who was employed to look after the lawns at Shugborough Hall from the late 1970s to the early 1980s. To this day he alludes to semi-veiled warnings made by senior staff at the hall at the time in question that went something very much along these lines:

> 'Do not to talk about the killings, the beheadings, the rites and the rituals. And most certainly do not discuss with anyone the sightings of the wild, hairy man-beast.'

Nevertheless, despite the ominous order of complete silence, the man does, at least, confirm that a decision was taken at the very highest level 'not to report anything to the police', and he further asserts that 'everything' was dealt with strictly in-house; aside, that is, from a visit by a local veterinarian whose services were occasionally used to treat the pet animals that lived at the hall, and who reportedly made a detailed examination of the dead water-fowl. Precisely what the results of that examination were, we unfortunately do not know, and probably never will.

The same source has been able to fill in the blanks relative to several other aspects of the story, however: Namely,

(A)   that the man-beast seen running wildly in the grounds exuded a foul smell that was somewhat akin to that of rotting vegetation;

(B)   that not a single one of the dead birds appeared to have put up a fight before decapitation (for example, there were no large piles of feathers laying around, no blood, and the birds looked to have been cleanly-cut and not torn open); and

(C)   that he had heard, from a colleague and friend, of 'something like this happening here once before, in the 1960s, with a big monkey running around'.

The Staff Speak Out

Some fifteen years ago or more now, I paid a visit to Shugborough Hall and had a brief opportunity to chat with a handful of the employees about the legend of the hairy wild man said to have been in their very midst, all those years earlier. Although none of them had any personal awareness of the story (which is not at all surprising, given that the chief events took place a decade and a half before I even thought about engaging them in conversation) they did admit to finding the whole thing very intriguing, and eventually related to me a series of entertainingly paranormal tales of various unknown entities said to haunt Shugborough Hall. Although, it must be said that these were all of a distinctly ghostly and spectral nature – of the typical 'grey lady' and 'hooded monk' variety - and most certainly not of a hairy and Bigfoot-like style.

While a direct connection to the presence of the Shugborough man-beast could never be firmly proved, one of the employees did recall a weird event that had supposedly occurred around four years previous to my visit. In this case, a horse had apparently been violently slashed on its back legs in a fashion that looked suspiciously like the work of a wild animal, such as a 'big cat' – or, possibly, as I thought both then and today, a latter-day equivalent of our old friend, George Edalji, who hardly lived a million miles away from the Cannock Chase. In fact, his Great Wyrley home was practically on the doorstep of the town of Cannock. Unfortunately, there were no more relevant details available; and so, therefore, I could do very little more than merely log the story for posterity, and in the event that further corroborating data might ultimately one day surface. To my lasting regret, it never has.

But, since then, another account has surfaced that does add to the overall mystery, even though it does not relate to the events of the 1960s or the early 1980s.

Hello, hello, hello; what's going on here, then?

In 2004, a further encounter with the elusive, hairy wild man occurred. The location was the road that runs from the hamlet of Milford to Shugborough Hall. And, in this case, the witness had impeccable credentials. She was a policewoman who, while on duty with a colleague on the night in question, was routinely patrolling the coiling old roads that run through the woods, and which surround the vast Shugborough estate. It was not long before midnight – yes, the veritable witching hour itself, no less - when both she and her partner were shocked by the sight of a strange beast that bounded across the road, only a short distance in front of them, and headed towards the expansive fields that dominate the old, historic hall.

In a 2006 off the record interview, the officer described to me the animal as being human-like in shape, an estimated, and incredible, eight and a half feet in height, covered in dark hair, but looking practically emaciated and near-anorexic in appearance. Her amazed colleague, who was driving, slammed on the brakes and brought the car to a screeching halt in the middle of the moonlit road. The shocked pair looked at each other for a moment; then, on regaining their composure they elected to do…absolutely nothing.

Shugborough: The lair of a beast. Copyright: Nick Redfern.

No-one would believe their story, the officer stated to me. They would likely receive nothing more than ridicule and endless jokes and jibes from their colleagues if they dared speak even a single word of the night's events. And, in addition to that, what purpose would it really serve to alert the staff at Shugborough Hall to the possibility that a creature acutely akin to Bigfoot was prowling around the area? Absolutely no purpose at all, they both quickly and quietly – and, perhaps, reasonably - concluded.

This self-imposed silence on the part of the pair begs an intriguing question: How many other people have had an up close and personal encounter with the monster of Shugborough Hall, but have also elected to say nothing, for fear of similar ridicule and hoots of derision? Maybe the number is none or but just a scant few. Perhaps, however, it runs to dozens; we may never really know the answer to that one.

There is one, final point worth noting. And it's a potentially highly significant point, too. Shug – as in Shugborough - is an ancient English term derived from an even older Anglo-Saxon word, scucca, which means demon. Shugborough: The borough of the demon. How very, very appropriate…

CHAPTER 4
NIGHTMARE IN 1971
'...they thought it was going to take them straight off to the Old Lad himself...!'

Eileen Gallagher relates how a friend of hers – named Janice – underwent, decades ago, some sort of very traumatic, late-night encounter with a British man-beast in the picturesque village of Child's Ercall. Found in north Shropshire, Child's Ercall has origins that date right back to Celtic times and its church – St. Michael's - to the 12th Century. But, in all of its many years, the village surely never before, and maybe never since too, encountered such a strange beast as that in the tale told to Eileen by her childhood best friend. So the story went, it was back in 1971, Janice was fifteen at the time, and living in a nearby village. Something abominable was about ready to radically upset the usual tranquil calm of old Child's Ercall…

Encountering the Beast

After an evening spent with her then-boyfriend at the home of his parents in Child's Ercall, Janice was happily riding her pedal-bike back home when she was shocked to see a large, hairy animal dash across the road directly in front of her, while simultaneously glaring at her in a distinctly menacing fashion as it did so. Eileen Gallagher recalled that Janice told her that the animal was no more than forty feet in front of her, was human-like in shape, was covered in long flowing dark hair, possessed a pair of bright yellow eyes that 'twinkled', and had a black-skinned and 'shiny' face.

Rather bizarrely, the Bigfoot-style entity seen by Janice in Child's Ercall was not the only weird creature said to have inhabited this otherwise utterly normal and pleasant little English village in times past. Legend has it that centuries ago a deadly mermaid was believed by many to inhabit an old pool there.

In 1893, the writer Robert Charles Hope described the story as follows:

'Off to the Old Lad himself!'

> '…there was a mermaid seen there once. It was a good while ago, before my time. I dare say it might be a hundred years ago. There were two men going to work early one morning, and they had got as far as the side of the pond in [a] field, and they saw something on the top of the water which scared them not a little. They thought it was going to take them straight off to the Old Lad himself! I can't say exactly what it was like, I wasn't there, you know; but it was a mermaid, the same as you read of in the papers. The fellows had almost run away at first, they were so frightened, but as soon as the mermaid had spoken to them, they

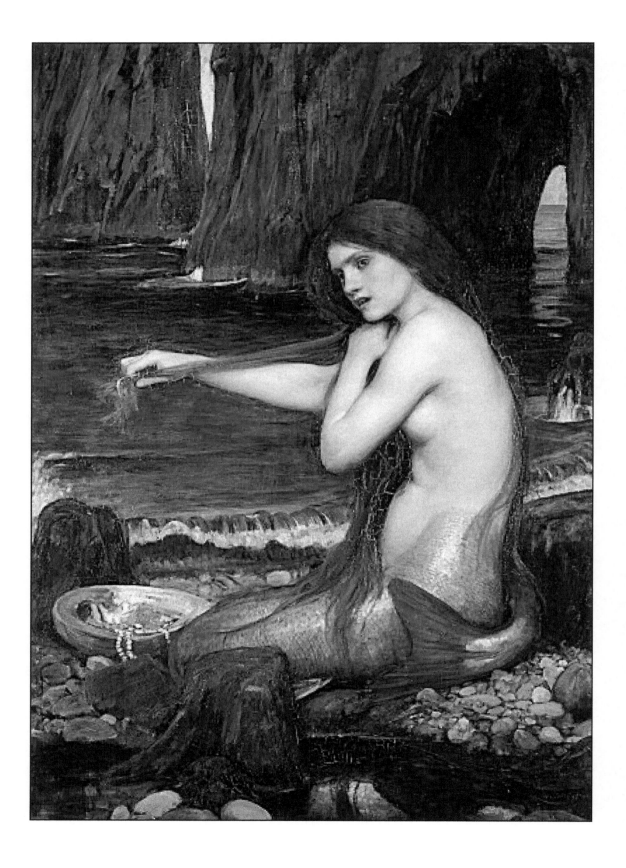

thought no more of that. Her voice was so sweet and pleasant, that they fell in love with her there and then, both of them. Well, she told them there was a treasure hidden at the bottom of the pond - lumps of gold, and no one knows what. And she would give them as much as ever they liked if they would come to her in the water and take it out of her hands.'

Hope continued:

'So they went in, though it was almost up to their chins, and she dived into the water and brought up a lump of gold almost as big as a man s head. And the men were just going to take it, when one of them said: "Eh!" he said (and swore, you know), "if this isn't a bit of luck!" And, my word, if the mermaid didn't take it away from them again, and gave a scream, and dived down into the pond, and they saw no more of her, and got none of her gold. And nobody has ever seen her since then. No doubt the story once ran that the oath which scared the uncanny creature involved the mention of the Holy Name.'

As will soon become apparent within the pages of this book, examples of cases where hairy humanoids have been seen in the same precise vicinity in Britain as water-based beasts absolutely abound. In fact, the very next case is a classic example, too. In the Theories section of this book, we will come to see – in astonishing style – precisely why this may well be.

OPPOSITE: Mermaids and man-beasts. Copyright: John William Waterhouse, 1901.

CHAPTER 5
THE CURSED CANAL
*'…a strange black creature with great
white eyes sprang out of the plantation…'*

Constructed in the early part of the 19th Century, England's historic Shropshire Union Canal, or the 'Shroppie' - as it has come to be affectionately and popularly known by those that regularly travel its extensive and winding waters – is some sixty-seven miles in length and extends from Ellesmere Port near the city of Liverpool right down to Autherley Junction at Wolverhampton in the Midlands.

The southern end of the old canal, that was originally known as the Birmingham and Liverpool Junction Canal, was the very last of the great British narrow-boat canals to be built, and is a true testament to the masterful engineering of Thomas Telford. Deep cuttings and massive embankments are the veritable hallmarks of the canal and they paint a picture that is as eerie as it is picturesque…

The Haunted Waters

The Shropshire Union Canal is quite possibly Britain's most haunted waterway, as the local folk that intimately know and appreciate the history and lore of the canal are only too well aware. At Chester's old Northgate, for example, and where the canal was dug into part of the town's old moat, a ghostly Roman centurion can be seen – when circumstances are said to be right, that is – still guarding the ancient entrance to the city. Then there is the 'shrieking spectre' of Belton Cutting, which is a veritable wailing, Banshee-style monstrosity that strikes cold, stark fear into the hearts of those who have the misfortune, and bad luck to cross its terrible path.

At the site of the former lock-keeper's cottage at Burgedin, on the nearby Montgomery Canal, come intriguing reports of the ghostly, ethereal figure of an early Welsh princess named Eira. And bringing matters relatively more up to date, there is the spectral American Air Force pilot whose aircraft crashed near the canal at Little Onn, at Church Eaton, Staffordshire during the Second World War. There is also the 'helpful resident ghost' of Tyrley Middle Lock at Market Drayton, which has allegedly been seen opening and closing the lock-gates for those novice, holidaying boaters that, from time to time, negotiate the waters of the long canal. But by far the most famous – or, perhaps, infamous would be a much more accurate word to use – ghostly resident of the Shropshire Union Canal is a truly diabolical and devilish entity that has become known as the Man-Monkey. That's right, the very same hairy creature that, back in January 1986, got me into this controversy in the first place!

OPPOSITE: Bridge 39: The domain of a British Bigfoot. Copyright: Nick Redfern.

The Monstrous Monkey of Bridge 39

It was within the packed pages of Charlotte Sophia Burne's book of 1883, *Shropshire Folklore,* that the unholy antics of what some have since perceived to be the closest thing that Britain may have to the North American Bigfoot and the Yeti of the Himalayas, were first unleashed upon an unsuspecting general public. According to Burne:

> 'A very weird story of an encounter with an animal ghost arose of late years within my knowledge. On the 21st of January 1879, a labouring man was employed to take a cart of luggage from Ranton in Staffordshire to Woodcock, beyond Newport in Shropshire, for the ease of a party of visitors who were going from one house to another. He was late in coming back; his horse was tired, and could only crawl along at a foot's pace, so that it was ten o'clock at night when he arrived at the place where the highroad crosses the Birmingham and Liverpool canal.'

It was then, Burne faithfully recorded, that the man received what was undoubtedly the most terrifying shock of his entire life – before or since, it seems pretty safe to assume:

> 'Just before he reached the canal bridge, a strange black creature with great white eyes sprang out of the plantation by the roadside and alighted on his horse's back. He tried to push it off with his whip, but to his horror the whip went through the thing, and he dropped it on the ground in fright.'

Needless to say, Burne added:

> 'The poor, tired horse broke into a canter, and rushed onwards at full speed with the ghost still clinging to its back. How the creature at length vanished, the man hardly knew.'

But the story was far from over, Burne learned:

> 'He told his tale in the village of Woodseaves, a mile further on, and so effectively frightened the hearers that one man actually stayed with friends there all night, rather than cross the terrible bridge which lay between him and his home.'

Burne's wild story continued that, by the time he reached the village of Woodseaves, the un-named man was in a state of 'excessive terror' and promptly retired to his bed for several days 'so much was he prostrated by his fright'. Burne also recorded that, on the following day, another individual travelled back to the sinister bridge and, sure enough, there was the man's whip, still lying at the very place where it had fallen to the ground after the nightmarish and bizarre encounter.

Almost inevitably, dark tales of the crazed beast and its infernal night-time activities began to spread like absolute wildfire throughout the little villages and hamlets of the area, as Burne quickly learned and recorded thus in her book: 'The adventure, as was natural, was much talked of in the neighbourhood, and, of course, with all sorts of variations.' Most regrettably, Burne failed to elaborate on the particular nature of these 'variations' and gossip.

But, it seems that the local constabulary had heard all about the nature and exploits of the hairy demon and knew exactly what was afoot, as Burne carefully chronicled:

> 'Some days later the man's master was surprised by a visit from a policeman, who came to

request him to give information of his having been stopped and robbed on the Big Bridge on the night of the 21st January.'

The 'master', who, apparently, was very much amused by this development in the escalating and seemingly mutating story, carefully explained to the visiting policeman that this was completely untrue, and that, in reality, it was his employee who had reported a strange encounter at the 'Big Bridge', but that there was most definitely no robbery involved at all. Interestingly, when the real details of what had occurred were related to the policeman, he was seemingly completely nonplussed, came to the realisation that no actual crime had been committed at all, and merely replied in a distinctly matter of fact fashion:

'Oh, was that all, sir? Oh, I know what that was. That was the Man-Monkey, sir, as does come again at that bridge ever since the man was drowned in the cut.'

Charlotte Burne also revealed that she personally had the opportunity to speak with the man's employer, but, also to our cost today, she did not expand upon the specific nature of the conversation within the pages of *Shropshire Folklore*. Nevertheless, Burne did describe the master as being a 'Mr. B_____ of L_____d'. And although the man's name remains unknown to us (and probably always will remain so), 'L_____d' is very possibly, and probably quite likely, a reference to the ancient Staffordshire city of Lichfield.

So what, precisely, was the strange, hairy critter that was seen wildly roaming the distinctly darkened corners of the Shropshire Union Canal by moonlight on that winter's night way back in January 1879? Was it truly some form of Bigfoot or Yeti-like entity? Could it potentially have been an exotic escapee of the simian kind, and possibly one that originated with a private zoo somewhere in the area, or even a travelling menagerie of the type that were indeed popular back then? Did it have wholly supernatural and paranormal origins, rather than purely physical ones? Or was it something else entirely? I will address those questions – and provide theories and answers - in later chapters, but, for now, let us focus our attentions on those encounters with the Man-Monkey that occurred in the years and decades after – and, in one case, before - its January 21, 1879 appearance on Bridge 39.

Roaming around Ranton

Peggy Baker's tale of the canal creature, related to me in the autumn of 1999, was brief, but equally as intriguing as that provided to Charlotte Burne more than a century earlier. On a weekend night in the winter of 1997, Peggy had been driving through the nearby village of Ranton with her daughter, Kathleen, when at around 11.30 p.m., the pair was shocked and scared witless by the surreal sight of a shambling, hairy man-beast that loomed out of the darkened fringes of the roadside, that 'threw its arms around in the air', and that proceeded to 'shout at us, like a big roar'. Not surprisingly, the terrified mother and daughter did not once slow down to get a closer look at the creature, but instead fled the scene with the utmost haste.

'I saw this bloody great thing'

Simon was a character that popped out of the cryptozoological woodwork in the wake of an article on the Man-Monkey that Irene Bott (formerly head-honcho of the Staffordshire UFO Group) and I wrote for the now-defunct *Chase Post* newspaper in the summer of 2000, and who provided an interview over drinks one evening at an old pub in the Staffordshire city of Lichfield. A jovial, anorak-and-green-wellington boot-wearing Bill Oddie-style bird-watcher and nature-lover, Simon told me and Irene in an initial and brief telephone call that he had been strolling by the Shropshire Union Canal, approximately three-quarters of a mile from Bridge 39, on a bright summer's day in 1982 when he heard what he described as 'a really loud noise from across the other side of the canal and in the trees'.

Notably, Simon added in the lengthier interview for us that:

> 'It was like [the scream of] a fox and I thought that's what it was.' That is until, as he described it, 'I saw this bloody great thing, like a gorilla, stand up [and] take off. I thought: Bugger me, what was that? But it was gone before I could think to do anything else about it. And, in any case, it was [on] the other side of the canal and I was nowhere near a bridge to get over there. But I shook after, I'll tell you.'

In answer to our questions, Simon said that the creature was not at all of the extreme height usually attributed to such cryptozoological entities as the Yeti of the Himalayas and the Bigfoot of North America, but was perhaps five to five and a half feet in stature at the very most (and possibly slightly less, even). And it appeared to be both highly agile and very muscular, and certainly not the sort of beast that a person would want to cross paths with on either a dark, and chilly winter's night in 1879, or on a bright summer's day in 1982.

An Earlier Encounter

Florence 'Florrie' Abbott grew up not far from the village Woodseaves, and, now pushing ninety and living in the city of Norwich, still distinctly remembers hearing uncanny tales of the Man-Monkey as a child in the late 1920s. Very interestingly, according to Florrie, one such tale that had been diligently passed down through her family told of a supernatural-like encounter with the Man-Monkey in the village of Ranton – only a short journey from Woodseaves – but in 1848, which was, notably, more than thirty years before the story chronicled by Charlotte S. Burne within the pages of *Shropshire Folklore* even surfaced.

As the story was related to me by an amusingly cantankerous Florrie (whose daughter was chiefly responsible for acting as the go-between that brought us together after the *Chase Post* highlighted the tale of the Man-Monkey as told by me and Irene Bott), it was an autumn night in 1848 when the witness – a young girl on Florrie's father's side of the family who was walking to her parents' home in Ranton – encountered in the shadows of the neighbouring property a five foot tall, man-like creature that was covered in dark, matted hair and that emitted strange grunting noises. For more than a minute or two, the pair stood staring at each other, both seemingly transfixed and rooted to the spot. Suddenly, said Florrie, the animal – if that is what it truly was – ambled off towards a nearby field and promptly vanished, quite literally, in a bright flash of light very much akin to that of a modern day camera flash.

In the Abbott household, it seems that the Man-Monkey was pretty much the local equivalent of the classic bogeyman, as Florrie well recalled:

> 'My brother and sister and I were all told this story as children and that if we were mischievous the Man-Monkey would come for us. The story was well known in our family when I was a little girl.'

A Wartime Monster

Another story that surfaced to me in 2000, and that most definitely deserves a mention here, came from a man who declined a personal meeting with me and even declined to reveal his name, but who, in a lunchtime telephone call, briefly told me how he had personally heard of an encounter with the beast of the bridge at the height of the Second World War. According to the tale, the man was a twelve-year-old in 1943 when a young evacuee – a boy of about nine or ten who hailed from somewhere in London's East End - came to stay with his immediate neighbours.

The pair regularly played in the woods and fields around Woodseaves during the summer of that year, and had jolly japes and adventures of a kind that would likely have made even the kids of Narnia, the Secret Seven, and the Famous Five envious. A significant degree of dark melancholy overcame the young Londoner, however, when he confided in my caller that, one night, he had overheard the husband and wife he was staying with quietly discussing a strange event that had occurred several days earlier: Namely, nothing less than the sighting by the husband of a large, hair-covered thing that 'walked upright', looked like a bear and that had been seen roaming menacingly through Woodseaves shortly after midnight.

The witness had apparently been deeply disturbed by the encounter and swore his wife to complete and utter secrecy. My source knew no more than that and had not spoken to the boy from London for more than half a century; for what it was worth, however, he said that he wanted to relate the details to me, as he thought I would find them interesting. I most certainly did find them interesting. I thanked the man and he quickly hung up the telephone, never to call again. So it goes in the field of monster hunting.

Bob and the Beastly Bridge

Bob Carroll told me that from the age of twenty-five until his late forties he had worked as a lorry driver – and, in the period from 1970 to 1977, specifically for a well-known paint manufacturing company. By the time of the interview, Bob was unable to recall the exact date of the incident at issue, which he wanted to

Waters of mystery and monsters. Copyright: Nick Redfern.

discuss with me, but he was pretty sure that it was either January or February of either 1972 or 1973, but certainly no later.

It was the early hours of the morning, at any rate, and Bob was driving to a spot where he was due to make a 6.00 a.m. delivery, having picked up a pallet of paint from a depot in Leicester the previous evening. Everything was completely normal until he approached...yes...that damned bridge. Stressing that 'it was all over in a few seconds', Bob said that it was his natural instinct to slow down as he reached the bridge; and, as he did so, he was shocked to see from his cab 'a hairy little man come storming through the trees and vanish down the canal'.

Bob was both surprised and amazed by the incredible speed and apparent agility of the beast as it bounded across the road and was subsequently, and quickly, lost to sight. He estimated that its height was four-and-a-half to five-feet at the very most, and that it looked 'well built', and was covered in what looked like black / blue coloured hair or fur. He did concede, however, that: 'Maybe that blue tinge was from the headlights though; it's hard to say now after so long.' Stressing that he had 'always been a gung-ho type', Bob pulled over to the side of the road, quickly turned on the hazard-lights of his lorry, and ran back to the scene of his bizarre experience.

> 'I was bloody daft,' he told me, with hindsight, 'because I say that I pulled over; but, really I was practically just stopped in the lane. If anyone had come along speeding around the bends there would have been a hell of an accident.'

Fortunately, on a country lane well into the early hours of the morning, such a calamity did not occur. On reaching the canal bridge, Bob quickly peered over both sides; however, the total lack of light made any attempt to see much of anything tangible nigh-on impossible. But there was one other odd thing that Bob was keen to tell me:

> 'The only thing that did happen at the bridge was I heard a noise while I was looking over the bridge. If you asked me to describe it – and my sister will verify I said the same to her years ago – I would say it was just like a baby crying. But it sounded a lot louder, and like it was evil or not right. And I got a funny feeling hearing it. It was almost like by sounding like a baby in trouble, it was trying to get me to come down to the canal; like it was luring me.'

Bob, probably very wisely, did not act upon the beast's cunning and macabre ruse. And, it may be relevant to note that Bob told me that when he returned to his vehicle, somewhat understandably shakily:

> 'It was like the battery was flat for a minute or two, then it kicked in, and I was off.'

In later chapters, we will see further evidence of how the British Bigfoot can seemingly affect both mechanical and electrical systems, as bizarre as such a scenario surely sounds.

A Tale of two Monsters

The remarkable tale of Paul Bell is, for me at least, a highly memorable one. Bell said that he was a keen fisherman and told me how in July and August 1976 he had spent several Saturdays out at the canal with his rods, reels, bait and his cans of Watney's Red and favourite beef and onion sandwiches, soaking in the intense heat of what was without doubt an absolutely scalding hot couple of months. I seriously doubt that anyone who is old enough to remember the summer of seventy-six will ever quite forget those truly extraordinary temperatures that briefly, and memorably, plunged the entire nation into complete and utter scalding chaos. But it was far stranger things than the occasional extreme nature of the British weather that Paul Bell had fixed on his mind.

He told me how, on one particular Saturday afternoon, he was sat near the water's edge on a small wooden stool that he always carried with him, when he was 'literally frozen solid' by the sight of 'what at first I thought was a big log floating down the cut, about sixty or seventy feet away'. According to Bell, however, it was no log; it was something else entirely. As it got closer, Bell was both astonished and horrified to see a large 'dark brown and black coloured' eel or snake-like creature – possibly ten feet in length or a little bit more – moving slowly in the water, with its head – that 'looked like a black sheep' - flicking rapidly from side to side. Although he had an old Polaroid camera with him, said Bell, he never even thought to take a photograph. Instead, he merely stared in both awe and shock as the animal cruised leisurely and blissfully past him, before finally vanishing out of sight. Bell stressed that the creature apparently did not see him ('or if it did, it never attacked me'), and did not appear to exhibit any outright hostile tendencies.

Having heard such accounts on several previous occasions – namely, of giant eels roaming British waterways, and particularly those of the West Midlands - meant that Paul Bell's story was not that unusual to me at all, even though it certainly involved what was without doubt an unknown animal of truly impressive proportions. But what elevated it to a far stranger level was the fact that Bell claimed, in quite matter of fact fashion, I have to confess, that the following Saturday he was fishing in practically the same spot when he 'got the feeling I was being watched' and saw something equally monstrous – yet manifestly different in nature and appearance. That's right, you guessed it correctly: The Man-Monkey.

Peering across the width of the canal, Paul was both horrified and petrified to see a dark, hairy face staring intently at him out of the thick, green bushes. The head of the animal was unmistakably human-like 'but crossed with a monkey' said Bell, who added that 'as soon as it saw me looking at it, up it went and ran right into the trees and I lost it'.
He further explained:

> 'That was it; a second or two was all at the most. But as it got up and ran I knew it was a big monkey. There's nothing else it could have been. But what flummoxed me more than seeing it though, was what was it doing there?'

And that was a question I sincerely wanted answering, too. At this stage, many might be inclined to ask: Is it just too much to accept when someone claims to have seen not one, but two, strange animals in the same, precise area? Maybe, for some; but, I will later reveal that sightings of hairy man-beasts and water-based monsters in the same area are curiously prevalent in Britain. And, there's an intriguing theory as to why, exactly, this should be so, which I will discuss in due course. Until then, though: On with the sightings.

Waterscape Revelations

In 2002, a report surfaced of an encounter with the Man-Monkey at the same wretched stretch of canal; it was one that had occurred back in the 1980s, but which remained hidden for years, until the witness finally decided to reveal the facts. A journalist for the website waterscape.com described the story – as told to their staff by the man himself - as follows:

> 'When British Waterways appealed for information about ghosts on the waterways in 2002, one respondent reported a more recent sighting of the ghost and thanked us for proving to his family that he was not seeing things! He told us that during a boating holiday on the "Shroppie" in the 1980s he took the tiller while the family were inside the boat preparing lunch. Passing under a bridge he looked up to see what he described as "a

huge black, hairy monkey" staring down at him. Astonished, he called his family out to see the creature. But by the time the boat had passed under the bridge, the creature had vanished. The man said he had been teased by his wife and children ever since over his sighting of the phantom monkey and was grateful to hear that others had seen it, too.'

A Latter Day Encounter

'I can only tell you what I saw,' fisherman Bob Jennings told me with impressive conviction in his voice, and with respect to his own encounter of the Man-Monkey variety in the summer of 2005. Once again, the location was Bridge 39, and out of the trees on the opposite side of the canal stepped forward an ape-like creature that was relatively skinny, around five feet in height, and possessed a pair of shining golden eyes. Bob added that: 'I was literally frozen to my chair; I nearly broke my rod gripping it as I stared at [the creature].'

Bob further revealed that as man and Man-Monkey continued to stare at each other, he got the distinct feeling that the creature was 'pure evil' and 'very intelligent'. He explained: 'Don't ask me how I know; but it wasn't just an ape. It seemed evilly clever and like it enjoyed scaring me.' Bob's fear was elevated to extreme levels when the Man-Monkey let out a blood-curdling, high-pitched howl that sounded something like 'how you might think an old woman would howl, if she did'. He added, perhaps with some justification and significance:

'Like how an old witch would scream.'

Bob said that the Man-Monkey then bent down towards the ground and 'pounded on the grass three or four times with his right fist', glared intently at him once again, and then 'shot off into the trees and went right through them'. It was gone. And so was Bob, who wasted no time at all in gathering up his rod, reel and other sundry items, and got the hell out of there. And, in a situation that very eerily paralleled the aftermath of the January 21, 1879 encounter with the legendary creature, Bob headed for the nearest pub, and a pint or several, in an effort to calm his frayed nerves. Realising that, at first, I had not fully appreciated the significance of his words, Bob explained that when he said the Man-Monkey ran 'right through the trees', he did mean that literally: Right through them. The creature may have appeared before him as a flesh and blood entity; however, it was distinctly spectral and was seemingly unhindered by the physical limitations that govern our existence.

Bob's story was not quite over, however. He said that two days after his encounter at Bridge 39, he was shopping in the nearby, old town of Newport when he caught sight of the beast once again. Bob was clearly embarrassed to relate this particular aspect of the story, since Newport is a bustling town during both the day and night, and is packed with shops, restaurants and pubs. And so, the idea that a five-foot-tall monkey could roam about the area without causing overwhelming mayhem and havoc in the process is completely inconceivable, by anyone's standards. But it wasn't quite like that, Bob assured me. Rather, it was while walking past a fourteenth-century stone cross in town known as the Butter Cross – which was specifically designed and built to denote Newport as a market town - that, out of the corner of his eye, Bob caught sight of the Man-Monkey standing next to the Cross and 'sneering at me'. The beast was only in view for a second or two and then vanished – quite literally. The oddest thing of all, Bob added, 'was that I looked around and it was like no-one else had seen it except me. Everyone else was doing their shopping, walking around, sitting outside and having a pint – the usual stuff you do in the summer'. Bob, shaken to the core, quickly returned to his motorbike and headed home at lightning speed. 'And I haven't been back, either,' he was careful to add. We should not, perhaps, blame him.

CHAPTER 6
WELSH WILD MEN
'...One man came up with the idea of consulting a magician...'

Moving on from the dark and menacing saga of the Man-Monkey of England's Shropshire Union Canal, let us now turn our attentions to the haunting wilderness of North Wales. Oll Lewis, of the Centre for Fortean Zoology (below right), has investigated a fascinating old legend pertaining to what can only be termed a definitive Welsh wild man.

Oll reveals that villagers in Nant Gwynant – which is a truly picturesque valley situated in Snowdonia, Gwynedd, North Wales - have for many a century told, in hushed tones, a turbulent and nightmarish story of definitive British Bigfoot proportions, and of how a dark and mysterious cave in the old valley – the Cave of Owen Lawgoch - came to be known, decidedly infamously so, as the abode of 'the hairy man'…

The Creature of the Caves

Oll's research has revealed that long, long ago, villagers and shepherds in the area of Nant Gwynant were plagued by a silent and stealthy thief who would break into their homesteads under the protective covers of shadow and darkness on a disturbingly regular basis. Those same villagers and shepherds would awaken to find that their goats and cows had been inexplicably milked, much-needed food was stolen, and a number of sheep were taken during the night, never to be seen again, their unfortunate fates surely sealed. The carnage and thievery, says Oll, 'went on for some years and every time anyone laid a trap for the thief it never took the bait and the finger of popular suspicion passed from ne'er-d'-well to ne'er-d'-well, with each suspect's guilt eventually being disproved'.

So, what – allegedly, at least – was the true nature of the nightmarish beast said to have been roaming the densely-treed, ancient valley? According to North Wales-based legend it was a creature of undeniably primitive proportions and terrifying appearance, one that seemed intent on tormenting the people of the picturesque area whenever, and however, possible, as Oll notes:

> 'One day a shepherd was returning from the mountains later than usual and spotted something strange; a huge, burly naked man covered from head to toe in thick red fur was resting on a neighbouring hill. The shepherd suspected that this out of place and strangely hirsute giant might be the thief that was plaguing the village, so the shepherd snuck past the man without being detected and ran back to the village as soon as he was out of sight.'

The story continued that when the shepherd in question breathlessly reached the heart of Nant Gwynant, he persuaded all of the available men-folk of the village to join him in a quest to, once and for all, rid the area of the creature that had elected to descend upon it and its people. Evidently, and unfortunately, not much thought went into this particular exercise. It basically involved little more than the hysterical posse charging up the green hill, and towards the wild man with crude, homemade weapons in hand, while simultaneously screaming at him at the top of their lungs. Not surprisingly, alerting the hairy man-thing to their presence was hardly the cleverest of all moves that the group could have made. The mighty beast shot away – on all-fours, interestingly enough – and, as Oll noted, in a fashion that suggested 'the skill and precision of a deer'.

A close and careful watch of the hill and its immediate surroundings was made from that day onwards, in the event that the man-beast might return to once again wreak diabolical havoc upon Nant Gwynant and its frayed and fried populace. It was, without doubt, a most wise decision. Barely a few days passed before the menacing entity returned, to both feed voraciously and spread fear and chaos across the immediate land.

This time, however, the villagers took a new and novel approach to tackling their quarry. The plan was to let loose a pack of vicious hounds upon the British Bigfoot-type animal, in the hope that the dogs would succeed where the men had overwhelmingly failed. Unfortunately, this action proved utterly fruitless, too. As soon as it caught wind of the scent of the hounds, the hairy thing was gone, once again bounding away in almost graceful fashion as it made its successful escape, and easily leaving the snarling dogs far, far behind. Oll reveals that a distinctly alternative plan of action was then put into place:

There's something in the woods. Copyright: Hans Burgkmair, circa 1500-1503.

'One man came up with the idea of consulting a magician. The magician told the villagers to find a red-haired greyhound without a single hair of a different colour and this would be able to catch the man. After much searching and bartering with local towns and villages the people of Nant Gwynant found a dog that fitted the bill and proudly took him home. When the villagers next saw the hairy man they were ready with the red greyhound and it was set loose to catch the hairy man. The hairy man escaped again by leaping down a small cliff.'

Were the people of Nant Gwynant cursed to forever have the marauding thing in their very midst? No. If the men, the dogs, and even the supernatural powers of a renowned and mysterious purveyor of ancient magic had failed to put paid to the monster-man and its terrible actions, then, quite clearly, another approach was sorely needed. It fell upon one of the women of the village to come up with a plan of attack to rid the area of the terrifying beast. Oll demonstrates what happened next:

'One woman was so angered by her frequent losses she decided to stay up every night and hide herself in the front room of her farmhouse to wait for when the hairy man decided to pay a visit. Sure enough after a few weeks the hairy man paid a visit to the wrong house and the lady was waiting with a hatchet. She remained hidden, until the man had squeezed his bulky frame half way through the window, before she struck the hairy man with her hatchet. The unexpected blow cleaved off the hairy man's hand in one blow and he recoiled back out of the window before the woman could smite him with a further whack. The brave woman dashed out of her door, hatchet in hand ready to finish the man off but by the time she had gotten outside he had fled.'

The wretched terror that had descended upon Nant Gwynant had finally reached its end, much to the overwhelming relief of the entire neighbourhood, as Oll reveals:

'When the village awoke the next day and the men learned what had happened they followed the trail of blood the hairy man had left behind to a cave beneath a local waterfall. As the big hairy man was never seen again it was assumed by the villagers that he had died in the cave, so the cave was named "the cave of the hairy man.'

This is not, however, the only time that North Wales has reputedly attracted the attentions and actions of hairy wild men and Bigfoot-type critters.

The Snowdonia Thing

I will be the very first to admit that the following account reads far more like a tall story, or an outrageous hoax, than it does of reality; and that's wording it mildly. But, if for no other reasons than (A) for the sake of completeness, and (B) because this book is an unbiased study of the British Bigfoot phenomenon, for what it's worth (or is not worth!), I am relating the words of the claimed witness, whose account was provided, anonymously to me, in 2001.

In a later chapter I will expand at length upon the issue of the extent to which hoaxing has played, and unfortunately, continues to play, a role in the matter of the British Bigfoot. In the meantime, however, here is the story, unedited, and provided to you, dear reader, just as it was provided to me more than a decade ago:

'I am a forester in North Wales, living for much of my time in a remote mountain bothy in Snowdonia. A bothy is a small mountain hut, and there's nothing I like more than to spend some quality time on my own, amongst the hills and nature. Over the years, I have received many reports of sightings of an extremely unusual creature, a "monstrous beast", as one visitor called it. This has puzzled me for a long time, and I became determined to seek out this beast for myself. It was while searching on the internet that I came across the British Beast on your website, and the thought occurred to me that maybe there is a population of these beasts spread across Britain.'

I have spent the last month or two preparing for an expedition base from my mountain bothy. The authorities refuse to give us any support, thinking that we are all crackpots. However, me and a group of colleagues managed to pull together enough resources to mount the expedition, which has just finished. I am afraid our success was limited, and there is much still to do but we did see the creature for ourselves. It attacked our camp one night, and much of our equipment was damaged. It was at least ten feet high, and stood on two legs. It seemed to be more bear-like than ape-like, it seemed to be investigating our camp when a dog we had with us tried to attack it. There followed a few minutes of absolute terror, as the beast was clearly quite distressed by our invasion, and sought an escape from what must have been a confusing situation. It was fortunate that no one was injured, and we are fairly sure that the beast is not inherently dangerous to people.'

A second email, received a couple of weeks later, also in anonymous fashion, reads as follows:

'We have returned to the campsite twice since the incident, to try and salvage what we could. One important point is that the beast could definitely not have been a bear, from a behavioural point of view; the only time a bear stands on two legs is to sniff the air, but this animal was rampaging about on two legs. We feel it is also vital to point out that the beast was in no way aggressive, but merely felt threatened by our presence. All of our camera equipment had been damaged beyond repair, and the terrain there is mostly rock, scree and heather, so there were no tracks etc. We have spent many hours trying to piece together what we would consider to be a fairly accurate description of the beast's appearance, bearing in mind we have been unable to rely on photographic evidence.'

'The beast was roughly ten feet tall, when standing on two legs and gave off a strong, musky type of smell. It had dark brown hair, probably fur, and massive hands. Its eyes appeared to be red in colour, and we could really sense the fear which the poor beast was enduring. For most of the time we were ducked down behind some rocks, and the campfire smoke was making it keep a fair distance away. It did attack our tent though, tearing through the sides. It was a dull and gloomy day, so when we began to take photos, the flash naturally went off. This really frightened it, and it began to head for us. So we ran off and were forced to leave the camera on its tripod. Alas, the beast picked it up and threw it against the rocks.

We feel that this bizarre animal is indeed very intelligent, and eagerly await some finer weather before embarking on another expedition. This disaster has not deterred us, and preparations are being made for next time. People are calling it the "Brecon Beacon Beast," despite it being nowhere near there. The local press seem to go for any excuse for a good alliteration!'

All attempts to trace the story to its original source, and to secure further commentary from the writer, resulted in nothing but overwhelming silence and a suspiciously – and suddenly - invalid email address. True or not - and if nothing else - this odd and controversial account most certainly adds to the colourful legends of the North Wales-based wild men.

CHAPTER 7
THE CREATURE OF THE LAKE
'...five of us saw an enormous man-shaped object
run from right to left...'

Beyond any shadow of a doubt, one of the most sensational of all the many and varied British Bigfoot controversies of recent years is that which concerns a hairy, man-like thing that has become known as the Beast of Bolam.

In the latter part of 2002 and early 2003, Jon Downes (below right) recalls that, with respect to both him and the staff of his Centre for Fortean Zoology;

> '...there occurred a huge "flap" of Big Hairy Men (BHM) sightings throughout the British Isles that we could not afford to ignore and that required our immediate attention. Indeed, such was the scale of this extraordinary wave of encounters that, even as we made firm plans for an expedition in March, a handful of new sightings of large, man-beasts from the Bolam Lake area of Northumberland, England, arrived in our e-mail In-Box in January that prompted us to undertake an immediate study of the evidence'.

On a cold, wintry morning shortly afterwards, Jon and his team from the CFZ hit the road, headed north, and the adventure duly and truly began...

Trailing the Beast of Bolam

When the creature craze was at its absolute height, and while he was personally on-site, Jon Downes prepared careful and copious reports, written in an in-depth style that expertly detailed the significant role played by the Centre for Fortean Zoology in the bizarre affair of the Beast of Bolam.

Those invaluable reports, made available for inclusion in this book, begin as follows, in Jon's very own words:

> 'We liaised very closely with Geoff Lincoln, an absolutely invaluable researcher based in the area. We gave him our planned arrival time, and asked if any of the eye-witnesses would be prepared to speak to us. Much to our ever-lasting delight, five out of the six were.

We think it should be noted here that the sixth is a soldier; and with the burgeoning situation in the Middle East spiralling rapidly out of control, it would be completely unreasonable to expect a serving military man to be at the beck-and-call of the CFZ.

Serendipitously, we were able to stay at a house owned by our County Durham representative, David Curtis. He and his wife, Joanne, were absolutely fantastic all the way through our sojourn in the North. The only sad thing about our stay with them was that Davy had to work most of the time; and so, therefore, was not able to join us during most of our activities.'

After what he described as a series of fairly dull misadventures best left unmentioned, Jon and the CFZ team then met up with Geoff Lincoln of British Hominid Research (pictured below at Bolam Lake indicating the location of one of the sightings) and Dr. Gail Nina-Anderson, a Fortean and art historian and made their way, in convoy-style, to Bolam Lake itself:

'It would be nice to be able to say that we were overwhelmed with a spooky feeling, or that the genus-loci of the location were in some way redolent of Fortean freakiness. But it wasn't at all. It was just what one would expect from a heavily wooded country-park in the North of England in the middle of January – cold, wet and grey.'

Geoff proceeded to show Jon no less than three locations where sightings of the beast-man had occurred:

'We carried out a thorough series of photographic mapping exercises, and did our best to fend off the incessant inquiries from the press. Just after lunchtime, a TV crew from a local television company arrived and filmed interviews with our investigation team. It was only after they had gone that we realised something very strange was happening.'

Jon was not wrong.

Electronic Madness and Avian Interference

After arriving on-site, a veritable wave of Fortean chaos erupted in the direct vicinity of Bolam Lake, as Jon recalls graphically:

'Although we had tested all of our electronic equipment the night before, had charged up batteries where necessary, and had even put new batteries in all of our equipment that needed them, practically without exception all of our new equipment failed. The laptop, for example, has a battery, which usually lasts between 20 and 35 minutes. It lasted just three minutes before failing. Admittedly, we received an enormous number of telephone calls during our stay at the lake, but not anywhere near enough to justify the fact that we had to change handsets four times in as many hours. The batteries in both Geoff's and our tape-recorders also failed. It seems certain that there was some strange electromagnetic phenomenon at work here.'

Later that afternoon,'

Jon continues,

'...we drove to a local pub where we met our first witnesses. Like all of the other people we were to meet over the next few days, they requested anonymity, and therefore in accordance with our strict confidentiality policy, we have respected this. Naomi and her son had been visiting Bolam Lake only a few days before. Not believing any of the reports that had appeared in the local media, they were both appalled and frightened when – while walking across the car-park itself – they had seen a huge creature standing motionless in the woods. They described an intense feeling of fear and trepidation, and rapidly left the area. They were incredibly co-operative, and agreed to come back to the lake with us the next day to stage a reconstruction.'

It was on that next day that undeniable high-strangeness affected the CFZ crew yet again, as Jon's notes clearly and carefully serve to demonstrate:

'We had a wake-up call at 5.30 a.m. the next morning, followed by a taxi-ride to a rest area five-hundred yards along the road from the Bolam Lake car-park, where we did a two-and-a-half minute interview for the BBC Radio 4 Today programme. One thing of great importance happened during the half-hour or so spent shivering by the side of the road waiting to speak to the BBC.'

Just before dawn, the crows, which live in a huge colony in the woods, started an appalling noise. Suddenly, the noise stopped, but was then followed by a brief succession of booming noises – like a heavily-amplified heartbeat from a *Pink Floyd* record – before the crows started up again. It is unclear whether these noises came from the vicinity of the lake itself or were made by the set-up of satellite dishes, and recording equipment that was loaded in the back of, and on top of, the BBC man's car. During the taxi journey back to Seaham, the driver remarked on the peculiar behaviour of the crows, and said that although he was a country-man himself and had spent his whole life living in this area, he had never heard anything quite like it.'

The Witnesses Revealed

The next step, Jon notes, was to seek out yet further witnesses to the monster and its actions:

'On arriving back at base, it was time for the entire CFZ expeditionary force to drive to the outskirts of the city of Newcastle, where we met with Geoff and a second witness in a café attached to a garden center. The witness, Neil, had been fishing at Bolam Lake one night four or five years previously. Together with two companions he had been making his way back to the car-park when they encountered a huge, dark, man-shaped object about 7-8 ft in height with what he described as sparkling eyes. The three fishermen did not stop to investigate but ran back to the car.

However, this was by no means the only encounter that Neil had reported to us. Together with one of his companions from the first adventure, he had again been night fishing at Bolam Lake during the summer of 2002. They had been camped out on this occasion, and had heard noises, which they assumed were from an enormous animal moving around in the bushes outside of their camp. Deciding that discretion was most definitely the better part of valour, they decided not to investigate any further; but when they broke camp the next morning they found that the fish they had stored in a bait-tin had been taken, and there were distinct signs that something very large had been lumbering around in the immediate vicinity.'

Possibly the most astounding story that he had to recount had taken place a couple of summers before our visit. He had been in the woods at the opposite side of the lake with his girlfriend. They had been making love, when his girlfriend told him she that she could see what she thought was a man in a monkey suit watching their sexual adventures from behind a bush. Neil, unsurprisingly, looked around the area but could find nothing.'

The Investigation Continues

And there was much more to come, too, as Jon's detailed files, prepared at the time, clearly demonstrate:

'We then continued to the lake. Neil had been amazingly co-operative, and had, like Naomi, agreed to stage a reconstruction with us. At the lake we liaised with the team from a local investigative group called Twilight Worlds and began a series of exercises, which would take up the rest of the day. Geoff had noted, the previous week, a series of apparently artificial tree formations similar to those "Bigfoot Teepees" noted by researchers in the United States. Together with Twilight Worlds, Geoff and CFZ stalwart Graham Inglis, went off to map these formations and to make a photographic record. They also took with them a Twilight Worlds member trained in using their EMF meter, together with a dowser. After our electrical mishaps of the previous day, we wanted to find out whether there were, indeed, any abnormal EMF fields in the area. Neither investigator found any unusual readings.'

Our next task was to stage a reconstruction of Naomi's sighting. Again a full photographic and video record was made, and EMF readings were also taken. Again no unusual readings were recorded either by the EMF meter or the dowser. We then repeated the exercise with Neil and reconstructed his first sighting.'

The Monster Hunters Meet the Monster

Little did Jon know it earlier that day, but as the afternoon progressed, something deeply profound and life-changing - for both Jon and the entire team, no less - was just about to occur. In his very own words, Jon details the truly extraordinary situation that suddenly, and undoubtedly breathtakingly, unfolded before the shocked eyes of just about one and all who were present:

'At about half-past-four, one of the members of *Twilight Worlds* reported seeing something large, human-shaped and amorphous in the woods directly in front of the car-park. As the dusk gathered at about 5 o'clock, we again heard the raucous noise of the crows that he had reported just before dawn.

Suddenly, once again, they fell silent and one of the Twilight Worlds members shouted that she could hear something large moving around among the undergrowth. All of the car-drivers present were ordered to switch on their headlights and to put them on full-beam. We did not hear any noise in the undergrowth; although other people present did. Eight people were watching the woods and five of us saw an enormous man-shaped object run from right to left, disappear, and then a few moments later run back again.'

**The site of Jon Downes' dramatic 2003 encounter with the monster of Bolam woods.
Copyright: Centre for Fortean Zoology.**

The most amazing aspect of the encounter, however, was that the hulking, racing thing was one-dimensional; shadow-like, and utterly lacking in any sort of 3-D substance, but, even so, still some form of mystifying entity in its very own right. The amazing event was over in an instant, but the overall investigation most certainly was far from being so.

The End of Days

With limited time now on its hands, the CFZ worked hard to follow up on as many leads, data, and testimony as was humanly, and conceivably, possible, as Jon's diary-style reports reveal:

> 'When the expedition returned on Monday, we conducted experiments to find out exactly how far away the creature – if it was a creature – was from the excited onlookers. We were able to make a fairly accurate estimate that the creature had been one-hundred-and-thirty-four-feet away at the time of our sighting. We also estimated that the creature had run along a distance of between twelve and eighteen feet. About five minutes after the encounter, we wandered across the car-park to the location when Naomi had reported seeing the creature. There, too, a sensation was felt of intense fear.'

As Jon noted correctly, after a startling encounter like that, anything else would have been an anti-climax. He added, however:

> 'Geoff Lincoln took the CFZ team to interview two further witnesses. The first was a young man living in the suburbs of Newcastle, who told us of his encounter with an enormous man-shaped being next to a hollow tree in the woods, some months previously. The incident had taken place while he had been walking his dog. He had been so frightened by his experience that he refused to ever go near the lake again. Finally, we went to another pub where we met another man called Neil. He had been with the first Neil at the time of his initial sighting. We were all impressed by his sincerity and by the way that he corroborated his friends' testimony in what seemed to us, at least, to be a very natural and wholly uncontrived manner. One day later, we all returned to the lake. We proceeded to carry out a thorough photographic survey of the final two sighting locations to ascertain – as far as was possible, at least – the size of the thing that had been seen on Saturday night, and its approximate distance from the eye-witnesses.'

> As the EMF scans had been remarkably unsuccessful, we tried to scan the area for magnetic anomalies using a pocket compass. Mike Hallowell, a friend and excellent researcher, registered a strange magnetic anomaly at the location of the fisherman's first sighting. However, it must be reported that when the team tried to replicate this later in the day, they were unsuccessful. '

> That evening, we interviewed a final witness: A woman in her late fifties who had been visiting the lake about five years before with her son who was then eleven years old. Like Naomi, she reported intense feelings of not exactly hostility; but what she interpreted as a message not to investigate a peculiar tree formation any further. She discussed these tree formations with us at some length. She had been surprised to find them at several locations throughout the woodlands. Our work was then finished and we returned home.'

The tale of the Beast of Bolam and its one-dimensional nature are matters most mysterious, indeed. We will return to them in a later chapter, and in which we will specifically try and make some degree of sense of the enigmatic affair. But, for now, though: On with the witness encounters.

CHAPTER 8
DARTMOOR'S HAIRY HANDS
'...A pair of hairy hands closed over mine...'

Around 1910, a distinctly strange and macabre saga began on what, today, is the B3212 road, which can be found in the vicinity of the English villages of Postbridge and Two Bridges. Both locales are situated amid the 368 square-mile mass of sprawling, mysterious English moorland known famously as Dartmoor, which was the foggy and boggy setting for Sir Arthur Conan Doyle's classic Sherlock Holmes novel, *The Hound of the Baskervilles*.

While Conan Doyle's massively entertaining story was only intended as fiction (albeit, a story based in part on legends and tales of real-life, spectral, glowing-eyed hounds of Hell said to haunt and prowl the ancient moors), the tale I am about to relate most certainly is not fiction. Rather, it is cold-hearted, hideous reality. In a highly disturbing fashion, a hairy, monstrous and unidentified force has, time and again, violently lashed out at unwary drivers passing through Postbridge and Two Bridges - and which, in one case, reportedly even resulted in a tragic death for an unfortunate road-user…

The Road Monster

In most of the cases on record at least, the unfortunate victims of the diabolical phenomenon known locally as the Hairy Hands, reported seeing large, hairy, 'disembodied hands', that looked half-human and half-ape, manifesting out of utterly thin air, firmly grabbing the steering wheel of their vehicles – or the handle-bars of their bikes – and unsurprisingly striking complete terror into their hearts, something which invariably resulted in them being violently forced off the country road and onto the moors. For a decade or so, the events were considered to be nothing more than a mild – albeit, certainly without doubt, sinister - curiosity for the superstitious people that inhabited the atmospheric depths of misty Dartmoor. That situation drastically changed in 1921, however, when overwhelming tragedy struck deep, suddenly and hard.

Death on the Moors

In June of that year, one Dr. E.H. Helby, who was at the time serving as the Medical Officer at the nearby Dartmoor Prison, met his death on the very same stretch of road when he lost control of his motor-cycle and sidecar. Sitting in the sidecar were his two children, and Helby had just about enough time to warn them to jump to safety – which they fortunately did – before he was thrown from his motor-cycle and instantly killed. Then, on the dull and misty day of August 26 of that very same year, a young British Army captain – who was described by the local media as being 'a very experienced rider' – was also thrown into the verge of the road, after he, too, lost control of his motor-cycle. Significantly, and incredibly, the captain stated at the time, in response to media questions that:

'It was not my fault. Believe it or not, something drove me off the road. A pair of hairy hands closed over mine. I felt them as plainly as ever I felt anything in my life – large, muscular, hairy hands. I fought them for all I was worth, but they were too strong for me. They forced the machine into the turf at the edge of the road, and I knew no more till I came to myself, lying a few feet away on my face on the turf.'

An Author and a Journalist Encounter the Hairy Hands

In the summer of 1924, the well known and widely respected Devonshire folklorist Theo Brown was holidaying in a caravan, approximately only half a mile from the road where practically all of the ominous activity had taken place. In later life, she graphically detailed the particularly nightmarish, and nighttime, encounter that she experienced while on that same holiday, and that is directly relevant to the mystery of the Hairy Hands.

Brown wrote of her ominous and unforgettable experience as follows:

'I knew there was some power very seriously menacing us near, and I must act very swiftly. As I looked up to the little window at the end of the caravan, I saw something moving, and as I stared, I saw it was the fingers and palm of a very large hand with many hairs on the joints and back of it, clawing up and up to the top of the window, which was a little open. I knew it wished to do harm to my husband sleeping below. I knew that the owner of the hand hated us and wished harm, and I knew it was no ordinary hand, and that no blow or shot would have any power over it. Almost unconsciously I made the Sign of the Cross and I prayed very much that we might be kept safe. At once the hand slowly sank down out of sight and I knew the danger was gone. I did say a thankful prayer and fell at once into a peaceful sleep. We stayed in that spot for several weeks but I never felt the evil influence again near the caravan. But, I did not feel happy in some places not far off [sic] and would not for anything have walked alone on the moor at night or on the Tor above our caravan.'

Then there was the tale told to the writer Michael Williams – the author of the book *Supernatural Dartmoor* - by journalist Rufus Endle, who maintained that while driving near Postbridge on an undetermined date, 'a pair of hands gripped the driving wheel and I had to fight for control'. Luckily, Endle managed to avoid crashing the vehicle; the hands, meanwhile, mysteriously, and in an instant, vanished into thin air. A very concerned Endle requested that the story specifically not be published until after his death.

The Monstrous Mystery Continues

Decades later, it seems, the diabolical Hairy Hands of Devonshire returned to terrorise the little villages and hamlets that, practically unchanged for centuries, still adorn darkest Dartmoor. Michael Anthony works for one of the largest suppliers of photo-copying machines in Britain, and spends a lot of time travelling the length and breadth of the country meeting clients and promoting – and hopefully selling and / or leasing - his company's products. Late on the night of January 16, 2008, Anthony was driving along the B3212 road when he had a terrifying encounter with the unknown. It was an encounter that easily paralleled the many and varied reports of the Hairy Hands that surfaced way back in the 1910s and 1920s.

According to Anthony, it was around 11.00 p.m., and he had been visiting a customer in Postbridge, who was establishing a new business in the area, and who wished to rent several copiers from Anthony's company. The evening had gone very well, a deal had been struck, contracts had been signed and exchanged, and a pleased and

Born to be wild.
Copyright: Jost Amman, 1589.

satisfied Anthony was now homeward bound to the city of Bristol. It turned out to be a journey that he would never, ever likely forget.

Anthony had barely left Postbridge, when his skin began to feel distinctly cold and clammy, and a sense of dread and fear completely enveloped him. And the fact that there seemed to be no logical reason for this, only heightened Anthony's fear and concern.

After all, he was merely making a leisurely, late-night drive home – something that usually cheered him after spending several days on the road and away from his wife and two young daughters. It would not take long before he found out what lay at the heart of this strange and sinister affair, however.

Like so many people before him, Anthony was about to have a dark, and very close, encounter with a pair of hands of the very hairy variety. He explained further that perhaps two minutes after the atmosphere in his car became oppressive, fear-filled, and even somewhat malevolent, he felt his hands begin to 'go numb'. He added:

'I actually thought I was having a stroke.'

Fortunately, it was no stroke. In some ways, however, it was far worse.

Anthony could only look on in both complete horror and disbelief as, just as had been the case so many decades earlier, a very large pair of hair-covered hands, 'or paws', as he intriguingly described them, encased his own, and then suddenly attempted to forcibly steer the car towards the edge of the road and onto the cold, moonlit moors. To his credit, Anthony struggled valiantly with the wheel and, on three occasions, fought off the actions of the spectral, hairy intruder in his midst.

Interestingly, after the third attempt, said Anthony, the hands simply vanished into thin air, amid a brief flash of light - that lit up the interior of the car – and an overwhelming smell of sulfur. The shaken driver floored the accelerator and did not stop until he reached one of the service stations on the M5 motorway. The mysterious hairy intruder, it seems, had struck once again. Fortunately, however, on this occasion it did not succeed in achieving its deadly goal.

There is a notable sequel to this affair, and it's one that's highly relevant to the overall subject matter of this very book. When Anthony later – and somewhat guardedly – mentioned his nightmarish encounter to his client in Postbridge, he was intrigued to learn that a relative of the man's brother in law had heard of sightings in the area during the 1940s of what was intriguingly, but unfortunately briefly, described as nothing less than a 'ruddy great chimpanzee'…

Something 'bloody odd'

Bob Shenton saw 'something bloody odd' on the wilds of Dartmoor back in the winter of 1967. He was driving across the moors late one night - at the time he worked as a plumber and was heading to a house to deal with a case of a burst water-pipe – and, while near the village of Postbridge, came across something decidedly strange. According to Bob, for the very briefest of moments, and as he approached Postbridge, he caught sight of what looked for all the world like a large ape-like figure crossing the road in front of him and vanishing into the shadows at the edge of the road. Interestingly, Bob described the creature as 'like a shadow', in the sense that it seemed one-dimensional in nature - which closely echoes the description of the very similar beast seen at Bolam Lake, Northumberland in January 2003 by Jon Downes, and as described in the previous chapter.

'A possible Bigfoot on the Moors'

In February 2012, yet another story with a distinct Dartmoor link to the British Bigfoot surfaced, this one from a man named John Cameron, who wrote me the following:

> 'Many years ago (1991 to be as exact as I can) I was on Dartmoor in the small hours, location forgotten but I recall being sat with the girl I was sort of seeing at the time and we were located around back of some public toilets (yeah, I know, real romantic but it gave us some privacy) and before us about two hundred plus meters away was a lake...

> As we were sat having a smoke I noticed a shape moving around down at what I believed to be the lake shore, it was night but the moon was bright so you could make out shapes and form but not features, anyway my brain first kicked in as to the fact that it must be a diver and it was late to be out diving, then I realized that this "person" had no lights about them to see where they were headed or, if they had been diving, to see underwater.'

John, who still resides in Devon, added:

> 'The form was definitely walking on two legs, that was apparent by the way it moved, but it was silhouetted against the lake so I could not make out features, being the inquisitive creatures that we are I began to move towards the shape, then I realized that whoever this was that was perhaps not the best idea, the form was still I assumed at or near the lake shore and seemed to be moving slowly not towards us but diagonally away to our left when the girl I was with suggested we should go I agreed that was a damn good idea.'

> The form itself was bulky but as to actual height etc I could not absolutely say, I just got the feeling that it was large, the thought occurred to me as we were leaving the area in my friends' car that perhaps it was a Bigfoot, that is all my mind could relate it to after ticking off the other options like an escaped prisoner from Dartmoor prison, there were no reports from around the time, a diver, at that time of night and with no lights, there was no other car in the small car park either for the diver to make his way to which also negated the possibility that it was another courting couple or someone out for a walk. There was another couple with us that night, but they remained in and around the car, and besides neither looked like the form that we saw.'

And finally...

The Hairy Hands of Wales

We have already seen evidence of legends and folklore pertaining to wild men on the loose in North Wales, and there is yet another report that may be of relevance to this aspect of the overall mystery. I have chosen to include the report in this chapter, however, as it is one of definitive Hairy Hands proportions, as you will imminently come to appreciate.

The location was Flintshire, and the time: the 19th Century. According to the story, which was publicised by Elias Owen – the author of *Welsh Folk-Lore* – the witness was a man named Richard Roberts, of Coederaill, Bylchau who had confided in the Reverend W. Jones – also of Bylchau – about what had occurred.

Instead of attending church on Sundays, Roberts got in the habit of roaming around the local fields near to where he lived, and on one Sunday morning in the autumn was out gathering nuts from bushes in a nearby wooded area. On reaching one particular bush that was practically weighed down with a mighty supply of nourishing nuts, Roberts reached into the bush and was ready to grab a handful when, out of the blue, a hairy hand appeared, also reaching for the very same bush.

Utterly terrified, Roberts fled the area, fearful that the hand was that of the Devil himself, and deeply worried that the horned one had come to punish him for not attending church. Notably, Reverend Jones tried valiantly, but unsuccessfully, to convince Roberts that what he had encountered was nothing stranger than an out of place monkey. And, for what it is worth, that is the tale. Whether true, or a concocted story to try and scare people into attending church, remains tantalisingly unknown. The deep parallels between this affair and that of Dartmoor's Hairy Hands, however, are surely as clear as they are undeniable.

With that said, if you should ever find yourself driving through Postbridge and Two Bridges on some dark and thundery night, and your vehicle is suddenly, and to your eternal horror, hijacked by a paranormal pair of hands of the hairy type, I suggest that if trying to regain control of the steering-wheel does not work, then bellow at full force the memorable words of Charlton Heston's character, Taylor, in the 1968 film, *Planet of the Apes*:

'Take your stinking paws off me, you damn dirty ape!'

Do man-beasts roam beneath London?

CHAPTER 9
LONDON'S UNDERGROUND
MONSTROSITIES
'...I think we didn't have control of the tunnels,
and someone up in the government knew...'

Britain's famous London Underground serves commuters travelling throughout Greater London, as well as select parts of Buckinghamshire, Hertfordshire, and Essex. It can also claim the title of the world's oldest underground system of its type, given that it opened up for business on January 10, 1863. Today, nearly 250 years after its initial construction, the London Underground has no less than 268 stations and approximately 250-miles of track, thus making it the longest – as well as certainly the oldest - sub-surface railway system on the planet. Moreover, in 2007, one-billion passengers were recorded as having used the Underground since 1863.

According to a number of select souls, however, the London Underground has played host to far more than mere tracks, trains and a near-endless number of travellers. Deep within the winding tunnels of this sub-surface labyrinth, bizarre and terrible things – many of a wild man variety - are rumoured to seethe and fester, and possibly even feed too. And British authorities are doing all they can to keep the lid on the chaos and carnage that threatens to spread deep below the streets of the nation's historic capital city…

Movie Monsters of the Underground
Stories of strange creatures – many of a definitively cryptozoological nature – lurking in the London Underground have circulated for years, and chiefly in fictional, on-screen format. Such examples include:

(A)   the 1967 production of *Quatermass and the Pit*, in which bizarre, mutated and diminutive ape men – who were the subject of advanced genetic experiments, undertaken millions of years earlier, by visiting Martians - appear in the London Underground of the 1960s in the form of spectral, manifested, inherited memories;

(B)   *The Web of Fear* – a *Dr. Who* adventure that surfaced in the following year, 1968, that sees the doctor and his comrades doing battle with robotic yetis on the Underground;

(C)   *An American Werewolf in London* – a 1981 film in which the beast of the title feasts on a doomed, late night rail traveller; and

(D)   *Reign of Fire*, a 2002 production starring Christian Bale and Matthew McConaughey, that revolves around literal fire-breathing dragons that burst forth from the old tunnels of the Underground and decimate Britain, and, eventually, the rest of the planet, too.

Some of the older tales of creature-like entities prowling the tunnels under London were incorporated into a less well known, fictionalised film. Its name was *Death Line*. Made in 1972, it starred horror film stalwarts Christopher Lee and Donald Pleasance, and related the saga of a collapse, in the latter part of the 19th Century, at a then new station being built at Russell Square – which happens to be a real station on the Underground. Unfortunately, when the disaster occurs, a significant number of workers – both men and women – are killed. Or, rather, they are presumed killed. And, when the company funding the project goes bankrupt, all efforts to try and dig out the bodies and give them a decent burial are quickly, quietly, and conveniently forgotten.

Had the plans gone ahead, the company would have learned to its horror that the workers did not die. Instead, they found themselves trapped underground, and forced to make new lives for themselves in their permanent, sub-surface home – which they do by living on just about anything and everything, and anyone and everyone, that dares to cross their path or stumble upon their darkened abode.

And as *Death Line* tells it, some eight decades on, the final few offspring of the original workers are still valiantly clinging on to life. Their existence, however, is a distinctly poor one: afflicted by a host of genetic abnormalities caused by in-breeding and a lack of regular nourishment, their minds are reduced to truly primitive levels and their bodies are overwhelmingly diseased and corrupted. As for their only source of food, it comes in the form of the occasional, unfortunate user of the Underground who, if the circumstances are in their favour, they can secretly grab, kill, and ultimately, devour.

Death Line is an entertaining and odd little film that seldom gets the airing it deserves, and it's one that leaves the viewer with much to think about and muse upon when it comes to the matter of wild people living among us. There are, however, those who believe the film is more than just mere fiction; far more than just mere fiction. Some are firmly of the opinion that the story it relates is 100 percent fact – albeit, admittedly, difficult to confirm fact - and that far below the capital, primitive man-beasts roam, forage, slaughter and feed.

Death in the Tunnels

Before his passing in 2007, Frank Wiley, who spent his entire working life in the British Police Force, told a bizarre and unsettling tale of his personal memories and investigations of a number of very weird killings on the London Underground, always late at night, in a particular period of time that covered 1967 to 1969. The killings, Wiley said, occurred on at least three stations, and were hushed up by the police, under the guise of being the unfortunate results of particularly vicious, late night muggings.

In reality, Wiley explained, the muggings were nothing of the sort at all. They were far, far more horrific in nature. There were, he recalled, seven such deaths during the time period that he was assigned to the investigations. As for the particular cases of which Wiley did have personal awareness, he said the modus-operandi was always exactly the same: the bodies of the people – a couple of who were commuters and the rest hobos simply looking for shelter on cold, windswept nights - were found, always after at least 10.00 p.m., a significant distance into the tunnels, with arms and/or legs viciously amputated – or possibly even gnawed off. Stomachs were ripped open, innards were torn out, and throats were violently slashed. A definitive man-eater – or worse still, a whole group of man-eaters – was seemingly prowling around the most shadowy corners of London's dark underworld after sunset. And it, or they, had only one cold and lethal goal: to seek out fresh flesh with which to nourish their ever-hungry bellies.

Could it have been the case that the killings were the work of a rampaging animal, possibly one that had escaped from a local, London-based zoo or a private menagerie, and that was now wildly on the loose far below the capital city? Or might the deaths have been simply due to desperate, suicidal people who threw themselves under the speeding trains, and whose remains were violently dragged into the tunnels, under the steel wheels of the racing carriages? Wiley strongly believed that neither of these scenarios provided adequate explanations.

There was a further, very good reason why the deaths were not ascribed to the work of wild beasts or suicides: namely, the presence of a terrifying-looking character seen at some point in 1968 by two workmen that were repairing a particular stretch of track on the Bakerloo Line (a fourteen mile long section of the London Underground that was constructed in 1906). The savage character, stated Wiley, was a bearded, wild-haired man, dressed in tattered, filthy clothing.

When one of the workers challenged the mysterious figure with a large ratchet, the man came closer, in a weird, faltering, stumbling style. To the horror of the pair, he held his arms out in front of him, bared a mouth of decayed teeth in their direction, and uttered a low and threatening growl. The strange figure then slowly backed away, eventually turning and then suddenly running deeper into the tunnel, until he was finally, and forever, lost from view. Unsurprisingly, and rather sensibly, the fraught workmen elected not to give chase, but instead raced to the nearest police station and summoned the authorities, who, said Wiley, questioned the petrified men vigorously.

The Stamp of Secrecy

Wiley further added that secret orders quickly came down to the police investigators on the case - from the British Government's Home Office, the work of which focuses on a host of issues relative to national-security - to wrap everything up, and very quickly, too. Intriguingly, Wiley maintained that secret liaison with Home Office personnel revealed that there were unverified rumours of deeper, very ancient, crudely built tunnels – that reportedly dated back centuries, and long, long before the advent of trains, railways and such like – existing far below the London Underground. There was even some speculation they may have been constructed as far back as the Roman invasion of Britain that began in A.D. 43. Precisely who had constructed the older tunnels, and who it was that might have emerged from them to wreak deadly havoc on the Underground in the 1960s, was never revealed to Wiley's small team of personnel.

He said:

> 'Probably no-one really knew, anyway. Only that someone, like the character seen by the workmen, was coming up from somewhere, killing, taking parts of the bodies, and then they were always gone again. It all got pushed under the rug when the Home Office said so. And when the last killing I was involved in [occurred], in 1969, I didn't hear much after that; just rumours there might have been more deaths in the '70's upward. I don't know.'

Wiley's last comments on his controversial claims, in 2004, went as follows:

> 'There's more to the [Death Line] film than people know. My thought then, and which it still is today, is someone making the film heard the stories, the deaths we investigated. They had to have; the film was too close to what happened. And I think we didn't have control of the tunnels, and someone up in the government knew. Perhaps it's still going on. That would be a thought.'

With Wiley's final sentence, I have absolutely no argument!

Confirmation of the Dwellers of the Underground?

The London Underground's British Museum Station closed its doors on September 25, 1933. For many years prior to its closure, however, a local myth circulated to the effect that the ghost of an ancient Egyptian haunted the station. Dressed in a loincloth and headdress, the figure would emerge late at night into the labyrinth of old tunnels. In fact, the story gained such a hold that a London newspaper even offered a significant monetary reward to anyone who was willing to spend the night there. Somewhat surprisingly, not a single, solitary soul took the newspaper up on its generous offer.

The story took a far stranger turn after the station was shut down, however. The comedy-thriller movie, *Bulldog Jack*, which was released in 1935, included in its story a secret tunnel that ran from the station to the Egyptian Room at the British Museum. The station in the film is a wholly fictional one dubbed Bloomsbury; however, the scenario presented in the film was specifically based upon the enduring legend of the ghost of British Museum Station.

Oddly enough, on the exact same night that the movie was released in British cinemas, two women disappeared from the platform at Holborn – which just happened to be the next station along from the British Museum. Strange marks were later found on the walls of the closed station, and more sightings of the ghost were reported, along with weird moaning noises coming from behind the walls of the tunnels. Not surprisingly, tales began to quickly circulate to the effect that the police had uncovered some dark and terrible secret - about a paranormal killer on the tracks - that had to be kept hidden from the populace at all costs. In other words, there was a strange, yet eerily-similar, precursor to the 1960's recollections of Frank Wiley, one that predated his own experiences by more than three-decades.

London Underground officials were, for a significant period of time, forced to dismiss the story, and there has always been an outright denial on the existence of a secret tunnel extending from the station to the museum's Egyptian Room. Nevertheless, the story was resurrected in Keith Lowe's novel of 2001, *Tunnel Vision*, in which the lead character states, while trying to both impress and scare his girlfriend at the same time:

> 'If you listen carefully when you're standing at the platform at Holborn, sometimes – just sometimes – you can hear the wailing of Egyptian voices floating down the tunnel towards you.'

Might the loincloth-wearing 'Egyptian' actually have been one of Frank Wiley's savage underground cannibals? And, if so, were the tales of a police cover-up an indication that officialdom may have secretly known about the capital city's wild men for far longer than even Wiley could have guessed?

Paranormal Activity on the Platform

In some respects, the story of Frank Wiley eerily parallels that of a man named Colin Campbell, who maintains that while travelling home on the London Underground in the mid-1960s, he had a nightmarish encounter with a very similar beast. According to Campbell, it was late at night and, rather surprisingly, he was the only person to get off the train at its scheduled stop on the Northern Line. As the train pulled away from the unusually deserted and deathly and eerily silent platform, and as Campbell made his way towards the exit, he claims to have heard a strange growl coming from behind him. He quickly spun around and was shocked to see a large, hairy ape-like animal lumbering across the platform towards the track, and seemingly mumbling to itself and no-one else as it did so.

Most bizarre of all, however, the beast was definitively spectral, rather than flesh and blood. Around three-

Creating an underground lair. Copyright: P. Justyne, 1861.

quarters of its body were above the platform, while its legs were curiously near-transparent and, incredibly, passed right through the platform. Campbell further asserts that as he stood in awe, too shocked to even try to move, the beast continued to walk through the concrete, right onto the tracks, and then straight through the wall directly behind the tunnel – all the time paying absolutely no attention to Campbell in the slightest.

Are savage, devolved humans really living – in literal cannibalistic-style – deep under London? And are the old tunnels really home to ghostly ape men of the type encountered by Colin Campbell back in the 1960s? Or are such tales simply borne out of legends provoked by the likes of *Dr. Who* and *Quatermass and the Pit?* If not the latter, then some might say that such accounts have a significant bearing upon the reports of the British wild man – particularly if the creatures have found ways to exit the tunnels from time to time, and have made their way around select portions of the city, and the surrounding countryside by the camouflage of a dark and disturbing night…

CHAPTER 10
THE TRAGIC TALE OF PATIENT X
'...I discovered the details of some
terrible human tragedies reaching back
over a century...'

From Jon Downes comes what is surely one of the strangest of all tales of a hairy, British wild man. Since the story is a lengthy and complex one that is full of an absolute multitude of twists and turns – not to mention deep conspiracy and Second World War-era secrecy and subterfuge - the most profitable approach is to allow Jon to relate the extraordinary findings for himself and in his own fashion.

They are findings that relate to a turbulent, terrible, and ultimately tragic, story told to Jon back in the early 1980s, when he was still in his early twenties and working as a psychiatric nurse at Starcross Hospital, Devon – Starcross being a small village which can be found on the west bank of the River Exe, Teignbridge. With that said, let us take a close and careful look at this emotion-filled tale of people long gone, shadowy secrets, deep stigma, and a wartorn era immersed in carnage and conflict...

Madhouse!
According to the British Government's National Archive at Kew:

> 'Originally known as the Western Counties Idiot Asylum [Author's note: I kid you not at all on that far less than subtle name!] this institution opened in 1864 in a house and two acres of land at Starcross, rented from W.R. Courtenay, 11th Earl of Devon. A committee appointed to collect donations and subscriptions, and to accept patients into the asylum, was chaired by the 11th Earl who was also its first president, positions he held until 1904.'

Kew's history of the hospital continues:

> 'By 1870 the building housed 40 residents, and an appeal for funds to build larger premises was launched. A new building, surrounded by 7 acres of grounds, was opened in June 1877. This was able to house 60 boys and 40 girls. Further additions were built between 1886 and 1909, and by 1913 a total of 1,451 patients had been admitted to the institution. In 1914, the asylum was incorporated under the

OPPOSITE: Hair today, not gone tomorrow. Copyright: Unknown, 1580.

Companies Act. It then became known as the Western Counties Institution, Starcross, and was certified as "a residential special school for mental defectives". Residents were trained in carving, weaving, basketry, lace-making and carpentry, and worked on the institution's agricultural holdings.

In the 1930s, properties at Dix's Field, Exeter and Steepway, Paignton were purchased for use as domestic training hostels for young women. A farm hostel was founded on Langton Farm at Dawlish and a seaside holiday home was opened. In 1948, the institution was transferred to the National Health Service, and became merged into the Royal Western Counties Institution Hospital Group, which coordinated all the residential mental deficiency services. The institution came under the control of Devon Area Health Authority from 1974 and of Exeter Health Authority from 1982. In 1986, in keeping with a national policy of transferring the majority of mentally handicapped people back into the community, the Royal Western Counties Hospital was marked for closure.'

A World War Wild Man

With that background on Starcross Hospital / 'idiot asylum' revealed, let us now focus on Jon Downes, who begins the remarkable tale as follows:

> 'A story, which, I am sure, was told me in good faith, and which even now I do not know whether to believe, apparently took place during the Second World War. There had, apparently, been a number of occasions when captured German aircrew and pilots who had been shot down over South Devon or the English Channel were kept, temporarily, in a remote wing of Starcross Hospital — which is roughly ten miles from the city of Exeter - until they could be transferred to the prisoner-of-war camp high above Starcross on the Haldon Hills.'

On one particular occasion, says Jon, the Home Guard had been searching for a fugitive German airman in the woods surrounding Powderham Castle, which is about half a mile away from the old hospital, and which was constructed between 1390 and 1420 by Sir Philip Courtenay. They had ventured into the deepest parts of the woods in search of their quarry when, suddenly, the small band of elderly men and boys who were too young to join the Army, saw what they believed was the fugitive airmen running through the woods in front of them. The leader shouted at him to stop, but it was all to no avail, as Jon reveals:

> 'The old man who told me the story was actually one of the Home Guards, and he told me that one of the party had been a teacher in Germany before the war and could speak the language. He ordered the man to stop, but the fugitive ignored him. In 1942, the war was not going well - at least as far as the British were concerned - and Home Guard units, especially in rural areas, were desperately under-equipped. Most of the patrol was only armed with pitchforks, although one had a dilapidated shotgun and the captain - who led the unit - had his old First World War service revolver.

> If it had been a normal patrol there would only have been about half-a-dozen of them, but large parts of Exeter had been levelled by successive waves of German bombers, and the opportunity for a population of a tiny village like Starcross to actually face the enemy on equal terms was an irresistible lure. According to my informant, the Home Guard patrol had been augmented by a gang of villagers baying for blood and desperate for revenge.

> The captain was an educated man, and had no intention of using force to capture the fugitive unless it was absolutely necessary. The man with a shotgun - a local farmer, who had lost two of his sons in the desperate weeks leading up to Dunkirk - had no such compunction. He was also drunk. Shouting, "I'll get you, you bastard!" He raised his weapon and fired. The dark figure ahead of them let out a grunt of agony and fell to the ground. The captain was furious. He immediately put the drunken farmer under arrest and confiscated his shotgun.'

It was at this point, Jon demonstrates, that the group came to a shocking realisation:

The man who had just been felled by the irate farmer was far stranger than anything that could have come out of Nazi Germany:

> 'The party then ran on towards what they thought was an injured German airman, but they found, to their horror, that it was nothing of the sort. Instead of a proud member of the Luftwaffe, they found a naked man in his early twenties covered in hair and plastered in mud.'

The Whistleblower Continues

Even forty years after the event, says Jon, it was obvious that his informant had been badly shaken by this highly unnerving experience. He was now an elderly retired nursing officer in his early seventies who, spared military service because of his profession, had eagerly embraced the Home Guard as his opportunity to fight 'The Hun', and it was equally obvious that that these years had been the happiest of his life. The rest of his professional career had been spent at the hospital, and he intimated to Jon that he had found the increasing struggle with a moribund bureaucracy exponentially tedious. So, when he was offered early retirement, he was quite happy to spend the rest of his days fishing, and propping up of the corner of the bar in the pub which had been named after Brunel's spectacularly unsuccessful foray into setting up a mass transit system.

You may very well ask: What happened to the hairy man who was supposedly felled all those years ago? Of his source and his strange and sensational story, Jon states:

> 'Apparently, he told me, the badly injured wild man was taken to Starcross Hospital in the middle of the night, and all efforts were made to make him comfortable. Then, in the early hours of the morning, apparently an unmarked black van had arrived, and two men in uniform and another wearing a long white coat, manhandled the mysterious victim on to a stretcher, loaded him into the back of the van, and took him to an unknown destination.
>
> My informant never heard anything about the case again. He did hint, however, that the authorities warned everybody involved to say nothing. And, in the prevailing culture of careless talk costing lives, they had all concurred. I was, apparently, the first person that he had ever talked to about the incident. And that was only because he had recently found out that sixty years of smoking had taken their toll and that he was doomed to die of lung cancer within the next eighteen months.'

As Jon's following words make abundantly clear, the revelations of his Deep Throat-like source had a profound and lasting effect upon the young and eager monster hunter:

'I sat back on the bar-stool in the pub we were frequenting at the time, and gulped at my pint. This was possibly the most bizarre thing that I had ever heard - in a life that had already seen several bizarre and inexplicable incidents. I had heard of Bigfoot - indeed, I had even been on a hunt for it whilst living in Canada - but I had never heard of such things in the United Kingdom. Could it be? I thought: surely not.

But my informant seemed genuine enough. He sat in the corner of the bar puffing away on a cigarette and wheezing gently like a dilapidated steam-engine. His face had the unmistakable translucent aura of somebody struck down by incurable cancer, and he sat telling me of these extraordinary events in a matter-of-fact tone, as if he was recounting the previous weekend's football results. Did he remember the exact location? If so, would he be prepared to take me there? I asked these questions diffidently, and to my delight he agreed. There was no time at the present, he told me; and, so, finishing our beers, we went outside and walked towards the castle grounds.'

Matters were about to be taken to a whole new level. Once again, I turn the story over to Jon. It is, after all, his tale to tell:

'If you're travelling towards Exeter from Dawlish, go through Starcross village and when you pass the *Atmospheric Railway* pub, go on past the large car park on the right-hand side of road, but instead of following the main road round to the left towards Exeter, take the right-hand fork which is sign-posted to Powderham. Carry on down this little road for about half a mile. On the left-hand side you will see an expanse of deer-park, which is bordered by a wide ditch full of brackish water that acts as a moat. Just before you come to a railway bridge, the moat peters out. And although it may not be there now, back in 1982 when I conducted the interview, there was a convenient gap in the fence. This was apparently well known to the local poaching community in the village, and formed their main entry point to the woods where Lord Courtenay and his family raised their pheasants. We wriggled through the gap in the fence to find ourselves blissfully trespassing in the forbidden grounds of the castle.'

Realising that even on such a brightly moonlit night it would be pretty much impossible to venture any further into the thick and uninviting woodland, Jon and his aged informant decided to turn around and carefully retrace their steps back to Starcross village. Jon says that as he was working for the next three days, he made arrangements to meet his companion, once again, in the pub the following weekend. This time, however, the atmosphere was distinctly different and profoundly frosty, as Jon makes acutely clear.

Commenting on his source, Jon recalls:

'He came around, and I rushed down to the *Atmospheric Railway* to fulfill our tryst. Sure enough, my friend of a few evenings previously was there, puffing away on a cigarette and drinking his customary pint of light-and-bitter. However, something had changed: I tried to broach the subject of the mysterious wild-man, but he was unwilling to talk about it. "I should not have said anything the other night," he muttered, "but I'm an old man and I wanted to share it with you.'

Jon had more than a few thoughts and opinions on the matter of this distinct about-face:

'Whether it was the intimation of his imminent demise, or just a memory of the promise that he had made back in the 1940s, I don't know. But, in stark contrast to his verbosity of our previous meeting, on this occasion he was adamant that he didn't want to talk about it. So, I bought him a beer, challenged him to a game of cribbage, and spent the rest of the evening doing the sort of things that blokes normally do in a pub.'

Not surprisingly, however, for someone whose cryptozoological pursuits were growing dramatically by the day, Jon just could not let the beastly matter drop. In actuality, for a while it's fair to say the whole thing became something of a definitive obsession for Britain's most famous creature seeker:

'The whole affair fascinated me. Over the next months I cautiously broached the subject of ape-men in Powderham woods with a number of the elderly men who drank in the pub, or who hung out in the hospital social club. None of them knew anything. Or, if they did, they weren't saying.'

And bad news was looming on the horizon too, as Jon sadly now recalls:

'The months passed, and the old man who had told me of the events in Powderham woods during 1942 was admitted to the cancer ward at the Royal Devon and Exeter Hospital in Exeter. I visited him on a few occasions - the last, a couple of days before he died. I smuggled him in a bottle of Guinness, and sat at the end of his bed as he drank it with relish. However, in view of his condition - and because I truthfully didn't think that I could get anything else out of him - I refrained from asking him any more about an incident which he obviously regretted having shared with me. I attended his funeral. I was one of the few people there. When his lonely black coffin trundled behind the curtain at the Exeter crematorium, I was convinced that the truth about this mystery would go up in smoke along with his elderly, cancer-riddled corpse. How utterly wrong I was.'

In Search of the Monster Files

Of the next chapter in this winding and weird story, Jon kicks off as follows:

'Christmas came and went. In the early weeks of 1983, I found myself going through the voluminous filing cabinets that held over a century's worth of patient records at Starcross. This was part of my training as a psychiatric nurse. And although I was supposed to be looking into the distribution of different syndromes of mental and physical handicap from which the patients at Starcross hospital suffered, much to my surprise I found what I strongly suspect to be the solution to my forty-year-old mystery.'

And it was here that the tragic truth spilled out:

'In amongst some of the older files, I found a number that referred to members of a very wealthy and noble local family. These were not the Earls of Devon; however, as the family is still very wealthy and extremely powerful, I do not feel comfortable with revealing their identity — at least not yet. It appeared that there was a strong vein of mental-illness in the family, and possibly more significantly, metabolic disorders running through the line. I discovered the details of some terrible human tragedies reaching back over a century. It turned out that an old lady, known affectionately to all the staff as Winnie – and who at the time I knew her, must have been in her early nineties - was a member of this noble family. She had committed the unpardonable sin of becoming pregnant at the age of thirteen, following her liaison with one of the stable-boys. This had happened way back before the First World War; and although history didn't relate what had happened to her boyfriend, she had been forcibly given an abortion and incarcerated for the rest of her life in Starcross Hospital.'

And there was far more misfortune to come:

'It turned out that, before the Mental Health Act of 1959 was passed, there were three criteria under which a person could be admitted to hospital without any real recourse of Appeal. These people were labelled as "idiots" (nowadays known as people with moderate learning difficulties), "imbeciles" (individuals with severe learning difficulties), and moral defectives. I looked at Winnie with new respect from then on, and, whenever I had the chance, I would give her a packet of cigarettes or some chocolate.'

Now, Jon comes to the meat of the tale, and of the origin of the hairy wild man of Starcross Hospital:

'The files also contained details of a number of her relatives. Several of them suffered from congenital generalised hypertrichosis, commonly known as Wolf-Man Syndrome. In extreme cases, this disease not only causes bizarre behaviour and radical mood swings, but the body of the victim becomes excessively hairy. Although several people from Winnie's family had been diagnosed as suffering from this syndrome, there were no hospital records absolutely proving that they had been resident at a hospital after the First World War. What I did find out, however, was that the bloodline definitely had not died out. The family was still very important in the Devon area. They were notable benefactors to local charities; and at one time, at least, members of the family had been on the governing board of Starcross hospital itself.'

As the condition is an inherited one, it seemed quite probable to Jon that the strain of congenital, generalised, hypertrichosis had not died out in the early years of the 20th Century. Rather, a more enlightened generation of the family had decided to treat these poor unfortunates at home, rather than subject them to the rigours of an institutionalised life. Maybe this, Jon mused, was the truth behind the story of the hairy man of Powderham.

He adds today,

'I thought it was quite likely that the unruly rabble that had accompanied the Home Guard on that fateful night in 1942 had actually shot a member of the local ruling family - in the mistaken belief that he was a German airman. This would explain everything. It would explain why the whole affair had been shrouded in secrecy. In those days, the part of the landowner and the patrician establishment was far greater than it is today.

There is still a stigma surrounding mental illness, mental handicap, and disability. This poor idiot, covered in hair, was still a member of the family who, after all, still paid the wages of most of the members of the posse that had hunted him down. Especially at a

OPPOSITE: When humans get hairy. Copyright: Aldrovandus, 1642.

time when the nation was facing the deadly peril of the Nazi hordes, the powers-that-be would not have wanted the populace at large to be aware that one of their own was an unstable, dangerous, hair-covered lunatic who had escaped from his care and was wandering, naked and belligerent, across the countryside.'

Thus ends the sad, enigmatic, and conspiracy-filled saga of the Starcross wild man, the decades-old secrets of a powerful family, official cover-ups, frightened figures, a shadowy informant who had hidden the truth for decades, and a young man – Jon Downes – who, more than thirty years ago, found himself so graphically exposed to the whole story (or, at least, considerable parts of it) in all its hideous and weird glory.

We're a Happy Family

Actually, the story is not quite over. The noted British naturalist Trevor Beer had an equally provocative account to relate that may, very possibly, be of some significant relevance to the tale described above. It concerned an event that reportedly occurred in the late 1950s, and that came from a man out walking his dog at the time of its occurrence. Although the year is different to that in the story told to Jon Downes, and the incident reportedly involved nothing less than a full-blown werewolf, rather than a wild man (although, to the untrained, terrified eye, is there really that much of a difference?), the location - Devon - was the same. Also the same are two further matters of significance. In the story told to Beer,

(A)   the hairy man-thing was shot; and
(B)   it was found to be a member of a well-known family in the area.

Beer described the story of the witness in these particular words:

'Climbing a hedge he stumbled upon an animal ravaging a flock of sheep and taking careful aim he shot it; the beast reared onto its hind legs to run off into the woods. The dog followed the animal into the trees where there was much hideous snarling unlike any creature he had ever heard before. Suddenly the dog came dashing out of the woods and bolted past its master who, firing a second shot into the trees, also ran for home in great fear.'

Beer added that the man

'...went on to explain his later studies of matters concerning the occult and his realisation that the animal he had shot was a werewolf and a member of a well known local family. [He] further states that he knows the family involved and that they called in help from the church over a decade ago but that they had to withdraw because of the terrible phenomena beyond their comprehension. Now the problem is at a stalemate, the family being aware of the nature of his character and chaining him and locking him behind barred doors every night.'

Are the similarities between this case and the one described to Jon Downes actually evidence of a single story that, over time, became somewhat distorted into two separate ones? Or, incredibly, could it be that the case Trevor Beer described involved yet another member of the affected and afflicted family to which Jon referred? Maybe, one day, we will know the full and unexpurgated truth of this intriguing and conspiratorial affair. Or, perhaps, like so many tales of deep cover-up, it will forever languish in mystery, intrigue and a closely guarded, locked filing cabinet marked Top Secret.

CHAPTER 11
SHUG MONKEYS ON THE LOOSE
'...When we saw what it was we just froze.
It was very frightening...'

Any mention of the mysterious locale that is Rendlesham Forest, Suffolk inevitably conjures up strange and surreal images of the famous, alleged UFO landing within the forest in the latter part of December 1980 – a startling event witnessed by numerous United States Air Force personnel stationed at a nearby military base, Royal Air Force Bentwaters. The bizarre affair has been the subject of a considerable number of books, numerous televisions shows, several investigations by military and governmental bodies, and unrelenting deep debate. Reports of strange lights, of small alien-like creatures seen deep within the heart of the woods, and of high-level cover-ups and sinister conspiracies, are all key ingredients of the case that has, for many, justifiably become known as the 'British Roswell'.

More than three decades on, the events in question continue to provoke intense debate and controversy, with some believing that extraterrestrials really did land on British soil on that fateful night, or as some believe, across the course of several nights. Others hold the view that everything can be attributed to mistaken identity (of a nearby lighthouse, no less!), while some prefer the theory that a dark and dubious military experiment, and subsequent disastrous mishap, may have been to blame for all of the fuss. More than thirty years on, the debate continues to rage, and doubtless it will continue to rage for many more years to come.

As for the forest itself, it covers an area that is around 1,500 hectares in size and can be found in Suffolk's coastal belt known as the Sandlings. It is comprised of large, coniferous trees, as well as heath land and wet land areas, and is home to the badger, the fox, the red deer, the roe deer and the fallow deer. According to some people, however, Rendlesham Forest is home to far weirder things, too.
Maybe, even, a strange form of British Bigfoot…

Rendleshug
Rendlesham Forest, as well as the Suffolk locales of West Wratting and Balsham, is reportedly home to something equally as strange – maybe even far more so – than a vehicle and creatures from another world. It is a beast that, locally, has come to be known as the Shug Monkey. Described as being a bizarre combination of giant dog, muscular bear, and large ape, the creature is said to take its name from either

(A)   an old English word – scucca – which means demon, and which, as we have seen already, also has a link to the naming of Shugborough Hall, Staffordshire; or

(B)   an old east-coast term - shucky – that translates, into modern day terminology, as hairy or shaggy. Maybe the name is even born out of a curious melding of both terms. But, whatever the true nature of the name applied to the foul, hairy entity, its presence in the woods of Suffolk is enough to strike deep terror into the hearts of those souls unfortunate enough to have crossed its path – which is something to which Sam Holland can most definitely attest.

Shortly after New Year's Day in 1956, Holland was walking through the Suffolk countryside with his spaniel dog, Harry, when he was horrified to see a bizarre-looking creature come looming out of the trees some forty feet in front of him. It walked upon four huge, muscular legs – 'like a lion's' – and its thick fur coat was both black and glossy. Incredibly, said Holland, the animal was easily ten feet in length, and so could not be considered anything even remotely resembling a domestic animal, or a known wild beast of the British Isles.

Holland, in a panicked state, thought for a moment that perhaps the animal was an exotic big cat that had escaped from a zoo or private estate; that is until it turned in his direction and he was finally able to see its terrible, frowning face. Likening it to that of nothing less than a silver-back gorilla, Holland said that the monstrous creature possessed a huge neck, intelligent-looking eyes, widely flaring nostrils, and immense, powerful jaws of a bone-crushing nature. For a moment or two, the animal looked intently at Holland and his whimpering little dog. Then, seemingly having lost any and all interest in the pair, the gorilla-faced nightmare simply continued on its way and into the depths of the surrounding undergrowth. Holland would later explain that the creature looked like a strange combination of ape, dog, bear, lion and rhinoceros. An absolute chimera of the highest order, one might be very inclined to say.

Needless to say, the British Isles are not home to any such animal that even remotely resembles the beast that Sam Holland says he stumbled upon all those years ago. In fact, it's fair to say that nowhere on the entire planet does such a creature dwell. Yet, Holland is adamant that his description of the monstrous entity and his recollections of the day in question are utterly accurate in each and every respect. Today, now well into his eighties and still spritely and fit, Holland believes that whatever the true nature of the beast he had the distinct misfortune to run into more than half a century ago, it was unquestionably paranormal rather than physical in origin. But from where, precisely, he admittedly has no idea whatsoever.

The Beast Leaves its Mark

Jon Downes has a tantalising tale to tell, too, of Rendlesham Forest's most monstrous inhabitant, the Shug Monkey:

> 'An ex-girlfriend of mine - an East Anglian paranormal researcher - was in possession of some video-tape which showed the paw print of some huge animal like that of a cat or a dog, but far bigger and with strange flattened finger nails rather than claws. She thought that it was a print from an alien big cat of some description, but my immediate thought was of the semi-mystical "Shug Monkey". When I later found that my friend and colleague, Jan Scarff, who was brought up in the vicinity of the air bases, also knew about the so-called "Shug Monkey" I became even more interested, and I have been collecting reports for some years.'

The Monster Returns

In March 2009, according to some, the Shug Monkey returned to its old, wooded stomping grounds. One of

**RAF Bentwaters: A near-neighbour of Rendlesham Forest, the home of the Shug Monkey.
Copyright: Nick Redfern.**

the witnesses, Jenny Pearce, said of her encounter with the creature of the forest during that month:

> 'I was on the green at Rendlesham Forest having a picnic with my three-year-old son and his friend's family. After the picnic we stayed to play and explore the woods. While we were in the forest I saw a large animal moving through the trees ahead. I thought it was a big dog, so I picked up my son because he has never really got into dogs and gets easily scared. But as it continued away from us it was clearly not a dog. It was much bigger and there wasn't anyone there to be walking it if it was a large dog.'

There is far more – or, more correctly – far less to this latter case than meets the eye, as will become acutely clear in a later chapter dealing with the controversial issue of hoaxing, malicious, good-natured or otherwise.

Orford's Awful Thing

It is truly ironic that many of those who are sceptical of the Rendlesham Forest UFO case of December 1980 are often keen to suggest that the airmen who were involved merely mistook the illumination from the nearby Orford Lighthouse for something more exotic. Why? Well, Orford itself is a veritable hotbed of weirdness and strange creatures of a wild man variety. Consider, for example, the following account of one Ralph, a monk and an abbot at Coggeshall, Essex. Recorded in the year 1200 in *Chronicon Anglicanum*, it describes the remarkable capture in the area of a wild man of the woods-style creature:

Hair-covered humanoids. Copyright: Julius Magnus Petersen, 1882.

'In the time of King Henry II, when Bartholomew de Glanville was in charge of the castle at Orford, it happened that some fishermen fishing in the sea there caught in their nets a Wildman. He was naked and was like a man in all his members, covered with hair and with a long shaggy beard. He eagerly ate whatever was brought to him, but if it was raw he pressed it between his hands until all the juice was expelled. He would not talk, even when tortured and hung up by his feet, Brought into church, he showed no sign of reverence or belief. He sought his bed at sunset and always remained there until sunrise. He was allowed to go into the sea, strongly guarded with three lines of nets, but he dived under the nets and came up again and again. Eventually he came back of his own free will. But later on he escaped and was never seen again.'

Or, maybe it – or, far more likely, given the large passage of time, one of its offspring - was seen again, albeit hundreds of years later. At some point during the summer of 1968, one Morris Allen was walking along the coast near, of all places, the town of Orford when, in the distance, he saw someone squatting on the sand and leaning over something. As he got closer, Morris said, he could see that the man was dressed in what looked like an animal skin and was tearing into the flesh of a dead rabbit. The man was dirt-encrusted, with long, tangled hair and had wild, staring eyes. Morris could only watch with a mixture of fascination and horror.

Suddenly the man held his head aloft and quickly looked in Morris' direction, as if he had picked up his scent. The wild man quickly scooped up the rabbit, bounded off into the grass and was lost from sight. For Morris Allen, however, it was an event never forgotten. Perhaps, the wild men and Shug Monkeys of Rendlesham Forest and its surrounding areas live on, taunting and tantalising us with the occasional sighting of their bestial forms.

The Shug Monkey on the Move

In August 1997, the sighting of a strange creature – that became known as the Fiskerton phantom - terrified four young girls from who were enjoying a holiday walk near the Lincolnshire village. Although there was much talk of the beast being a big cat of some sort, the consensus on the part of the girls - Rachel Rowan, 12, Nicki Handley, 11, Nicola Proctor, 9, and Joanna Brogan, 10 – was that it was far more bear-like. Notably, cat-like and bear-like were descriptions used by Sam Holland in relation to the beast he came face to face with in Rendlesham Forest back in the 1950s.
One of the girls told the press:

> 'We saw something moving, so we went to take a look. When we saw what it was we just froze. It was very frightening. It looked like it was eating a pheasant. It had some very big teeth and great big claws. After a few seconds we ran off, but later when we went back to see if it was still there it had gone. It had left some big paw prints though.'

At the time, the girls were staying at a caravan park situated adjacent to the *Tyrwhitt Arms* pub at Short Ferry, which is near to Friskerton, and in states of near-hysteria, the girls raced to the pub for help. The manager of the *Tyrwhitt Arms*, Dave Brumhead, spoke out as follows:

> 'There was no way this was a schoolgirls' prank, they were really shocked. We had another sighting that evening near to where the girls had been. A motorist stopped his car in the middle of the road after he thought he had seen something. It's all very strange.'

Yes, it was strange. Was it a big cat, a small bear, or a wandering Shug Monkey? We may never really know the answer to that conundrum. Interestingly, a character called Fiskerton appeared on a U.S. cartoon series called *The Secret Saturdays*, which followed the adventures of a family of cryptozoologists, the Saturdays of the show's title. In the show, which ran on the Cartoon Network from 2008 to 2010, Fiskerton is a seven-foot tall 'gorilla-cat'.

Terror at the Tay Bridge. Copyright: Unknown, circa 1878-1879.

CHAPTER 12
A BRIDGE TOO WEIRD
'...the drowning at the Tay Bridge was followed by
sightings of a strange, hairy entity...'

According to a Glasgow electrician named Danny Thomas, on a particular evening in January 1879, his great-great-grandfather, who had apparently suffered from some form of severe mental affliction, committed suicide by hurling himself off Scotland's Tay Bridge, and right into the harsh depths of Dundee's Firth of Tay. The date of the suicide – January 1879 – amounts to the exact same time-frame in which the Man-Monkey was seen prowling around the Staffordshire countryside near the village of Woodseaves, which may be only a coincidence or something more, as we shall see in a later chapter.

But there is much more to come right now: In the immediate days that followed the family's tragic loss, ominous reports began to quietly circulate within the close-knit confines of the neighbourhood of a shaggy-haired man-beast that was seen roaming the Tay Bridge late at night, and that came to be known locally as the Shuggy – a term that instantly evokes thoughts of Rendlesham Forest's Shug Monkey and the Bigfoot-infested grounds around Shugborough Hall, Staffordshire. And that, as you will see – as with the encounter at the Shropshire Union Canal in 1879 – the drowning at the Tay Bridge was followed by sightings of a strange, hairy entity hardly went amiss in these quarters, either...

Disaster on the Bridge
As far as the known data are concerned, at least, the story goes like this: Almost two miles in length and carrying a single rail track, the bridge – completed in February 1878 to the plans of Sir Thomas Bouch – was the longest in the world at that time. Proposals for such a bridge dated back to 1854, and its foundation stone had been laid with ceremony on July 22, 1871. The first engine duly crossed the bridge on September 22, 1877, and the bridge was officially opened by Queen Victoria on June 1, 1878. Ulysses S. Grant worded it correctly when he commented that it was 'a big bridge for a small city'. But that situation soon changed – and most definitely not for the better.

It was an appropriately dark and stormy night on December 28, 1879 when, at around 7.15 p.m., and as a veritable storm of truly deluge-style proportions was blowing right down the length of the estuary, the central navigation spans of the Tay Bridge collapsed and plummeted into the Firth of Tay – taking with them a train and six carriages that resulted in no less than seventy-five untimely and tragic deaths. Legend and urban-myth that still circulates in Dundee to this very day holds that - had illness not intervened - none other than Karl Marx himself would have been aboard the doomed train.

A Court of Inquiry set up at the time decided that: '…the fall of the bridge was occasioned by the insufficiency of the cross bracing and its fastenings to sustain the force of the gale'. Had the wind-bracing been properly concluded, said the Court, the bridge might very well have withstood the intense battering of the mighty storm. Regardless of the real nature of the tragedy, however, the trail of death was still far from over. Plans were duly made for a new bridge to be built – according to the designs of one William Henry Barlow. The first stone was laid on July 6, 1883; and, by the time of its completion, no less than fourteen of the construction workers were dead, all from a variety of accidents.

It must be said that Danny Thomas was most definitely not an adherent of the theory that the Tay Bridge disaster could be attributed to something as down to earth as the stormy and relentless British weather. No: It was his firm belief that the dark and sinister forces of the Shuggy were at work on that most tragic of all nights. Moreover, Danny was of the opinion that the precise cause of the Tay Bridge disaster of December 1879 was his great-great-grandfather; returned, after his January 1879 death, to our plane of existence in the spectral form of some vile man-beast that haunted the darkened corners of the bridge – positively oozing negative energy and creating an atmosphere of death, doom, tragedy and decay as it did so, albeit briefly for a few weeks following the collapse of the once-mighty bridge.

As we shall see later, Danny is far from being alone when it comes to positing a connection between the recently deceased and the presence and actions of marauding monsters of an ape-like nature and appearance.

CHAPTER 13
SLITTING MILL'S HAIRY TROLLS
'...it was a bit like we were being hunted...'

I am not at all sure that the following case is directly linked to the controversies surrounding Bigfoot or unknown apes in Britain. But, as it does involve the sighting of unidentified, hairy humanoids in our very midst, I can only conclude that here is just about as good a place as any to relate the admittedly odd details, such as they are.

While there can be little doubt at all that the vast majority of the reports that appear within the pages of this book are both controversial and sensational, the following is certainly one of the weirdest of all. Understandably, given the bizarre set of circumstances, the family in question is highly reluctant to speak out publicly, aside from being willing to reveal the very basic aspects of the case.

Doubtless, the arch-sceptic or debunker would conclude that this determination on the part of the family not to discuss their case on the record is an indication that I have been the victim of an audacious hoax or a practical joke. And, while such a scenario can never be outright dismissed, I can only state that having now spoken to the husband and wife concerned on several occasions by 'phone, and twice in-person at their present home in Stoke-on-Trent, I do not doubt the veracity of the case or of their honesty and sincerity. But, that does not mean I can make a great deal of sense of their experience. With that stated, I urge you to read on…

A Festive Encounter

It was in the early hours of a winter's morning in 1975 when Barry and Elaine, a married couple then in their late twenties and with two small children at the time, were driving towards their then-Slitting Mill, Staffordshire home after attending a Christmas party with friends and family in the nearby town of Penkridge. As the pair headed towards the small village (its population today, four centuries after its initial foundations were laid, is still less than three hundred), their car's engine began to splutter and, to their consternation and concern, completely died. Having managed to carefully coast the car to the side of the road, Barry proceeded to quickly open the bonnet and took a look at the engine – 'even though I'm mainly useless at mechanical stuff', he states.

There did not appear to be any loose-wires, the radiator was certainly not over-heated, and a check of the car's fuses did not provide any indication of what might be the problem. But, as the family was less than half a mile or so from home at that point, Barry made a quick and decisive decision, as he explained:

> 'We had a picnic blanket in the boot [of the car] and I got it out. I got back into the car
> and I said to Elaine something like: "Let's cover you up and the kids with the blanket."
> They were in the back sleeping and [were] only four and six at the time. So I said to

A monstrous road. Copyright: Nick Redfern.

[Elaine]: "You stay with them, and I'll run back home and get your car, pick the three of you up, and then we'll leave my car here, and we can get someone out from a garage to look at it tomorrow."'

At that point, however, their plans were thrown into complete and utter disarray. According to Barry, Elaine let out a loud scream, terrified by the sight of a small figure that ran across the road in front of them at a high rate of speed. She takes up the story:

'I just about saw it at the last second, and then another one followed it, and then a third one. The best way I can describe them to you is like a hairy troll or something like that. We had some moonlight and they were like little men, but with hunchbacks and big, hooked noses and not a stitch on them at all. Not a stitch, at all; just hair all over them. I'd say they were all four-feet-tallish, and when the third one crossed by us, you could see them at the edge of the trees – wary, or something, anyway.'

Missing Time
At that point things became very hazy indeed, says Barry:

'We both know from memory they came forwards, towards us, very slowly to us, and I've thought since they were interested in us or wanted to know who we were. They came very slowly, and it was a bit like we were being hunted, to me. Elaine was hysterical; and with the kids with us, I wasn't far-off, either.

'But that's all we remember. The next, it's all gone; nothing. Neither of us remembers seeing them go, and the next thing it was about two o'clock and the car started fine, then. It felt like something had happened to us, but I couldn't quite put my finger on, you know what I mean? But the memory thing is the biggest problem, even now. What was it? I did have a dream later about them surrounding the car, but that's it, really. But they were there and we did see them, right up by the Stone House [Author's Note: A reference to a large, old abode – locally well-known - that sits on the edge of the village

Trolls on the loose? Copyright: John Bauer, 1915.

of Slitting Mill and that dates back to 1584, two centuries prior to the emergence of the village in the 1700s].'

Barry states that, to this day, and now both in their mid-sixties, both he and Elaine still feel very uneasy about the loss of memory they both experienced back in 1975, but he is keen to affirm that:

'I know, and we know, we both saw them. The kids don't remember a thing, thank god. They were horrible little things. All that hair: Trolls, goblins, something. But they were there and they were real.'

Neither Barry nor Elaine have ever experienced any further such incidents or encounters with the unknown, but they have never forgotten those disturbing events deep in the heart of Slitting Mill on a chilly, winter night all those years ago.

There is one point on this case that may be worthy of some comment, and it relates to the specific time of year when the event occurred: Christmas. Indeed, right after a Christmas Party. As Kithra notes:

'Some of the characteristics of the Green Man can be found in some of the figures from mythology, such as John Barleycorn [the personification of barley, as well as of beer and whisky, both being derived from barley], the Green Knight [a heroic figure in the 14th Century heroic poem, Sir Gawain and the Green Knight], and Puck [a definitive nature spirit of fairy-like proportions], amongst others. And, in modern times, perhaps even Peter Pan, and the original Father Christmas who, until not that long ago, was dressed in green rather than red, and shown garlanded in ivy [Author's Note: Italics Mine].'

The Game of the Name

In her 2012 title, *Real Wolfmen*, Linda Godfrey notes:

'Author Jim Brandon wrote in his 1983 book *The Rebirth of Pan* that there exists a curious worldwide repetition of location names associated with odd happenings. He calls it a "network of name and number" and wonders whether certain names based on old, powerful words somehow attract unknown entities and unexplainable events.'

It might be said that Shug – as in Shugborough Hall being a derivation of the devilish Scucca - is a perfect example. But, it's not just place names. The names of individuals seem to be a part of this huge and unfathomable cosmic joke, too. And on this matter, it's worth noting the following, extracted from a now-declassified British Royal Air Force Police document of 1962, written by a Sergeant C.J. Perry. He outlined the facts relative to the late-night experience of a man who, just like Barry and Elaine at Slitting Mill in 1975, experienced an encounter of the paranormal kind that resulted in car trouble.

In Sergeant Perry's own words to the Air Ministry at Whitehall, London:

'At Aylesbury on 16th February 1962, at 1530 hrs, I visited the Civil Police and requested information on an alleged "Flying Saucer" incident. I was afforded every facility by the Civil Police authorities and although no official report had been made, details of the incident were recorded in the Station Occurrence book.'

The details, Sergeant Perry noted, were that the witness:

'...a car collection driver, was travelling along the Aston Clinton road at about 0330 hrs, on 9th February 1962 when he came upon an object like a hovercraft flying approximately 30 feet above the road surface. As he approached he was travelling at 40 mph but an unknown force slowed him down to 20 mph over a distance of 400 yrd [sic], then the object suddenly flew off. He described the object as being about 40 feet wide, oval in shape with a number of small portholes around the bottom edge. It emitted a fluorescent glow but was otherwise not illuminated.'

Perry added that the man in question:

'...reported the incident to a police patrol who notified the Duty Sergeant, Sergeant Schofield. A radio patrol car was dispatched to the area but no further trace of the "Flying Saucer" was seen. It was the opinion of the local police that the report was perfectly genuine and the experience was not a figment of imagination.'

What makes this experience so notable is that the name of the witness was Ronald (wait for it!) Wildman.

Staffordshire's mysterious German Cemetery. Copyright: Nick Redfern.

CHAPTER 14
DISORENTIATION IN THE WOODS
'...The silence was strange, the landscape unfamiliar...'

A high plateau bordered by the Trent Valley to the north and the West Midlands to the south, the huge and picturesque Cannock Chase has been an integral feature of the Staffordshire landscape for generations. Following an initial invasion of Britain in A.D. 43, Roman forces advanced to the south to what is now the town of Cannock and along a route that would become known as Watling Street, a major, and historic, Roman road. The surrounding countryside was very heavily wooded even back then, as is demonstrated by the Romans' name for the area: Letocetum, or the Grey Woods.

In 1872, John Marius Wilson said of the Cannock Chase, in his *Gazetteer of England and Wales*, that the

'...ancient forest...extends to the vicinity of Bednal, Lichfield, and the Trent, with an area of about 25,000 acres; and was anciently a hunting-ground of the Mercian and the Norman kings. It long was covered with wood; but is now bleak, moorish, and wild; yet is so rich in coal and ironstone as to have been much encroached upon both for mining and for cultivation. Large portions of it present the attractions of a hill country; and some spots have ancient standing-stones, supposed to be Druidical.'

Designated as an area of outstanding beauty, today the Chase runs to approximately twenty-six square miles, is home to a herd of more than 800 deer, and gained deep notoriety in the late 1960s when the remains of three young girls were found buried on the Chase. A Walsall, West Midlands, man named Raymond Leslie Morris was found guilty of one of the killings – of seven-year-old Christine Darby - and was strongly suspected of having killed the other two, who were six-year-old Margaret Reynolds, and Diana Joy Tift, who was just five; although such was never definitively proved by police investigators. But outstanding beauty and terrible tragedy are not the only things that have shaped and sculpted the history of Cannock Chase...

Disorientation on the Chase

One of the most fascinating stories of a potential British Bigfoot nature to have ever caught my attention is that of a man named Mike Johnson who, in 2001 – and in what sounded like a distinctly altered state of reality – sighted a very weird, tall, grey-coloured entity with elongated arms on Britain's Cannock Chase. Mike begins his account:

'I studied Ecology at the University of Wolverhampton from 1997 to 2001 and was heavily involved in surveying vegetation on the Chase for the University and the Staffordshire Wildlife Trust. In June 2001 I was at the Chase a little due north of the German War Cemetery when something very strange happened. [It was] an event which I've never been able to explain.

The land at this location had been plantation forest that had been cleared some years earlier. I was searching for an example of the Midland Hawthorn I had been told was growing at this location. The weather was clear visibility, excellent, and the time was approximately 14.00 hours. While searching I was aware that the area had gone oddly quiet; normally you can hear birds and traffic. At this time I saw a herd of perhaps fifty deer come hurtling across a ridge perhaps eight or nine hundred meters away from me. They were running quite fast to an area of mature plantation forest to my right.

I was cheered by the site of them, as in the past I had only a rare glimpse of small groups of deer. At this time I was aware that the area in which I was standing seemed unfamiliar. The path which I had travelled down from the cemetery was on my left due west, as opposed to the east, which it should have been. The sun's position, which should have been high in the west, was now directly north. Several landmarks, such as the ridge, were still in situ and recognizable from previous trips. However, the area to the south, which rises towards the cemetery, was now due west. To all intents and purposes, it was as if someone had taken a slice of the landscape away and moved the sun.

I was aware that sometimes when in terrain such as this you may become disorientated and lost. I had a comprehensive map and compass and sat down to take stock of my position. The compass was unmoving with not a flicker of life, so I took the suns position as due west and tried to find my position on the map looking for landmarks and ridge lines. The view in front of me was not that of the map; and the path which I took from the German Cemetery was not the path I was looking at.'

Before moving on with the rest of Mike's story, a word or several about the German Cemetery, to which he refers: Situated near Broadhurst Green, the cemetery is a memorial to no less than 5,000 German servicemen, whose graves are marked by headstones, constructed out of Belgian granite and set in plots of heather. A tribute to the spirit of cooperation that exists between the Commonwealth War Graves Commission and the Volksbund Deutsche Kriegsgraberfursorge – the German War Graves Commission - the cemetery has its origins in 1959, the year in which Germany made the first, initial approaches with a view to finding a site on the Chase near the existing Commonwealth Cemetery that contains the graves of 388 men from both the First and Second World Wars, including near three hundred German soldiers.

In March 1962, the County Council made a gift of the land to the German Government, with the design of the cemetery and its surrounding buildings placed in the hands of Professor Diez Brandi of Gottingen, Germany, and Harold Doffman and Peter Leach, who were partners in a Stafford firm of architects.

As a result of the construction of the cemetery, between 1964 and 1966 the bodies of numerous German servicemen, such as sailors buried at seaports around the British coast, airmen shot down inland, and soldiers – most of whom were prisoners of war buried in churchyards around the country – were transferred to the cemetery, which today boasts thousands of visitors per year, including some of a very strange type, as the next part of Mike's story makes acutely clear.

'The silence was strange, the landscape unfamiliar, and I was effectively lost only seven hundred metres from my car parked at the cemetery. I noticed a group of three elderly walkers rambling in the distance and thought I'd wait until they were closer. They were walking towards me, as far as I could tell; then I would take stock of my position with their knowledge. About ten minutes passed as I watched them approach. They got to about five hundred metres away from me when I realised I could hear every word they said; it was as if they were standing in front of me.

There was a tall man in cream trousers and a shirt with a small rucksack, and two women aged maybe fifty to sixty with waterproof coats tied around their waists. As I watched them, they simply popped out of existence. One second they were there and the next gone. I assumed they had descended into a gully and had gone out of sight but I watched for a few minutes and they didn't appear. Then I noticed them approximately two hundred metres to my left of my peripheral vision; but now they had someone extra with them.'

A Creature Looms Into View

It's now that Mike's account takes on decidedly weird proportions:

'This character was tall, with very thin arms and legs, dressed in what I presumed were grey trousers and a tight long sleeved shirt of the same colour. He - I presumed it was a he - walked to the rear of them and when they stopped for a second he stopped also. Observing the group, I now came to the conclusion this added walker was not what he seemed. His hairless head was elongated and neck spindly, and his arms reached practically past his knees; I could not discern a facial feature. The clincher was when one of the ladies stopped and drank from a bottle of water: he approached her quite closely and I realised he was around three metres tall.'

At this point I had a feeling of intense disorientation and the added walker turned to look at me and put a hand on the lady's shoulder - this gesture seemed protective, as if to show me they were under his protection and I dare not interfere. I turned away to pick up my rucksack and approach the group, and when I looked up again I saw the original path to the German Cemetery was again in situ, with a large German Shepherd dog bounding down it, followed by a group of children and adults. The sun had returned to the west and all landmarks were again in vision. The walkers had gone and so had the landscape with them. I practically legged-it up the path to the car park and drove away. To this day I've never gone back.'

Comments and Observations

Looking back on what occurred, Mike said:

'I must state that the incident was so strange that even today I can't explain any of it. I hope it is of some interest to your investigations. It has certainly been cathartic for me personally.'

In a follow-up exchange with Mike, he told me:

'Animals or beings, [I'm] not quite sure what it was I saw. I'm a pretty good observer of details and in a sense had a better look at the animal. As you know animals have a keen sense of environment: they have to in order to survive. An animal will keenly survey the surrounding area quickly and repeatedly using all its senses. This creature was, in my opinion, sentient and had a complete sense of self. Why the walkers had no interaction with it, I have no idea. Why the walkers "jumped" a few hundred meters and appeared with the creature: again no clue at all.'

Mike continued astutely, and in a fashion with which I was in full agreement:

'Personally, I cannot accept that a literal "Bigfoot" type animal of a flesh and blood nature, at least in the way we understand the term, can live on the Chase or anywhere in the U.K. It would, of course, require a substantial colony of such creatures, and evidence of massive ingestion of plants, leaves, etc to feed such a population. Yet, this appears not to be happening.

Since the observation of the events, I have turned the matter over and over in my mind, trying to ascertain the how's and therefore's [sic] of the event. The environment was changed for a few minutes; of that I have no doubt. Was the change purely on an observational level and only observed by me? I think that's a definite hypothesis. I haven't really got a sense of the extra-normal and my past history is just that of a normal existence in Wolverhampton. Another hypothesis is that I was in the right place at the right time.

My personal belief is that many of these "animals" are indeed more paranormal in nature. I hate to use terms like "inter-dimensional", as that conjures up all sorts of science fiction-like scenarios; but it is indeed a fact that many such reports do seem to suggest a brief merging of two realities when these encounters occur. Looking at the observations, one known environment took on the characteristics of a second unknown environment for a time which resulted in a sighting of a sentient unknown being and three "known" beings. That's a few too many unknowns for an ex-ecologist to stomach, I'm afraid.'

The Encounters Continue

The high-strangeness was not quite over for Mike, as he explained:

'A year later I was at Loch Garten in the northeast of Scotland close to the Cairngorms [Author's Note: Interestingly, the Cairngorms mountain range is reputed to be home to a spectral Bigfoot-type creature known as the Big Grey Man, about which a great deal more later]; in beautiful surroundings, and in an area of untouched ancient pine forest when I had the strong feeling that something wasn't quite correct about the environment and, in particular, one area ahead of me. No strange adjustments of the landscape, no figures striding across the greenery; but the overwhelming feeling of something not right with this one area. Nothing to report visually, or any other way: just a tingle that whatever that area was - and it was simply an area of mature Scots Pine and Alder, as I remember - it didn't belong there. The same thing happens maybe a few times a year when I'm out and about.'

Mike concluded:

'Having had a few more experiences, I can say that yes, the Cannock event certainly changed my experience of certain sites and environments. My depth perception changes during the "tingle". An example or description: if you look at the corner of a room where the ceiling meets the two walls you see an inside corner. I see an

Pisky-led enchantment. Copyright: John Bauer, 1912.

outside corner. That's the best way to describe the feeling.'

Being Pisky Led

It's worth noting too that the very unnerving phenomenon of deep disorientation in a wholly familiar environment as described by Mike is nothing new in the slightest. His strange experience at the German Cemetery on the Cannock Chase - where he clearly seems to have been rendered into a distinct state of altered reality that affected his ability to accurately gauge his location - very much brings to mind the words of Margaret Ann Courtney, a noted expert in Cornish folklore.

In 1890, she said of the games and manipulative behaviour of fairies, goblins and a wide assortment of what have become known, collectively, as the 'little people' or the 'wee folk':

> 'When mischievously inclined pisky often leads benighted people a sad dance; like Will of the Wisp, he takes them over hedges and ditches, and sometimes round and round the same field, from which they in vain try to find their way home (although they can always see the path close at hand)...'

It's also worth noting that while, today, the 'pisky' to which Courtney referred – a diminutive entity that can be both mischievous and malevolent, and whose origins date back centuries – conjures up imagery in the minds of many of tiny, playful beings that flitter and flutter around inviting streams and glades on wings of gossamer, such is actually not always the case. In times long gone, one particular form that the pisky would adopt was that of a hideous troll – perhaps, it might be suggest, not unlike the hairy trolls of Slitting Mill as described in the previous chapter. That Slitting Mill is literally only a few, mere minutes' drive from the Cannock Chase's German Cemetery makes this particular matter all the more worthy of wonder and intrigue.

CHAPTER 15
THE CLEADON CREATURE
'...Two spectacular cryptids in the one village, only a few short years apart...?'

I n August 2001, Mike Hallowell, (below right) a very well respected researcher of numerous anomalies – mystery animal-based and otherwise - penned an article for the Centre for Fortean Zoology's in-house magazine, *Animals & Men*, on the subject of the sighting of a large cat of unknown origins in Cleadon, which is a village located in South Tyneside in the northeast of England. The origins of the village date back more than one thousand years, and it happens to be situated only a few short miles from where Mike and his wife reside. The sightings of the giant cat, which were never satisfactorily resolved, began in January 1999 and attracted Mike's attention for years.

Then, during December 2009, Mike commented on a new development in the saga; although it was a development that most observers and commentators of the mystery would probably never, ever have anticipated. As Mike began, regarding the latest strand in the curious saga:

> 'Over a decade after the Cleadon Big Cat first strutted onto the cryptozoological stage, something has happened to resurrect it.'

Or, he added:

> 'Maybe not, as it's all a bit confusing.'

It certainly is that, alright...

Cleadon Curiosities
With the above said and outlined, let us address the story of Mike himself, who, on December 10, 2009, told of how several days earlier he spoke with a friend and research colleague, John Triplow, who informed Mike of a website that contained 'an intriguing BHM [Big Hairy Man] story, not unlike that of the infamous Beast of Bolam Lake, which I actively investigated with a CFZ team in early 2003', and which was the subject of an earlier chapter of this very book.

What puzzled John – and that also deeply flummoxed Mike – was that this particular sighting of a large, hairy man-beast allegedly occurred right in the heart of Cleadon village, in the very same year that the large black cat was reportedly prowling, in sinister and similar fashion, around the neighbourhood. As for why it so flummoxed Mike, let's take a good and close look.

He noted, correctly, that the Borough of South Tyneside is the smallest Metropolitan Borough in the United Kingdom, and is comprised of only half-a-dozen villages and towns, a handful of farms, and, if one is brutally honest, not much else at all. Aside, that is, from one thing. And it's a very significant thing, too. The area, Mike revealed, 'also happens to be one of the hottest spots around for paranormal research, and I've written a good few books, articles and columns dealing with the wacky stuff that seems to happen here more than anywhere else I know'.

As for the story of the Cleadon man-beast, Mike said that the witness in question reported seeing in the darkness of the night in question (a night, the precise date for which, has yet to be ascertained) what appeared to be a large, two-legged animal covered in a thick coat of fur, as well as a second individual – but this one undeniably human - apparently out walking their pet dog. Mike added that 'it seemed more than a little odd to me that this BHM sighting should occur in the same village that had only a short while previously been the setting for the infamous Cleadon Big Cat incident. Two spectacular cryptids in the one village, only a few short years apart?'

It was a most puzzling question to be sure, and one that Mike dug into further, as he attempted to resolve the nature of what, exactly, was afoot:

> 'My suspicions were further fuelled by the presence of someone walking a dog when the Cleadon BHM was allegedly seen. During my investigation into the Cleadon Big Cat case, the press (the *Shields Gazette*, January 14, 1999) reported that a woman who had been walking her huge Burmese mountain dog on Cleadon Hills believed that she – or rather her pet – may have been mistaken for the big cat. I was subsequently able to discount this, but the fact that both the Cleadon Big Cat story and the account of the Cleadon BHM included a dog-walker on Cleadon Hills at the time of each sighting again made me wonder if the two stories had been melded together.'

And there was yet another similarity, too, as Mike came to realise:

> 'One of the witnesses in the Cleadon Big Cat case claimed that he'd seen the animal running past his hedge, approximately fifty feet away. If one substitutes the words "tree line" for "hedge" and "fifty yards" for "fifty feet", the two accounts are unnervingly similar.'

Had the two stories – one of a huge man-beast and the other of a large, exotic cat - somehow become confused and intertwined in a fashion that, to this day, is still not altogether clear? Just like the true nature of the beast, the answer to that question remains unknown.

CHAPTER 16
A MONSTROUS CASTLE
'...For about twenty seconds the beast stared at both husband and wife...'

Late one evening in September 1986, Mick Dodds and his wife were driving his mother-in-law back to her place of abode, which was a small but picturesque cottage in the Staffordshire village of Stowe-by-Chartley. All was completely and utterly normal until Dodds passed by the ancient and ruined Chartley Castle that overlooks the A518 road.

Constructed on land that came into the possession of the Earls of Chester as far back as the 11th Century, Chartley Castle is a stone motte-and-bailey fortress founded in the thirteenth century by Ranulph Blundeville, the then Earl of Chester. Supported by the motte are, today, the still-standing remains of a rare cylindrical keep, with the inner bailey curtain wall still strongly flanked by two huge half-round towers, a gate-house, and an angle-tower. A strong counter-scarp bank and cross-ditch divides the inner and outer baileys, with another ditch and bank encasing the whole castle. Notably, Chartley Castle is to where – on Christmas Eve, 1585 – Mary, Queen of Scots, was taken before being moved to Fotheringhay for execution on February 8 of 1586. And, according to Mick Dodds, Chartley Castle just might be home to a literal British Bigfoot...

A Creature Roams the Castle

Mick Dodds says that after dropping his mother-in-law off at her home, he and his wife began the journey back to their own abode, and what they assumed would be a stress-free, night-time drive through Staffordshire's engaging countryside. How completely and devastatingly wrong the pair was. According to Dodds, as they drove along the road, and with Chartley Castle rapidly closing in, he was forced to violently and suddenly slam on the brakes as a huge stag ambled slowly – yet majestically, too – across the road directly in front of them. The sight of the massive beast was enough to both amaze and gob-smack Dodds and his wife in equal amounts. But that was nothing at all compared to what supposedly happened immediately thereafter.

Dodds, realising how bizarre the next aspect of his story was surely going to sound to me, apologised profusely before he even began relating the complex details. In return, I told him that no apology was necessary. Instead, I explained to him, I would much prefer to merely hear the facts, and then try and firmly evaluate them for myself. And so, with that out of the way, Mick Dodds duly began.

As the huge stag made its slow yet deliberate way across the road, his wife suddenly screamed at the sight of what looked like a large chimpanzee that bounded after the stag from the darkness of the field that sat to the right of their car. Halfway across the road, the chimpanzee stopped suddenly, looked directly at the terrified

Chartley Castle: The haunt of a man-monster. Copyright: Nick Redfern.

husband and wife and, to their utter horror and consternation, charged their vehicle – but, at the very last moment, backed away from actually causing any structural damage to the car, or physical harm to the fear-stricken pair. Dodds said that in his overwhelming panic to quickly put the vehicle into reverse gear, he stalled its engine, and then, even worse still, ended up completely flooding it as he raced to try and re-start the car. As an inevitable result, the Dodds were briefly stranded in the road with a hairy monstrosity looming wildly in front of them. For about twenty seconds the beast stared at both husband and wife, and on two other occasions again headed for their vehicle at full speed, 'like it was going to attack', before finally bounding off to the left, and, so it appeared at least, in a direction that specifically followed that of the huge stag – which, by now, was seemingly long gone.

Now, to a curious sequel in this distinctly odd affair…

The Dance of the Horns

There is one other aspect of Mick Dodds' story that I have omitted until now. Some may find it to be of significance; others might suggest its connection is down to mere chance, coincidence, and nothing else whatsoever. Make up your own mind, as you most probably will. On the very same day of their encounter at Chartley Castle, the Dodds family spent several hours in the ancient Staffordshire village of Abbots Bromley, where, for the very first and only time, they attended a famous and equally ancient ritual.

Although certainly only a small village, Abbots Bromley has become well-renowned – actually world-renowned - for its famous 'Horn Dance' that is held every year on 'Wakes Monday', which follows the first Sunday - or 'Wakes Sunday' as it is known - after September 4. While the full and unexpurgated facts pertaining to the Dance and its origins have been somewhat obscured by the inevitable passage of time, the following can most certainly be said: The 'horns' that are themselves utilised in the dance are, in reality, reindeer antlers, that date back to at least 1065. And Wakes Monday aside, they can be found on continuous display in the village's St. Nicholas' Church. At 8.00 a.m. on each and every Wakes Monday, twelve performers comprised of:

(A)   six men whose job it is to hold the horns aloft throughout the dance;
(B)   a musician;
(C)   a young boy equipped with bow and arrow;
(D)   a 'Hobby Horse';

'...commence upon their magical and mystical parade through the old streets of the village to a specific location where the dance duly kicks off in fine style. Music is supplied by a melodeon player; while the Hobby Horse beats a careful and rhythmic time with constantly snapping jaws.

Abbots Bromley's famous Horn Dance. Copyright: John Benjamin Stone, 1906

The high point of the dance occurs when the 'Deer-Men' face each other, and with horns duly lowered, act out a mock form of combat.

Much merriment and celebration inevitably follows, with the dancers and the ensuing throng making their way to the various village inns and houses – and which continues well into the evening, and that is ultimately brought to a resounding close at around 8.00 p.m. with what is known as the Service of Compline. In other words, a damned good time – and one that harks right back into the fog-shrouded heart of British history and folklore - is truly had by one and all.

It must be said that while the Horn Dance is without a doubt the major event of the year for the village folk of Abbots Bromley, the precise origins of the centuries-old ceremony are still somewhat obscure and vague. Some students of the Dance are firmly convinced that it was put into place to commemorate the assigning of hunting rights to the people of Abbots Bromley in centuries long past. Meanwhile, others see the Horn Dance as possibly being a relic celebration that honours the granting in 1226, by Henry II, of the three-day-long Berthelmy Fair.

And, then, a third theory suggests the possibility of even older and truly archaic origins for the Horn Dance. According to some, the Horn Dance may even represent one of the very last of the surviving rituals that celebrate Britain's long-gone mysterious, and prehistoric, past. For example, the 'shooting' of the bow at the 'Deer-Men' is perceived in some quarters as being an act that has its origins fixed firmly within the world of ritual magic, when prehistoric man utilised both wild dance and ancient sorcery in a swirling and heady concoction designed to ensure a successful hunt for food.

But, whatever the ultimate truth of the affair, even today, as I can attest, in the somewhat sterile and technology-driven years of the early twenty-first century, to personally attend Abbots Bromley's Horn Dance is to take an instant, curious and joyous journey into England's past when myth, magic and folklore were all-dominating and all-important. How curious that Mick Dodds and his wife should have encountered a British Bigfoot on the very same day as they attended a longstanding ritual that pays homage to, many believe, prehistoric man, and which involves wild 'Deer Men' and even Maid Marion, whose links to the legend of Robin Hood – himself perceived as a Woodwose-style character – are known worldwide.

I still keep in touch with Mick Dodds and his wife to this very day, and they both continue to stand by their accounts of that September 1986 encounter with a strange hairy man-beast at Chartley Castle. And, based on what both husband and wife had to say, who am I to argue?

It's worth noting, too, that Chartley Castle is not the only British castle at which a weird monkey- or ape-like animal has been seen. Carolina Manosca Grisales notes:

> 'Sometime before 1967, a Mr. Beer took photographs at Berry Pomeroy Castle, Devon, one of which on being developed showed the unexplained image of a woman in medieval dress carrying a monkey. Unfortunately Mr. Beer gave his photograph to the poet Robert Graves, who was so disturbed by it that he burned it.'

Most unfortunate, to say the very least! And, we are certainly still not yet done with castles and creatures – as will become apparent soon enough.

CHAPTER 17
GO WILD IN THE COUNTRY
'...The area where he is living is thickly-wooded... the sort of area where it is easy to disappear...'

Jon Downes notes of wild men seen in the counties of Devon and Cornwall that:

'From the Cannibals of Clovelly to the Brew Crew of Treworgey[1], the whole area has attracted people who wish to live outside of our recognized society; and these people have often degenerated into a wild and lawless existence, sometimes even reverting to a surprisingly primitive lifestyle.'

They are not of the hairy and sub-human variety that we have encountered thus far. They are, however, by definition, men living wild, sometimes very wild, and in recent times, too; in fact: very recent times. And, thus, in their own odd and unique ways they, too, have become staple parts of the legend of the British wild man. We'll start with those alleged cannibals, to which Jon refers...

The Cannibals of Clovelly: Sorting Fact from Fiction

Preserved in an eight-page chapbook in the Pearse-Chope collection at Bideford is a sensational and controversial story of one John Gregg and his assorted family of murderers and thieves. The text is estimated to date from the latter part of the eighteenth century and it recounts the story of how the Gregg family took up residence in a cave near Clovelly on the north coast of Devon in the 1700s, and from where they were to live for an astonishing twenty-five years.

So the legend goes, during this period they passed their time by robbing more than a thousand unfortunates, and merrily devoured the corpses of all those they robbed. Such was the horror the story generated that even the king himself – along with four hundred men – allegedly resolved to bring to an end their prehistoric-like and abominable existence. The cave was supposedly discovered and reportedly contained, according to the chapbook, 'such a multitude of arms, legs, thighs, hands and feet, of men, women and children hung up in rows, like dry'd beef and a great many lying in pickle'. Gregg's distinctly less than charming family was found to consist of a wife, eight sons, six daughters, eighteen grandsons and fourteen granddaughters all begotten by incest - and many said to have been as mad as hatters - and all of who were taken to Exeter and on the following day executed at Plymouth without trial.

---

1. A band of drugged and drunken ruffians who travelled around the free rock festivals at the end of the 1980s. The Treworgey Tree Fayre in 1989 was a particularly notorious festival in Cornwall from which , together with a potent brand of beer called 'Special Brew', they got their name. JD

It was suggested very convincingly by A. D. Hippisley-Coxe, in his 1981 book *The Cannibals of Clovelly: Fact or Fiction* that this bizarre and horrific tale was simply that: a tale, and one created to ensure that the superstitious locals kept away from the myriad local caves used by smugglers at the time. And, indeed, the area around Bideford and Clovelly was a hotbed for smuggling.

Broadly, the same legend appears in a number of other chapbooks – such as *The Legend of Sawney Beane*, that places the scene of the action in Galloway, Scotland. The tale of Sawney Beane was first recorded in 1734 in *A General and True History of the Lives and Actions of the Most Famous Highwaymen* by Captain Charles Johnson, a pseudonym of none other than Daniel Defoe, who had visited north Devon in his *Tour Through the Whole Island of Great Britain* and from where, in 1714, he reported that he 'could not find any foreign commerce, except it be what we call smuggling'.

So, we have a story of people gone wild – and horrifically so, in the saga of the Clovelly cannibals – but one so steeped in legend, folklore and probably a very high degree of fabrication, that the complete picture will probably never become clear to the point where it satisfies everyone who has sought out the truth of the matter. But that most certainly cannot be said for every case. Sometimes, stories of people living wild in Britain can be utterly vindicated.

The Pantyffynnon Enigma

On April 29, 2009, the *Daily Mail* newspaper published an article with the eye-catching and lengthy title of **Police launch hunt for 'Wolfman' behind mini crimewave who lives on rabbits and berries in woods**. Had the legendary Green Man returned to Britain? Was the Woodwose of Sproughton, Suffolk on the move? Well, let's see, shall we?

The Daily Mail's article began in intriguing, definitive, scene-setting style:

> 'The one man mini-crime wave is also suspected of a string of thefts of shopping from parked cars and clothes from washing lines during his furtive forays into the civilised world over the last two years. Police have tried to catch him during searches on foot and have even sent up a helicopter with heat-seeking equipment to track him down, but he has so far always managed to avoid capture. He knows the miles of paths through the dense woodland near Ammanford, South Wales, where he lurks, so well that even when officers are on his trail, he manages to give them the slip. Abandoned hideouts made from board with plastic roofs have been found, suggesting he moves around to avoid arrest.'

He became known, locally and infamously, as 'The Wolfman'.

We are the Angry Mob!

In the tiny hamlet of Pantyffynnon, which was one of the mystery-man's favourite hunting grounds, outraged and worried locals planned on taking steps – definitive direct action, actually - of their very own to seek out the strange and elusive man of the woods. Planning a course of attack that nigh-on combined:

(A)   the proactive approach taken by 'V' in the *V for Vendetta film*, and

(B)   the breathless antics of torch-wielding eastern Europeans in those old, 1930s and 1940s black and white monster movies, the people of Pantyffynnon were, almost, baying for the wild man's blood. One villager said, in ominous tones:

> 'We want him caught before something serious happens.'

Wild thing! Copyright: Unknown

For their part, the local police vowed to apprehend the man – 'sooner or later', a decidedly vague and open-ended statement which hardly satisfied many - and loudly appealed to locals not to start scouring the woods themselves. As evidence of this, one Sergeant Charles Gabe sternly warned any would-be heroes 'not to take the law into their own hands or approach this man'.

Seeking Rambo with the Force Helicopter

Sergeant Gabe added:

> 'We've found one or two hides where we believe he has been sleeping. We think he catches rabbits and eats berries or whatever else he can get his hands on. But although we've had the police helicopter overhead using heat-seeking equipment we've still been unable to locate him. This is a massive thickly-wooded area - and one he obviously knows well. On one occasion a couple of our guys came close to nabbing him but he scarpered back into the woods. But we are sure he will be caught sooner or later.'

When questioned for comment, local councillor Hugh Evans said:

> 'It's a very strange case and no-one seems to know who he is. But he must be a bit of a Rambo type and pretty tough to have survived the bitterly cold winter living out in the open. The area where he is living is thickly-wooded and forested - the sort of area where it is easy to disappear.'

Evoking surreal imagery of some *Stig of the Dump*-type character, the Daily Mail added:

> '"The Wolfman" lives in the woodland on an area of reclaimed coal slagheaps known locally as "The Tips."'

Meanwhile, a Dyfed-Powys Police spokesman tactfully said, in typically bureaucratic terminology that was suggestive of far more than they were willing to impart at the time: 'We want to question him over several alleged incidents.' For a while the wild man and his equally wild antics vanished – perhaps into the underground lair that many believed had become his home. He wasn't destined to stay buried for too long, however. In the latter part of 2010, the mystery man resurfaced from the heart of those dark woods.

The Return of the Native (With Apologies to Thomas Hardy)

> 'The hunt for a West Wales "wolfman" is back on – after stumbled across what is thought to be his lair,'

Noted *Wales Online* on October 10, 2010. The 'unknown vagrant', it was reported, was up to his old tricks, something that led to the revelation that:

> '...officers from the Dyfed-Powys force this week confirmed they are looking into possible fresh sightings after walkers reported stumbling across a woodland shack stuffed with food, clothes and electrical equipment'.

One of those who was willing to speak publicly on the return of the wild man was John Jones, a builder from Pantyffynnon, who told *Wales Online*:

> 'We've been told that some walkers found a tin shed full of food and clothes, so we assume that is one of his hideouts. Lots of people have been looking for where he is, but the woodland is so dense it's not an easy place to search. There have been one or two sightings of this longhaired, bearded person who is so scruffy and unkempt; *he's like a wild man* [Author's Note: Italics Mine].'

There was also talk of milk being stolen, of food taken from freezers in outside storage areas in the dead of night, and of what were intriguingly, but briefly, described as 'odd sightings'. But was the wild man simply some eccentric, solitary soul that had decided to leave the restrictive boundaries and conventions of society far behind him? Not everyone was quite so sure that's all he was.

Gwilym Games, a regional representative - for Wales – of the Centre for Fortean Zoology, noted correctly that:

> 'There is a long history of werewolves in Wales and even an earlier mention in the Amman valley.'

Despite this undeniably intriguing aside, nothing else surfaced on this particular aspect of the mysterious matter, and once again the wild man vanished into obscurity, or, far more likely, into the heart of the thick woods that dominate the area.

As per usual, the police continued on their plodding path of 'making enquiries'. They proved to be utterly fruitless. But, there was one further development in the story. One week after the *Wales Online* article surfaced, a Pantyffynnon solicitor named Peter Rhys Jones said that the wild man was harmless, and nothing stranger than an ex-serviceman who he, Jones, had once represented. Once again, things then went quiet for a while. But, in 2012, there was a dramatic development in the story that confirmed what Peter Rhys Jones had to say about the man's military background.

In February of that year, it was revealed that the man living wild was one Wayne John Morgan, aged thirty-seven, formerly of the British Army and someone well-trained to survive in the harsh and unforgiving wilds of the Welsh outdoors. A police spokeswoman said:

> 'He has not been seen by his family for four years, but now concerns have been raised about his welfare.'

adding:

> '...as he is living rough, he may be hungry and on the look-out for food. If you are suspicious that any food items are missing from your stores, or whether any outbuildings such as garden sheds and garages have been disturbed, then please contact us.'

Mike Lewis, editor of the *South Wales Guardian*, stated of the latest news on the affair:

> 'One magazine specialising in the paranormal even sent a reporter to assess whether this was a real-life werewolf...But strip away the legend and what's left? A missing man, a police appeal and a worried family anxious for news. 'The Guardian' has covered some strange stories during my five years at the helm, but the one about "The Wolfman" of Pantyffynnon tips must rank among the strangest.'

By May, with still no news – despite fairly widespread, renewed media publicity - things were looking bleak. The local press highlighted the opinion of people in the area that there was 'no chance' Morgan was still hiding out in the woods – citing the then recent, bitterly cold weather as one specific reason - while his obviously very anxious family prayed and hoped for good news. At the time of writing, unfortunately, that is where matters still stand in this tragic and sad affair.

A Hidden Village and a 'Lost Tribe'

There is one final affair worth noting that, in a tangential way, at least, is tied in to this story of people living wild lives in the heart of Wales to this very day. Back in 1993, Julian and Emma Orbach purchased a 180-acre piece of land in west Wales' Preseli Mountains. Ultimately, the hillside compound, which was surrounded and camouflaged by trees and bushes, became home to more than twenty like-minded souls, all of who wished to live outside the regular confines of what passes for society. They constructed grass-covered, wooden buildings, became very much self-sufficient and, for all intents and purposes, created a self-enclosed community, the existence of which very few, if indeed hardly any, had even the barest inkling. That the secret village resembled something straight out of the Middle Ages or - as the media noted, when the story broke – Tolkien's *Lord of the Rings* only added to the curious and near-magical nature of the area.

Astonishingly, the Orbachs, as well as their friends and colleagues, lived in blissful peace and stealth for no less than five years before anyone in authority even realised what was going on. In fact, the only reason why the story ever surfaced at all was because, in 1998, a survey aircraft in the area happened to take aerial photographs of the area and caught sight of their hidden hamlet - which, most unfortunately for the Orbach family and their friends, finally blew their cover. It didn't take any time at all before the humourless wrath of local government reared its ugly head.

With no planning permission having ever been obtained for the village, the government was adamant that the buildings and each and every bit of the little, isolated locale had to be destroyed – or else. And, as a result, thus began a years-long campaign in which the unsmiling men in black suits sought to 'just follow orders', while those that called the Narnia-like area their home, fought to remain there, untouched and unspoiled by officialdom and the Nanny State. At one point, bulldozers were even brought onto the scene, just ready and waiting for the cold-hearted command to flatten the eight buildings that comprised the secret village in the wilds of the Preseli Mountains.

Fortunately, it did not come to that. Finally, in 2008, a full decade after the existence of the village first became public knowledge, and fifteen years after the first steps to create it had been taken, the government caved in. By then, far more mindful of so-called 'green' issues than it had been in earlier years, officialdom agreed that providing the villagers followed certain rules and regulations laid down by the government, and could demonstrate that they were improving the biodiversity of the area and conserving the surrounding woodland, they could stay where were they were, and their *Lord of the Rings*-type dwellings could remain intact and forever free of bureaucratic meddling. Sometimes, sanity does actually prevail, even within government!

Of course, the above does not have a direct relevance to the matter of Bigfoot or specifically Woodwose-type wild men in Britain. But, what it does serve to demonstrate is that people can, and - as these two examples amply demonstrate – people have lived in the wild for years, in situations where they remain outside of society, and pretty much unknown to anyone and everyone else, including even the ever-watching eyes of government. And, if they can, maybe others have too. The wild places and wilder people of Britain, perhaps, are not quite as extinct as many might well assume...

CHAPTER 18
MONSTER OF THE MAGIC RING
'...Tell me that isn't a big black shape walking towards me...'

Reports of hairy wild men absolutely abound throughout the English county of Staffordshire, but there is one area of the county that seems to attract a great deal more than its fair share of such activity. Its name is deeply familiar to one and all throughout the area as Castle Ring. Located

Welcome to the ring of monsters. Copyright: Nick Redfern.

near to the village of Cannock Wood, Castle Ring is an Iron Age structure commonly known as a Hill Fort. It is 801 feet above sea level, and its main ditch and bank enclosure is fourteen feet high and, at its widest point, 853 feet across.

It has to be admitted that very little is known about the mysterious and long-forgotten people who built Castle Ring, except to say that they were already in residence at the time of the Roman invasion of A.D. 43 and remained there until approximately A.D. 50. Some suggest that the initial foundations of Castle Ring may even have been laid as early as 500 B.C. Moreover, historians suggest that the creators of Castle Ring might have represented a powerful body of people that held firm sway over certain other parts of Staffordshire, as well as significant portions of both Shropshire and Cheshire at the time in question.

While its enigmatic builders exited our world millennia ago, and left us with very little solid knowledge of who they were or what they actually represented, Castle Ring can claim to play host to far stranger entities, including…well, by now, do I really have to tell you? Really? I strongly suspect that, at this stage, I probably don't…

A Glowing-Eyed Monster

On May 1, 2004, Alec Williams was driving passed the car-park that sits at the base of Castle Ring when he witnessed a hair-covered, man-like entity lumber across the road and into the trees. A shocked Williams stated that the sighting lasted barely a few seconds, but that he was able to make out its amazing form:

> 'It was about seven feet tall, with short, shiny, dark brown hair, a large head and had eyes that glowed bright red.'

Interestingly, Williams stated that as he slowed his vehicle down, he witnessed something akin to a camera flash coming from the depths of the woods and heard a cry that he described as 'someone going "Hoo."'

The Media Takes Note

Just over one year later, on June 8, 2005 to be precise, in an article titled **Hunt For Dark Forces at Chase Monument**, *Chase Post* journalist Sarah Taylor reported that 'paranormal investigators are set to swoop on one of the area's oldest monuments to find out what dark forces lie beneath it'. As the newspaper noted, 'a team of real-life ghost-busters' had determined that the area of Gentleshaw that surrounds Castle Ring lay upon what was described as a 'psychic fault'. Certainly, the whole area surrounding Castle Ring has been a hotbed of weird activity for years – and not all of it revolves around weird beasts.

For example, commenting on the mountain of strange activity at the Ring, Sue Penton – of Paranormal Awakening, a group affiliated to the Association for Scientific Study of Anomalous Phenomena – said:

> 'There have been reports of strange music being heard up there. It is such a high place there have been lots of UFO sightings there, too.'

The comments of Sue Penton were echoed by Graham Allen, then of the Etchinghill, Rugeley-based Staffordshire UFO Group:

> 'Obviously, Castle Ring is the highest point on the Chase which makes it a good place for UFO spotting. There have been numerous incidents of UFOs, which could be because you are more likely to see something from a high point.'

Allen elaborated to the press on what he knew about the mysteries of Castle Ring:

> 'There have been reports of something landing there in the 1960s. From a research point of view there are a high number of reports around ancient sites. One argument could be that ancient sites have been located there because of the incidents of UFOs and natural phenomenon. There could be locations where there could be magnetic influences in the ground which have been attributed to earth lights.'

Moreover, relatively close to Castle Ring is an old, disused windmill, which, it is widely believed by local folklorists, was built upon nothing less than an ancient, pagan burial ground. Ghosts of the miller's children, who allegedly suffocated in a flour silo, are said to haunt the mill to this day, and legend tells of a strange black, humanoid figure that manifested just before the tragedy occurred. Could this perhaps have been the very same, dark figure that Alec Williams saw near Castle Ring in 2004?

Equally as strange are the reports that come from the nearby village of Cannock Wood – from which Castle

Welcome to the ring of monsters. Copyright: Nick Redfern.

Ring lies in a northwest direction – of a ghostly nun reported seen in the vicinity of an ancient well where water was once dutifully gathered by local villagers.

The 'Big Black Shape'

In September 2005, local media reported that the aforementioned Paranormal Awakening investigation group had recently completed a nighttime investigation of Castle Ring in an attempt to chronicle the strange activity that had been reported there for years. It was an investigation that proved to be immensely profitable.

A spokesperson for the group said, after the experience was completed:

> 'The Cannock Chase local authorities were kind enough to give permission for PA to conduct its research. Indeed, we are extremely grateful to them for being so open-minded as to allow us to conduct our research at this historical and most important monument. The group's results are stunning and have created yet more questions than we have answers. We appear to have obtained a very strange mix of UFO and genuine paranormal activity.'

As for the specific nature of that activity, this was made public midway through February 2006. *The Chase Post* elaborated on the revelations:

> 'A paranormal investigations group say they have evidence of strange, dancing lights and ghostly figures at the area's most ancient monument.'

On one tape, said the 'Post', one of the group's members is heard to exclaim:

> 'Tell me that isn't a big black shape walking towards me.'

The 'Post' added that:

> 'A mystery make voice responds, "There is!"'

Lest we forget, large, walking, dark shapes and strange lights were both staple parts of Alec Williams' May 2004 Bigfoot-like sighting at Castle Ring, too.

CHAPTER 19
THE BEAST OF DERBYSHIRE
'...they brought the car to a screeching halt and came face to face with an enormous creature...'

During the course of undertaking research for a book dealing with landscape-based mysteries, one informant told well-known Fortean authority Andy Roberts of a terrifying mountain-based experience that occurred to him during the early 1960s. The source was a boy at the time, and out with a friend to investigate one of the many aircraft wrecks from the Second World War that still, today even, litter the 2000-foot-high Bleaklow plateau in the Derbyshire Peak District. While visiting the crash site, the man suddenly heard his friend shout. But the reason for his cry had nothing to do with the remains of old, wrecked aircraft...

Th'owd Lad Comes Calling

The man told Andy:

> 'I looked and saw, all in one instant, grouse exploding out of the heather towards us, sheep and hares stampeding towards us and behind them, rolling at a rapid rate towards us from the direction of Hern Clough, a low bank of cloud or fog......but what was truly terrifying was that in the leading edge of the cloud bank - in it and striding purposefully towards us -- was a huge shadow-figure, a man-like silhouette, but far bigger than a man, as high as the cloudbank, as high as a house. And the terror that hit me and was driving the birds and the animals and my friend was utterly overwhelming - like a physical blow - and I have never felt the like since!'

The two boys had never heard of the very similar phenomenon of a sudden outbreak of all-encompassing fear that the Big Grey Man of Ben Macdhui provokes – about which, more soon - and the man's friend attributed the terrifying incident to 'Th'owd Lad,' a Pennine-based term for none other than the Devil himself.

> 'We fled,'

the man added, and continued thus to Andy:

> 'We plunged over the crags above Gathering Hill - and every time I go back and look at those crags, I wonder why we didn't break our necks. We fled in mindless terror down that mountainside towards the Shelf Brook and Doctors Gate - and all the sheep and wildlife that could run or fly went careering down with us in utter panic. And then, about half way down, we seemed to run out into the sunlight - and it was all over! All of the panic was gone. The sheep

The Wild Man roams. Copyright: Sluper, 1572.

stopped, put their heads down, and started to graze. Everything returned at once to normal. But back up there, on Higher Shelf Stones, wisps of mist were still coiling round.'

The man did, however, have his own views, thoughts, and ideas about what might have been the cause of this particular form of what has become known as 'mountain panic'. These were the only additional words he could offer to Andy:

'Don't ask me to rationalise. Or rationalise it away - which is what it amounts to. I've come to the conclusion that sort of thing amounts to no more than a cop-out, a late twentieth century defensive mechanism - it's safe if it can be explained. As if "explaining away" were like defusing a bomb. I do think that every now and then, some of us - maybe all of us - stumble into an encounter with elements deeper and older than we are, and they are not, by their nature, benevolent, though they may be. This certainly wasn't.'

Terror at the Reservoir

Also on matters of a Peak District nature, Jon Downes reminisces on another case from this particular area:

'One of the most credible reports brought to my attention,'

Jon reveals,

'...came from a family that had a daylight encounter with a large and hairy beast in the Peak District in 1991. This all occurred as they were driving near Ladybower Reservoir on the Manchester to Sheffield road. On a hillside, one of the family members had spotted a large figure walking down towards the road. But this was no man. Well, they brought the car to a screeching halt and came face to face with an enormous creature about eight feet tall, that was covered in long brown hair with eyes just like a man's. Its walk was different, too, almost crouching. But just as the man-beast reached the road, another car pulled up behind the family and blasted their horn – apparently wondering why they had stopped in the middle of the road. Suddenly, the creature – which I presume was startled by the noise - ran across the road, jumped over a wall that had a ten-foot drop on the other side, and ran off, disappearing into the woods. Now, I know that the family has returned to the area but has seen nothing since.'

The case to which Jon refers was also studied deeply by paranormal investigator Martin Jeffrey, who was able to speak in person with the family in question – who he described as being 'one of the most sincerest families I have ever met' – and was able to determine that the incident occurred on a Sunday afternoon in November 1991. Martin, too, got confirmation from the family of the 'crouching' nature and gait of the mighty beast, and who additionally told Martin of the monster that:

'...We don't think he's dangerous...just a creature left behind by evolution.'

Of possible relevance to this 'crouching' aspect of the story, Jon Downes recalls another series of events that occurred in decades past that sound noticeably similar:

'Hangley Cleeve, in Somerset, has been the scene of very similar sightings. They occurred in a local quarry, and another on the nearby barrows, where what was described as a large, crouching man-like form, covered in dark, matted hair and with pale, flat eyes was seen.'

Konungs skuggsja: Priceless papers. Copyright: Kristian Kalund, 1905.

CHAPTER 20
A CACKLING CREATURE IN AN IRISH CASTLE
'...these people run along the trees almost as swiftly as monkeys or squirrels...'

Neil Arnold says: 'There is nothing like a chilling ghost story,' adding that 'one of my favourite ghoulish tales comes via Reverend Archdeacon St. John D. Seymour, and concerns a bizarre entity once said to have haunted an Irish castle.'

The story, Neil notes;

> '...is mentioned in *True Ghost Stories* by Marchioness Townshend and Maude Ffoulkes, who comment that "the truth of this story was vouched for to Mr. Reginald Span by the Vicar of the Anglican Church, Arizona, as it happened to some friends of his when they once rented a picturesque castle in the South of Ireland."'

And, with that said, read on…

Man and Beast

So the very weird saga goes, late one particular night, many years ago, a certain 'Mrs. A' was sitting alone in one of the castle's bedrooms, awaiting the return of her husband. Suddenly, there was the distinct and unmistakeable sound of one of the doors banging in the corridor outside the room. More disturbingly, footsteps could be heard, too. Someone or something was creeping around the old castle. Grabbing a lit candle, Mrs. A carefully and slowly opened the door and, to her eternal horror, saw a darkened, shadowy form heading towards the staircase.

Evidently, the entity realised its presence had been noticed, and it turned to face the by now fear-stricken Mrs. A. It was at this point that her terror was elevated to stratospheric proportions: the thing was apparitional in nature, and possessed the head of a man, but the body of a mighty, hair-covered ape. For a moment or several, it glared malevolently at Mrs. A, before vanishing into nothingness. The story is not over, however.

Several nights later, the woman's husband also saw the animal-man, after his attention was drawn to the shadows of the landing, from where distinctly unsettling and creepy laughter was emanating. On looking up, Mr. A was confronted by a beast that – just as the man's wife said – had the body of a large and hairy ape and the head of a man – and a most ugly man, too. Interestingly, Mr. A evidently got a better look at the creature than did Mrs. A, and he could see that the hair of the monster appeared to be of a red/brown colour. In what sounds like some sort of bizarre nightmare, as the man headed up the stairs to confront the man-thing, the terrible laughter got louder and echoed through the old halls of the castle. Not surprisingly, at the last moment the man thought far better of his actions and raced for the safety of the bedroom.

For a few days, things were mercifully quiet. It was a situation that was not destined to remain so for too long, however. While arranging flowers one afternoon in the drawing-room, Mrs. A suddenly felt a pair of hands on her shoulders, and, thinking it was her daughter she spun around, only to be confronted by the cackling creature, looming over her at a height that easily exceeded six feet. Mrs. A screamed for help, and, as a friend came running, the strange and unearthly entity vanished into absolute nothingness – just as it had before. And for the family, by now enough was well and truly enough: they packed their bags and returned to the United States.

Perhaps of relevance to this story, noted Fortean and Dubliner, Ronan Coghlan, says that:

> 'There is an Irish word, gruagach, which can mean a magician, giant or ogre, but that actually means "the hairy one". The question must be asked if this contains any sort of reminiscence of hairy man-beasts prowling the Irish countryside.'

It may very well, given what Ronan has to say next:

> 'A Norse work of the 13th Century mentions the capture of a wild man in Ireland with a mane running down its back.'

Ronan, as he always does, speaks correctly. The work in question was called *Konungs Skuggsja*, or, alternatively, *Speculum Skuggsjo*, and describes the Irish wild man by the name of the gelt, and his peculiar condition as geltacht.

A careful examination of the old book reveals the following about this Irish entity:

> 'There is also one thing which will seem very wonderful about men who are called gelt. It happens that when two hosts meet and are arrayed in battle-array, and when the battle-cry is raised loudly on both sides, that cowardly men run wild and lose their wits from the dread and fear which seize them. And then they run into a wood away from other men, and live there like wild beasts, and shun the meeting of men like wild beasts. And it is said of these men that when they have lived in the woods in that condition for twenty years then feathers grow on their bodies as on birds, whereby their bodies are protected against frost and cold, but the feathers are not so large that they may fly like birds. Yet their swiftness is said to be so great that other men cannot approach them, and greyhounds just as little as men. For these people run along the trees almost as swiftly as monkeys or squirrels.
>
> Now, however, when he arrived out of battle, it was seldom that his feet would touch the ground because of the swiftness of his course, and when he did touch it he would not shake the dew from the top of the grass for the lightness and the nimbleness of his step, He halted not from that headlong course until he left neither plain, nor field, nor bare mountains, nor bog, nor thicket, nor marsh, nor hill, nor hollow, nor dense-sheltering wood in Ireland that he did not travel that day, until he reached Ros Bearaigh, in Glenn Earcain, where he went into the yew-tree that was in the glen.'

Thereafter, we are told, the gelt lived as a definitive outcast, roaming the land of Ireland in search of three things, and three only: Water to drink, water-cress to dine upon, and ivy-bushes on which to sleep.

There is one final Irish story to relate here. Like the opening one in this chapter, it, too, comes from Neil Arnold. But, unlike that first case, this one is focused upon not an ape with the head of a man, but a group of men with the heads of apes, and a solitary one sporting the visage of a stag! Neil says of this truly bizarre saga:

> 'Ghost stories are better suited to the soundtrack of a crackling log fire on a dark and stormy night. However, some spooky tales are so absurd that they are probably better off not told, in case they cause permanent nightmares.'

> So bizarre is the story that one may feel that it stretches the limits of believability. But even so, let us visit County Waterford for an Irish ghost story. It was recorded that many years ago one Christmas Eve, a man named Eli Hayson was settling down for bed in his house which sat alongside the River Suir, when he heard sounds as if someone was running alongside the waterfront.'

> Eli went to the window and peered out into the moonlit night and noticed that his brother Jack, who he thought was at sea on the Thomas Emery, running along the pathway by the river. Eli then noticed that out of the shadows came a group of men that seemed to emerge from the inky waters in pursuit of his brother. Eli could see that his brother was in some distress and tried to shout out to warn him, but to his horror he noticed he could not speak. It was only when his brother reached the door that Eli realised the true horror of the situation. The figures were clearly not all human; in fact, several of them had the head of an ape, and another the head of a stag perched on its shoulders. Were these merely masks? It didn't seem so.'

> Eli's brother was accosted by the hideous forms, and as a grey cloud swept across the moon, all suddenly became still and as Eli searched for his brother, and any signs of the attackers, there was no trace. The next day Eli convinced himself that the terrifying episode had been a dream but the following day learnt from the captain of the Thomas Emery that his brother had fell overboard and drowned. Jack, it seems, had been sleepwalking, even though this possibility was dismissed by Jack and Eli's father.'

The story does not end there, as Neil notes:

> 'Many years later Eli was drinking in his local pub at Cork when he was told by the landlord that an elderly chap wanted to speak to him. The man's named was a Mr. Webster, and he revealed to Eli that twenty years previous his son Tom had been warming himself by a campfire in the vicinity of the river when he saw a trio of what appeared to be men walking along the pathway. Tom hid himself in the undergrowth and watched as the figures passed and it was then he realised with the utmost horror that two of them had the head of a gorilla and one the head of a stag.

> Bravely, Tom followed at a distance and noted that the figures, which were wearing sailor's garments, descended some steps into the gloom of the water and lumbered

into a dinghy and set off for a ship marooned in the harbour. Tom followed in a small boat. The beings climbed aboard, and Tom followed shortly afterwards and hid amongst some barrels. A few minutes later a scream filled the still air and Tom watched as a young man raced across the decks, pursued by the three hideous figures.

Before Tom could act the terrified man leapt overboard into the black, icy waters. At that point Tom's cover had been blown and the figures apprehended him. At close quarters Tom realised that the vile monstrous heads were, in fact, masks and that the three men were simply pranksters hoping to petrify the man who had jumped overboard. Two of the masked men wanted Tom dead, but the third man decided he should be released as long as he did not tell anyone of his weird encounter. Although Tom swore not to tell anyone, so haunted was he by the encounter that years later, on his death-bed he told his father about what happened. Bizarrely, when Eli asked the old man what date all this had taken place, he turned out that it was, in fact, the same night he had seen his brother, Jack, running from the three men.'

While it is incredibly difficult to know what to make of this affair – hoax, urban legend or reality – I do find it intriguing that it should have involved a group of men wearing ape-masks, and one the head of a stag. Shades, one might say, of the monkey-based experience of Mick Dodds and his wife at Chartley Castle, Staffordshire in 1986, which happened to occur right after their attendance at Abbots Bromley's Horn Dance – an event renowned for its stag-horn-wearing men.

CHAPTER 21
SASQUATCH ON THE CHASE
'...It came level and jumped at the car...'

The startling, pisky led-like encounter of Mike Johnson near the Cannock Chase's German Cemetery in the summer of 2001, and the many and varied sightings at the nearby Castle Ring aside, there are other parts of what broadly comprise Staffordshire's Cannock Chase, including its depths and fringes, that have played host to things large, hairy, and man-like…

Eyes that Glow

In 1995, Jackie Houghton was living in Cannock, and working as a waitress in the nearby town of Stafford. On February 18 of that year, and at around 1.00 a.m., she was driving across the Cannock Chase, back to her flat, and along the main road that links the towns of Rugeley and Cannock, after her shift at the restaurant was over. As she approached the turning for the village of Slitting Mill, however, she was suddenly forced to violently swerve the car and only narrowly avoided collision with a large, shambling creature that stepped out into the road at a distance of about two hundred yards from her.

Considering that she was travelling at high speed, said Jackie, it was a wonder that she didn't hit the huge thing. The encounter only lasted just a few seconds, but it was long enough for her to catch sight of the animal in the headlights of her vehicle. She was certain that it was not anything quite as down to earth as a large stag, but was bipedal, tall, very hairy, and had a head dominated by two, fiery, red eyes. In an instant, said Jackie, the beast vanished into the cover of the surrounding trees, leaving her distinctly shaken and stirred. We should not forget that the small hamlet of Slitting Mill – right around where Jackie had her experience - played a significant role in a 1970s-era encounter with a group of hairy, troll-like creatures. And there are many others beyond Jackie who have experienced the Cannock Chase Bigfoot in all its vile and close-up glory.

A Beast at the Boulder

Gavin Addis claims a sensational encounter with a Bigfoot-like entity at one of the Chase's most famous attractions. Its name is the Glacial Boulder. Constructed out of granite, the boulder is both large and impressive. It is also made curious by virtue of the fact that there are no natural granite outcrops anywhere in the area. Certainly, the nearest rock of this type can be found in the Lake District, more than 120 miles to the north, and on Dartmoor, Devonshire, no less than 165 miles to the southwest. The boulder, however, has been matched conclusively to a rocky outcrop at Cniffel in Dumfries & Galloway, which is over 170 miles from the Chase in the Southern Uplands of Scotland. At some point during the last Ice Age, the boulder, it is presumed, was carried by the great glaciers down the country and to its present, and final, resting location on what is now the Cannock Chase.

According to Gavin, on a winter's night in 1997, he and his girlfriend were parked in his car near the

Staffordshire's Cannock Chase: a hotspot for the British Bigfoot. Copyright: Nick Redfern.

boulder, doing what courting couples do amid the darkness and shadowy trees that the Cannock Chase provides at night, when his girlfriend let out a loud scream. Standing atop the boulder was a large hairy man, waving his arms wildly at the sky. Gavin jumped into the front seat of the car and floored the accelerator. Tyres spun, dirt flew into the air, and the car shot away at high speed, but not before the creature succeeded in jumping onto the bonnet of his car. For five minutes, it hung on, before finally being thrown to the ground. Gavin looked in his rear-view mirror and could see that the creature was already back on its feet and running into the woods.

For the sake of telling both sides of the story, it must be said that several people in the Fortean community who have met Gavin Addis in person are convinced that his sensational and undeniably over-the-top tale is simply that; merely a wind-up and nothing more. For his part, Gavin has been careful and vocal to point out in response that he has nothing to gain – and, arguably, everything to lose – by fabricating such a strange story of almost being locked in near-battle with a Bigfoot. And, in that respect at least, he is not at all wrong.

Saying that you have seen a creature resembling Bigfoot on the Cannock Chase – and which, at the height of the encounter, proceeds to clamber on to the bonnet of your prized car, too - is, unfortunately, unlikely to result in anything other than the rolling of eyes and hoots of derision.

'It was coming towards the car'

The next report of any real substance from the dark confines of the Cannock Chase surfaced in January 2003, when Peter Rhodes of the *Express and Star* newspaper wrote an article on an extraordinary encounter on the Chase that almost chillingly paralleled that claimed by Gavin Addis some six years previously. Rhodes reported, under the graphic and memorable headline of Night Terror with a British Bigfoot:

> 'Whatever it was, it scared the living daylights out of Craig Blackmore.

His mother Val says:

> 'I have never seen Craig like that before. He came home shaking, absolutely petrified and white, as though he'd seen a ghost.'

What Craig – and a friend – had actually seen was not a ghost but a 'huge, ape-like creature at the side of the road on Levedale Lane between Stafford and Penkridge'. Craig told Peter Rhodes that:

> 'I was driving my [Ford] Fiesta down the road towards Penkridge and as we approached a house, the security light came on. I saw something in the corner of my eye. It was coming towards the car, running very fast. It wasn't a dog or a deer. It was running like a human would run, but it was really hairy and dark. It came level and jumped at the car but just missed. My friend turned round and said it was huge and had run through the hedge and across the field. I turned the car around but there was no sign of it.'

Craig's mother added:

> 'I thought maybe Craig had been drinking, or perhaps someone had spiked a drink. But that hadn't happened. He is a very truthful boy. He would not say something had happened if it hadn't. And anyway, his friend was in the same state of shock.'

Peter Rhodes noted:

> 'Although the event had been terrifying, Craig, a 19-year-old HGV mechanic, did not report it to the police. He told a few friends ("they all laughed") and tried to forget the experience.'

Rhodes also spoke with British-based Bigfoot investigator Geoff Lincoln, who told the *Express and Star* that:

> 'Bigfoot in Britain is an odd subject and very often the target of ridicule. But sightings are taking place and I am currently looking into two other reports in 2002, one in Northumberland and another in Lancashire.'

To Craig Blackmore, Lincoln offered a simple message (and one that Peter Rhodes said was 'worthy of *The X-Files*'):

> 'You are not alone.'

Interestingly, this particular case closely echoes one from 1994 that occurred in Scotland and which was investigated by Mark Fraser. The location was the area around Torphins, near Aberdeen, and involved three young men that had actually undergone an earlier encounter with a Bigfoot-like entity in the area, and who, while driving, encountered a large, dark-coloured, hairy man-beast at the side of the road, which proceeded to pursue them at an incredibly fast rate of knots. As with Craig Blackmore and his friend, the outcome was fortunately not disastrous for the three terrified souls: after a brief chase, the beast simply gave up the chase and came to a halt in the road.

Perhaps those who are suspicious of the account of Gavin Addis at the Glacial Boulder in 1997 should now consider maybe reevaluating their views, taking into consideration the startling similarities present in the encounter at Torphins in 1994 and that of Craig Blackmore and his friend who – I was told by Peter Rhodes – preferred anonymity, even though his name was given to the *Express & Star*, and to me by Rhodes.

Monsters and The Morning Show: The BBC Takes Note

In 2003, specifically following the publication of, and the publicity given to, the encounter of Craig Blackmore, none other than BBC Television personality, weatherman, and star of *The Morning Show*, Ian McCaskill became embroiled in the mystery of the Cannock Chase Bigfoot when, with cryptozoologists and CFZ-stalwarts Jon Downes and Richard Freeman, he headed to the area in search of the mysterious creature. The BBC was full of good-humour as it reported on McCaskill's adventurous romps on and around the Chase with the Fortean pair:

> 'Apparently he's hairy, giant and ape-like. And not at all the sort of person you want to bump into in a deserted place, on a dark night. Unfortunately, "Bigfoot", or the "Yeti" as it's become known, is out and about, on the prowl, and could be coming to a place near you. Never fear, for The Morning Show's gallant Ian McCaskill was here. In the first week of February, he went off to Cannock Chase in Staffordshire to hunt down the eight-foot Yeti spotted recently in the area.
>
> Ian joined monster hunters Jon Downes and Richard Freeman, from the Centre for Fortean Zoology based in Exeter. Richard, a qualified zoo keeper and centre founder Jon describe themselves as "Britain's foremost professional monster hunters".
>
> They were following up the recent sighting on the side of the road near Stafford. It was only miles from another "Bigfoot" appearance four years earlier. Although they have been mocked, a U.K. website devoted to Bigfoot research contains many reports, including yet another Staffordshire sighting. Lots of sightings occur near telecom towers, and one of the theories is that apparitions are caused by radiation surges from these towers.'

Granted, the segment of the show that focused on the Cannock creature was presented in the light-hearted, mystery-soaked fashion that was always intended, but it did at least ensure that stories of the British Bigfoot reached a prime-time, and fairly large, daytime audience.

Terror at the Tent

In the summer of 2005, Tom, a resident of the town of Bloxwich – which is only about a twenty-minutes or so drive from the Cannock Chase - spent several nights camping with two friends deep in the woods near the Chase's German Cemetery. Having made their camp, the friends headed off into

OPPOSITE: The Pye Green BT Tower has been the reported site of several encounters with the man-beasts of Cannock Chase. Copyright: Nick Redfern.

town to purchase various items that they would need for their time in the great outdoors. On their return, however, they were angered – and disturbed – to find that 'something' had paid a visit to their campsite while they were gone. Charcoal bags, clothes and more had all been 'flung around' the campsite in a highly haphazard fashion, as if by some form of irate, wild animal.

The trio duly set to work and cleaned up the area, then got on with the day's activities. Around 2.00 a.m. the following morning, however, and after they had retired to bed, they were jolted awake by a hideous, animalistic scream that emanated from the woods. It was unlike anything Tom and his friends had ever heard before. Somewhat concerned, the following day they once again headed to town for provisions. But on their return they were faced with an even greater puzzle: Their possessions were as they had left them but now their tent was gone.

Some might very well say that the strange scream may have been that of a fox, but Tom is adamant that it was something far weirder in nature. He also reiterates the fact that the group was camped very deep in the woods and, therefore, the chances of anyone stumbling across their camp were virtually zero. As Tom rightly notes, if people were responsible for the activity at the campsite, why were the group's valuables not stolen along with their tent? And, moreover, what would lead someone to haphazardly fling their possessions around their tent on the previous morning? Clearly, the answers to those questions are unlikely to ever be forthcoming now. Tom, however, is certain in his mind that something was out in the woods on those bright days and dark nights, watching, screaming and taking a keen interest in the activities of both him and his friends.

Commenting on the Creature

It is intriguing to note that when reports of Bigfoot on the Cannock Chase caught the attention of the local media during the early months of 2006, they were not dismissed out of hand by local wildlife experts. Granted, those same experts were not at all prepared to accept that the legendary ape-man had made a home for himself on the Chase, but they were willing to accept that people were probably seeing something out of the ordinary. One of those was Derek Crawley, chairman of the Staffordshire Mammal Group.

Crawley, on February 22, said that:

> 'From the reports it would seem too big to be an escaped ape. A lot of people seem to be saying it has red, staring eyes. It may be a big cat in a tree. The person who saw it may have been confused and mistaken the branches for arms.'

At the same time, Chris Mullins, of Beastwatch UK called for a further investigation, and had the following to say in response to the theory of Derek Crawley:

> 'There is definitely something weird going on and the theory that some of them could be big cats in trees is a genuinely interesting one.'

One week later Chris Mullins had more to add:

> 'Theory has it that a Bigfoot couldn't possibly exist in our country due to the small area of rough country. However, I believe they could be creatures that may well dwell underground. According to reports that I've taken myself, all sightings have been at night or in very poor light – this may be due to their eyes being sensitive to light.'

Mullins continued:

> 'As far as their eyes glowing red are concerned, I cannot possibly put a logical explanation to this. I must admit I don't follow the big cat theory as I've not only studied but even witnessed a big cat in the UK. Their eyes tend to reflect a golden yellow to almost white and I have never heard of a big cat's eyes reflecting red as yet.'

...what would it have done if we didn't get away?'

On September 2, 2008, the Birmingham-based *Sunday Mercury* newspaper published a lengthy letter from a resident of Cannock that told an extraordinary tale. Of course, the fact that the newspaper chose to withhold the name of the writer doesn't help when it comes to trying to validate the encounter, but given that the story is a fascinating one – and a deeply relevant one to the subject of both this book and this particular chapter – I include it without edit. And here it is:

> 'Last year around June time, me and two other friends were supposed to go to a 24-hour basketball event for charity. Us being lads we decided to skive and go and sit down the lane in my car, and do what typical teenage lads do.
>
> Anyway, so me and two others were parked up in a little pull-in, down a lane in Gentleshaw not too far from Burntwood, Cannock. We were parked in this pull-in facing the road, with trees either side of us, and a gated-field behind. It was around two o'clock in the morning and we had the interior light on in the car, when my friend in the front passenger seat said he could see something moving outside, on the right side of the car.'
>
> We turned off the interior light to get a better look and could definitely see something moving in the trees in the distance. Our first thoughts were a person or an animal, all we could see was something large moving around. This thing must have been about 10-15m away. (I didn't exactly have time to measure!) I turned the car headlights and hazard lights on, to see if I could see anymore. This thing was the shape of a human, but stood about 7-8ft, it was hard to tell with it being dark and such a distance away.'
>
> At first sight it was crouching, not completely to the floor, but approx half way and facing directly at the car. It was too dark to see whether it was staring at us, but I'm guessing it was! As soon as it realised we had seen it, it stood up straight, hesitated and ran towards us. Well as you can imagine I wasn't sticking around. This thing was definitely not human, it was huge! It wasn't just tall, but broad and stocky too. I haven't got a clue what its face was like, or its skin or fur, or whatever it had. It wasn't light enough.
>
> My back passenger darted to the other side of the car, and nobody said a word. As it came towards us it was rustling big bushes, shaking pretty big trees, it was just like in a horror movie. I drove out of the pull-in and turned left down the lane, this thing was keeping up with the car, but in the trees. I was trying so hard not to look in my mirrors, but I could see it in the corner of my eyes, I don't know whether it was flying or jumping or what.
>
> Its strength and quickness was unbelievable. Obviously I wasn't thinking that at the time, I just wanted to get the hell out of there! I drove to the bottom of the lane doing about 80mph, and it just vanished as soon as I came up to a pub at the bottom of the lane. I didn't stop until I entered a residential area.

The fear was unreal, I have never been so scared, and didn't think I would ever experience anything that would scare me so much. I felt physically sick, cold and shakey. I just didn't want to believe what I had seen. None of us discussed it, I think we were all in denial! I completely blanked it from my mind after that, and didn't discuss it again until 3 days ago, when the front seat passenger brought it up in conversation, and now I can't forget about it.

I hate re-living it, but I thought I would let others know of my experience. I'm not asking you to believe me, because to everyone else it probably seems so far fetched, but I know what I saw and so do the other two lads. I'm not at all saying I saw "bigfoot" but I know 100% this thing was not human. I know other stories say the thing they saw had red eyes, but I didn't see red eyes, I wasn't close enough to see. Glad I wasn't too.

What haunts me now, is... What would its face have looked like? Where is it? It must have been watching us, and what would it have done if we didn't get away?'

The Club-Wielding 'Chimp' of the Hill

Etchinghill, that towers over the Staffordshire town of Rugeley, was the site of an encounter with a chimpanzee-like animal that was seen early on the morning of May 7, 2009 by a man driving to work, and who, in a brief email sent to me eleven days later, described the animal as being:

'... a big old chimp, about four feet tall, with a big piece of wood in his right hand [Author's Note: The latter point about the wooden weapon surely provokes Woodwose-type imagery, as described by Kithra in Chapter One of this book]'.

The witness continued:

'He was black and hairy all over and shot off as I drove past. It was definitely some sort of biggish monkey though.'

It may not be entirely coincidental that Etchinghill has an appropriately intriguing history.

An article that appeared in the *Lichfield Post* on January 15, 2010, and titled The Little-Known History of the Hill, makes that point amply clear:

'Towering over Rugeley, Etchinghill stands proudly, just as it has for hundreds of years, overlooking the town and a central part of the community. But, the historic site which lies in an area of outstanding natural beauty and is listed as one of Staffordshire's RIGS (Regionally Important Geological and Geomorphological sites). Etchinghill has had many uses over the years and has not always been, the picturesque beauty spot it is today. In its time, the hill, which was formed during the ice age, has been home to armed forces, visitors from across the region as well as a race track but there are many people who know little of the importance of the site. Etchinghill stands 454 feet above sea-level on the edge of Cannock Chase and is capped with an outcrop of rock covered on its lower slopes to the north, south and west with gorse, bracken and heather and on the east by fields.'

When exactly horse racing began at Etchinghill is unclear; however, what is known is that infamous poisoner Dr. William Palmer was once a clerk at the site. Foot races were being run on a course at Etchinghill as early as in the reign of King Charles II when noblemen and gentry employed especially fleet footed men as "footmen" - men who ran before and after their masters' coaches. The course was also present from 1820- 1856 and ran along the foot of the hill, along what is Mount Road, down towards Chaseley House out over towards Shooting Butts Farm and back down to the Hill. At the foot of Etchinghill, the old rifle range had its iron targets which were whitewashed and then painted with black paint.'

And scientists from Birmingham University excavated the site over a period of two months in 1974 after the discovery of two skulls in a cave at Bowers Farm opposite the bottom of Etchinghill. What they found was astonishing. They discovered 267 flints, among them, scrapers for the preparation of game, many microliths which were used as the tips or barbs of arrows and a single serrated flint knife. There was also evidence that the site had been used for knapping and tool manufacture. The cave site turned out to possess the third largest late Mesolithic flint assemblage known in the county.'

As with the various man-beasts seen at Staffordshire's Castle Ring, at the Glacial Boulder, and at Chartley Castle, it seems that the creature of Etchinghill is similarly drawn to locations of a distinctly historical and ancient nature…

Kit's Coty: A magnet for the wild man. Copyright, Neil Arnold.

CHAPTER 22
A REAL LIFE STIG OF THE DUMP
'...they were all spooked by the massive humanoid
which appeared near the chalk quarry...'

'When I were a lad,'

Says author and Kent-based cryptozoologist Neil Arnold,

> 'I watched and collected some of the weirdest examples of children's television; from eerie documentaries, to low-budget dramas, from supernatural series to psychedelic cartoons. One of the most intriguing and certainly most influential things I watched was *Stig of the Dump*, adapted from the Clive King classic novel which was originally published in the '60s. Despite being a huge fan of both series and book, I never realised that such a work may well have been based on an area close to my heart, and my house – Blue Bell Hill in Kent. In the book there is mention of Sevenoaks, but only recently I re-read the book and to my amazement found some odd cases of synchronicity which often pepper local folklore.'

Could truth be stranger than fiction? Did Clive King secretly know something of real hairy wild men dwelling deep in the heart of the Kent countryside? And, if so, did he then weave some of that reality into his engaging page-turner? According to what Neil has to say shortly, very possibly, yes. But, before we get to the heart of the mystery, a bit of background, from Neil, himself, on what got him hooked on cryptozoology…

The Makings of a Monster Hunter

When I told Neil that I was writing a book on the British Bigfoot, he was most keen to have his views aired. And, given that, collectively, those same views provide us with very insightful commentary on the controversy, I was pleased to undertake an extensive interview with Kent's most famous creature seeker. Neil told me:

> 'My interest in cryptozoology began when I was around eight or nine. I didn't know what Cryptozoology was, but I was chilled one dark night in front of my parents' TV after watching the U.S. low-budget docu-drama, *The Legend of Boggy Creek*, a Charles B. Pierce film concerning an alleged Bigfoot-type creature said to roam the bayous of Arkansas. The way it was filmed and the creepy atmosphere and sincerity of the actors - most of whom who were actual witnesses - opened my eyes to what strange things could lurk in the wilds of the world.'

The young Neil Arnold was now on a definitive roll:

'Around the same time I was given a book by a relative called *A Dictionary of Monsters & Mysterious Beasts* by Carey Miller. The book contained great illustrations of mythical monsters I'd seen in films, such as *Clash Of The Titans*, such as the minotaur, harpies etc, but I was intrigued by stories in the book concerning the Loch Ness Monster, the Yeti and lesser known creatures at the time such as the Nandi Bear. My dad and granddad were always telling ghost stories, especially when we visited eerie lakes on a summers' evening for a spot of fishing. But they also told me about so-called "big cats" on the loose, and I collected my first report as a nine-year old; as decades previous there'd been the legend of the "Surrey Puma" and in the '80s the "Beast of Exmoor". I wanted to investigate these stories, because I realised that whilst Bigfoot and the Yeti may have roamed lands out of my reach, there were mysterious creatures being seen on my doorstep. If it wasn't for my dad and granddad, I wouldn't have become a full-time monster hunter, author and lecturer pertaining to strange animals.'

And, with Neil's introduction to monster-hunting and Bigfoot detailed, let's see what he has to say about the strange saga of Clive King's *Stig of the Dump*.

The Story of Stig

'For those of you who are not familiar with this delightful tale,' begins Neil, 'it concerns a young boy named Barney who, whilst staying with his nan, somewhere in Kent, discovers an old chalk quarry which just happens to be inhabited by a Neanderthal-type humanoid who Barney calls Stig. When we are first introduced to Stig, one could almost visualise a completely hair covered humanoid, something akin to a small Sasquatch.

Over the course of the fascinating book Barney and Stig become great friends, but like so many great kids' programmes and books of that era, from the '60s to the '80s, we are often left to wonder as to whether Stig was a real creature or all part of Barney's strange imagination. Either way, upon re-reading the book, I was amazed at how the author had mentioned several "fictional" items which I would eventually uncover as fact many decades later.'

The Standing Stones

Neil continues with the curious parallels between the fiction of *Stig of the Dump* and the reality of what has taken place in certain parts of mysterious Kent:

'On a less cryptozoological note, we are introduced to the 'Standing Stones' in Chapter Nine [of King's novel], which could be a reference to Kit's Coty House, a set of Neolithic stones said to be older than Stonehenge, which jut from a field at Blue Bell Hill. These stones have a lot of folklore attached to them. Some suggest that the stones are used as a calendar, or could be a mark of where a great and bloody battle once took place. Others believe the stones to have once been used for sacrificial means, and there are those who opt for the more fanciful rumour that they were constructed by witches on a dark and stormy night.

When we are first introduced to Stig, Barney, with a bump on the head along the way, falls into a steep chalk quarry (there are such quarries at the base of Blue Bell Hill) and accidentally stumbles upon the den of the creature called Stig. Oddly, for almost a century there have been reports from the quarries around Blue Bell Hill of a "Wildman" of sorts.'

There have, indeed, as Neil demonstrates…

Wouldham Gone Wild

'A woman many years ago, growing up in the neighbouring village of Wouldham,' explains Neil, 'often spoke about how in the 1960s her grandmother would tell her bedtime stories of the local "hairy man" seen near the standing stones. The woman mentioned that her grandmother had grown up with these stories and had seen the man-beast herself. In the 1970s a woman named Maureen saw a hair-covered, hulking great creature with glowing eyes one night whilst tending to a campfire with her boyfriend.'

In 1992,'

adds Neil,

'...a similar beast was seen at Burham, a neighbouring village of Blue Bell Hill, by several men on their way to the pub. The men were all members of the Territorial Army and not prone to flights of fancy, but they were all spooked by the massive humanoid which appeared near the chalk quarry. In 2008 a man-beast was seen by a female motorist in Kent. She was so terrified by the creature she almost crashed her vehicle.'

And, as Neil's work and research in relation to Clive King's much-cherished story reveals, there are still further aspects of cryptozoology that seem to pop up within the pages of the engaging novel:

'Stig Of The Dump also makes a couple of references to leopards, and in particular one specimen which Stig captures and skins in the local quarry. Barney finds the skin of the exotic cat in Stig's den and one begins to wonder whether Barney has stepped into some ancient period or Stig has killed an animal that has escaped from a private collection.'

As anyone with an appreciation of British history and mystery will be acutely aware, sightings of large and exotic cats in the British Isles absolutely proliferate. They even date back centuries, and in precisely the same area that has so fascinated Neil, as he now shares with us:

'Interestingly there are several reports of large cats on the loose around Blue Bell Hill dating back to the 1500s. I saw a black leopard three times (twice in 2000 and once in 2008) near Blue Bell Hill, but interestingly the area where Stig would have killed his prey is the same area which once housed a local zoo. During the early part of the 1900s several children playing on the Downs reported seeing a black leopard. Some people believe it escaped from the zoo, then owned by Sir Tyrwhitt-Drake, although this was never proven. The children reported that the authorities came out, flushed the animal from the undergrowth and shot it dead.'

Sir Tyrwhitt-Drake, notably, was an odd but amusing character with whom we will cross paths again, shortly. Until then, however, back to Neil:

> 'During the 1700s a large animal was said to have killed a rambler on the Pilgrim's Way, an ancient track-way which runs through Blue Bell Hill. The "beast" was also recorded by a local Reverend as being the size of a calf. Some believe the animal was a hellhound but I'm of the belief it was a large cat, misunderstood at the time and confined to superstition.'

On this particular aspect of the story, Neil closes thus, and in thought-provoking fashion:

> 'A number of children's programmes and books a few decades ago always hinted at some bizarre, psychedelic landscape of imagination, dream and eerie drama. I just wonder if Clive King knew of such local folklore and built the story around it, or by accident manifested some of the forms which have become embedded into local lore. Either way, Stig... is a magical story and a great place to start for any would-be adventurer and explorer, like I was all those years ago.'

Certainly, having read the classic novel myself as a child, teenager, and adult, I have to heartily endorse Neil's words! And, we are far from being finished with Neil. Actually, we have scarcely begun.

CHAPTER 23
SOUTHERN ARCHIVES
'...It's clear to me that we aren't dealing with tales of escaped monkeys...'

Neil Arnold is someone who turns up regularly in the pages of this book, and with very good reason and much justification, too: he's someone who gets out into the field, undertakes a great deal of on-site investigations, and, as a result, has compiled a vast amount of data on mysterious creatures seen in the British Isles, and particularly so in the county of Kent – in which Neil and his wife, Jemma, reside – and other parts of the south of England too, as will now become demonstrably clear…

A Creature Seeker Comments

'The south-eastern region of England,'

says Neil, specifically of British wild men and Bigfoot,

'...has had sporadic reports over the years. [It] still harbours forest area and also heavy woodland, and these woods are steeped in history and folklore [and] figure quite heavily with some reports. But a majority always seem to come from already eerie and mystical places, where in the past there have been ghost sightings, rumours of other strange creatures and also areas that seem to attract legends of black magic, ancient stones, white witches, pagans, etc.'

And, with that said, let's dig deep into Neil's archives, which he has generously shared with me, and, as a result, with you too.

An Encounter in Essex

From October 2010, comes the following story, written to Neil by Sally of Essex, and presented for you in unedited form:

'On the 14th October I was driving home from work. It was approximately 9:30 p.m. and I turned the corner into the Ferry Lane Industrial Estate in Rainham. I was coming from the A13 end, approaching *The Cherry Tree*. I was about one hundred and fifty yards away from a "shape" that was manifesting before my eyes and if I'm truthful, if I'd blinked I would have missed it. From the two seconds that it was in front of me, I will try to explain what I saw.'

'From the railings, a shape approximately the size of a large-shouldered man started to take a human form. It seemed to be made of a dark nicotine-brown smoke, the edge of the shape seemed lighter in colour. Its legs looked strong in their form and the shoulders were broad. The strangest thing was the head, as it was very small in comparison to the body, arms and legs.

The "creature" minded me of the Yeti – the Abominable Snowman of the Himalayas. Then just as quick as it had manifested it seemed to be sucked back into the railings as if nothing had happened. I pondered what it might have been. A trick of the light. My headlights causing an optical illusion. The weather was clear and mild, there was no fog or other cars, or people. I have driven round that area several times since but have never seen it again...very, very strange.'

The Sussex Things

'The county of Sussex is saturated with strange beastly folklore; from reports of dragons, to "big cats", and from phantom bears, to even Bigfoot,'

Neil notes, and with a great deal of justification, too:

'One such tale that did the rounds a few years ago took place at Friston Park, in East Sussex. The sighting occurred near Newhaven on November 18th, 2002, at 2:30 a.m., as a Phil Hayman had parked his lorry up to stretch his legs when he spotted a large figure in the woods. The form was illuminated by a red light situated on a forestry machine in the woods. Mr. Hayman was unsettled by the presence and hurried back to his cab but still had time to shine his torch at the being as it rushed off into the darkness. Phil claimed that the creature wasn't human because he saw no skin colour reflected in the flashlight beam, and suggested it may have been covered in hair for it was dull in colour.'

Neil admits that the above report 'probably doesn't prove that an unknown bipedal creature haunts Sussex woodlands', but he does add that 'the following encounter is one that will make you think again'!

He details it like this:

'In the summer of 1948, E.J.A. Reynolds, a young boy, had a bizarre encounter whilst setting rabbit traps in a wooded area of Horsham. Whilst he was hiding in the undergrowth and keeping watch on the traps, a small man no more than two feet in height appeared a few yards away from the thicket. The being was covered in hair except for its face. Its nose was pointed and it had incredibly long arms. It did not notice the terrified youngster. The figure then turned and headed back into the woods. Even weirder, the youngster claimed to have seen the creature again a few days later. He was travelling on a bus in the area and noticed the hairy being walking across the lawn of a large garden.'

Wild Things

'I have ten or eleven amazing reports from here in [the British county of] Kent alone, which I couldn't believe,'

Nick Redfern and Neil Arnold. Copyright: Nick Redfern.

reveals Neil.

> 'One was from a woman I used to work with who had seen one in the woods about one hundred yards from my house - which was very, very strange - and the woman hadn't told anybody about it for thirty years. In these British Bigfoot reports, the witnesses are all seeing things with red, glowing eyes, and these reports are hard to categorize. Although people are seeing big hulking things that are covered in hair, I don't actually think they are the same things that people are seeing in America; because I personally think that the American Bigfoot is actually flesh-and-blood.'

And, now, Neil outlines a few of those cases from his files:

> 'Wouldham is a small village in Kent which sits right next to Blue Bell Hill, which for me remains the countries weirdest village,' explains Neil. In his opinion, here's just one of the many reasons why Wouldham is a place to be considered definitively weird: 'In my book [The Mystery Animals of the British Isles: Kent], I noted several bizarre tales concerning witnesses who'd seen red-eyed man-beasts and very recently a lady, who now resides in Norfolk, contacted me to say that when she was

a child growing up in the '60s at Wouldham, her grandmother used to tell her intriguing tales.

One of these,'

Neil divulges,

'...was said to date back to the 1920s and her grandmother, who passed away, made notes of this. The lady said that her grandmother used to tell her about the "hairy man" of Wouldham. A humanoid often seen in local woods by children, and certainly adults were made aware of this being. It was completely covered in hair and the story had become embedded in her psyche and was triggered again when she purchased my *The Mystery Animals of the British Isles: Kent* and saw, at the front, an image of a hairy humanoid standing at Blue Bell Hill's Kit's Coty House, an ancient structure on the landscape.'

As for what, exactly, all of this may mean, Neil offers the following:

'It's clear to me that we aren't dealing with tales of escaped monkeys, but indeed something very much embedded in the fabric of the place, as some kind of folkloric creature which has existed for possibly centuries. It seems, as well, that the more I write about the creature, the more it stirs up. Around 1997 / '98 there was a report in the local newspaper of a gorilla-type creature seen at Blue Bell Hill, and I recall scoffing at the report and believed it was simply down to media drama. Now, it seems that there is, and always has been, a strange humanoid prowling the dark lanes and thickets of a place that I've been obsessed with since I was a kid, [when] my dad used to take me there and terrify me with tales of the phantom hitchhiker.'

'A hulking, hairy creature'

In August 1975, at Walderslade, Chatham, Kent, says Neil:

'A female witness named Maureen, who was eighteen at the time, was with her boyfriend, late at night, in local woods near Sherwood Avenue. They were chatting and her boyfriend decided to bend down and light a fire. As he was doing so, Maureen saw two glowing points of light just a few feet away that she took to be eyes. They belonged to a hulking, hairy creature that she could just pick out in the darkness, and it stood a couple of feet above her, making this creature around six to seven feet in height.'

Maureen watched the figure, but was too transfixed to alert her companion, and then, the eyes seemed to lower and the form disappeared behind the undergrowth, but she sensed it was still there, so, without trying to worry her partner, she simply asked to leave.'

She never spoke of the encounter for some thirty years often asking herself afterwards if she'd seen the Devil! Scepticism may arise over such matters but across the U.K. there are legends of such "wild men", and as you will read in other cases from Kent, such glimpses of red eyes and hulking humanoids, albeit scarce, do occur.'

CHAPTER 24
THE BIG GREY MAN OF THE MOUNTAIN
'...something beyond the wit of man haunted that mountain...'

> 'Ben Macdhui, at 1309 metres (4296 ft), is the second highest mountain in the U.K. and lies in the heart of the mountain range known as the Cairngorms,'

Says Andy Roberts, the leading authority on the strange enigma of what has become known as Scotland's Big Grey Man. Andy continues:

> 'The mountain comprises of a high plateau with a sub-arctic climate and is often covered in snow for months at a time. Weather conditions can be extreme and unpredictable. Sadly the Cairngorms have been defaced by ski-lifts and restaurants but until recently have remained remote, requiring considerable physical effort and mountain-craft to navigate successfully. The wild nature and relative inaccessibility of the area has contributed to their popularity and the Cairngorms have been a playground for climbers, walkers, skiers, naturalists and those who love the high and lonely places for hundreds of years. Ben Macdhui has several spellings and its English translation is Gaelic for hill of the son of duff.'

And, adds Andy:

> 'Like any other area of land be it mountain, plain, or urban townscape Ben Macdhui and its environs have a large body of oral and written folklore which encompass phenomena which broadly fall into the Fortean and paranormal fields.'

Welcome, my friends, to the world of the Big Grey Man…

The Beginning of a Legend

> 'The past eighty years,'

Andy rightly notes;

> '…has seen the Big Grey Man of Ben Macdhui become a staple for authors and journalists writing about Scottish legends. With the exceptions of the Loch Ness Monster and the Bonnybridge UFO hotspot it is arguably Scotland's best known example of strange phenomena. So much has been written about the Big Grey Man that one could be forgiven for believing it is a well-attested experience with tens if not hundreds of witnesses. If only it were that simple! When put under the microscope, away from the conventions of story-telling or the obligations of having to make a profit, the Big Grey Man

of Ben Macdhui, like the majority of other Fortean phenomena, takes on a completely different appearance.'

Andy notes that witnesses to the phenomenon known as the Big Grey Man - or the BGM - describe how they have variously encountered footsteps, a distinct sensation of a threatening 'presence', and an over-powering sense of panic whilst on the mountain called Ben Macdhui. The experience is graphic enough to compel witnesses to flee in sheer terror, often for several miles. And taking into consideration the fact that the encounters almost exclusively takes place on rocky, dangerous ground, often in weather conditions involving mist and snow, Andy stresses that 'we should not underestimate the power of the experience'.

Although the first recorded Big Grey Man experience did not take place until 1891, and was not made public until 1925, there are a few precursors and legends that help place the phenomenon in some geographic, folkloric and historical context, as Andy now reveals.

A Spectre Appears

'In 1791 poet James Hogg, known as the Ettrick Shepherd, described seeing a huge figure on Ben Macdhui whilst tending his sheep,' records Andy. 'As he watched the halo which had formed around him due to the combination of sunshine and mist he suddenly noticed a huge, looming figure. It was vaguely human in shape and he imagined it to be the devil. Hogg fled in terror, not stopping until he reached fellow shepherds. The next day he saw the same figure under similar climatic conditions.'

Hogg dramatically described the eerie experience himself, and, fortunately, his report still exists and is available for scrutiny:

'It was a giant blackamoor [an antiquated term for a person of dark skin], at least thirty feet high and equally proportioned, and very near me. I was actually struck powerless with astonishment and terror. My first resolution was, if I could keep the power of my limbs, to run home and hide myself below the blankets with the Bible beneath my head.'

Instead of fleeing, however, Hogg stood firmly his ground, fully determined to trace the source of the figure. Cold fear gave way to utter astonishment, however, when he removed his hat and found the strange entity mimicking both this and all his subsequent actions. Hogg, trying to rationalise the experience, came to believe that the affair could be explained by an uncommon natural phenomenon known as the 'Brocken Spectre'. And, for the uninitiated, here's Andy to tell you more about it:

'The Brocken Spectre, so named because the summit of the Brocken in Germany's Harz Mountains was one of the places it was first recorded from, is a dramatic natural effect with many variations. Essentially it is formed when the observer's shadow is cast onto mist by sunlight. The experience is dependent on the relationship between factors such as the brightness and angle of the sun, thickness of the mist, presence and intensity of rain or wind and the position of the observers. The resulting effect can range from the simple "shadow" effect of the viewer to grossly distorted, moving images of what appears to be one or more giants. In all cases, however dramatic or terrifying to the witness, the

OPPOSITE: Andy Roberts, an acknowledged expert on the mysteries of Ben Macdhui. Copyright: Nick Redfern.

Brocken Spectre is just one of nature's free light shows. It has been invoked by many writers to "explain" the BGM and may have some relevance in a number of the experiences.'

But, as Andy is keen and careful to stress, 'the Brocken Spectre is only a small part of the whole story'.

The Goliaths of Scotland

Andy's research has demonstrated that legends exist of giants in the Cairngorms some of which may have fuelled the larger and enduring body of data relative to the Big Grey Man:

'High above Loch Einich, on the slopes of Sgor Gaoith, to the west of Ben Macdhui, is a natural feature called Am Bodach, the Old Man. There is also another stone bearing the name A'Chailleach, the Old Woman. One of the legends attached to these stone giants is that they are locked in eternal combat, doomed to hurl stones at each other. Stones bearing these names are common in Scotland and the legends pertaining to them are similar. The notion of giants in and on the landscape, either personified by rock formations or as creatures from mythology, is entrenched in the folklore of these Isles. With the Big Grey Man of Ben Macdhui we have one of the few which is part of a living tradition. Whether it is a breathing entity, remains to be seen.'

And it's now that we get to the heart of the mysterious 'man' of the mountain.

Encounters on the Mountain

Andy explains.

'Hugh Welsh, camping with his brother by the summit cairn of Ben Macdhui in 1904 heard the type of footsteps which later became synonymous with the BGM. They heard the noise both and night and in daylight describing it as being like "...slurring footsteps as if someone was walking through water-saturated gravel.'

Welsh also recalled they were:

"...frequently conscious of something near us, an eerie sensation of apprehension, but not of fear as others seem to have experienced". They questioned the head stalker at Derry Lodge who told them, "That would have been the Fear Liath Mor you heard.'

Fear Liath Mor is Gaelic for Big Grey Man, and, as Andy states with some significance:

'If this account is true it is the first known reference to the BGM by name. That it was proffered as an explanation by a local stalker may indicate a larger body of tradition regarding the Big Grey Man which has gone unrecorded.'

Moving further into the twentieth century, George Hall, in the pages of his book, *Leaves from a Rambler's Diary*, recounted the experience of an unnamed friend who worked in the Cairngorms, and who also had some sort of curious encounter. Hall, unfortunately, provided very few details. But, as Andy has commented, we have to remember that this was prior to any wide, public knowledge of, or even interest in, the Big Grey Man. Thus, the story was likely not perceived as being as significant as many might suggest it is today, given the body of data that now exists on the Big Grey Man.

But, Andy offers, it appears that Hall's unknown friend:

'had an odd experience on Ben Macdhui involving a "presence" which frightened him to such an extent he left the mountain, after which the sensation faded.'

The Mountain Man Reaches the Media

The *Cairngorm Club Journal* for 1921 noted the eye-opening contents of a then recent letter sent to the *Aberdeen Free Press* in which the writer:

'....called attention to a myth prevalent in Upper Deeside to the effect that a big spectral figure has been seen at various times during the last five years walking about on the tops of the Cairngorms. When approached, so the story goes, the figure disappears. Moreover, it has got a name - 'Ferlie More', to wit.'

Andy, commenting on this particular quote from the *Cairngorm Club Journal*, says:

'Obviously the name "Ferlie More" is a derivative of the Gaelic Fear Liath Mor, or Big Grey Man, again perhaps suggesting the tradition of a local giant.'

And the cases kept on coming. Yet again, back to Andy, who reveals a further layer of the puzzle:

'In 1924, Dr. Ernest A. Baker's book, *The Highlands with Rope and Rucksack*, appeared. Here, Baker relates the experience of a friend whose job took him into the mountains, a deer stalker or perhaps a shepherd. Alone on Ben Macdhui one day he became aware of a terrifying presence which, as Affleck Gray [the author of the book, The Big Grey Man of Ben Macdhui] recounts, "disturbed him in a manner which was beyond his experience". Gray makes the point that this was no ordinary fear but something so powerful that Baker's friend fled Ben Macdhui, the terror only subsiding when he reached low ground. Baker also reports how one mountain climber had told him that he would under no circumstances spend any time on Ben Macdhui alone, even in daylight.'

Categorising the Phenomenon

That, in essence, is just some of the history of the BGM; but what about the evidence for the existence of, well, whatever the Big Grey Man might or might not be? To have at least a chance of answering that question, we must, once again, return to the research of Andy, who says of this particular aspect of the phenomenon:

'In discussing the BGM, the researcher is immediately confronted with the problem of exactly what can be admitted as evidence for its existence. Affleck Gray's book lists numerous alleged BGM encounters and draws in a plethora of other ghosts and paranormal phenomenon encountered on Ben Macdhui. This heady mix gives the impression there are far more BGM encounters than there actually are. There is also the problem relating to the geography of the mystery. Many encounters and experiences attributed to the BGM are not actually on Ben Macdhui but from surrounding mountains and valleys. So the first step in any discussion about the BGM is to define what constitutes a BGM experience.'

And Andy's very own definition goes like this:

'The experience must contain any or all parts of the core phenomenon. This core phenomenon consists of the following elements: A giant figure; footsteps being heard; a sensation of terror or panic, strong enough to cause flight; [and] the experience must have taken place on the mountain of Ben Macdhui or in its immediate environs.'

Andy's list of what does – and, by default, does not – constitute an encounter with the Big Grey Man is significant. Andy explains that these particular requirements for a BGM encounter immediately discount:

'...much of the phenomena discussed in Gray's book such as the many odd sounds, singing, chanting, musical notes etc., as well as the sightings of figures (especially the ones described as of human size) at a distance and unaccompanied by other phenomena. The sounds are almost certainly attributable to natural phenomenon such as the actions of wind, snow and water in an extreme environment. The 'figures' seen at a distance are just that and may well be other climbers. Gray discussed this problem at length and eventually accepts this is likely to be the case'.

Andy does, concede, however, that:

'This definition could be construed as being unnecessarily dismissive of what might be seen as supporting evidence. I will be the first to admit its inadequacies, but when dealing with a phenomenon as mutable (both by witnesses and its commentators) as the BGM it is essential to have some parameters within which to work.'

When Seeing and Hearing is (for a while) Believing

As a keen hill-walker, and someone well-versed and experienced in mountainous and hilltop territories, Andy is right on target when he offers the following statement:

'Anyone who has spent any time in wild, mountainous or open country will be well aware of the problems of visual and aural perception; particularly when alone, especially in poor visibility or in bad weather. The mountaineering literature is scattered with many good examples of these perceptual tricks, of figures being seen, of presences being felt and so on.'

As a perfect and prime example of what Andy is talking about, it is worth quoting the experience of veteran Scottish mountaineer and author W.H. Murray, which also took place in the Cairngorms. In Murray's own words:

'When we started on the last rise to Cairn Toul there came a wider clearance than usual. Suddenly Mortimer gripped my arm and pointed uphill through the misty chasm. "Look!" he exclaimed, "Two men crossing to Glen Einich." Upon looking up at the slope I was duly surprised to see two climbers a long way ahead of us.....I watched them traverse a full fifty feet from east to west across the snow-slope, one about ten yards in front of the other.....We advanced and saw them halt, apparently to wait for us. At a hundred yards range they turned out to be two black boulders. So great was our astonishment that we failed even to laugh at ourselves.'

The Collie Affair

In Andy's opinion:

'There are only six "good" first or well-attested accounts which fit the criteria. Of these only three took place on the summit or summit plateau of Ben Macdhui. Only two of the six include a "Big Grey Man", or similar figure. Of those, one was later relegated by the witness to either being imagined or as a confabulation of panic and mist.'

Andy adds:

'Despite rumours that the BGM was experienced frequently by climbers in the late 19th century, the only record from that century is that of Professor Norman Collie's 1891 encounter. This experience is the one most often quoted by writers on the subject and the one which brought the BGM to the general public's attention.'

As far as the background of the man himself is concerned, Andy says:

'Collie was Professor of Organic Chemistry at University College, London. A climbing contemporary of Aleister Crowley he was a keen all-weather mountaineer well used to the rigours of the Himalayas, Alps, Rockies and Scotland. Collie was a rigorous scientist who was closely involved with the discovery of the gas neon, and was responsible for taking the first X-ray for surgical purposes.

Collie did not go public in the U.K. with his experience until 1925, although there is circumstantial evidence his was the tale recounted in [Dr. Ernest A.] Baker's book, as the two were climbing partners. Speaking at the Annual Dinner of the Cairngorm Club on November 28th that year, he recounted his frightening experience on Ben Macdhui. His story was published within days by an Aberdeen newspaper and shortly afterwards in the Cairngorm Club Journal.'

The account from Collie, that appeared in the *Press and Journal* and in the pages of the *Cairngorm Club Journal*, runs as follows, and makes for truly undeniable, atmospheric reading, regardless of how one personally interprets the many and varied complexities present in both the BGM legend and Collie's own telling of his experience:

'I was returning from the cairn on the summit in a mist when I began to think I heard something else than merely the noise of my own footsteps. For every few steps I took I heard a crunch, and then another crunch as if someone was walking after me but taking steps three or four times the length of my own. I said to myself: This is all nonsense. I listened and heard it again but could see nothing in the mist. As I walked on and the eerie crunch, crunch, sounded behind me I was seized with terror and took to my heels, staggering blindly among the boulders for four or five miles nearly down to Rothiemurchus Forest. Whatever you make of it I do not know, but there is something very queer about the top of Ben Macdhui and I will not go back there by myself I know.'

The only other first-person account of this experience, notes Andy, comes from the obituary published following Collie's death in 1942. Again, Collie's words spell out the undeniably unsettling nature of the encounter; one which clearly left a deep impression upon him:

'One day at Eastertime I was climbing Ben Macdhui. It was very misty and I was only able to see a few yards from me when not very far from the summit, I suddenly heard footsteps on the snow behind me. Confident that some man was following me, I waited for him to join me, but the moment I stopped the footsteps also stopped. When I started on my way again, once more I heard the footsteps clearly. More than ever convinced that some man was on my track I turned and ran back for some distance, but found no-one.

Once again I started on my way to the summit and once again I heard footsteps which stopped whenever I stopped. When at last I reached the summit the footsteps did not stop but came nearer and nearer until they came right up to me. At that instant I was seized with an intolerable fright and I ran my hardest down the mountainside. No power on earth will ever take me up Ben Macdhui again.'

And there are other aspects to the Collie affair that need to be highlighted, too, if we are to gain a full understanding of the one case, that perhaps more than any other on record, has become so inextricably tied to the legend of the BGM. Fortunately for us, Andy does highlight them:

'Baly, Collie's obituarist had, at times, worked and climbed with him and his unreferenced account gives the impression it was obtained verbatim from Collie. But it differs slightly from the account in both the Press and Journal and the *Cairngorm Club Jour*nal, changing the story slightly. *The Press and Journal* article and Baly's obituary have been the two sources from which all subsequent re-tellings of Collie's experience have been taken.

Another element often used by writers dealing with the BGM,' reveals Andy, 'is to suggest that although Collie didn't speak publicly about his experience in the U.K. until 1925, he had originally revealed his story in an obscure New Zealand newspaper at the turn of the century. Despite no-one having seen or referenced the original source - usually given as an article entitled *A Professor's Panic* - it is, nevertheless, used to add weight to the story. It is first mentioned in an article about the BGM by Ronald W. Clark in *Scotland's Magazine*, [in] November 1961.'

Andy stresses a significant point, however:

'There is no evidence, according to his biographer, that Collie visited New Zealand until the 1930s.'

And what of the rumours that it was not just footsteps that Collie encountered. There are stories and rumours that Collie may have experienced more; far more, in fact. Andy, however, places such stories into their correct, and more down to earth, context when he says:

'Yet another variation which has crept into the Collie story is that he saw the "something" which was causing the footsteps. This canard stems from Seton Gordon's retelling of the experience. Gordon used the phrase "Collie encountered this spectre", seeming to infer a visual encounter. But this statement is not backed up by Collie's 1925 account, and it is clear from Gordon's overall context that Collie saw nothing. His experience was purely the hearing of footsteps, followed by blind panic.'

Then there is the controversial theory that the entire affair was nothing but a BGM-sized hoax, an issue that Andy has also addressed during the course of his quest to get to the heart of the BGM puzzle:

'It has been suggested that Collie invented the whole story having, according to Rennie McOwen, "a mild reputation as a prankster."'

OPPOSITE: Creatures of the mountains. Copyright: Unknown, 1487.

But, yet again, accounts differ. Affleck Gray believed Collie to have been 'sardonic and dry as dust', adding that 'he did not suffer fools gladly'. Whatever the real nature of Collie's character, and whatever the minor variations in the story, it does appear, Andy is willing to conclude:

> '...that Collie did have a terrifying experience and one which had a dramatic effect on him. He was convinced that there was "something very strange" about the summit of Ben Macdhui, something he clearly believed was supernatural in origin. His biographer spoke to Collie's niece about the matter and she confirmed that she had heard the story from him many times and that "Uncle Nor believed in it completely.'

Interestingly, Andy has something else to report of relevance, too:

> 'Collie, for all his science, was not a reductionist though and well understood the atmospheres created by wild places. Years prior to revealing his Ben Macdhui experience he wrote "...there are places that one dreads, when one trembles and is afraid, one knows not why and fears stand in the way". In her discussion of the matter Collie's biographer concludes that,' "Collie remained emphatic - something beyond the wit of man haunted that mountain.'

Interest Sparked and 'Perfect Nonsense'

Not surprisingly, the coverage given at a public and media level to the Collie story, provoked further interest in the saga of Ben Macdhui's Big Grey Man, as Andy records:

> 'Shortly after the newspaper coverage of Collie's Cairngorm Club speech the Press & Journal ran a piece entitled Opinions on the Elusive "Big Grey Man". Several Cairngorm Club members, with hundreds of Ben Macdhui ascents between them, opined on the legend. Robert Clarke claimed he had heard the story direct from Collie in 1915 and as a result made enquiries in the area among the older deer stalkers and crofters. He found that it was virtually unknown on Deeside to the south but that it was "still current among the older residents on Speyside, where it had apparently had its rise.'

Inevitably, not everyone was in agreement, or even felt the story worthy of merit or much comment. As evidence, we have the following from Andy:

> 'William Gordon, then president of the Cairngorm Club, regarded such stories as "perfect nonsense", although having heard the story direct from Collie himself. Gordon is quoted as saying: "It was not even a tradition entertained, as such, among the members of the club, nor had he ever encountered residents on the Deeside or Speyside districts, abutting upon the Cairngorms who gave forth the story or hinted at anything of the kind.'

Arguments as to whether or not there was a pre-existing tradition of the BGM raged in newspapers, magazines and climbing journals for the next few years, but no specific oral or written tradition pre-dating Collie's experience has ever surfaced.

The Kellas Controversy

The second account of the BGM, Andy's studies have demonstrated, originated from one Dr. Henry Kellas. Unfortunately, neither he nor his brother, who was with him at the time of the encounter, ever personally recorded their experience. And, on top of that, Henry Kellas died on the 1921 Mount Everest

Reconnaissance Expedition; thus ensuring he would never be in a position to comment on the veracity, or otherwise, of the tale that has been specifically attributed to him.

Andy, commenting on the Kellas case, tells us that:

> 'Their account, also widely featured in the BGM legend featured, first appeared in print as a letter in the pages of the *Press and Journal* in December 1925, following hot on the heels of Collie's speech to the Cairngorm Club.'

As for the account in the *Press and Journal*, here it is, presented in unedited form:

> 'The correspondence in your paper on the subject of the Ferla Mohr has encouraged me to state the story as given to me by the late Mr. Henry Kellas, my lifelong friend, with whom I once climbed Ben Macdhui. He and his brother, Dr. Kellas, had been chipping for crystals in the late afternoon well below the cairn, and were together on the slope of a fold of the hill. Suddenly they became aware of a giant figure coming down towards them from the cairn. They saw it pass out of sight in the dip on the side of the fold remote from themselves, and awaited its reappearance. But fear possessed them ere it did reach the top, and they fled. They were aware it was following them, and tore down by Corrie Etchachan to escape it. Mr Kellas said there was a mist on part of the hill, but refused to believe that the figure could be the shadow of either his brother or himself, causing an optical illusion. He asked why not two figures if that had been the case. But he never spoke of "crunching" or of footsteps being heard by either himself or his brother.'

It's important to note that, as Andy stresses:

> '...this is not a primary source for the story and must be treated as such. But if we allow for it being a genuine account with a degree of accuracy, it is the first recorded sighting of a giant figure. Kellas' certainty that it couldn't be a Brocken Spectre, because there were two witnesses to one phenomenon, is not borne out by the factors which govern the Brocken's appearance and would have depended on where he was standing in relative to his brother. The conditions of mist and light mentioned in the account would have been optimum for a Brocken to be seen. But Brockens only move if the observer(s) move(s), and, going on the details given, it is difficult to ascertain whether Kellas and his brother were standing or moving. Given that they were chipping for crystals the likelihood is that they were stationary at the time.'

Andy also states of this particular story:

> 'The date of the Kellas brothers experience is unclear. Affleck Gray points to it being twelve years after Collie's encounter, placing it in 1903. There is also some confusion as to the exact circumstances. The *Press & Journal* account gives it as being on a late afternoon. Gray mentions that it was late on a clear June night. A clear June night in those latitudes, even after midnight, would have been very light. Gray does not reference his alternate version and I have been unable to contact him or locate his papers on the subject. But the panic engendered by the experience, whatever its origin, seemed to be real enough and like Collie the Kellas brothers fled: And not just

a few yards, or even hundreds of yards; but several miles, risking life and limb over rough and dangerous terrain.'

A Mountaineer Speaks

The *Scots Magazine* reported on the story of one Alexander Tewnion, who had his own experience with the BGM phenomenon during the Second World War, specifically in 1943. He told the magazine, in the form of a letter:

> 'Of all the experiences that have come my way, one stands out above all others in its strangeness. This was when I shot the Fear Liath Mor, the Big Grey Man of Ben Macdhui. It happened like this. In October 1943 I spent a ten day leave climbing alone in the Cairngorms. Rations were short then, and I carried a revolver and ammunition to shoot any hares or ptarmigan that came my way. One afternoon, just as I reached the summit cairn of Ben Macdhui, mist swirled across the Lairig Ghru and enveloped the mountain. The atmosphere became dark and oppressive, a fierce, bitter wind whisked among the boulders, and, fearing a storm was imminent, I took hurriedly to the Coire Etchachan path. Above Loch Etchachan the path angles easily downhill. I was swinging along at about five miles an hour when an odd sound echoed through the mist - a loud footstep, it seemed. Then another, and another. Spaced at long intervals!'

His story continued:

> 'I am not unduly imaginative, but my thoughts flashed instantly to the well-known story of Professor Norman Collie and the Fear Liath Mor. Then I felt the reassuring weight of the loaded revolver in my pocket. Grasping the butt I peered about in the mist, here rent and tattered by eddies of wind. A strange shape loomed up, receded, came charging at me! Without hesitation I whipped out the revolver and fired three times at the figure. When it still came on I turned and hared down the path, reaching Glen Derry in a time I have never bettered since. You may ask, was it really the Fear Liath Mor? Frankly, I think it was. Many times since then I have traversed Macdhui in mist, bivouacked on it in the open, camped near its summit for days on end on different occasions - often alone, and always with an easy mind. For on that day I am convinced I shot the only Fear Liath Mor my imagination will ever see.'

Not surprising at all for someone who has dedicated so much time and effort to unravelling the complexities of what lies behind the BGM controversy, Andy has his comments and thoughts to air on this case, too:

> 'Tewnion's experience is widely quoted in the BGM literature. The fact that someone would be so scared as to pull a gun on the phenomenon and fire it, gives considerable weight to the "reality" of the experience. It also contains all the criteria for a BGM experience. It cannot easily be explained in terms of a Brocken Spectre. Yet few writers quote Tewnion's letter to Affleck Gray in 1966 when he wrote': "To this day I am convinced that I saw something but I am equally convinced that something was only a towering wisp of mist which I imagined to be a menacing ghost.'

'I stood up and was conscious of a crunching noise...'

Peter Densham, says Andy:

'...recounted his BGM experience verbally to many friends but did not write an account himself. Eventually it was recorded by his friend, mountaineer and author Richard Frere. The encounter took place in May 1945 when Densham was in charge of aeroplane rescue in the Cairngorms during World War Two.'

As Densham proceeded to eat a piece of chocolate, he had, in his very own words:

'...sudden impression there was someone near me - an impression which is sometimes experienced by mountaineers. I did not pay much attention to the impression knowing it was fairly common. After a little I had the impression of something cold on the top of my neck. I had the hood of my anorak down. I thought this feeling of cold was due to the air having become more moist, but I still seemed to feel a pressure on my neck. I stood up and was conscious of a crunching noise from the direction of the cairn on my left. I went forward to investigate this noise.

When I got near to this cairn I began to think of the Grey Man and his footsteps. I thought this experience very interesting and until within a few feet of the apparent source of the sound I was not the least frightened. Suddenly, however, I was overcome by a feeling of apprehension and after a little my overpowering wish was to get off the mountain. I found myself running at an incredible pace, and then realised that I was running in the direction of Lurcher's Crag. I tried to stop myself and found this was extremely difficult to do. It was as if somebody was pushing me. I managed to deflect my course, but with a great deal of difficulty, and I managed to strike the direction between the left of the Lairig Ghru and Coire an Lochain. I ran down the ridge all the way to the Allt Mor Bridge, and all the way past Glenmore, and I was right on the other side of the loch before I stopped running.'

So, what we can we say about this particular experience? Back to Andy for a few choice comments and observations:

'Densham's account flags up several points. The most significant is that although his experience is firmly enshrined within BGM lore, like Collie he did not see anything at all. Densham's experience consisted solely of feeling a presence and being gripped by a fear. As with other BGM experients the fear was so compelling that it caused him to run blindly for several miles, narrowly avoiding certain death if he had run over Lurcher's Crag.'

'The phrase: "I found myself running at an incredible speed" suggests he was fully aware of what was happening, yet so overpowered by it he could not stop it. Also, according to Affleck Gray, Densham was aware of the BGM legend and "scornful" of any power which could make a man flee in terror. He later had another unusual experience on Ben Macdhui involving phantom voices. He attributed both incidents to a "psychic" origin, the "effect on his consciousness of undefined properties of the mountain" and contended that Ben Macdhui was "...the most mysterious mountain I have ever been on.'

The BGM on the Move and a Missing Missive

Andy describes the cases above as being amongst 'the most important ones relating to the BGM which have come to light as being from Ben Macdhui and which incorporate elements of the core phenomenon'. He correctly notes, however, that there are a couple of tales that 'may have some relevance to the mystery', but which did not occur specifically on the legendary mountain itself.

Ben Macdhui: A place of terror. Copyright: The Creator.

Explains Andy:

> 'Joan Grant, spending the stalking season of 1928 in the Cairngorms with her husband, set off walking through the Rothiemurchus Forest towards the Cairngorms. The day was too hot for any serious climbing and so after a while they set off back down to Aviemore.'

As for their experience, here it is, for you to digest and consider, in all its enigmatic and monstrously captivating glory:

> 'Nothing could have been farther from my mind than spooks when suddenly I was seized with such terror that I turned and in panic fled back along the path. Leslie ran after me, imploring me to tell him what was wrong. I could only spare breath to tell him to run faster, faster. Something - utterly malign, four-legged and yet obscenely human, invisible and yet solid enough for me to hear the pounding of its hooves, was trying to reach me. If it did I should die, for I was far too frightened to know how to defend myself. I had about half a mile when I burst through an invisible barrier behind which I was safe. I knew I was safe now, though a second before I had been in mortal danger; knew it as certainly as though I were a torero who has jumped the barrier in front of a charging bull.'

As intriguing as it undeniably is, Andy suggests that we should tread very carefully when it comes to analysing and interpreting the Grant story:

> 'Grant's account frequently becomes entangled in BGM lore even though it took place several miles from the summit of Ben Macdhui, did not involve a sighting and was not witnessed by, or even conveyed to, her companion. Grant was a writer of historical fantasy who had a strong belief in reincarnation and similar ideas and it has been suggested that her encounter was more the product of a fertile mind than of any genuine experience.'

Grant also noted that she knew of other such encounters with the mysterious phenomenon:

> 'A year later one of my father's professors described an almost exactly similar experience he had when bug-hunting in the Cairngorms. He was a materialist, but he had been so profoundly startled that he wrote to The Times - and received a letter from a reader who had also been pursued by the "Thing.'

And there's an issue with this story that, for some, might be seen as a slight one, but for others, could be perceived as being deeply problematic. Andy tells it like this:

> 'Affleck Gray checked *The Times* for the relevant period and I have done so myself. No account similar to the one mentioned by Grant appears to exist.'

This does not, of course, mean it was never printed, Andy admits, but it is without doubt typical of the sort of elusive information which very often typifies alleged paranormal experiences. In the wider Fortean field, Andy notes,

> '...a good example is the mystery surrounding the famous "Thunderbird" photograph, the search for which has become an item of Fortean interest in itself!'

Into the 21st Century

On July 28, 2004, a highly sensational, but admittedly entertaining, story appeared in the pages of none other than the *Daily Star* that well and truly thrust the BGM right into the 21st Century. The article began in eye-catching style: 'A ghosthunter rescued from Scotland's second highest peak has claimed he was attacked by a mysterious yeti. Tom Robertson, 68, was led to safety by mountain rescuers after a ten-hour ordeal on Ben MacDhui in the Cairngorms. He and a pal had been hunting for the legendary Big Grey Man of Ben MacDhui – Mountain of the Black Pig in Gaelic.'

As for the encounter itself, Robertson – author of *Ghosthunter: Adventures in the Afterlife* - was quoted as saying:

> 'At about 1.00 a.m. after we climbed in to our sleeping bags we heard the footsteps of something coming to the tent and heard mumbling noises outside.' Moments later, Robertson added that the side of the two-man tent, perched 4,000ft up the peak, caved in: 'I looked up through the air vent in the roof and saw a large arm crashing down. The figure of what seemed like a yeti was standing over the tent, then all hell broke loose and it was trying to get on at us. I remember something landed on my foot. My toes are black, kind of bruised. I have never been so scared in all the 60 years I have been interested in such things. I don't know what it is but it wasn't human. I reckon it could be the Grey Man or something from outer space.'

Robertson and his friend, Derek Blake, we are told, did not hang around to find a definitive answer to the unearthly encounter and fled the scene. Moving on…

Summing up on the mystery of Ben Macdhui, Andy Roberts says:

> 'These accounts are the main body of experiences comprising the BGM experiences. Explanations for the BGM have been tossed to and fro in numerous editions of many Scottish newspapers as the interest in the BGM has risen and fallen. Books such as Gray's detail theories ranging from the BGM as space-visitor or faerie-like elemental to outright hoax. No real evidence is ever put forward to back these claims up and they rest entirely on belief and speculation.'

There is more - in fact, a great deal more - to be said by Andy on the matter of the BGM, however, and it will surface soon enough in the Theories section of this book that deals with explanations for the 'panic on the mountain' syndrome that seems to so adversely affect eyewitnesses, and dominate the experiences, on the mysterious heights of Ben Macdhui. But, while we are pretty much done (but not completely done, as the opening paragraphs of the following chapter demonstrate) with the BGM for now, we are most certainly not finished with Scotland...

CHAPTER 25
BIGFOOT IN SCOTLAND
'...It is fortunate you do not know the truth for
if you did you would never be happy...'

'When considering any physical evidence connected to the BGM,'

Says Andy Roberts,

'...it is worth noting that some accounts refer to photographs of unknown
footprints taken in the Spey Valley. Although the location of the photographs
is some fifteen miles from the summit of Ben Macdhui, it has been claimed or
inferred by some writers that they may of the BGM. Indeed Rennie cites a
ghillie as saying (upon seeing the footprints) they were "Bodach tracks". This
comment, made by a local man may indicate the survival of a tradition
connecting unexplained phenomena to the legendary "Bodach" or old man, of
wider Scottish legend. As these tracks have been proffered as physical evidence for
the BGM in the literature, they and their possible origins need addressing.'

'...a whole succession of tracks in "line-astern" were appearing miraculously before my eyes...'

The actual source of the photographs to which Andy refers is the book *Romantic Speyside*, penned by J.A. Rennie who, in its pages, describes how on December 2, 1952 and around a mile outside of the village of Cromdale, he came across mysterious tracks which, as he recalled and noted in his book:

'...were running across a stretch of snow covered moorland, each print 19 inches long
by about 14 inches wide and there must have been all of seven feet between each
"stride". There was no differentiation between a left and a right foot, and they
preceded in an approximately single line.'

Andy highlights that Rennie likened the prints – perhaps quite unsurprisingly and very understandably - to the controversial, so-called 'Devil's Hoofprints' found across Devonshire during the winter of 1855, which have been an absolute Fortean staple and favourite for decades.

His interest decidedly piqued, Rennie followed the tracks for about half a mile, until they:

'...terminated at the foot of a pine tree, for all the world as though the strange
creature making them had leapt up into the foliage of the tree'.

Twenty yards further on, Rennie picked the tracks up again. He followed them across a field and down to the river's edge, where they terminated opposite the village churchyard. Rennie rushed home for his camera and showed the resulting photographs to baffled locals.

'Writers often cite Rennie's photographs as evidence for the BGM case,'

Offers Andy,

'... but fail to quote further from his account at this point, which is regrettable as he goes on to give highly useful information.'

Without doubt, the additional data is most important, as Andy makes clear:

'Whilst working in Northern Canada in the 1920s Rennie came across similar tracks whilst crossing a frozen lake. These tracks reduced his French / Canadian companion to a state of gibbering terror as he believed them to belong to the Wendygo [also variously spelled as Wendigo, Windigo, Weendigo, Wihtikow, and even Wanka!], a Bigfoot-like creature. Rennie was baffled by the tracks until later that winter when he saw the mysterious tracks for the second time. But on this occasion he saw them being made.'

We now refer to Rennie's own words on the startling occurrence:

'There on the flawless, smooth white of the snow, a whole succession of tracks in "line-astern" were appearing miraculously before my eyes. No sign of life anywhere, no movement even, other than the drifting clouds overhead and those tracks springing suddenly into being as they came inexorably towards me. I stood stock-still, filled with reasonless panic.

The tracks were being made within 50 yards of me -20-10-then, smack! I swung round brushing the water from my eyes, and saw the tracks continuing across the lake. In that moment I knew that the Wendygo, Abominable Snowman, Bodach Mor, or what have you, was forever explained so far as I was concerned.'

Rennie went on to give his explanation for the cause of both of those tracks and the ones he had seen many years later in Speyside:

'Some freakish current of warm air, coming in contact with the low temperature, had set up condensation which was projected earthwards in the form of water blobs. When these landed in the snow they left tracks like those of some fabulous animal.'

Commenting on Rennie's words and theory, Andy suggests that:

'Given that Rennie saw these tracks being made and felt water falling from the air, it is reasonable to assume that both the Canadian tracks and the tracks seen near the Cairngorms were the result of a rare meteorological condition.'

The Glamis Ghoul

Situated just west of Forfar, Glamis Castle is referred to by Shakespeare in Macbeth; Macbeth of its title having killed Duncan there in 1040. And it is also at the castle where assassins murdered King Malcolm II in 1034. In addition, Glamis Castle was the childhood home of both Queen Elizabeth II and the Queen Mother, and the birthplace of Princess Margaret. And then there is the castle's very own monster. Jon Downes notes that:

'...the castle is, of course, the site of yet another, well known and semi legendary beast known as the Monster of Glamis. It's said that the creature was supposed to have been the hideously deformed heir to the Bowes-Lyon family and who was, according to popular rumour, born in about 1800, and died as recently as 1921.'

Jon digs further into the puzzle:

'Legend has it that the monster was supposed to look like an enormous flabby egg, having no neck and only minute arms and legs but possessed incredible strength and had an air of evil about it. Certainly, there is a family secret concerning the monster, which is only told to the male heir of the Bowes-Lyon family when they attain majority. But according to the author Peter Underwood,

Glamis Castle: The legendary home of a ghoul. Copyright: Morris' *Country Seats*, 1880.

who has looked into this case, the present Lord Strathmore knows nothing about the monster, presumably because the creature has long been dead, but he always felt that there was a corpse or coffin bricked up behind the walls.'

There is another other matter worth noting too that may be of deep significance: according to James Wentworth Day, an author who extensively researched and wrote about the legend, the creature of the castle was 'hairy as a doormat'.

According to folklore and oral tradition, the existence of the creature was allegedly known to only four men at any given time, namely the Earl of Strathmore, his direct heir, the family's lawyer, and the broker of the estate. At the age of twenty-one each succeeding heir was told the terrible secret and shown the rightful – and horrendously deformed – Earl, and succeeding family lawyers and brokers were also informed of the family's shocking secret. As no Countess of Strathmore was ever told the story, however, one Lady Strathmore, having indirectly heard of such rumours, quietly approached the then broker, a certain Mr. Ralston, who flatly refused to reveal the secret and who would only say by way of a reply:

'It is fortunate you do not know the truth for if you did you would never be happy.

'...it reared itself on its haunches after the manner of an ape...'

Was the strange creature of the castle a terribly deformed soul with some bizarre genetic affliction, a captured wild man or something else? While the jury, inevitably, remains steadfastly out, it's an intriguing reality that in 1912, in his book, *Scottish Ghost Stories*, Elliott O'Donnell published the contents of a letter that he had received from a Mrs. Bond who had spent time at Glamis Castle and who underwent an undeniably weird encounter. In her letter to O'Donnell, rather notably, she describes a somewhat supernatural encounter with a beast possessed of distinct ape-like qualities.

Mrs. Bond wrote to O'Donnell the following words:

'It is a good many years since I stayed at Glamis. I was, in fact, but little more than a child, and had only just gone through my first season in town. But though young, I was neither nervous nor imaginative; I was inclined to be what is termed stolid, that is to say, extremely matter-of-fact and practical. Indeed, when my friends exclaimed, "You don't mean to say you are going to stay at Glamis! Don't you know it's haunted?" I burst out laughing. "Haunted!" I said, "How ridiculous! There are no such things as ghosts. One might as well believe in fairies."
Of course I did not go to Glamis alone - my mother and sister were with me; but whereas they slept in the more modern part of the castle, I was, at my own request, apportioned a room in the Square Tower. I cannot say that my choice had anything to do with the secret chamber. That, and the alleged mystery, had been dinned into my ears so often that I had grown thoroughly sick of the whole thing. No, I wanted to sleep in the Square Tower for quite a different reason, a reason of my own. I kept an aviary; the tower was old; and I naturally hoped its walls would be covered with ivy and teeming with birds' nests, some of which I might be able to reach - and, I am ashamed to say, plunder - from my window. Alas, for my expectations!

Although the Square Tower was so ancient that in some places it was actually crumbling away--not the sign of a leaf, not the vestige of a bird's nest could I see anywhere; the walls were abominably, brutally bare. However, it was not long before my disappointment gave way to delight; for the air that blew in through the open window was so sweet, so richly scented with heather and honeysuckle, and the view of the broad, sweeping, thickly wooded grounds so indescribably charming, that, despite my inartistic and unpoetical nature, I was entranced-- entranced as I had never been before, and never have been since. "Ghosts!" I said to myself. "Ghosts! How absurd! How preposterously absurd! Such an adorable spot as this can only harbour sunshine and flowers.

I well remember, too - for, as I have already said, I was not poetical - how much I enjoyed my first dinner at Glamis. The long journey and keen mountain air had made me hungry, and I thought I had never tasted such delicious food - such ideal salmon (from the Esk) and such heavenly fruit. But I must tell you that, although I ate heartily, as a healthy girl should, by the time I went to bed I had thoroughly digested my meal, and was, in fact, quite ready to partake of a few oatmeal biscuits I found in my dressing-case, and remembered having bought at Perth.

It was about eleven o'clock when my maid left me, and I sat for some minutes wrapped in my dressing gown, before the open window. The night was very still, and, save for an occasional rustle of the wind in the distant tree-tops, the hooting of an owl, the melancholy cry of a peewit and the hoarse barking of a dog, the silence was undisturbed.

The interior of my room was, in nearly every particular, modern. The furniture was not old; there were no grim carvings; no grotesquely-fashioned tapestries on the walls; no dark cupboards; no gloomy corners;--all was cosy and cheerful, and when I got into bed no thought of bogle or mystery entered my mind.

In a few minutes I was asleep, and for some time there was nothing but a blank-- a blank in which all identity was annihilated. Then suddenly I found myself in an oddly-shaped room with a lofty ceiling, and a window situated at so great a distance from the black oaken floor as to be altogether inaccessible from within. Feeble gleams of phosphorescent light made their way through the narrow panes, and served to render distinct the more prominent objects around; but my eyes struggled in vain to reach the remoter angles of the wall, one of which inspired me with terror such as I had never felt before. The walls were covered with heavy draperies that were sufficient in themselves to preclude the possibility of any save the loudest of sounds penetrating without.

The furniture, if such one could call it, puzzled me. It seemed more fitted for the cell of a prison or lunatic asylum, or even for a kennel, than for an ordinary dwelling-room. I could see no chair, only a coarse deal table, a straw mattress, and a kind of trough. An air of irredeemable gloom and horror hung over and pervaded everything. As I stood there, I felt I was waiting for something - something that was concealed in the corner of the room I dreaded. I tried to reason with myself, to assure myself that there was nothing there that could hurt me, nothing that could even terrify me, but my efforts were in vain - my fears grew.

Had I had some definite knowledge as to the cause of my alarm I should not have suffered so much, but it was my ignorance of what was there, of what I feared, that made my terror so poignant. Each second saw the agony of my suspense increase. I dared not move. I hardly dare breathe, and I dreaded lest the violent pulsation of my heart should attract the attention of the Unknown Presence and precipitate its coming out. Yet despite the perturbation of my mind, I caught myself analysing my feelings. It was not danger I abhorred so much, as its absolute effect - fright. I shuddered at the bare thought of what result the most trivial incident - the creaking of a board, ticking of a beetle, or hooting of an owl-- might have on the intolerable agitation of my soul'

In this unnerved and pitiable condition I felt that the period was bound to come, sooner or later, when I should have to abandon life and reason together in the most desperate of struggles with - fear. At length, something moved. An icy chill ran through my frame, and the horror of my anticipations immediately reached its culminating point. The Presence was about to reveal itself. The gentle rubbing of a soft body on the floor, the crack of a bony joint, breathing, another crack, and then - was it my own excited imagination - or the disturbing influence of the atmosphere - or the uncertain twilight of the chamber that produced before me, in the stygian darkness of the recess, the vacillating and indistinct outline of something luminous, and horrid? I would gladly have risked futurity to have looked elsewhere--I could not. My eyes were fixed--I was compelled to gaze steadily in front of me.

Slowly, very slowly, the thing, whatever it was, took shape. Legs - crooked, misshapen, human legs. A body - tawny and hunched. Arms - long and spidery, with crooked, knotted fingers. A head — large and bestial, and covered with a tangled mass of grey hair that hung around its protruding forehead and pointed ears in ghastly mockery of curls. A face - and herein was the realisation of all my direst expectations - a face - white and staring, pig-like in formation malevolent in expression; a hellish combination of all things foul and animal, and yet withal not without a touch of pathos.

As I stared at it aghast, it reared itself on its haunches after the manner of an ape, and leered piteously at me. Then, shuffling forward, it rolled over, and lay sprawled out like some ungainly turtle — and wallowed, as for warmth, in the cold grey beams of early dawn. At this juncture the handle of the chamber door turned, someone entered, there was a loud cry - and I awoke - awoke to find the whole tower, walls and rafters, ringing with the most appalling screams I have ever heard - screams of something or of someone - for there was in them a strong element of what was human as well as animal - in the greatest distress.

Wondering what it meant, and more than ever terrified, I sat up in bed and listened,--listened whilst a conviction - the result of intuition, suggestion, or what you will, but a conviction all the same - forced me to associate the sounds with the thing in my dream. And I associate them still.'

CHAPTER 26
THE LITTLEFOOT PHENOMENON
'...It was about four feet tall and with really big feet...'

Moving on from Bigfoot, what about Littlefoot? Certainly, it's an undeniable fact that reports emanating from Britain tell of encounters with not just large and lumbering, hairy entities, but with distinctly smaller critters, too. Centuries-old Welsh folklore, for example, tells of the Bwbach, an approximately three foot tall, hair-covered humanoid perceived by the folk of that era as a brownie or nymph.

Supposedly, like so many of similar ilk, they would undertake chores and little jobs around the homes of humans, providing they were the recipients of two things: respect and nourishment, the latter usually in the form of oats, milk and cream. And they had a deep hatred of those who avoided alcohol and led teetotal lives!

Mr. Sikes and the Bwbach.
Wirt Sikes was U.S. Consul to Wales, a noted expert on Welsh folklore, and the author of an acclaimed 1880 book, *British Goblins*. In its pages, Sikes wrote of the hairy little Bwbach that it:

> '...is the good-natured goblin which does good turns for the tidy Welsh maid who wins its favour by a certain course of behaviour recommended by long tradition. The maid having swept the kitchen, makes a good fire the last thing at night, and having put the churn, filled with cream, on the whitened hearth, with a basin of fresh cream for the Bwbach on the hob, goes to bed to await the event. In the morning she finds (if she is in luck) that the Bwbach has emptied the basin of cream, and plied the churn-dasher so well that the maid has but to give a thump or two to bring the butter in a great lump. Like the Ellyll which it so much resembles, the Bwbach does not approve of dissenters and their ways, and especially strong is its aversion to total abstainers.'

The Bwbach is largely forgotten today, but encounters with small, hairy, man-like figures in Britain are certainly not – as we saw in the Horsham, Sussex case of 1948, as detailed in an earlier chapter by Neil Arnold. Jon Downes says of such matters:

> 'I have many similar reports of such creatures being seen in Devonshire woodland. And the following one is a real cracker because it has so much separate and credible corroboration to it...'

Duendecitos

Hairy dwarves have long been reported in the UK.
Copyright: Francisco Goya, 1799.

The Green-Faced Monkey

The location, Jon reveals, was Churston Woods, which is situated close to the English holiday resort of Torbay:

> 'Over a six week period, in the summer of 1996, fifteen separate witnesses reported seeing what they could only describe as a green faced monkey, running through the woods. Granted, some of the descriptions were quite vague, but most of the witnesses told of seeing a tailless animal, around four to five feet tall, with a flat, olive-green face that would run through the woods and occasionally would be seen swinging through the trees. Now, to me at least, this sounds like some form of primitive human, but again, of course, such things simply cannot exist in this country – and yet they seem to. And this area – Devon, Somerset and Cornwall - is rich with such tales, you know.'

For what it's worth, there's an update to this saga that surfaced a decade and a half after the Churston woods controversy subsided. Back in 2011 I highlighted at one of my blogs the photograph that you can see below, which was mailed anonymously to me back in the early to mid 1990s, if memory serves me correct, which I think it does. Anyway, after publishing the picture on the Net, I ended up getting a very weird late night 'phone call, in February 2012, from someone who claimed it was a legitimate picture of none other than the green-faced monkey of Churston Woods. How they knew this was not revealed, and no further data - beyond a slightly absurd Deep Throat-like message warning me not to meddle with 'the beast' – was revealed. But, I present the photo for you, just as it was given to me. Frankly, I think it looks like a cross between Donald Duck, the Dover Demon, and some discarded leftover from a 1970s-era episode of *Dr. Who*. You may agree!

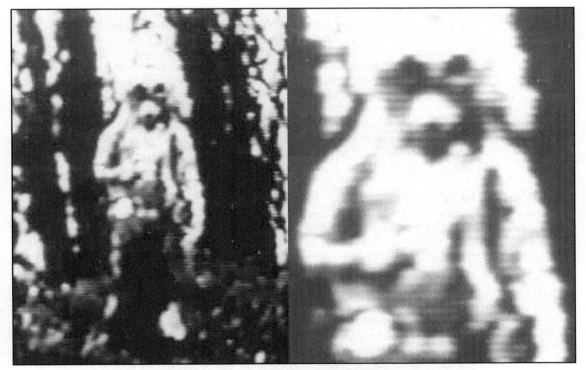

Almost certainly a hoax! Copyright: Unknown.

The Hairy Sprite of the Cemetery

'It all started in the late 1950s,'

Began Jason Hill, when he related the details to me in 2008:

'My dad was visiting a friend in Heath Hayes [a town very close to Cannock Chase, Staffordshire]. This friend sadly died in the early 1990s; so I am afraid the details are secondhand. Even so, my dad is not the sort of person for tall tales; and the details he repeated to me last Sunday were the same as he told me thirty plus years ago. It was back in 1959 and dad was at his mate's house talking when his friend's mother pipes up: "Look! In the newspaper: your little green man!" The newspaper story - dad thinks it was the Express & Star or the Cannock Advertiser - told of a little girl from Pye Green [an area of Cannock] running back home to her mother in tears...

'When questioned,' Jason added, 'she said a little green man had run from the undergrowth and frightened her. Dad waited his chance and raised the question. His friend, who was very embarrassed, said that in the summer of 1958 he played cricket for GEC [the General Electric Corporation] at Stafford, his place of work, and cycled back home, later than normal across the Cannock chase. On a weaving part of the road he saw something in the headlight of his cycle. The "something" he saw ran into the road, stopped, and then ran back into the trees. He described it as a "little green man.'

'When I first heard it, at the age of nine or ten, I thought it was great; but I grew up and thought it was a pile of rubbish - until a conversation with a friend about strange creatures on the Chase revealed he had a story to tell. Driving past the German Cemetery he felt something fall on the back of the car, like a big branch from an overhanging tree. He looked in the mirror and for a split second saw what he described as a 'gremlin or sprite,' little and hairy.

'The more I think about it, the less it makes sense and seems logical. In fact, if I had thought it through, I probably would not have contacted you. But somewhere in a fifty year old story that has stood the test of time, and a twenty year old version, lies something. But what?'

The Wonder of Wanstead

In November 2008, an extremely strange story surfaced from Wanstead - a suburban area of the borough of London. According to witness testimony, a small Bigfoot-type creature was supposedly seen wandering in Epping Forest, a 2,476 hectare area of forestland which, by name at least, was first referenced in the 17th Century, but that has existed since Neolithic times and which, in the 12th Century, was designated as a Royal Forest by King Henry III.

Neil Arnold describes how the distinctly odd story began:

'The animal was first sighted during early November by eighteen-year-old angler Michael Kent who was fishing with his brother and father in the Hollow Ponds area of Epping Forest, on the border of Wanstead and Leytonstone. The teenager claimed that whilst walking towards his brothers, he heard a rustling in the bushes and saw the back of a dark, hairy animal around four feet in height, that scampered off into the woods.'

Another of those that caught sight of the diminutive beast was Irene Dainty, who claimed a face to face encounter with the thing on Love Lane, Woodford Bridge. She told the press:

> 'I had just come out of my flat and just as I had turned the corner I saw this hairy thing come out of nowhere. I really don't want to see it again. It was about four feet tall and with really big feet and looked straight at me with animal eyes. Then it leaped straight over the wall with no trouble at all and went off into the garden of the Three Jolly Wheelers pub. I was so terrified that I went to my neighbour's house and told her what had happened. She couldn't believe it and asked me if I had been drinking, but I said of course I hadn't – it was only about 3.00 p.m.'

Further reports subsequently surfaced, some of which were far more of a four-legged variety, maybe even bear-like, rather than actually being suggestive of Bigfoot. But, it was this issue of the 'really big feet' that kept the media-driven controversy focused on matters of a mini Sasquatch-type nature. Ultimately, just like so many similar such affairs, sightings of the beast came to an abrupt end and the matter of the Epping Forest monster was never satisfactorily resolved.

Questions, Questions, Questions...

Was the hairy sprite of Cannock Chase some form of unknown primate that had stealthily made the woods its secret home? What of the creature of Epping Forest, the unknown animal of Churston Woods, and the Horsham horror of 1948? How about the Bwbach of Wales? Are we seeing, in these cases, evidence of juvenile British Bigfoot beasts? Or is there a far more down to earth theory to explain the presence of Littlefoot in our very midst? As far as the first three questions are concerned, until (or even if) solid evidence surfaces to validate or deny such controversial scenarios, we must leave these matters firmly on the back-burner. But, to the latter question, there most certainly is a theory that may offer at least some answers to the sightings of smaller, hairy, ape-type beasts roaming Britain. We start with the baboon.

Do baboons roam the wilds of the UK? (Public Domain/Wikimedia Commons)

CHAPTER 27
THE BABOONS OF BRITAIN

T he very idea that the green and pleasant British countryside may well be playing host to hidden populations of wild baboons sounds manifestly bizarre and unlikely in the extreme, which, for the most part anyway, it surely is! And, yet, sightings of baboon-like animals certainly do surface from time to time, and from across much of the entire nation. That these same sightings, of what are actually African and Arabian Old World monkeys, span centuries and are comprised of encounters with both (A) flesh and blood entities and (B) beasts of a distinctly spectral and paranormal nature, and may have, very occasionally, been mistaken for definitive British wild men of small stature, only adds to the mystifying, monkey-based strangeness, as you will now come to firmly appreciate.

Baboon vs. Wild Man
Neil Arnold has noted several old tales of a wild man variety that may actually have had their origins in encounters with out of place baboons. Neil says that:

> 'During the reign of Queen Anne [of England, Scotland, and Ireland, from 1702-1707], it was rumoured that, at Charing Cross [London], a "wild man" was on show. The beast was said to have danced on a tight-rope, remaining perfectly balanced to the beat of the music. The creature was also said to have smoked tobacco!'

Neil reveals more:

> 'During the eighteenth-century a "man-tiger" from the East Indies was exhibited in London although many believed such a creature to be a baboon. A little, black hairy 'pigmy' was also recorded and exhibited at the White Horse Inn, Fleet Street. The being was two feet in height. During the end of the eighteenth century a five foot tall quadruped, deemed the "missing link", and allegedly found in Mount Tibet, was also showcased in the capital.'

On the Loose!
A baboon provoked unbridled chaos in 1856; it was an affair that was noted by *The Times* of July 14 under the heading of **Baboon Hunt on a Ships Rigging.** This three and a half foot tall specimen, Neil Arnold learned:

> 'escaped onto the docks at Wapping on the Wednesday and was pursued by many. The animal, had, according to the paper, been acquired by a naturalist. When the man went to collect his animal it proceeded to dart up the rigging. Several men from varying vessels began the hunt, which amused many on-lookers. The agility of the animal was clear as it effortlessly sprang and leapt out of the outstretched arms of its pursuers. After a few

hours, the baboon then simply decided it had had enough and descended to a cabin, but at once startled a steward who claimed that the Devil had in fact come aboard. A sack was eventually thrown over the creature and the naturalist reclaimed it'.

The wild adventure was over!

Neil, digging deeply and diligently into the heart of old newspaper archives, adds the following, which reveals the details of yet another baboon-based affair in the British Isles:

'In the *New York Times* of 19th December 1889 there was mentioned of "A Baboon at Large in London."'

The creature, Neil demonstrates:

'was witnessed in the vicinity of Westminster Bridge road after escaping from Sanger's Amphitheatre around 1:00 pm. The animal ran along Lambeth Palace road snapping at onlookers. It was said to have caused wounds to the face of six-year old George Jugger, a wound to the eyelid of twelve-year old William Buckley, and also knocked over a William Wyles'.

Finally, and with much relief to the local populace, the animal was recaptured.

Mr. Bishop's Baboon

In 1913, Elliott O'Donnell – the author of more than fifty acclaimed titles on spooks, spectres, and supernatural mysteries - penned the classic title *Animal Ghosts*, which included in its pages the decades-old story of a phantom baboon seen in a large, old, imposing country house-style abode near the English town of Basingstoke, Hampshire.

In O'Donnell's own words:

'A sister of a well-known author tells me there used to be a house called The Swallows, standing in two acres of land, close to a village near Basingstoke. In 1840 a Mr. Bishop of Tring bought the house, which had long stood empty, and we went to live there in 1841. After being there a fortnight two servants gave notice to leave, stating that the place was haunted by a large cat and a big baboon, which they constantly saw stealing down the staircases and passages.'

O'Donnell continued with his tale:

'They also testified to hearing sounds as of somebody being strangled, proceeding from an empty attic near where they slept, and of the screams and groans of a number of of people being horribly tortured in the cellars just underneath the dairy. On going to see what was the cause of the disturbances, nothing was ever visible. By and by other members of the household began to be harassed by similar manifestations. The news spread through the village, and crowds of people came to the house with lights and sticks, to see if they could witness anything.'

'One night, at about twelve o'clock, when several of the watchers were stationed on guard in the empty courtyard, they all saw the forms of a huge cat and a baboon rise from the closed grating of the large cellar under the old dairy, rush past them, and disappear in a dark angle of the walls. The same figures were repeatedly seen afterwards by many other persons. Early in December 1841, Mr. Bishop, hearing fearful screams, accompanied by deep and hoarse jabberings, apparently coming from the top of the house, rushed upstairs, whereupon all was instantly silent, and he could discover nothing.

'After that, Mr. Bishop set to work to get rid of the house, and was fortunate enough to find as a purchaser a retired colonel, who was soon, however, scared out of it. This was in 1842; it was soon after pulled down. The ground was used for the erection of cottages; but the hauntings being transferred to them, they were speedily vacated, and no one ever daring to inhabit them, they were eventually demolished, the site on which they stood being converted into allotments.'

'There were many theories as to the history of "The Swallows"; one being that a highwayman, known as Steeplechase Jock, the son of a Scottish chieftain, had once plied his trade there and murdered many people, whose bodies were supposed to be buried somewhere on or near the premises. He was said to have had a terrible though decidedly unorthodox ending - falling into a vat of boiling tar, a raving madman.'

In closing, O' Donnell asked the important questions:

'But what were the phantasms of the ape and cat? Were they the earth-bound spirits of the highwayman and his horse, or simply the spirits of two animals? Though either theory is possible, I am inclined to favour the former.'

There ends the story. Interestingly, however – and directly connected to O'Donnell's questions about earth-bound spirits returning to our plane of existence in animal form - there existed a deep belief in Staffordshire and Shropshire in the 18th and 19th Centuries that sightings of the notorious Man-Monkey of the Shropshire Union Canal were linked to the death of a man who had drowned in the waters of the canal shortly before the sightings began in January 1879.

Are restless human spirits really returning from the depths of the grave and manifesting in the form of marauding, ghostly monkeys and apes? In a later chapter, we will return to the matter of ancient, and surprisingly widespread, beliefs in the British Isles that human spirits could return to our world in precisely those animalistic forms. But, for now: Back to the British baboons…

Chaos in the 20s!

During the summer of 1924 in Barnet, notes Neil Arnold, a baboon escaped:

'from an animal dealer named Chapman and found itself right in the heart of Barnet Police Court. The baboon then proceeded to climb through a ventilation grate and make itself cosy in a cell before two keepers arrived at the location and caught it in a net.'

Game over! For a while, anyway...

It's not every day that you see a headline in *The Times* newspaper that reads like this: An escaped baboon – antics at a Crystal Palace station. And, yet, that is precisely the title of a story that appeared in the pages of the Times on September 23, 1926, and which began as follows:

'An escaped baboon in the booking office of the Crystal Palace High Level (Southern Railway) Station yesterday for a time considerably enlivened the proceedings in the morning rush period. After the discreet withdrawal of the booking clerk, the monkey, a female, was for several minutes in complete possession of the office, and employed the time first in ransacking it, and then at the window attending to the wants of passengers in her own way. Before she was recaptured many passengers had missed their usual trains, and many others had travelled without tickets, intending to pay at their destinations.'

The newspaper continued that the beast, which was estimated to have been around two years of age, was quickly captured and hastily placed inside a wooden cage 'by Messrs. De Von and Co., the naturalists, of Kings Cross road, to the private menagerie of Mr. H.G. Tyrwhitt Drake at the Crystal Palace.'

It was not all smooth sailing, however, as *The Times* made very clear:

'The cage and monkey travelled by train from St. Paul's Station early yesterday morning, and at the High Level Station the cage was put in the combined cloakroom and booking office "to be called for". Soon afterwards, according to the booking clerk, the baboon shook the bars of the cage so violently that it fell over on its side. The monkey then kicked the bottom out of it, and sprang up to the gas bracket, showing her fangs to the clerk, who went away to find help.'

Yes, chaos had broken out at the old station. And it duly continued at a manic and comical rate, too. *The Times'* reporter, clearly relishing the entertaining nature of the story he or she had unleashed upon the readers of the newspaper, revealed the next stage of the animalistic soap-opera-like saga:

'Watched by a porter through the ticket window, the baboon was seen to swing off the gas-bracket and make a tour of inspection of the office. She turned out the ticket pigeon-holes and threw the tickets about the floor, opened bags full of copper change money, biting some of the coins to find out if they were good to eat, and, finally, stationed herself at the window and busied herself with the ticket punching machine. The numerous faces now clustered on the safe side of the window perhaps annoyed her, for soon she began to gather tickets and money in handfuls and hurl them out.'

The final word on the matter from *The Times*:

'The station master appeared, and announced that all who wished could travel without tickets and pay at the other end. Then he and a porter boarded up the office window, and a little later menagerie keepers came.' The curious creature caper was over, and the baboon was destined for a new home with the aforementioned 'Mr. H.G. Tyrwhitt Drake of Crystal Palace.'

Mr. H. G. Tyrwhitt Drake – actually, Sir Garrard Tyrwhitt-Drake, to give him his correct title - was a most curious character, and one whose undeniable oddness was appropriately apt for such a manifestly strange saga. As well as holding the position of mayor of Maidstone on no less than twelve occasions, he established Maidstone Zoo, and was an undeniably and definitive English, upper-class eccentric. For example, he had a fascination – that bordered upon a full-blown obsession – for zebras. To the extent that, on one bizarre occasion, he ordered one of his staff to paint black and white stripes on an unfortunate donkey, purely for the purpose of his, Drake's, own obscure and odd entertainment. One suspects the donkey was hardly enamoured by the experience!

And there is one other monkey-related story that concerns events at Drake's zoo. This one was connected to the nightly bombing raids on England by the Nazis during the Second World War. On October 14, 1940, *The Times*, in an article titled **Animals and Air Raids,** noted that:

'Some very interesting reports have come from the Maidstone Zoo. The animals show no reaction to the

British Bigfoot seeker, Neil Arnold. Copyright: Neil Arnold.

most violent air activity or AA fire. On the other hand, the two chimpanzees though they do not mind the guns, stamp and shriek at the sound of the siren.'

Quite what the painted donkey might have thought of the hostile actions of Hitler's aerial hordes, if indeed the animal was still living by 1940, remains a mystery!

A Beast Lurks in the Woods of Brassknocker Hill

The strange saga all began in July 1979, amid wild rumours that a terrifying monster was haunting the dark woods of Brassknocker Hill, situated near to the old British city of Bath. Described variously, and in both excited and hysterical tones, as a long-fanged, four-foot tall creature resembling a baboon, chimpanzee, spider-monkey, gibbon or lemur, the creature was of far more concern to some than it was to others.

Locals Ron and Betty Harper were hardly in good moods when they discovered that the mysterious creature had stripped whole sections of their old, mighty oak tree bare of bark. To the kids of Brassknocker Hill, however, the hunt for the beast provided them all the excitement they needed of a jolly adventure of Enid Blyton proportions – particularly so when, only one month later, the number of trees targeted had reached an astonishing fifty, and the woods were plunged into an eerie silence after almost all the local birds summarily fled the area, presumably for far safer and beast-free pastures.

Meanwhile, eighty-one-year-old Brassknocker Hill resident Frank Green, clearly hyped up to the max and desperately trying to live out his Dirty Harry fantasies, took a far more grave and serious view of the strange situation. He took up nothing less than a day and night shotgun vigil, and told the media in loud and worried tones:

> 'I am very fond of some animals, but I reckon this creature could be dangerous and I am taking no chances.'

Fortunately, or unfortunately – depending on one's personal perspective on the monstrous matter - Green did not have the opportunity to blast the baboon-like beast to kingdom come, or, indeed, to anywhere. It skilfully avoided all of his attempts to track it down, much to the relief of the police, who were hardly enamoured by the idea of a grouchy, old-age pensioner roaming around Brassknocker Hill with a loaded shotgun in search of a marauding, unknown creature.

Nearby Monkton Combe became the next locale terrorised by the Beast of Brassknocker Hill. A small, old village situated approximately three miles from Bath, the main claim to fame of Monkton Combe is that the village's railway-station appeared in the 1931 film, *The Ghost Train*, penned by Arnold Ridley (Mr. Godfrey in the BBC's classic, wartime-set comedy series, *Dad's Army*), and also in the 1953 Ealing comedy production, *The Titfield Thunderbolt*. As for the creature, it was seen by a man who was driving through the area late one night, and who offered the anonymous description to the press that the animal he crossed paths with was of a significant size, seemed somewhat bear-like in appearance, briefly stood on its thick and substantial hind legs, and possessed a pair of large eyes that were surrounded by great white circles of fur or hair.

Getting in on the growing sensationalism, a Dutch newspaper – *Het Binnenhof* – ran a story that, translated into English, practically suggested an assault on Brassknocker Hill of the type of proportions one would expect to see in a Tokyo-shattering on-screen attack by Godzilla! The sensationalised title of Het Binnenhof's eye-catching article, that provided an entertaining summary of the affair, was: Beast of Bath Destroys British Wood! Far more cataclysmic than the real picture, the story and its attendant title guaranteed not just local and countrywide interest, but now international coverage, too.

By the time the following summer arrived, the mystery seemed to have been solved: a policeman, one Inspector Michael Price, caught sight in the woods of what he thought was nothing less than a large chimpanzee running around; although the identification of the animal was never fully confirmed, thus leaving the cage-door open to the possibility it had been a baboon, after all. The local press quickly sought out comments from the police. And they got them, too:

> 'We were sure this mystery creature would turn out to be a monkey of some sort,'

Said Inspector Price himself, clearly and happily wallowing in a brief wave of very odd publicity:

> 'After all, men from Mars aren't hairy, are they?'

Quite! But rumours of strange and savage activities at Brassknocker Hill persisted, much to the glee of the local media.

Two years later, the stories returned, only this time - rather curiously - the tales of a baboon, or some other type of monkey, on the loose were replaced by sightings of something very different. A stag, polecat, or even a Japanese deer, were among the many and varied candidates for the new beast of the hill. Then, one morning in the summer of 1984, reports started coming in to the news-desk of the *Bath Chronicle* newspaper of a strange-looking creature holding up traffic on Brassknocker Hill. Once again, for the press, the game was afoot, to reference a certain famous and fictional detective.

'I grabbed my notebook,'

said reporter Roger Green, who later became the editor of the Littlehampton Gazette.

'Colin [Shepherd] the photographer grabbed his camera, and we rushed out to the hill. The reports were pretty credible, so we were convinced that there was something there,' Green recalled. 'It was with slight trepidation that we entered the woods. After several minutes of stalking, we came across the "beast," by then calmly grazing in a field. It was an Alpacca, a type of llama, and had escaped from a paddock. It was later reunited with its owner by the police.'

But, quite obviously, this did not explain the earlier sightings of a baboon-like animal, which – under no circumstances, at all - could have been confused with a llama! Needless to say, the mystery was never resolved, and the baboon, if that is what it really was, vanished, died, or moved on to pastures and tree-bark new. Its place of origin, obviously, was forever a mystery.

The Prestwick Pest

On January 17, 1999, a very unusual story surfaced in the pages of Scotland's *Ayrshire Post* newspaper. Titled Baboon sighted near Prestwick Airport, it began as follows:

'A motorist spotted what he believed was a "Baboon-like creature" on the Shaw Farm Road in Prestwick, not far from the airport. Police rushed to the scene, and as the officers got to within 30 yards of the animal it disappeared into the undergrowth.'

The sighting had reportedly occurred some eleven days before it hit the headlines, and provoked a great deal of fascination when the police revealed to the media the details of its X-Files-like dossier on the enigmatic affair. A spokeswoman for Strathclyde Police told the *Ayrshire Post*:

'We received a call from a local man who said he'd narrowly avoided hitting a baboon-like creature on Shaw Farm Road, Prestwick. A patrol car was sent out and after a search of the area the officers reported seeing an animal of some sort, although they couldn't be sure what it was.'

Given that the eyewitnesses to the beast and its antics included members of the police - the officers described it as looking like something that was part-dog and part-monkey, which is a distinctly apt description for the appearance, build and gait of a baboon - the matter was taken very seriously, and newspaper staff noted that careful but futile checks were made at the airport, which, rather interestingly, had received a cargo of livestock only days earlier. A baboon, however, said an airport spokesperson, in response to feverish questions from the press, was most certainly not part of that same cargo.

As the mystery grew, and with no answers anywhere near in sight, checks were also made with numerous zoos across Scotland, but none had lost a baboon - or, more correctly, none admitted to having lost one. Although Richard Grady, then the director of Glasgow Zoo, pledged to get to the bottom of the mystery, he did not. The beast vanished as mysteriously as it had first appeared near the airport.

The final word on the matter came from a senior policeman, who told the press, always eager for an entertainingly weird story, and one that ultimately, albeit briefly, threatened to eclipse Scotland's most famous mystery beast - the Loch Ness Monster - in the publicity stakes that:

> 'The officers were very careful how they phrased the sighting over the radio. The mickey-taking could have been merciless and they didn't want to make monkeys of themselves.'

If nothing else, the saga of the elusive baboon of Prestwick Airport provided a bit of light relief and entertainment for the local constabulary, and a deep degree of mystery and intrigue for just about everyone else. Once again, a strange, out of place baboon-like animal was briefly sighted in the British Isles, before racing off into the mysterious darkness, and void from which it first surfaced.

Moving on from baboons, we see yet further evidence - in the shape of all manner of monkeys on the loose - of what might go some significant way towards explaining at least some of the British Littlefoot sightings.

CHAPTER 28
OLD NED'S DEVIL AND THE DR'S ZOO
'...I think I saw a monkey run across the road in front of me this morning...'

More than a century ago, Dr. John Kerr Butter was both a resident of the town of Cannock, Staffordshire and a keen and renowned zoologist. It is a little-known - and truly startling - fact that Butter possessed a highly impressive collection of exotic animals that were housed at his place of residence on the town's Wolverhampton Road, and which, astonishingly enough, included giraffes, monkeys, elephants, ostriches, emus, geese, kangaroos, and a Madagascan cat-like creature called a fossa that is related to the mongoose. Butter had even tamed a wild ocelot that he kept on his property, a certainly considerable feat that justifiably earned him the distinction of being made a Fellow of the Royal Zoological Society.

Somewhat amusingly, Butter would regularly make house-calls to his patients sat atop a trap that would be wildly pulled around Cannock by a fully-grown zebra! And for those patients that were able to make it to his surgery, they would invariably be greeted at the door by Antony, the doctor's favourite pet monkey…

Butter's Beasts

Dr. Butter was also a recognised expert on big cats and he provided regular animal welfare for the varied travelling menageries that visited the town of Cannock, as well as the surrounding towns and villages. In addition, Dr. Butter was a devoted collector of strange artifacts, which included bear-skins, an ink-stand constructed from the jaw of an alligator, and countless jars full of preserved animal organs. But there is still more to come: much more, as it so transpires.

On one occasion Dr. Butter went to do battle; namely, at the turn of the twentieth century, in the Boer War. And it is a known and verifiable fact that at least some of his animals did disappear from his property during this particular period when he was far away from home. Moreover, at the outbreak of the First World War in 1914, all of Dr. Butter's remaining animals promptly vanished – as a direct result of the nation's dwindling food supplies, something which ensured an unfortunate lack of adequate sustenance for Butter's ever-overflowing menagerie. Notably, there is no record whatsoever of what happened to the doctor's huge and varied collection of exotic beasts in this crucial period of British zoological (and perhaps even crypto-zoological) history.

Is it possible that Dr. Butter – who was an undoubted, life-long animal lover – secretly released his beloved beasts back into the wild, perhaps on a dark night, when the prying eyes of the folk of Cannock would no longer be upon him? Needless to say, of course, if a fully grown elephant or a zebra were

Ocelots in Staffordshire. Copyright: U.S. Fish & Wildlife Service/U.S. Government.

roaming the wilder parts of Staffordshire in the early part of the twentieth century, we surely would have heard about it long ago. That no such claim has ever been made, however, suggests strongly that these particular creatures, at least, found new homes in local zoos, or perhaps in travelling circuses.

But, it is an undeniable reality that Cannock Chase has for decades been the reported home of large, exotic cats and kangaroos, or possibly wallabies - animals that most assuredly were housed at the doctor's property on Cannock's Wolverhampton Road. The possibility that at least some of today's creatures roaming the area might very well be the direct descendents of those same animals lovingly kept and cared for by Dr. Butter - who may very well have wished them their freedom, rather than risk having them 'put to sleep' - must rank highly, even if some prefer to dismiss such admittedly fantastic and controversial ideas.

And what was the fate of Antony, the doctor's beloved monkey? Certainly, no-one knows or is telling. If Antony was also released into the wilds of Staffordshire, is it possible that Butter had released other, somewhat similar creatures - chimpanzees, perhaps - into some of the dark woods and forests of the area in earlier times, say around, oh, January 1879, and near a certain bridge on the Shropshire Union Canal? And, if so, is it remotely possible that they have been secretly breeding and living in stealth ever since?

Admittedly, this is a purely hypothetical scenario (and, some might say, a wholly outlandish and over the top scenario, too), and there is certainly no hard data at all to prove or disprove anything of substance on this particular issue - beyond that from the latter part of the 1800s to the early years of the 20th Century, distinctly exotic animals from all across the world were kept at a location on the doorstep of Cannock Chase, and not at all far from the infamous Bridge 39 near Woodseaves. And, lest we overlook it, all of those same animals vanished under circumstances unknown, lost or forgotten.

If Dr. John Kerr Butter was in any way implicated in the strange affair of the Man-Monkey or the small monkey-like animals seen on the Chase, then he certainly took his strange secrets to the grave with him when he died - in his mid-sixties - in 1920.

Old Ned's Devil

In a somewhat strange and roundabout way, the following story has a connection to both me and to the Man-Monkey. It came to me via my dad, Frank, who got it from a close friend of his: Eddie. The two of them, to this very day, work together on weekends as volunteer guides at the aerospace museum at Royal Air Force Cosford, Staffordshire. Eddie knows that I have a somewhat unusual job and passion (to say the least!), and a few years ago he shared with my dad a story, the origins of which date back to the 19th Century, and to Eddie's great-uncle.

That the story related to an incident involving something that was rumoured to be an out of place monkey roaming around just outside the elegant and majestic city of Birmingham, certainly made me take a high degree of notice. And yes, this story may be said to be one of definitive 'friend of a friend' proportions. But, for what it's worth, here it is, in the words of legendary cryptozoologist and friend, Dr. Karl Shuker - the author of *Karl Shuker's Alien Zoo* and many more titles - with whom I shared the known details in 2007:

> 'Around the end of the 19th Century, Eddie's great-uncle Ned was driving a pony and trap on Rolfe Street, Smethwick, late one night when he heard some strange noises behind him. Suddenly, a weird-looking animal leapt out at him, but he supposedly fought it off with his horse-whip. The creature was killed, placed in a glass case, and displayed in the Blue Gate pub on Rolfe Street for some time, where the locals dubbed it "Old Ned's Devil". Sadly, however, this mystifying specimen, for which no morphological description exists, apparently vanished years ago, and nothing more is known of it.'

The story, of course, with its attendant tale of the man sat atop a trap and striking the beast with his whip, is incredibly reminiscent of the January 1879 saga of the Man-Monkey at Bridge 39 on the Shropshire Union Canal, which means we cannot rule out the possibility that, in some poorly understood fashion, the tale of Old Ned's Devil might be a distorted story of the beast of the Shropshire Union Canal. But, for now anyway, let's give it some degree of benefit of the doubt.

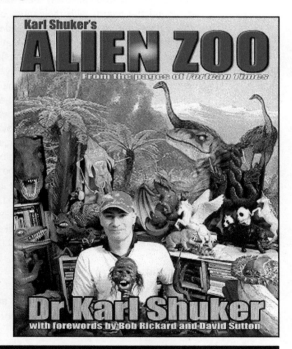

Recognising the potential significance of the affair, Karl began to make enquiries of his very own: he wrote about it at his blog, in the hope it might have brought forth additional data (it did not), and he also emailed the scant details to Professor Carl Chinn, the leading historian of the Black Country, which encompasses such fantastic locales as Sandwell,

Dr. Karl Shuker: On the track of Old Ned's Devil. Copyright, CFZ Press.

Dudley, Wolverhampton, Walsall, and the outskirts of Birmingham. Unfortunately, even the attempts of Professor Chinn failed to open any more doors, and, today, the story remains very much in stalemate mode, just as it was when it was told to my dad, by Eddie, back in 2006. But, there are two other pieces of information I want to share, since - in a roundabout way - they have their parallels with the saga of both the Man-Monkey and Old Ned's Devil.

The Mystery of Monkey's Jump

Situated just west of Dorchester is a place called Monkey's Jump, at which, today, a roundabout and cafe exist, but which may have been the original crossroads in the area (crossroads, interestingly, play integral roles in many tales of a paranormal nature). A number of theories exist to explain the name, including the possibility that it was provoked by the escape - many decades ago - of a monkey from a travelling circus. Another, more intriguing, story, however, tells of a woman, driving a pony and trap from Bridehead to Dorchester, at some point during the First World War. According to the story, on-board the trap was the woman's small, pet monkey that duly escaped at what is now Monkey's Jump, scarpered up a tree, and which, after refusing to come down, was eventually shot for being a German spy!

Back to the Bwbach

Still on the matter of horses, carts and strange beasts, I feel the need to refer back to the Welsh Bwbach, a hairy, diminutive creature discussed and described in the opening lines of the previous chapter. Back in 1880, Wirt Sikes – in *British Goblins* – noted a case with intriguing parallels to that of Old Ned's Devil, the Man-Monkey affair of 1879, and the saga of Monkey's Jump.

Wirt detailed the story in the following words:

> 'There was a Bwbach belonging to a certain estate in Cardiganshire, which took great umbrage at a Baptist preacher who was a guest in the house, and who was much fonder of prayers than of good ale. Now the Bwbach had a weakness in favour of people who sat around the hearth with their mugs of cwrw da and their pipes, and it took to pestering the preacher. One night it jerked the stool from under the good man's elbows, as he knelt pouring forth prayer, so that he fell down on his face. Another time it interrupted the devotions by jangling the fire-irons on the hearth and it was continually making the dogs fall a-howling during prayers, or frightening the farm boy by grinning at him through the window, or throwing the maid into fits. At last it had the audacity to attack the preacher as he was crossing a field. The minister told the story in this wise: "I was reading busily in my hymn-book as I walked on, when a sudden fear came over me and my legs began to tremble. A shadow crept upon me from behind, and when I turned round - it was myself! - my person, my dress, and even my hymn-book. I looked in its face a moment, and then fell insensible to the ground." And there, insensible still, they found him. This encounter proved too much for the good man, who considered it a warning to him to leave those parts. He accordingly mounted his horse next day and rode away. A boy of the neighbourhood, whose veracity was, like that of all boys, unimpeachable, afterwards said that he saw the Bwbach jump up behind the preacher, on the horse's back. And the horse went like lightning, with eyes like balls of fire, and the preacher looking back over his shoulder at the Bwbach, that grinned from ear to ear.'

Thus, Wirt's account ends.

There are several threads to all these stories that are worthy of note. In the tales of the Monkey Jump creature, Old Ned's Devil, and the Man-Monkey of the Shropshire Union Canal, we see the presence of either a pony and trap or a horse and cart; while the Welsh tale of the Bwbach involved a horse and rider. And, in all these cases, the animals seem to have been of relatively small stature: even the Man-Monkey has been given a height of between four-and-a-half and five-feet, for the most part. Then there is the matter of the Dorset monkey shot for being a German espionage agent. This is clearly an update of an even earlier, and very famous, story that dates way back to the Napoleonic Wars, when a monkey - said to have been dressed in the uniform of the French military of the day - was supposedly hanged in Hartlepool for being a French spy.

Somewhere, in all three of these tales, I am sure there are ultimate truths still to be found and understood. Today, however, those truths, whatever they may be, are so deeply entangled in distortion, myth, legend and folklore that it seems most unlikely we will ever have the full, true answers we seek.

The Beast of a London Borough
Then there is this account, related to Neil Arnold by a woman named Liz, from 2009:

> 'I think I saw a monkey run across the road in front of me this morning (11th August 2009) as I was driving from Bexley to Bexleyheath. It was a sort of greeny, browny stone colour with hanging fur from its skinny limbs and it ran across the road with a slightly sideways skip on back legs and one front leg. It didn't move like a cat but it was so quick that it had gone before I was aware what was happening. I looked down the drive of the house it had run towards but of course saw nothing. It wasn't very big, sort of large cat sized but would probably be about 20 - 24 inches tall had it been standing.'

A Monkey in Maidstone
> 'A Mr. Price,'

Said Neil, in 2009,

> 'reported that a year or so ago, in the wilds of Maidstone, he was awoken one night by a startled domestic cat. Upon reaching his bedroom window and looking out he was amazed to see a "monkey" bound along and head off towards the woods. Mr. Price had seen a large puma a few years before, but the last thing he expected was a monkey. In height he stated that the creature was Labrador-size, but the length smaller than a domestic cat, as on all fours it leaped by.'

> 'The witness stated that the primate was larger than a capuchin, which inhabits South America. The Weeper Capuchin however, which lives in the north-eastern region of South America, can measure up toeighteen inches in length, whilst the Brown Capuchin (which inhabits much of north, east and central South America) is similar in size. Mr. Price said the animal was brownish in colour but hard to tell under the street lights, and it seems very likely the animal had escaped from a private menagerie.'

And, now, on a journey that has taken us from wild men to green men, and from giant ape-men to little hairy things, it is time for us to turn our attentions away from strictly the stories of the British Bigfoot and, instead, direct them into the domain of the theories that exist to explain the nature of the monsters and beast-men. Just like the creatures themselves, the possibilities are many and varied, but always wild!

THE
THEORIES

Chapter 29
The British Bigfoot: A Flesh And Blood Animal?
'...Britain cannot, does not, and never will, harbour a species of ape - known or unknown...'

F.W. 'Ted' Holiday was the author of such ground-breaking and paradigm-shifting books as *The Dragon and the Disc*, *The Great Orm of Loch Ness*, and *The Goblin Universe*, all of which should be considered absolutely vital reading for cryptozoologists and Forteans, both seasoned and new.

He famously stated the following with respect to the thorny matter of mysterious, hairy hominids in our very midst:

> 'Real animals stay alive by eating. Giant primates, such as the gorilla, feed almost continuously during daylight, and in no dainty fashion. Bigfoot, however, allegedly lives in coastal evergreen forests which produce low-energy food of the poorest quality. It is impossible to imagine this miserable fare could sustain a race of eight-foot-high anthropoids.'

Holiday's undeniably wise, and wholly justified, words were made in particular relation to the controversy surrounding the Bigfoot phenomenon in North America; yet, they are equally as relevant to the problem of such animals allegedly residing in the British Isles – and, quite possibly, even more relevant, too...

Feeding, Hiding, Surviving and Thriving: A Mammoth Problem.
If the British Bigfoot is a 'real' entity in some sense of the word, then it's highly ironic in the extreme that the one theory for its existence that many people might assume to be the correct one - namely, that it is a creature of flesh and blood proportions that science and zoology have yet to classify or categorise - is, actually, the one least likely of all to provide a definitive, or even a remotely, potential, viable answer.

Prevailing theories within the domain of mainstream cryptozoology (a description which some might consider to be the ultimate oxymoron!) certainly differ on the finer points of what Bigfoot is or is not, and what it may be or may not be. But, for most of those who adhere to the idea the creature is a living entity in the way most of us understand and interpret the term, the beast is some form of unknown ape, or, possibly, a surviving example of the presumed-extinct great ape known as Gigantopithecus, which roamed India, China, and Vietnam hundreds of thousands of years ago.

OPPOSITE: Richard Freeman, Zoological Director of the Centre for Fortean Zoology.
Copyright: Nick Redfern.

And, while we can never rule out such possibilities when it comes to Bigfoot in the United States, the Yeti of the Himalayas, the Russian Almasty, China's Yeren, and the Australian Yowie, on the matter of the British beast things are a tad more problematic. Well, no, actually, they are extremely problematic!

Big Feet in a Little Country

First, there is the problem of size. Not just of the creature (an issue that we will address shortly), but the scale of the country in which it is said to live. At its absolute longest point - from Land's End, Cornwall, England to John o'Groats, Caithness, Scotland - Britain only extends to 603 miles (or, if you use the winding roads and travel by vehicle, 838 miles). And the population density of its sixty-million-plus people is 717 per square mile. Are we really to believe and accept that in such a small country, but one with a significantly-sized population, it has proved consistently impossible to find, classify, capture or kill at least one British Bigfoot or wild man? With 717 people, on average, inhabiting every square mile of the country, where are these immense beasts hiding? And, precisely how are they managing to remain consistently out of our hands?

And, on top of that, we are faced with the major problem of food. Or, more correctly: what food?

Non-existent Nourishment

If we take the stance that the British Bigfoot is a form of ape, one of the biggest and most important questions that needs answering is: on what does the creature live? There sure as hell is not a lot of wild bamboo in Britain - a food source that mountain gorillas, for example, thrive on. In fact, if one takes a good, long walk around any number of places where the British creature has been seen - such as the Cannock Chase, Dartmoor, Bolam Lake, the Shropshire Union Canal, the Cairngorms, the mountains of Wales, and both Rendlesham Forest and Sherwood Forest - what we actually notice is a marked lack of food that is rich in nourishment and vitamins. A fully grown mountain gorilla partakes of more than 140 types of plants, shoots, stems and leaves, and can eat up to sixty pounds of vegetation...each and every day. When one takes a look at their massive bulk, this is not surprising at all. But here's the big problem: the average British Bigfoot is no smaller than the typical mountain gorilla. In some cases, it even dwarfs the mountain gorilla! Yet, we come back to that big problem in Britain: where is the food that allows - and must have allowed for centuries, given how long reports date back into recorded history - these immense 'animals' to live?

Well, maybe the British beasts have adapted to surviving on the type of nourishment that one typically finds in the average farmer's fields, or orchards, in Britain. Not impossible, you might say, but if whole colonies of well-built, muscular beasts of six to eight feet tall are having to eat upwards of sixty pounds of vegetation every day, of every week, of every year, of every decade, of every century - just to stay alive - then why aren't the nations' food-suppliers up in arms about all the mysteriously missing cabbages, sprouts, carrots, apples, potatoes, beans, and more? The answer is devastatingly simple, but equally devastatingly problematic when it comes to Bigfoot in Britain. The reason: nothing of great significance is going mysteriously missing on a massive, regular, country-wide scale, that's why.

Taking another approach to resolving the problem of food, could it be that the British animal has really diversified and has, over numerous generations, developed a keen taste for meat, and not much else? Certainly, farm animals – sheep and the like - would make for the ideal fodder, if that is the case. And wild creatures, such as foxes and deer, are sometime found dead, partially or wholly eaten, or just badly mutilated, in locales including Cannock Chase and Rendlesham Forest. These particular events, however, are often seen as the work of so-called big cats, or they are the results of far more down to earth scenarios that involve cars, vans and lorries running into them late at night, and their drivers hastily and stealthily exiting the scenes, after which the smaller wild animals of the area then feed eagerly upon the carcasses, and the remains.

The British Bigfoot, Gorillas and food: A big problem! Copyright: H.B. Scammel, 1890.

In 2007, it was revealed by Staffordshire County Council that, on average, a staggering 170 deer are killed each and every year on the Cannock Chase. That's a figure of almost one every two days per year. But, here's the important thing: those deaths are, for the most part, nearly always easily explainable via the aforementioned accidents involving various vehicles - very often driven by people speeding along the long, wide road that links the towns of Hednesford and Rugeley, and which cuts a dramatic and picturesque swathe right through the heart of the very Chase itself.

The other important factor here is that there is zero evidence to suggest the bodies of these many animals are being stealthily hauled away by mysterious beasts after being hit by racing drivers. Yes, they may very well get gnawed and nibbled on by small, wild animals after dark, but on practically every occasion, they remain where they fall, which is generally in a smashed state on the tarmac, or, on the grass at the side of the road, having been hurled there by the pulverising force of metal hitting flesh and bone at high speed. It is then the unenviable job of the council to dispatch workers to clean up the usually grisly mess, a task they perform very regularly, and which anyone can see them doing, if such is their warped idea of entertainment.

The only other possibility to account for how a Bigfoot just might survive by eating deer on Cannock Chase - and, I stress, I do not believe this to be the case, at all - is that Staffordshire County Council is engaged in a gigantic *X-Files*-type conspiracy to hide mountains of evidence that, each and every year, the bodies of hundreds of deer - after having been hit by cars, vans and lorries - are being grabbed by scavenger-style Bigfoot beasts all across the area, and then heartily and voraciously devoured.

Such a scenario would most certainly make for a wonderfully entertaining cryptozoological novel, but for the world of reality? Forget it! And, let's not lose sight of the fact that sightings of the British Bigfoot hail from all corners of the country, so such an unlikely conspiracy would have to be one of nationwide proportions -

and which would make the possibility of keeping it under wraps even more unlikely.

Then there is the matter of habitat. Aside from stumbling upon the very occasional, so-called 'Bigfoot Tepee', nothing of any real substance has ever surfaced to offer a viable solution to certain, critically important questions: where on earth does the British Bigfoot live? Where do they mate? Where do they rear their young? The more we address such important questions, the less credible are the answers that come to the fore. Or, at least, they become less credible when we try and pigeon-hole the existence of the beasts into the flesh and blood camp.

And, if you think that's just my opinion, then you're dead wrong.

'There's nothing in the fossil record'

Jon Downes, too, is sure that, although there is without doubt a British Bigfoot phenomenon of very real proportions, it is one that falls outside the domain of matters of a flesh and blood nature. And here he is to tell you precisely why:

> 'Britain is a very small country and one of the best explored in the world. And there simply is not enough wild land for an unknown species of higher primate to live in. New species of animal do get discovered in Britain, but they are always small. The biggest thing to be discovered in Britain in recent years is a population of lizard, which is about nine inches long, living on the cliffs in Dorset. And the idea of a relatively small lizard living on cliffs in Dorset is pretty outstanding; but the idea of something the size of a gorilla living in Britain, in the wild, is ridiculous. And in the places where they have been reported, there simply is not enough food available for them to eat. Most of the higher primates are herbivorous, and there is not enough vegetation to supply the quantities and nutrients that a viable population of large primates would need. And even if they had adapted to living here on deer and rabbits, there just isn't enough land for them to hide in and live in.
>
> Bolam Woods, is only around forty acres. It's ridiculous to suggest that an animal the size of a gorilla could live there, so close to civilisation, and not be found. But, here's one of the most important things of all: There's nothing in the fossil record to indicate that a great ape has ever lived in Britain. Now, in Asia, where there is a fossil record of Gigantopithecus in the areas where the Yeti has been reported today. And, so, it is logical for the Yeti to be there. But, the lack of fossil evidence, not enough food, and not enough land, all rule out the idea of a great ape existing in Britain.'

A Monster Hunter is Born

As a boy in the 1970s, Richard Freeman - Goth, *Dr. Who* devotee, and the zoological director of the Centre for Fortean Zoology - holidayed with his grandparents in Devon, England. One summer, when Richard was about nine, his grandfather got talking to a retired trawler man in Goodrington Harbour. The old man recounted his life as a fisherman and one particular incident that was firmly and forever stuck in his mind. Some years previously he and his crew were trawling off Berry Head, where the seas of Britain are almost at their deepest.

Such are the depths of this part of the English Channel that the area is commonly used as a graveyard for old ships and the drowned wrecks of these vessels have made an artificial reef that has attracted vast amounts of fish. Good catches are, therefore, almost guaranteed, and the area has become a popular place for fishermen to drop their nets.

On one particular night, the crew had trouble lifting the nets and began to worry that they had got them entwined about a rotting mast. Soon, though, they felt some slack and duly began to haul the nets up. The men thought that their catch was a particularly good one, so heavy were their nets. As their nets drew closer to the trawlers lights, however, a frightening sight took shape. The crew had not caught hundreds of normal sized fish but one gigantic one.

> 'It was an eel, a giant eel,'

A wide-eyed, young Richard was told:

> 'Its mouth was huge, wide enough to have swallowed a man; the teeth were as
> long as my hand,'

Said the fisherman. Even now Richard still remembers the words of the ancient mariner and is convinced that this was not a tall story designed to entertain gullible tourists:

> 'While it was still in the water,

Said the frightened fisherman,

> 'it was buoyed up but as soon as we tried to pull it on board the nets snapped like
> cotton and it vanished back down. I was glad it went, I've been at sea all my life but
> I've never been as scared as I was that night. I can still see its eyes, huge, glassy.'

From that moment onwards, Richard's life was forever changed. And, as a result, he has a good deal to say about the British Bigfoot, all of it most enlightening:

> 'The very idea of there being a race of large, ape-like creatures living undiscovered in
> Britain is a complete nonstarter. You obviously can't have one animal; you would
> have to have a base-population breeding. But, there are just not enough wilderness
> areas in Britain. People who have never been to Britain don't seem to realise this.
> They seem to have this idea that it's all moorlands and woodlands and quaint little
> villages and castles. But, it's not. Even in the wilds of Scotland, Wales or Devon where
> it is like that, you couldn't hide something like that. It would have been found, and
> probably hunted to extinction, years and years ago. We're not talking about a
> Tibetan plateau or the forests of the Himalayas or central China. We're talking about
> a highly-populated, highly-industrialised, small, western European country. We
> should also see them feeding; and we should find their tracks, and biological traces
> like dung. But there's nothing. But people are seeing something.'

That 'something', which Richard believes offers a viable explanation for the British Bigfoot, is an issue that we will return to in the final chapter. Until then, yet even more on why the hairy beasts of these lands are not at all what they initially appear to be.

Observations from Neil Arnold

In early 2012, I extensively interviewed author and researcher Neil Arnold with respect to his views on whether or not the British Bigfoot is a flesh and blood entity, or something far, far stranger. As someone who has immersed himself deeply in the subject – and who has personally spoken with and interviewed many witnesses to such 'creatures' - Neil's words are, just like those of Richard Freeman, invaluable.

Neil says of Bigfoot in the part of England in which he resides, Kent:

'A majority of things I investigate - i.e. big cats - are real animals, but sometimes I receive reports of creatures which clearly cannot exist, such as British "wild men", hairy, bipedal creatures with glowing eyes. These creatures are not zoologically, biologically, scientifically possible. And so they are either the product of hoax, misinterpretation or some obscure manifestation connected to the witness or the layout of the land.'

The inconsistent nature of the British Bigfoot, Neil believes,

'...suggests a paranormal entity of sorts rather than elusive flesh and blood creature. I believe this is exactly the same for the rest of Britain - and it's important to analyse this from an angle beyond flesh and blood, scientific possibility - because the theory that these "British Bigfoot"-type creatures are "real" is absurd, and probably more absurd than suggesting they are ethereal,' says Neil. 'I've never seen a ghost, and I believe it takes a certain type of person to see a spirit, demon, etc. I think we need to look at the witness before we start trying to find where these wild men are living.'

Neil does not, however, rule out the possibility that at least some of the Earth's mysterious man-beasts might be of definitively flesh and blood origins, however:

'I'm of the opinion that what we know as Bigfoot in the Pacific Northwest, or the Yeti in the Himalayas, could be a flesh and blood, yet undiscovered, species of upright walking ape. This certainly seems the case with the Orang Pendek of Sumatra, which has been seen by zoologists, such as Debbie Martyr. However, Britain cannot, does not, and never will, harbour a species of ape - known or unknown. It is important to eliminate certain theories and details before we start saying such things are real or not. There's not a shred of evidence for ghosts and there'll never be a shred of evidence to support the English "wild man", except for those occasional startling eyewitness reports. As we know, not everyone is genuine, but there are people out there who are genuine and very sure that what they've seen is not down to a hoax or misinterpretation.'

'Each year, since the early '80s,'

Neil expands,

'I receive one or two reports that defy description or zoology. And, in most cases, witnesses seem genuine in what they've experienced: A creature between six and eight feet tall, covered in hair, muscular, bipedal, and having glowing yellow or red eyes. In some cases, these could be down to people dressed up, but the majority seem to suggest something unexplained.'

Neil makes a comment that squarely sums up his position on the entire controversy:

'There's not one report, in my opinion, pertaining to U.K. wild men that could suggest a real, flesh and blood creature. The U.K. could not support a colony of apes, let alone an undiscovered species of upright walking ape or unknown form of man. Like ghosts, the U.K. wild men reports seem to be more connected to the human psyche, or are the product of misinterpretation, or have deep-rooted connection to the land. Centuries ago there were legends of the Woodwose, a type of medieval wild man, but this seemed to exist as a nature spirit.'

Adding further commentary on this matter, Neil says:

> 'Jonathan Downes categorised such figures as "zooforms" - spiritual entities that have animal characteristics. This obscure category has been vital in collating unexplained creatures which clearly do not fit into zoological or cryptozoological types: hellhounds, ghostly animals, mothmen and other winged humanoids, and British wild men are zooform phenomena, possible demonic apparitions that have existed for centuries, but rarely taken seriously.'

He concludes:

> 'Such entities have now become part of modern folklore like the dragons, harpies, centaurs, satyrs, etc., of old. These are not flesh and blood animals but no doubt belong in the same melting pot as fairies, elementals and the like. This doesn't mean such things do not exist - but they simply do not exist as viable flesh and blood creatures in the woods. Although: Weird things are seen in the woods, oceans, lakes and skies of the world. It's as if we, as a race, put them there, but as a zoological form they are invalid. Whilst in a few rare cases a gorilla or monkey may escape into the wilds of the U.K., the reports from all over the U.K. suggest that such wild men are more akin to ghostly phenomena rather than natural animals.'

The Big Grey Man of Ben Macdhui as a Flesh and Blood Animal

Of the Cairngorm's most infamous alleged inhabitant possibly being a living, breathing entity, Andy Roberts offers the following statement, which leaves us in no doubt at all where he stands on this particular matter:

> 'One of the main contentions has been that the experiences are evidence of a flesh and blood creature of the same type as the Yeti, Bigfoot or Alma. I doubt this very much. Even being charitable with the evidence and broadening the content of acceptable cases to include anecdote and third and fourth hand stories within a twenty mile radius of Ben Macdhui, it is almost certain that the BGM is not a corporeal creature.'

Providing further support to his reasoning, Andy correctly notes that:

> 'There are no photographs, no bones, no fur or skin samples, no evidence of a family group, no droppings, no evidence of any predatory action on the local mammal population. Not even a reasonable number of good consistent accounts seen within a defined area.'

And although the Cairngorm plateau is a wild, oft-inhospitable place, since the boom in outdoor activities of the last thirty years or so, Andy explains,

> '...the area is frequently visited by relatively large numbers of people at all times of day, night and year. It seems logical that if the BGM was physical in nature some tangible evidence would have come to light by now. When dealing with the possibility of other large, relict hominids such as the Yeti, etc., being flesh and blood creatures the argument is considerably strengthened by the existence, however ambiguous, of photographs, videos, footprint-casts, skin and hair samples, etc. None of these exist in respect of the BGM and until they do it is reasonable to assume that we are not dealing with a physical creature.'

So, if not a beast of flesh and blood, we are forced to look elsewhere for the answers to the conundrum of Bigfoot in Britain.

CHAPTER 30
FAKERY IN THE U.K.
'...Bigfoot almost caused me to lose my baby...!'

Before we get to the far more esoteric and definitively Fortean theories for the British Bigfoot, let us first take a look at the one angle which, more than any other aside from the flesh and blood theory, many people might be inclined to suggest plays a highly significant role in the controversy. It is, of course, that of hoaxing.

I am personally convinced that most witnesses to British-based Bigfoot and wild man sightings are utterly genuine and have shared their mystifying accounts in an attempt to earnestly resolve the true nature of the conundrum that crossed their respective paths. Unfortunately, however, that is not always the case.

There is always some joker who wants to pull a fast one, play a prank, or confuse the nature of the phenomenon - or, maybe, all three at the same time. Sometimes this is done from a purely humorous perspective, and with no malicious intent involved. Occasionally, however, such pranks almost end up causing deep and long-lasting tragedy, as we shall soon see…

The Games Begin

In late 2005, Phyllis Galde, the editor of *Fate* magazine, commissioned from me an article for her publication on the subject of Bigfoot in Britain. Not surprisingly, it was titled Bigfoot in Britain (what else?). Not long after the feature appeared in the printed, newsstand version of the magazine, it was also placed on the *Fate* website. And, as a result of the now-online article focusing to a significant degree on the many and varied reports of Bigfoot in and around Cannock Chase, it caught the attention of Mike Lockley, then the editor of the unfortunately now closed down *Chase Post* newspaper, which - for years - covered the large area of the Chase and its immediate, surrounding old towns, villages and hamlets, and regularly reported on paranormal, ufological, and cryptozoological mysteries in the area.

Astutely recognising an eye-catching story whenever he saw one, Mike splashed the details of my *Fate* article across the pages of the Post in January 2006, noting that:

> 'Bigfoot fever first struck in our area when respected "X-Files" reporter Nick Redfern
> started investigating the existence of a strange creature after a spate of sightings
> over the Chase.'

On February 14 - in an article titled: Is There Truth in Bigfoot Sightings? - the *Birmingham Mail* newspaper got in on the anomalous animal action, too:

OPPOSITE: Bigfoot in a suit: The problem of hoaxes. Copyright: Nick Redfern.

> 'Reports were circulating today that a strange beast is roaming Cannock Chase – and now paranormal investigators are investigating.'

The Mail also recorded:

> 'All of the locals who spotted the mystery beast give the same description: a giant, hairy creature with blazing red eyes.'

It was then that the fun and games began; although, for some Bigfoot researchers, it was a period they would most likely prefer to forget! Mike Lockley noted in the February 9 edition of the newspaper that:

> 'Anyone who can provide me with a picture of Bigfoot will get a free Indian meal.'

It didn't take long at all – barely mere days – for numerous photo-shopped images of Bigfoot on Cannock Chase to reach the office of the newspaper. One came from a man named Andrew Soltysik, who wrote an exciting note to accompany his Photoshop-created image of a silverback gorilla roaming the wilds of the Chase. Soltysik said:

> 'By chance I was walking my dog, Rusty, up by the raceway and the poor fellow came racing towards me, tail between his legs and shaking with fright. Moments later, over the brow of the hill, I saw what I can only describe as a beast. I was able to take a shot of him before I myself turned and ran.'

Commenting on his photograph, which easily provoked imagery of definitive King Kong-like proportions, Soltysik noted:

> 'You can tell from the scale of things that he must be far in excess of the 6ft 8ins mentioned in your story. To be honest, I was too frightened to hang around, his exact height wasn't too important at the time! I think that in his quest for survival on Cannock Chase he must have picked up a discarded bag of chips wrapped in the Chase Post and noticed the story within. Perhaps he's a little upset that his cover has now been blown. Whatever his reasons, he didn't seem in a very joyous mood. I returned about half an hour later but could find no trace of him. Over the weekend I intend to hunt him out. I know of a few caves, hideouts and tree camps where he may be setting up home. Wish me luck!'

Mike Lockley, clearly pleased to the max by the monstrous response his coverage had provoked, once more stressed to the good folk of Cannock that there was a free curry awaiting anyone who might be able to provide a real photo of Bigfoot on the Chase. If such was not forthcoming, however, said Mike,

> '...we'll select the one that gives us the best laugh'.

I probably do not need to tell you that even more Photoshop-driven pictures of gorillas, King Kong and Star Wars' Chewbacca poured into the offices of the Post - as did a multitude of humorous letters, faxes and emails.

'M. Willis' – which may, or may not, have been a made-up name - of the nearby town of Hednesford told 'Post' staff:

> 'Some weeks ago I was walking in the woods of Beaudesert Old Park, when a large hairy being crossed my path. As it passed it turned and glared right at me. I never forgot those

eyes, and some days later I opened the Chase Post and the truth hit me. The creature I had seen was none other than Big Dave [a well-known columnist] from the Post. Was he on an undercover story or has he got a weird hobby?'

And, as Mike Lockley noted:

'Cannock man Mr. Hanysz even sent us a snap of what he believes could be the beast. Whether it's our furry friend or one of the Chavs at chucking out time, the jury is out again.'

Hoaxing and game-playing? Yes! But it was all good fun, of course, and not taken seriously, aside from those humourless souls in the field of cryptozoology who looked down on such shenanigans with a very dim view. But, the matter of harmless pranks aside, near-tragedy was waiting just around the corner. And I do mean that literally.

A Bun in the Oven and a Man in a Suit

Quite possibly the strangest of all headlines to ever have graced the pages of the *Chase Post* jumped out at its readers on March 23, 2006. It read: Bigfoot almost caused me to lose my baby! And, of course, it evoked memories of *The Sun's* infamous and masterful piece of front-page reporting of March 13, 1986 - which appeared, rather eerily, almost exactly two decades earlier to the day - that was entitled Freddy Starr Ate My Hamster! Few, I'm sure, can forget that one.

Utterly relishing the opportunity to relate to its readers a tale of proportions that easily surpassed the surreal, the Post began in fine fashion:

'Police chiefs have hit out at the dangers posed by the spoof "Bigfoot" craze after a teenager almost lost her baby when a joker clad in a gorilla suit jumped in front of her car. And the concerns have been echoed by a leading councillor and conservationist, who fears the "irresponsible idiots" are causing harm to wildlife as well as people.'

No, it was not April Fools' Day; although many might have been forgiven for thinking it was exactly that! So the story went, the controversy kicked off in the heart of the village of Brocton, which is situated only a very short distance from Shugborough Hall - the man-beast encounters at which we have discussed already, and which, to some degree, we may now be forced to look at in a new light, given the data that follows.

It was barely sixty minutes before the witching-hour struck when a 19-year-old pregnant girl and her parents were driving through picturesque Brocton, having had a Saturday night out in a restaurant in nearby Milford - a locale whose other brief claim to infamy occurred in September 1990, when Sir Peter Terry, the former Governor of Gibraltar, was shot and severely injured at his Milford home by the Provisional IRA.

When questioned later by police, the girl said:

'We noticed a BMW parked in the road. Suddenly it flashed its lights. Just then, out of nowhere, this person dressed in a gorilla suit jumped out in front of our car, flailing their arms like mad. Then they started running at the car like mad. It was terrifying.'

She continued:

'Looking back it was obviously a fake suit, but late at night, in an isolated area like that, it was a very scary experience. In broad daylight, I suppose it could be quite funny, but this was 11 o'clock at night with no-one around. It's very lonely there. If that had been someone with a heart condition, they could've had a heart attack. I screamed so loud. It was a real scare. It left me with fears that the trauma of it could have fatally harmed my baby.'

The girl's irate dad was up in arms (as opposed to his daughter, who was up the duff) and told the *Chase Post:*

'If I'd have caught the idiots, I'd have pasted them.'

The local plod weren't exactly laughing either. When contacted by the newspaper for comment on the matter, a spokesperson for Staffordshire Police HQ replied in stern tones:

'We take it very seriously because it may result in a Public Order Offence. The person [in the gorilla suit] may very well be in high spirits, but this would be viewed as a criminal offence.'

And Councillor John Burnett made sure he put in his considerable two-penneth, too:

'This is the behaviour of an irresponsible idiot. At this time of year, there are all manner of ground-nesting birds in that area; the partridge, the pheasant, woodlarks, skylarks - many rare birds whose habitat and nesting could be destroyed by this kind of activity.'

The Bigfooters Moan

Not surprisingly, such antics and high-jinks were hardly welcomed with open arms by the Bigfoot-hunting community. Actually, they weren't welcomed, at all. Not that the staff of the *Chase Post* was bothered in the slightest, as it was, undeniably from their perspective, all good fun and exposure for the newspaper. One commentator on the Chase Bigfoot affair said:

'There are interesting aspects of the whole Cannock Chase mystery that could be investigated and that would prove genuinely interesting. But clearly dicking about on Photoshop for five minutes is easier than getting out and researching a story. The sad fact is that all this will do is make people less likely to come forward for fear of being ridiculed so the whole story grinds to a halt and the actual solution to the mystery remains elusive.'

There was yet another 'equally damning' comment, too, which the 'Post' quickly and eagerly published:

'I keep waiting to see how low my opinion of the coverage of the Cannock Chase Bigfoot story can get and every time I think they can't get any lower they somehow manage it. The stories are accompanied by the god awful collection of Photoshopped snaps with pictures of gorillas and Chewbacca pasted into a forest scene.'

Mike Lockley, noting the absurdity of the situation, and responding in kind, was wholly unmoved by the backlash, and he defended the position and reporting of his staff like this:

'We at the *Chase Post* are not so quick to condemn. We believe people should be given the right to send us in pictures they believe show their encounters with the mystic beast. To all those doubters, we ask you this: If you've never seen Bigfoot, how can you tell a person he does not resemble Chewbacca or King Kong? We rest our case.'

Perhaps Mike had a very good point!

And the comments of Lockley only served to raise to dangerous levels the blood pressure of those in the Sasquatch-seeking community whose sense of humour had been removed, lost, or never existed in the first place - and which probably pleased the *Chase Post* and its monster-loving editor no end!

'Your Orangutan's been in the paper'

Also from Cannock Chase, but one year later - 2007 - the very strange story of Marcus, the monkey of the Marquis' Drive, surfaced. Marcus was actually a toy orangutan that had been found on the Chase 'entangled in a pile of fly-tipping rubbish' by Raymond and Angela Clarke - the former who, having 'rescued' poor, dumped Marcus, decided to monkey around himself, and placed the cuddly-toy on the branch of a nearby tree, where it could sit and survey the pleasant, green surroundings. Then the mystery began. While the Clarkes were on holiday, Marcus decided to take his own little vacation. He mysteriously moved - well, okay, we all know he was really moved by human hand - to another branch of the tree, then to another, and another, over the course of several days - one of which was situated at a very high level. But, no-one seemed to know who was responsible. There were also unverifiable tales of Marcus having been seen posing for the cameras and chilling at various other locations on the Chase, before being returned to his preferred Marquis' Drive, the site of Cannock Chase County Council's Visitor Centre and Café. Someone was showing Marcus a fine and fun view of the area while the Clarke's were away. It was only when they returned home that it became clear that not only had Marcus been befriended by a mysterious character seemingly intent on giving the little fellow a good tour of the area, but the bizarre story had even caught the attention of the local media. Mrs. Clarke told the press:

> 'It has caused us no end of fun and we couldn't believe it when it appeared in the newspaper; it's been fantastic. We had no idea about the fuss it had caused. And when we returned from holiday all of our friends were saying "Your Orangutan's been in the paper."'

And there's really not much I can add to that!

A Cumbrian Caper

The Beckermet area of Cumbria was allegedly the location of a January 1998 encounter that many within British Bigfoot research circles eventually came to view with deep suspicion. A letter that appeared in the *Whitehaven News* of March of that year told a story that, at first glance, made for notable reading, since it allegedly came from a local person who claimed an encounter in the area with a definitive Bigfoot-like beast:

> 'It was about 5.00 p.m. and starting to get dark so my visibility was not that good, but as I walked past the woods I heard the snapping of branches. Thinking it was an animal, I stopped to try and see it. Looking through the trees I noticed a large creature covered in a sort of ginger brown hair that seemed to be drinking from a pond about 150 meters into the woods. As the lighting was getting bad I was straining to make out what it was, but as I stopped and stared, it appeared to notice me. At this point it reared up onto its hind legs and made off slowly further into the woods. I would estimate its height when upright, to be around 6 feet 6 inches.'

While the story was undeniably eye-catching in nature and content, discrete inquiries on the part of several researchers with staff at the Whitehaven News revealed that there were deep suspicions the letter was actually the work of another newspaper seeking to pull a fast one on its rival.

A Winter's Tall Tale

I mentioned in an earlier chapter how, in March 2009, stories surfaced suggesting that the Shug Monkey had returned to its old haunts in Rendlesham Forest. One of the witnesses, Jenny Pearce said of her alleged encounter with the legendary animal:

> 'I was on the green at Rendlesham Forest having a picnic with my three-year-old son and his friend's family. After the picnic we stayed to play and explore the woods. While we were in the forest I saw a large animal moving through the trees ahead. I thought it was a big dog, so I picked up my son because he has never really got into dogs and gets easily scared. But as it continued away from us it was clearly not a dog. It was much bigger and there wasn't anyone there to be walking it if it was a large dog.'

As interesting as this most certainly was - at first glance, at least - the story was not true. In fact, Jenny Pearce and her young child didn't even exist. The whole thing turned out to be a publicity stunt, one dreamed up by the Red Rose Chain Theatre Company to promote their outdoor staging of Shakespeare's *A Winter's Tale*, which includes the famous stage direction: 'Exit, pursued by bear.' Jimmy Grimes - both actor and designer - said that faked accounts, and Photoshopped footage posted to You Tube (along with bogus comments below the footage), helped carry the caper along at a fine and merry pace - the purpose of which was to raise publicity for their production of *A Winter's Tale*.

Grimes added that the story was intended to come out on April Fools' Day, and explained that:

> 'No-one really knows that much about the play. In Shakespeare's day they probably would have had a real live bear at the Globe. But this tiny little stage direction is probably the most famous part of the play and it's something we thought we could use to get kids interested.'

What can we say, except: 'Exit, no Shug Monkey!' On this occasion, anyway…

Cases like those cited above certainly demonstrate that we most assuredly do need to be very careful when it comes to how, and under what specific criteria and circumstances, we accept as genuine those accounts of the British Bigfoot that reach our eyes, ears, letter-boxes, and in-boxes. Certainly, I also have extremely grave doubts about the authenticity of the story of the 'Snowdonia Thing', as described in the chapter of this book on Welsh wild men. And, Gavin Addis' 1997 story of the Bigfoot seen at the site of the Cannock Chase's Glacial Boulder has also provoked suspicions of hoaxing. But, it's important to remember that we have a wealth of credible data, from equally credible sources that - in my own, personal view - suggests while the angle of hoaxing has certainly played a small role in the matter of Bigfoot in Britain, the sheer number of reports, and the fact that they extend back centuries, is indicative of a real phenomenon that, overall, has nothing - whatsoever - to do with pranksters and fakery; good-natured, malicious, near-disastrous, or somewhere in between a blurry mixture of all three.

The Sword-Wielding Wild Man of the Caves

I have left until last - when it comes to hoaxes, at least - a strange story to which I was exposed in 1997. It involved an anonymously-posted photo which, in reality, is just a life-sized model that can be found in a

Cave creature fantasies. Copyright: Unknown.

certain, famous series of caves in England, and which is meant to offer a bit of 'sword and sorcery'-style entertainment for those who visit the caves in question. But what was interesting was the intricately woven tale that accompanied the picture when it was posted to me. I forget the precise details now, but it all revolved around the claim that intelligent, sword-wielding, dwarfish man-beasts were roaming the many and varied caves that exist deep below the British Isles. The letter ran to two or three pages and was a highly entertaining piece of horrific hokum written in a definitively atmospheric, Lovecraftian style. But, if you too are ever on the receiving end of this particular photo and its accompanying letter, just enjoy it for what it is: a piece of man-made entertainment, coupled with the written ravings of someone with - apparently - a very good imagination, but way too much time on their hands, and nothing else!

Mistaking a Monster on the M5

Before moving on to theories that go beyond just those pertaining to flesh and blood beasts and outright hoaxes, there is one additional area that must be addressed. It's that of mistaken identity. It barely needs mentioning that there aren't many things in the British Isles that one could conceivably mistake for Bigfoot, and so - for that very reason important reason alone - the number of cases I have on file is very limited. Actually, 'cases' is the wrong word to use, since I only possess one, solitary account that can be said to fall into this particular category. But, rather weirdly, it is a story that I was able to solve within mere seconds of receiving it from the witness in late 2009.

The report came from a woman named Samantha who, on a Thursday night in the final days of July 2009, was driving to her Edinburgh home after visiting family in Redruth, Cornwall. It was, then, to be an absolute mammoth drive home, one destined to take Samantha considerable hours to complete in her compact Fiat. But, it certainly wasn't a boring journey.

According to Samantha, while speeding (to the extent that one can speed in a Fiat) up the M5 'somewhere before getting to Bristol, I think', she was shocked to the core by the sight of what she described to me as 'a 15 foot high Bigfoot running along a field next to the M5 with his arms wide out!!!' And yes, Samantha did use three exclamations marks! Since it was impossible for her to stop and turn around, she quickly 'phoned her family on her mobile – all of who responded in sceptical but most definitely jovial fashion. But, for Samantha, the experience was as nerve-jangling as it was amazing.

This case is one from which we can learn a great deal. If not a Bigfoot, then what on Earth could it have been that Samantha briefly viewed as she drove along the M5 and while the light faded perilously fast? Well, I'll tell you what it was: Willow Man, a forty-foot-high figure made of steel and coated with black maul willow. It was sculpted by Serena de la Hey and was unveiled in 2000. Unfortunately, Willow Man - also known as the Angel of the South - was burned down by an arsonist in May 2001; however, within five months a replacement was firmly in place. And it did indeed stand in a field next to the M5, specifically near the Somerset town of Bridgwater.

Moreover, on a cloudy and cold morning only a couple of weeks after Samantha's encounter, me and Dan Holdsworth - a regular attendee at the Centre for Fortean Zoology's yearly Weird Weekend conference in Woolsery, Devon - were driving back to the Midlands from Jon and Corinna Downes' abode in the village of Woolsery, when we caught sight of the huge, man-like form in the very field in question. And, with Dan at the wheel, I even managed to hastily capture a solitary image of Willow Man with my digital camera as we zoomed by, and which I reproduce for you right here. As you can see, it's tall, dark, has its arms spread wide, and is in running mode. All just as Samantha had said. The big difference is that Dan and I had the full benefit of broad daylight to see the creation, whereas Samantha's view was sorely limited by the dark shadows of the rapidly descending night. I can also say that approaching the 'creature' at high speed most certainly did create the optical illusion of it charging along at a fairly significant rate of knots. When I emailed Samantha my slightly blurry photo, she said she was in no doubt that this is indeed exactly what she saw, but admitted to being mightily disappointed that she had not had a close encounter with a British Bigfoot, after all! It's also worth noting that Samantha significantly misjudged the size of the creation. What she believed to have been in the region of fifteen feet high was actually forty. This suggests we should be very careful how we interpret witness reports when it comes to judging size, scale, height and so forth. To be sure, it was a cautionary experience for both Samantha and me.

Moving on to yet another theory for the beast of the British Isles, you will recall that in the previous chapter Neil Arnold noted:

> 'Whilst in a few rare cases a gorilla or monkey may escape into the wilds of the U.K., the reports from all over the U.K. suggest that such wild men are more akin to ghostly phenomena rather than natural animals.'

With Neil's words in mind, let's see what evidence exists - or does not exist - for what I call 'escaping apes' in this fair land?

OPPOSITE: Mistaking Bigfoot on the M5 Motorway. Copyright: Nick Redfern.

Knaresborough (Wikimedia Commons)

CHAPTER 31
THE MYTH OR MENAGERINES AND
MISSING ANIMALS
'...They all come from Knaresborough
Zoo, you know...'

As all of the data detailed in Chapter 28 clearly demonstrates, the very idea that a colony of large, ape-like animals of definitively flesh and blood nature could successfully (A) live, (B) feed, (C) breed, (D) thrive, and (E) elude one and all for centuries in a country that stretches to only 601.5 miles and that has a packed population of in excess of sixty million, is not just most unlikely, but is manifestly absurd in the absolute extreme.

There is a startling possibility, however - and granted, it is a remote possibility - that on one occasion a fully grown gorilla may really have lived, albeit very briefly, in the wilds of Britain, and only a little more than 130 years ago. If the incredible story has even the remotest semblance of truth attached to it, then the presence of the animal may very well have provoked the legends of one of the nation's most famous and enigmatic of all its mysterious ape-men: The Man-Monkey of the Shropshire Union Canal...

A Bid for Freedom

On a particular day in 2009, Fortean expert and author Mike Dash was leafing through a copy of the December 8, 1878 edition of *Sheldrake's Aldershot & Sandhurst Military Gazette*, and came across a fascinating story in its pages that sat below the eye-opening headline of: CAPTURING A GORILLA IN SHROPSHIRE. The article began in an appropriately controversial fashion:

> 'For a fortnight past the district around Madely [Author's Note: This should be Madeley] Wood, Salop, has been in a state of intense excitement, by the alleged depredations committed by a gorilla, which is said to have escaped from a wild beast menagerie travelling to Bridgnorth. The animal was stated to have first made his appearance in the neighbourhood of that town, where in the darkness of the night it was severally seen by a clergyman and a policeman, both of whom fled. It is also said to have appeared at several places in the immediate neighbourhood.'

If the story was true, then it seems to have led to a spectacular case of mistaken identity, and near-tragedy, too, as the `Gazette's` writer noted:

> 'A few evenings since the occupier of a house in Madely [sic] Wood went to bed at

a reasonable hour, with the greater portion of his family, leaving his "gude wife" up, who took the opportunity to visit a neighbour, leaving the door open and a candle burning.'

'Returning in a short time, she was horrified at seeing a bent form, with a goodly array of gray hair around its face, crouching over the expiring embers of the fire, apparently warming itself, the light having gone out. Too frightened to shriek, she ran to her neighbours, who quickly armed themselves with pokers, iron bars, guns, and pitchforks and other instruments of a similar character, and marched in a body to capture the gorilla.'

The 'gorilla' - on this occasion, anyway - turned out to be nothing of the sort, as the article made clear to one and all:

'The form was seen sitting at the fire, but evidently aroused by the approaching body, rose to its full height and revealed the figure of an eccentric character well known in the neighbourhood as "Old Johnny," who seeing the door open had quietly walked in to light his pipe, accidentally "puffed" the candle out, and was very near being captured, if not exterminated, in mistake for an escaped gorilla.'

The on-the-loose animal, reported the `Gazette`, 'has not been heard of since'.

Monsters and Menageries

Well, this highly important discovery of Mike Dash was indeed fascinating, particularly so given the fact that the story surfaced in print only one-a-half months before the Man-Monkey was seen at Bridge 39 on the Shropshire Union Canal. That Bridge 39 is situated just a short distance from Bridgnorth - on the way to which the gorilla supposedly escaped from its clearly less than sturdy confines - makes the matter even more intriguing. Significantly, the old Staffordshire village of Ranton - which also plays an integral role in the Man-Monkey affair - is located less than thirty miles from Bridgnorth. And, given that the beast supposedly escaped on its way to Bridgnorth, rather than specifically at Bridgnorth, this suggests that the distance between the place of its escape, and Bridge 39, may have been far less than thirty miles. Indeed, an argument could be made that it was perhaps, barely no distance at all.

There are, however, certain other issues that need to be addressed, as Mike Dash astutely noted. Of the December 8, 1878 article in *Sheldrake's Aldershot & Sandhurst Military Gazette*, Mike said:

'Old Johnny and his humorous encounter make for an interesting story, and it's easy to see why the journalist who wrote the piece focused on him. As published, though, the article ignores the central question of what became of Shropshire's mysterious "gorilla". The wild-beast-escaped-from-a-travelling menagerie is a common motif in out of place animal stories, as Mick Goss demonstrated years ago in a Fortean Times article on the mysterious crocodile of Cefn Caves - itself just over the border in north Wales. But it would be an ambitious showman who kept an animal as dangerous as a gorilla in a travelling show.'

It most certainly would. And Mike was right on the money: Numerous stories, tales and rumours of 'circus escapees' (in Britain, in the United States, and elsewhere) have been dutifully trotted out time and time again to try and account for baffling sightings of strange, hairy, ape-like animals having been seen in areas where they have no business, at all, roaming.

I briefly mentioned in a previous chapter how the curiously named Monkey's Jump, near Dorchester, may have got its origins from the story of a monkey that escaped from a menagerie in the area. That story is scant in detail, and very much open to interpretation, as I noted. The following, however, are not.

'It was very tall, moving on two legs and covered in thick hair...'

While I don't personally think that the following case is a provable example of the escape of some form of ape from a British zoo, the fact that it occurred right in the vicinity of just such a place, and one that happens to house the second largest collection of primates in the entire world, is admittedly, somewhat intriguing.

The story comes from one James Culwick, who told me that, back in 1992, when he was fifteen, he and several of his friends had a curious experience at Norton Juxta Twycross, Leicestershire. A very little village indeed, Norton (the Juxta part of the name comes from the Latin for next to) is bounded on its east side by the Ashby Canal and is situated only a very brief distance from England's famous Twycross Zoo - an 80-acre facility, which was founded in 1963 by Mollie Badham and Natalie Evans.

James recalls the distinctly strange affair:

> 'There was a church in this village [Author's Note: A 12th Century structure, the Holy Trinity Church], and behind the church was a small wooded area and fields, where we used to generally mess about and have a sneaky beer or two. One sunny day though myself and two friends (no beers involved) were messing about having a laugh as teenagers do when one of my friends shouted that he had suddenly seen something move through the undergrowth.'

> 'He was genuinely shocked by what he saw as he claimed it was very tall, moving on two legs and covered in thick hair. On hearing my friend shout, I spun round as I had my back to him, I recall, and I too caught sight of something truly strange. It was only a glimpse, however, but I do remember seeing something through the leaves which was tall with scraggy brown fur. All I can remember is that immediately after the sighting I was shocked and so was my friend. We were quite scared and also perplexed because whatever we saw vanished after making its appearance. What is also worth noting is that my other friend saw nothing at all, very odd.'

That the beast was described by James as being of significant height, effectively rules out some wandering, escaped little monkey from Twycross Zoo as being the cause of all the commotion. And surely something of much bigger proportions would not have gone unnoticed by the zoo's personnel. Nevertheless, it is worth noting the words of the staff of the zoo itself:

> 'We have the largest collection of primate species of any zoo in the world, outside Japan. Twycross is the only U.K. zoo to hold all four species of great ape, including bonobos [Author's Note: Also called pygmy chimpanzees]. We also have a very successful breeding record and many of our primates can be observed in breeding groups with individuals of various ages and stages of development.'

Did one of the zoo's many primates briefly escape into the small woods around Norton, only to be quickly captured and the whole thing covered up? Or was the beast seen by James and his friends something far stranger? Two decades later, I suspect neither James nor we will ever have solid answers for those questions. I cannot, however, fail to note the irony in the fact that, until 1990 - only two years before James' encounter - none other than the Centre for Fortean Zoology's Richard Freeman worked at Twycross Zoo in the position of head curator of reptiles! If only Richard had stayed at the zoo a little longer and had known what was possibly lurking in those woods and fields…

Circus Accidents and Escapees

Taking a trip across the Atlantic, there is the Beaman Monster of Kansas City, Missouri, USA. Close to Beaman is the city of Sedalia, where, allegedly, in 1904, a train crashed in the vicinity, and which just happened to be carrying a large number of circus animals, including a mighty gorilla that stood twelve feet tall! Of course, the fact that gorillas don't grow anywhere near twelve feet in height did not stop the legend from developing suggesting they do! The descendents of this Goliath-like animal (and, presumably, a similar escapee of the opposite sex) are, locals conclude, today's man-monsters of Beaman.

Then, on January 28, 1921, an article, titled Chase Gorilla to Mountains, appeared in the pages of the Gettysburg, Pennsylvania, *USA Times*. In part, it stated:

> '"Gorilla" warfare which was started last week in the vicinity of Idaville, when Adams County residents, well armed, pursued what is believed to be an animal that escaped from a circus car when it was wrecked, not long ago, was renewed by citizens of Rouzerville Wednesday night when an armed posse scoured the Blue Ridge slopes in the hope of getting a shot at the beast.'

No-one should be surprised to learn that the beast of Idaville seemed to be wholly impervious to bullets, skilfully evaded each and every pursuer on each and every occasion, and finally made good its escape forever.

Said to lurk deep in the swamps of Louisiana, USA, the Honey Island Swamp Monster, as it has become infamously known, has been reported roaming the area since the early 1960s. Local folklore tells of the crash of a train in the area during the early years of the 20th Century. And guess what? The train was supposedly transporting a variety of animals on behalf of a travelling circus, which included a number of chimpanzees that made a quick and spectacular bid for freedom in the wake of the crash. The result: the now free chimps bred with the local alligator population (yes, you did read that right!), and spawned the nightmarish monster of the swamps.

And, the above stories of apes having escaped from circuses - and, in the process, provoking monster legends - are just three of dozens; the unlikely list goes, quite literally, on and on. It's not restricted to ape-men either. A further, perfect case in point is Britain's seemingly ever-growing population of cats of the wild, the exotic and big variety.

The Zoo Cats That Never Were

In his classic title *Cat Flaps*, Andy Roberts discussed a wave of 'big cat' sightings in the English county of Yorkshire in the 1980s. One particular series of encounters led a certain commentator to quietly inform Andy, in what sounded like a slightly conspiratorial fashion, that:

> 'They all come from Knaresborough Zoo, you know.'

Of course, there was no evidence, at all, that the now-closed down zoo had lost any big-cats; yet tales and theories along these very lines often spring up in such fraught and Fortean situations, and particularly so when people are striving and struggling to make some sense of what may well be afoot in their very midst. They become staple parts of the folklore, mythology and gossip of the area, and, ultimately, are sometimes perceived by whole swathes of the populace as being nothing less than undeniable, collective reality.

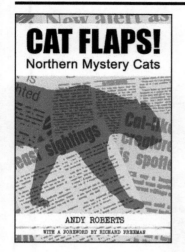

Andy Roberts' *Cat Flaps.* **Copyright: CFZ Press.**

So, is that what happened in England in late 1878? Had someone - or, as the `Gazette's` story suggests, several people - seen a weird Bigfoot-like entity in Shropshire that was subsequently explained away (without any actual evidence to support the notion), as being a gorilla that escaped from a non-existent travelling menagerie? Or, incredibly, was the story actually true?

Could there really have been a mobile circus from which a gorilla made a successful bid for freedom all those years ago? And if so, did it ultimately find its way one dark and winter night in January 1879 to the heart of the Shropshire Union Canal, where it scared the life out of the man who had the misfortune to encounter it, while crossing Bridge 39? Could it really have been the case that the animal briefly made its home in the wilds of Shropshire before probably, and almost certainly inevitably, succumbing to starvation and the effects of a harsh British winter of the type that dominated the land before global warming set in?

We can never totally rule out such an unlikely (and, as we have seen, widespread) scenario, but, even if it was true, it would most assuredly not explain the seemingly spectral nature of the beast reported at the canal. Nor would it account for how sightings of the same beast have continued until the present day. Unless, that is, what people are seeing in the modern era is the ghostly form of the long dead gorilla; one that is forever doomed to haunt and wander the tree-shrouded, old canal. Bringing tales of ghostly apes into the mix is, undeniably, a whole different and varied kettle of enigmatic fish! But what is particularly interesting is that apes believed to be spectral and ghostly in nature have surfaced from other parts of Britain for centuries. Let's now take a look at this particularly controversial matter, as it relates to life after death of the animal kind.

**In 1994, a spectral ape manifested at Scotland's Dundonald Castle.
Copyright: Unknown, 1903.**

CHAPTER 32
WELCOME TO THE GHOST APES
'...Maybe Bigfoot is a "phantimal...'

The Man-Monkey of the Shropshire Union Canal and the Irish ape with the human head aside, a study of British folklore, history and mythology reveals a veritable host of additional tales pertaining to old and new encounters with spectral, monkey-like animals. And what a swirling cauldron of strangeness it is, too...

The Eerie Apes of Marwood and Martyn

Jon Downes notes that the so-called Ghost Ape of Marwood, was, when alive, a pet of a local landowner who, one day, grabbed the landowner's young son and climbed a tree with him, utterly refusing to come down. And, after being killed for its actions, the monkey supposedly returned, in ghostly form, to haunt the surrounding area.

Jon continues on with another, yet somewhat similar, affair:

> 'The well known spectre of Martyn's Ape, at Athelhampton Hall in Dorset, is supposed to have been the pet of a member of the Martyn family that was either accidentally bricked up alive during building work, or was entombed when the daughter either committed suicide in a locked, secret room, or was walled up by an unforgiving parent - depending on which account you read and accept. The Martyn family built the earliest part of this house in the fifteenth century; and, interestingly enough, their family crest was of an ape sitting on a tree stump. The family motto was: He who looks at Martyn's ape, Martyn's ape will look at him.'

The crest in question still exists: it can be found above the main arch of the vestibule that marks the entrance point to the hall. Mark North, an expert on Dorset folklore and a noted author on the county's many and varied anomalies, notes that the ape sits 'with a solemn expression upon its face'.

The Cornwall Critter

Certainly one of the most bizarre of all the cases that falls into the domain of this particular category dates from 1789 and is referenced in an old document that came from the private collection of a noted family of landowners in Cornwall. The details are unfortunately very scant indeed, but, nevertheless, of deep significance, given what we have read thus far, and what is still yet to come. It concerned an immense monkey-like creature seen on several occasions at Crowlas, near Penzance.

The creature was seen by local folk late at night, on at least three occasions, and was described as being around eight feet in height and made a strange whistling noise that was interpreted as a call - to who or what, mercifully, remains unknown. Most notable of all: when the creature was last seen, at the height of a violent thunderstorm, it literally disappeared in an almighty flash of light.

Cornwall is also home to additional man-beast mysteries.

The Other Beasts of Bodmin

Any mention of the infamous Beast of Bodmin Moor inevitably conjures up memorable imagery - for those, like me, who recall the story and followed it - of large black cats roaming the old land and leading the British Army and the media of the early 1980s on a very merry dance both night and day. But maybe the beast is not alone. Maybe there are actually two beasts, but of very different types. Several years ago, I received an email from a man who had an intriguing, but unfortunately, very brief story to relate. The details, from Keith Fletcher of Derby, concerned a story told to him back in the mid-1980s - by a work colleague who hailed from Cornwall - of a huge ape seen roaming Bodmin Moor six or seven years prior to when Keith heard the story, which would have placed the events somewhere in the latter part of the 1970s. In this case, said Keith, the animal vanished into what was described as 'a small black cloud and just sort of disintegrated, like a ghost' [Author's Note: Italics Mine].

Moving on, but still very much on definitive Bodmin Moor turf - and, very possibly, even directly linked to the words and memories of Keith Fletcher - big cat researcher Marcus Matthews has gone on record with a story that is well worth citing right here. In Marcus' very own words:

> 'I have learned from a relation that in the 1970s and 1980s there were always rumours of an escaped orang-utan ape in the area. Farmers coming home from the public houses were used to seeing a strange pair of eyes looking at them, and a hairy human-like figure disappearing quickly.'

It's worth noting, too, that the eighty square-miles that comprise the atmospheric granite moorland of Bodmin Moor have been a beacon for bizarre tales and legends for centuries. Not surprising at all, given the wild, ancient atmosphere that pervades the old, desolate moor, and its many, attendant tors, hills, stone circles and Bronze Age monuments. In other words, one might well argue if there is any part of the country guaranteed to have tales of monstrous beasts attached to it, it's surely Bodmin Moor!

Haunted by Monkeys

Carolina Manosca Grisales says that 'shadowy forms' and 'chattering monkeys' reportedly,

> '...disturbed a Carlton TV crew in 1998 filming in Rectory Lane, Datchworth, Hertfordshire, helping establish the village as the most haunted in the county.'

She continues:

> 'A boat containing a woman and a pet monkey supposedly appears on a lake of several acres near a mansion in Leicestershire, according to *Another Grey Ghost Book* (1915) by Jessie Adelaide Middleton. The phantom lady was said to have been accidentally shot by her duck-hunting husband, the boat sunk and the monkey drowned.'

The Vanishing Beast of the Hill

And what are we to make of the spectral ape of Dundonald Castle, Scotland? Situated atop a large hill that overlooks northern Kilmarnock, the castle's origins can be traced back to the 1100s, when one Walter, the High Steward of King David I, constructed a wooden fort high on the hill. Then, a century later, a far more formidable and sturdy structure was built, and Dundonald Castle steadily began to take shape. During the Wars of Independence with England in the fourteenth century, much of the castle was decimated, and razed to the ground. It was, however, rebuilt according to the wishes of King Robert II, and still remains standing centuries later. But that is not all. A remarkable and terrifying encounter with a spectral ape took place near the castle in 1994. The witness was a woman named Josephine Aldridge who encountered a huge, gorilla-like animal on the hill that, after being in sight for a few moments, faded away into nothingness - just like so many other British Bigfoot.

A Macaque Named Satan

Carew Castle, located in Pembrokeshire, Wales, has an intriguing and notable history. Although originally a Norman creation - and one that was added to, and modified in varying degrees, over the centuries - evidence exists to suggest the area on which the ancient castle was built was seen as having prime strategic and military advantage as far back as 20 B.C. It's also said to be the haunt of a ghostly gorilla, monkey, hairy ape-man, or...well, take your pick; the choices are many!

While a number of reports exist - and which span four centuries, no less - of people seeing, hearing, or sensing the presence of the spectral monster, amongst the biggest questions are: how, and under what particular circumstances, did the legend surface? And: what was, and maybe still is, the true nature of the beast? For the answers, we have to travel back in time to the 1600s and the actions of the castle's then-lord, Sir Roland Rhys, who could boast of being nothing less than a fully-fledged, former pirate of near-Jack Sparrow proportions.

So the tale goes, on one of his sea-fearing adventures, Rhys acquired a 'Barbary ape' - or, given that it is actually a monkey and not an ape – a Barbary macaque, its correct but less well-utilised title. Living on Gibraltar, and on the Atlas Mountains of Algeria and Morocco, Barbary apes are not large animals, by any stretch of the imagination. Averaging around only two-and-a-half feet in height and two stone in weight when fully grown, there is not much chance of such an animal being mistaken for Bigfoot. Or is there?

Witnesses to the Carew creature have, as early as 1801 and as late as 1969, described the hairy fiend as a shadowy, bulky, gorilla-like animal, which is absolutely at complete odds with what the old tales tell us about the nature of the animal that is believed to have provoked the legend in the first place. But, before we jump the proverbial gun, let us return to the saga of Sir Roland Rhys, who - with some hindsight - sounds very much like the cruel and maniacal Hugo Baskerville of The Hound of the Baskervilles infamy.

A bad tempered drunk, and one with a deep propensity for violence, bullying and cruel humour, Rhys would host huge banquets, invite friends and local dignitaries over to dine with him, and then mercilessly taunt them, goad them, and pummel them with insults. And, more often than not on such nights, he would parade, for one and all to see, his very own macaque, which went by the memorable moniker of - wait for it - Satan. By all accounts, Satan was highly intelligent, devious, cunning, and could eerily mimic Rhys' laughter which he, Satan, would also direct at Rhys' guests - many of whom were highly fearful of the wild beast that would appear in their midst dressed in nothing less than butler-style, posh garb. And, no: I am not making this up!

Death Strikes

Legend suggests that it was a dark, stormy, rainy, and wind-filled night (in a saga like this, could it really have been anything less?) when there was a loud and echoing knock on the old, mighty, wooden door of Carew Castle. Rhys, blind drunk on a staggering amount of spirits even by his impressive standards, made his stumbling way to the door. He was confronted by a Flemish tradesman who, having rented land in the area from Rhys, brought over his rent money which was then overdue by several days. Or, rather, the man had brought part of the money with him. Hard times had unfortunately befallen the man and he pleaded with Rhys to be given a few more days to try and get the outstanding payment together. Rhys, unsurprisingly for such a cold-hearted character, was having none of it whatsoever - not only because of the money issue, but also because Rhys' son was seeing the man's daughter, a relationship upon which Rhys deeply frowned. So, he took a most different approach to resolving the matter. It was a terrible and bloody approach, too.

In a fashion that eerily paralleled the scene in *The Hound of the Baskervilles* where Hugo of that name lets loose his pack of hunting dogs on the daughter of a local yeoman who has dared to snub his - Hugo's - advances, Rhys loosened the chains that kept the monkey from roaming too freely and wildly, and goaded it to attack the petrified man - which it duly did, tearing into his flesh in a savage and violent fashion. Fortunately, the man managed to escape the clutches of the laughing, dwarfish, hairy butler. He staggered out of the door, weak, dizzy and disoriented from both shock and significant blood loss, and collapsed in a helpless heap in the grounds of the castle. Even more fortunately, a kindly servant - one hardly enamoured by the violent actions of his master and his attendant hairy fiend - bandaged the man's wounds and intended on giving him shelter in his own quarters until the turbulent storm finally subsided. But the night's calamitous events were not yet over. The main-course was just about to surface.

As the servant helped the man gain his footing and guide him to shelter and safety, loud cries and crazed laughter broke out in the main dining hall. The servant raced to the room and was faced with a terrifying sight: by the time the man flung open the door, Rhys was dead, his throat brutally torn open - and not at all unlike that of Hugo Baskerville in Sir Arthur Conan Doyle's novel, when he was attacked and killed by the glowing-eyed, fiendish dog of the book's title.

The body of Satan, somewhat appropriately, when one takes into consideration the name of the maniacal monkey, was burning fiercely in the great, stone fireplace that dominated the room. But, neither creature nor master was destined to stay quiet for long. Even the very grave itself could not contain them. To this day, their hysterical cackling, maniacal laughter, and spectral forms, continue to be heard and seen in and around Carew Castle - and particularly so on wild and windy nights that so closely resemble the long gone thunderous eve upon which alcohol-fuelled Sir Roland Rhys and savage, mad Satan met their infernal, terrible ends.

Whether or not Sir Arthur Conan Doyle took any of his inspiration for *The Hound of the Baskervilles* from the saga of Carew Castle and Sir Roland Rhys is an issue very much beyond the scope of this book. It is worth noting, however, that Doyle did incorporate the legend of one Richard Cabell, an evil squire who lived at Brook Manor, north of nearby Buckfastleigh, Devon in the 1600s, into the pages of his acclaimed novel. And I will say that the parallels that exist between certain, integral parts of both The Hound of the Baskervilles and the unsettling saga of Roland Rhys and Satan are uncanny and most certainly worthy of further study and scrutiny. What is not beyond the scope of this book, however, is the fact that while a ghostly ape has been seen in and around the castle on a number of occasions, its sheer size, shape, bulk and gait are all significantly at major odds with what one would see in a small Barbary macaque - whether physical or spectral.

Could it, instead, be that the legendary story of Sir Roland and his utterly mad butler / pet was simply an invention to try and rationalise and explain away the presence of an ape-like entity seen in the area that defied any and all conventional explanation? Let's see what Jon Downes has to say about this particular possibility.

The Dead Returned?

With what I personally believe to be a high degree of justification and common sense, Jon says of cases such as those cited immediately above:

> 'Unlike the phenomena in other parts of the world, each of the historic British Bigfoot and mystery ape cases have a convenient little folk story, or ghost story, attached to them to explain the presence of these apparitional creatures in the relevant region. Now, my theory is that none of these assertions is correct. I earnestly believe that these stories were invented by village folk in centuries past to try and explain the sightings of monkey-shaped apparitions that would fleetingly appear from time to time and then would vanish as if into thin air.'

Keeping Jon's provocative words in mind, might we, then, consider all of the incidents and stories in this chapter to be clear evidence of life after death in both monkeys and apes? When we chatted in 2010 about such issues as animal spirits and whether or not our furry, flying, and swimming friends might have souls, paranormal expert and good friend Joshua P. Warren - the author of the highly-relevant book, *Pet Ghosts* - told me that he had extensively investigated a series of encounters with apparitional, ancient animals on farmland at Lancaster, South Carolina – one of which seemed to resemble nothing less than, of all things conceivable, a ghostly pterodactyl.

Ghost-hunter Joshua P. Warren at his Paranormal Headquarters. Copyright: Nick Redfern.

Josh told me he had mused very deeply upon the possibility that the paranormal presence of certain extinct animals might very well help explain at least some sightings of monstrous beasts in our presence to this very day - and particularly so those that seemingly appear and vanish in the blink of the proverbial eye.

'Maybe Bigfoot is a "phantimal,"'

said Josh to me, utilizing a term he uses to describe ghostly beasts,

'perhaps even the ghost of a prehistoric creature, similar to the enormous extinct ape, Gigantopithecus, or maybe even the spirits of primitive humans.'

And, in a similar fashion, Josh explained to me, he was not at all adverse to the idea that the world's most famous lake-monster, Nessie, might actually represent some form of 'ghostly plesiosaur', rather than a literal, living animal, or even a colony of animals.

This latter point was closely echoed by the investigative author Jim Marrs. While digging deep into the subject of the U.S. Government's secret research into the realms of so-called remote viewing and psychic spying, Jim learned that elements of the official world had secretly attempted to focus their skills upon solving the riddle of what it is that lurks within the deep and dark waters of Loch Ness, Scotland. It was a very controversial operation, however, as Jim noted. And it led to an utterly amazing conclusion, as he further revealed:

'Several sessions targeting the famous Loch Ness Monster revealed physical traces of the beast – a wake in the water, movement of a large body underwater. Their drawings even resembled a prehistoric plesiosaur, often identified as matching descriptions of Nessie. But when the viewers tried to discover where the object came from or returned to, they hit a dead end. The creature seemed to simply appear and disappear. Considering that reports of human ghosts date back throughout man's history, the Psi Spies seriously considered the possibility that the Loch Ness monster is nothing less than a dinosaur's ghost.' [Author's Note: plesiosaurs were not actually dinosaurs].

Neil's Observations
Commenting on the matter of life after death in animals, Neil Arnold says:

'I've investigated numerous reports of ghostly bears across England over the years. I've often been of the opinion that if people see ghosts of humans then they must surely be able to see ghosts of animals, the most common seem to be spectral pets: dogs, cats, and also horses and birds. However, I've gathered reports over the years of a number of ghostly, wilder animals from lions to apes. Ghostly bears have been reported all over the U.K. Maybe these are lost souls that suffered greatly at the hands of bear-baiting centuries previous.'

Neil is careful to stress, however:

'I don't believe the reports of alleged U.K. wild men cross into ghostly bear territory. For one, bears, in their natural form, are not bipedal. When they do stand on their hind legs they cannot walk far and certainly have no apparent stride. Bears also have muzzles. In the cases of phantom bears I've looked at, in every case a bear has been described, nearly always on all fours and not bipedal.'

Do the spirits of long-extinct animals still roam the Earth - whether on land, in the air, or within the mysterious depths of ancient lakes and oceans? Could such a theory account for the on-going presence of a gorilla-like animal at Bridge 39 on the Shropshire Union Canal? And might the same theory account for the Ghost Ape of Marwood, Martyn's Ape, the beast of Dundonald Castle, Scotland, and Sir Roland Rhys' extraordinarily mad and violent pet macaque, Satan, the laughing, hair-covered butler? Maybe we should not rush to dismiss such thought-provoking possibilities wholly out of hand.

And just to make matters even more confusing and controversial, there is a variation on this issue of the dead returned to our plain of existence. In centuries past, there were widespread beliefs in Britain that the spirits of deceased human beings - never mind just animals - could come back to our world in the form of terrible creatures, some of which closely resembled grossly mutated monkeys and apes, as you will now come to see.

CHAPTER 33
FROM MAN TO BEAST
'...Man has in him two spirits – an animal spirit and a human spirit...'

Dr. Dave Clarke, a long-time Fortean, who has a PhD in folklore, says:

'One enduring folk belief is that human beings, as well as devils, witches and fairies could shape-shift and appear in animal form. This type of story appears in trial records, pamphlets and folklore throughout the middle ages where animal familiars are identified with the devil. Earlier accounts lack the preoccupation with demonic creatures. An early list of shape-shifting apparitions was prepared by a Cistercian monk in North Yorkshire around 1400. It contains accounts of ghosts changing forms from human to crow, dog, goat, horse and even a haystack. These are described as human souls trapped in purgatory, appealing for help from the living to escape their predicament.'

And with respect to the 1879 encounter with the spectral beast of the Shropshire Union Canal, Dave reports:

'This account identifies the Man-Monkey as a human revenant who returns to haunt a bridge in animal form. The manner of its appearance, in the form of "a strange black creature with great white eyes" and the fear created by its actions leaping on the back of the horse, resonates with contemporary accounts of ghostly activity elsewhere...'

British Shape-Shifters

Was the soul of a man who, according to local police knowledge, apparently 'drowned in the cut', really roaming the area in the guise of a spectral monkey-like entity of the type that Dave Clarke described? As far back as the 1800s, Charlotte Burne, who was personally responsible for bringing the story of the Man-Monkey to the attention of people in her classic title *Shropshire Folklore*, most certainly thought so. Or, at the very least, she certainly acknowledged that belief systems of this precise type were in circulation and accepted by many as nothing less than gospel. Burne's thoughts and conclusions on the nature of the Man-Monkey, as well as the rumours circulating that the presence of the animal was in some fashion connected with the death by drowning in the canal of an unknown man, were recorded in 1883. They went as follows:

OPPOSITE: Shape-shifting nightmares. Copyright: Unknown, circa 18th Century.

'I believe this to have originated in the classical and medieval notion of werewolves, living men who could assume the shape of a wolf at pleasure,' Burne began. 'Sometimes also a corpse would arise from its grave in the form of a wolf, and might do incalculable damage if it were not at once beheaded and cast into the nearest stream. This is a Prussian fancy, and the English King John too is said to have gone about as a werewolf after his death. Wolves have been extinct in England long enough to have disappeared from popular tales though not so many centuries as most people suppose, but the Man-Monkey seems very like the old fable in a new guise [Author's Note: Italics Mine].'

O'Donnell's Opinions on the Dead Returned

Elliott O'Donnell, as I have already noted in the chapter of this book dealing with British-based encounters involving out of place baboons, was the author of numerous classic titles on all manner of mysteries, but it is his 1912 book, *Werewolves*, that has a bearing upon the very matters described, and commented upon, by Dr. Dave Clarke and Charlotte Burne. O'Donnell presented a fascinating body of data in his near-legendary book, which is essential reading for anyone wishing to acquaint themselves with hard to find data on British man-beasts, albeit more of a wolf variety than ape-like. Nevertheless, O'Donnell's words are deeply applicable to this particular chapter.

He wrote:

'It is an old belief that the souls of cataleptic and epileptic people, during the body's unconsciousness, adjourned temporarily to animals, and it is therefore only in keeping with such a view to suggest that on the deaths of such people their spirits take permanently the form of animals. This would account for the fact that places where cataleptics and idiots have died are often haunted by semi and by wholly animal types of phantasms.'

O'Donnell's words relative to 'idiots' and 'such people' might not be perceived by the tedious politically-correct brigade of today as being particularly heart-warming, but they do, without doubt, offer a theory that is fascinating to muse upon. And, there are other parallels, too, that can be found in folklore. They also deal with the matter of man becoming terrible animal when physical life ends, and at which point a new life - and a highly strange life, I might add - duly begins.

Suicidal Tendencies

Writer and researcher Andrew Gable, who is the Centre for Fortean Zoology's representative for Maryland and Pennsylvania, USA, says:

'On November 3 [2009], Mindi and I took a trip to Reading to do a bit of early Christmas shopping. While there, we decided to stop at the old Union Canal, so we could check out Lock 49. On August 17, 1875, Louise Bissinger, distraught over her husband's infidelities, took her three children on an outing along the Tulpehocken Creek [Pennsylvania]. She had a basket tied around her waist, and when she reached the area of Lock 49, she grabbed her children tightly and plunged in. The children were still alive when witnesses arrived on the scene, but they drowned before the bodies could be pulled from the canal. The bodies were taken to Gring's Mill nearby. Later reports had it that while Mr. Bissinger mourned the deaths of his children, he callously was unmoved by the death of his wife. The stories have it that the ghostly forms of the Bissinger children are seen walking along the canal's towpath.'

Andrew continues:

> 'Nick Redfern's book Man-Monkey is about the traditions of a shambling humanoid - what could be called a Bigfoot, though it is likely that it, like other British sightings, are something else - along the Union Canal in Shropshire, England. One aspect mentioned was the humanoid as the ghost of a suicide whose body was found in the canal. I had mentioned to him the coincidence of another Union Canal with a suicide in its history, as well. This possible presence of some sort of humanoid furthers the coincidence.'

'Do it, do it!'

Neil Arnold has provided me with the details of a highly unsettling case involving what is clearly an ape of the paranormal and malevolent variety - and, from its physical description, one not at all unlike the Man-Monkey, even down to the slim build, dark colour, and shining eyes - and its link to a near-suicide, one that thankfully, was thwarted at the very last moment. Over to Neil:

> 'In the case of some zooform phenomena, it seems that we are dealing with negative energy as a conjurer of monsters. For instance, the county of Essex has several cases of weird manifestations presenting themselves, but they are forms which clearly are not of some biological or zoological order. At Wallasea Island there was once a place called the Devil's House which sat on the bleak marshlands flanking the River Crouch.
>
> The house, was more for a farm-like abode and took its sinister name from its owner, a chap named Daville, although author Eric Maple notes that "according to the old records it was known as Demon's Tenement as far back as the time of Charles II".
>
> At first the building seemed like many a haunted house in that local folk would refuse to stay in it because of the strange atmospheres and sudden drops in temperature. On other occasions weird sounds were heard, such as the flapping of wings and an overwhelming sense of dread would follow. Such a fear seemed justified when a sergeant, serving in the First World War decided to put the legends to bed and stayed the night in the building. The following morning the sergeant was found in such a terrible state, his pale complexion and refusal to speak had locals worried.'
>
> Another man claimed that he had heard to sound of wings flapping suggesting some giant yet unseen bird was soaring above but the ghostly reputation of the place took a knock when one evening it was reported that a hideous spectre with horns and a long tail was explained by a stray bullock which had sought shelter in the hayloft after being pursued by a dog.'

And, now, as Neil reveals, we come to the story of that aforementioned supernatural ape, and a case of an attempted suicide that never quite came to pass:

> 'During one particular harvest a local labourer experienced a terrible creature whilst working in one of the barns. He had heard his name being called on

several occasions and the sudden drop in temperature told him that something wasn't right. Although spooked, the man continued his work when suddenly he felt as though he was possessed and had a sudden urge to commit suicide.'

The labourer found a piece of old rope, fastened it around his neck as a noose and climbed a ladder to tie the rope around a beam. A voice rasped, "Do it, do it," in his ear, but then something even more bizarre happened. Looking upward the man saw a terrible ape-like creature swinging from the timbers. The phantom ape had bright yellow eyes that glowed in the gloom. It appeared rather slim in form and was completely black in colour. This hideous apparition seemed to jolt him out of his suicidal trance and scrambled down the ladder and fled the barn.'

As for what might have been afoot, Neil says:

'Locals believed the ghastly experiences that had taken place in the building were the product of Devil worship which had taken place years before. Such negative energy, depending on the individual who experiences it, seems to have the ability to prey on the human psyche and cast out weird, absurd holographic-type entities which feed on fear. Such devils can take on many forms, either as unseen poltergeists which hurl items around the place or attack their victims, to nefarious familiars ranging from disfigured demonic cats, headless black dogs, and goodness knows what else.'

'There crouched a figure of evil'

Commenting on the above affair, Richard Freeman relates the details of yet another beastly barn saga:

'A very similar creature, perhaps of the same type (whatever that is!) was seen in the mid-1800s by Irish historian Dermot MacManus' father when he was around fourteen and recorded by him in his book Middle Kingdom: The Fairie World of Ireland. His father had returned from his school in England for the Christmas holidays. He was playing hide and seek with his older brother, Arthur, around the farm on which they lived. It was afternoon and still light. Whilst tiptoeing through the granary he heard the horses in the stables below stamping and snorting as if they were alarmed by something.

Investigating he saw that the horses were panicking and shying away from a trapdoor above a manger where food was thrown down. Looking up he saw a horrific creature not twelve feet from his head.'

In the words of Dermot MacManus himself:

'There crouched a figure of evil with baleful eyes, blazing red like coals of fire. It was huddled in a compact ball, as a boy his own size might look squatting on his haunches. My father remembered only those awful eyes, the squatness of the awful body hunched in the dark cover of the manger, and one awful hand, a human hand but how different! It gripped the edge of the manger and as a dirty greyish-brown. The fingers were bone and sinew and ended not in human nails but curved, pointed claws.'

Richard Freeman concludes:

> 'The scared youth jumped back into the granary, slammed the trap door and ran to warn his brother. They both fled back to the house.'

Black Dog Parallels

In his definitive book on the subject, *Explore Phantom Black Dogs*, author and researcher Bob Trubshaw wrote the following words:

> 'The folklore of phantom black dogs is known throughout the British Isles. From the Black Shuck of East Anglia to the Mauthe Dhoog of the Isle of Man there are tales of huge spectral hounds "darker than the night sky" with eyes "glowing red as burning coals". The phantom black dog of British and Irish folklore, which often forewarns of death, is part of a world-wide belief that dogs are sensitive to spirits and the approach of death, and keep watch over the dead and dying. North European and Scandinavian myths dating back to the Iron Age depict dogs as corpse eaters and the guardians of the roads to hell. Medieval folklore includes a variety of "Devil dogs" and spectral hounds.'

Ancient British lore holds that the phantom black dogs had the ability to appear and vanish in the blink of an eye, just like a number of British Bigfoot. The ghostly dogs would almost unanimously frequent the same locations time and again, and particularly old bridges, waterways, paths and crossroads - again, just like certain mysterious apes in Britain. And certain spectral hounds sometimes exhibited signs of outright hostility - something of which the Man-Monkey of 1879 was most certainly guilty. And that's far from being the end of the matter.

Shocked by the Shug

Perhaps the most famous of all of the phantom hounds of old Britain are those that are said to have frequented - and, in some cases, still frequent - the ancient roads and pathways of Norfolk, Essex, Suffolk, and Sussex. Their names include Black Shuck, the Shug Monkey, and the Shock. The Shuck and the Shock are classic black dogs; whereas, interestingly enough, the Shug Monkey - as we have seen - is described as being a combination of spectral monkey and immense hound, amongst several other beasts, too, as Sam Holland's testimony of his 1956 encounter with such a beast in Suffolk has clearly demonstrated.

Even their very names have intriguing origins: while some researchers consider the possibility that all of the appellations had their origins in the word Shucky - an ancient east-coast term meaning shaggy - others, as I have already noted, suggest a far more sinister theory; namely that Shock, Shuck, and Shug are all based upon the Anglo-Saxon scucca, meaning demon; a most apt description, for sure. More notable: in the case of Danny Thomas, the Man-Monkey-like beast that he was so in fear of, and that he firmly believed was solely responsible for the Tay Bridge disaster of December 1879, became known as the Shuggy - a name that must surely have had the same, obscure point of origin as that of the Shug Monkey and Black Shuck.

Equally of note and relevance, the phantom black dog would often appear just before, or during, a thunder-storm. We might very well postulate, perhaps a thunder-storm not unlike that which led to large-scale tragedy and disaster at the Tay Bridge on that long-gone fateful and fatal night in December 1879. And, remember, a massive ape-like beast was seen, and duly vanished, during a powerful thunderstorm in the vicinity of Penzance, Cornwall in 1789. And just to hammer home the connections even further, phantom black dogs have, on occasion, been interpreted as the souls of departed human beings returned to our plane of existence in the form of vile, nightmarish beasts, as I will now demonstrate, courtesy of two choice examples.

The Dogmen of Newgate

Bob Trubshaw notes:

> 'Newgate Gaol was the scene of a haunting by "a walking spirit in the likeness of a black dog.'

So the story went, says Bob,

> 'Luke Hutton, a criminal executed at York in the late 1590s, left behind an account of the phantom hound. Published as a pamphlet in 1612, The *Discovery of a London Monster, called the black dog of Newgate* suggested the dog was the ghost of a scholar imprisoned in Newgate who had been killed and eaten by starving inmates.'

A Beastly Brother

Then there is the weird tale of William and David Sutor. The dark saga all began late one night in December 1728, when William, a Scottish farmer, was hard at work in his fields and heard an unearthly shriek that was accompanied by the briefest of glimpses of a large, dark-coloured dog. And on several more occasions in both 1729 and 1730, the dog returned, always seemingly intent on plaguing the Sutor family. It was in late November of 1730, however, that the affair ultimately reached its apex. Once again the mysterious hound manifested before the farmer, but this time, incredibly, it was supposedly heard to speak in English, and uttered the following, concise words:

> 'Come to the spot of ground within half an hour.'

The shocked William did so; and there waiting for him was the spectral animal.

> 'In the name of God and Jesus Christ, what are you that troubles me?'

Pleaded the terrified William. The hound answered that he was none other than David Sutor - William's brother - and that he had killed a man at that very spot some thirty-five years earlier.

William cried:

> 'David Sutor was a man and you appear as a dog.'

To which the hound replied:

> 'I killed him with a dog; therefore I am made to appear as a dog, and I tell you to go bury these bones.'

Finally on December 3, and after much frantic searching and digging, the bones of the murdered man were finally found at the spot in question, and were duly given a respectful, Christian burial within the confines of

OPPOSITE: Beware of the black dog. Copyright: Abraham Fleming, 1577

A straunge,

and terrible Wunder wrought
very late in the parish Church
of Bongay, a Towzn of no great distance from the citie of Norwich, namely the fourth of this August, in ye yeere of
our Lord 1577. in a great tempest of violent raine, lightning, and thunder, the
like wherof hath been sel-
dome sene.

With the appærance of an horrible shaped thing, sensibly perceiued of the
people then and there
assembled.

Drawen into a plain method according to the written copye.
by Abraham Fleming.

the old Blair Churchyard. The dog - David Sutor in animalistic, spectral form, legend maintains - vanished, and was reportedly never seen again.

The Warrington Wild Thing

And, there is yet another story of a hairy man-beast that some believed to have been a human transformed via supernatural means. Interestingly, this one - just like in the original Man-Monkey story of 1879, the tale of Old Ned's Devil, and that of the legend of Dorset's Monkey Jump - involves a creature encountered by someone riding a horse and trap in centuries past. Neil Arnold relates the details:

> 'The town of Warrington, which sits on the banks of the River Mersey, is also a borough and unitary authority area of Cheshire. According to an obscure story from the 18th century [one that, in the 1940s was told to writer and researcher Wally Barnes, author of the book *Ghosts, Mysteries & Legends of Old Warrington*], a terrifying man-beast once stalked a farm in Warrington. One such farm, once known as Peggy Gronachs Chicken Farm harboured a bizarre story. According to Barnes, Peggy Gronach was '"...the most evil, ugly and haggard old wretch ever seen in the vicinity".

> According to legend Peggy Gronach was a witch who escaped the original 17th century witch hunts which took place in Norwich. When Peggy moved to Warrington, she was the dread of the local community: Her run down shack would spook many a passer-by and no-one was ever brave enough to venture through the undergrowth. However, one day a group of young children were playing near the old farm and decided that, for a dare, they would approach the cottage. When they were within a few metres a terrifying roar emanated from the building and staring through the grime-laced window pane was a hideous face. Then, Peggy emerged from the farmhouse and began screaming at the children who, of course, fled the area.'

> When the terrified children returned home to their parents, they spoke of the great roar, to which their parents responded that the crone must have owned a ferocious dog. However, the children were adamant that what they saw peering from the house was a hair covered man with burning eyes, pointed ears and horns on his head.

> However bizarre the report may have seemed, the following month, according to Barnes, *'...a farmhand was driving a horse and trap about a mile from the cottage when without warning the horse reared up. The farmhand then saw a hideous ghoul-like creature under a tree ready to pounce'* [Author's Note: Italics Mine].'

> Local villagers began to spread rumour that Peggy Gronach had supernatural powers and that to explain the man-beast, they believed she could transform herself into the terrifying man-beast which had been reported around the area. Shortly after the farmhand's encounter, a local farmer reported that one of his cows had been attacked. He found it dead and its head was hanging on my thread – only a very powerful creature could have committed such a crime. So, the local vicar, accompanied by "a gang of religious zealots" visited Peggy's remote cottage in the hope of driving her away from the village. However, upon arrival they found no trace of the old hag nor the hairy

monster, the only sign that some '"thing" had been around was the carcass of a half-eaten goat.

'There were no further sightings of the terrible monster, or Peggy Gronach, and the building was knocked down. Barnes however, ends the tale with a chilling climax, stating that, "Many years later workmen dug up the remains of a giant bullock – or was it a bullock? Bullocks do not have human skulls. Think about it.'

Neil's wraps up his thoughts on this most odd affair:

'This intriguing tale may sound far-fetched, but maybe, just maybe, out there in the sticks of old Warrington, there still lurks a frightful, hairy monster, a creature which, during the day either retires deep into the woods, or transforms itself into the shrivelled form of Peggy Gronach.'

The Final Word

The last missive on this admittedly highly controversial aspect of the British Bigfoot controversy goes to Elliott O'Donnell:

'According to Paracelsus, Man has in him two spirits - an animal spirit and a human spirit - and that in after life he appears in the shape of whichever of these two spirits he has allowed to dominate him. If, for example, he has obeyed the spirit that prompts him to be sober and temperate, then his phantasm resembles a man; but on the other hand, if he has given way to his carnal and bestial cravings, then his phantasm is earthbound, in the guise of some terrifying and repellent animal.'

While O'Donnell's words were meant as a collective warning to his many and faithful readers, frankly, the latter sounds far more appealing and adventurous than does coming back as some chain-rattling spectre of human proportions. Give me terrifying and repellent, rather than sober and temperate, any day of the week!

Silent Invasion

The Pennsylvania UFO-Bigfoot Casebook

Stan Gordon

CHAPTER 34
THE BRITISH BIGFOOT AND UFOs
'...If UFOs travel by worm-holes, and if Bigfoot does the same, that might allow for a connection between the two...'

Stan Gordon is a well-known, long-term researcher, writer and authority on many things of a Fortean nature - as is clearly evidenced by his excellent and insightful 2010 book, *Silent Invasion: The Pennsylvania UFO-Bigfoot Casebook*, which was sent to me for review in January of that year. Now, I know for sure that any book suggesting Bigfoot may somehow be inextricably linked with the UFO phenomenon is bound to raise distinct hackles in certain quarters, but such reports undeniably exist, so examine them we must...

When Aliens and Mystery Animals Meet
The fact of the matter is that there is surely not a Bigfoot researcher out there who has not been exposed to even just a few creature cases that absolutely reek of undeniable high-strangeness, and that place the hairy man-beasts into definitively Fortean - rather than zoological or cryptozoological - realms, whether in Britain, the United States, Australia, or elsewhere. But, whether or not those same Bigfoot researchers are willing to give such reports some degree of credence is a very different matter.

Fortunately, there are a number of researchers who recognise that as much as it would be undeniably preferable to place Bigfoot in a purely flesh and blood category and nothing else whatsoever, there is a significant and hard to deny body of data and testimony that points in a very different direction. And it's a direction that, to his credit, Stan Gordon does not shy away from. Indeed, Stan's book is a first-class study of a truly weird wave of Bigfoot / UFO activity that swamped the good folk of Pennsylvania, USA in the period from 1972 to 1974.

Silent Invasion is a swirling cauldron filled with dark and ominous woods; glowing-eyed beast-men prowling the countryside by night; strange lights in the sky; UFO landings; neighborhoods gripped by terror and fear; and much, much more, too. And, it's thanks to Stan's research, as well as his in-depth files prepared back when all of the dark drama was at its very height, that we're now able to appreciate the curious chaos and calamity that collectively hit the unsuspecting people of Pennsylvania all those years ago.

But, that's not all: Macabre Men in Black, paranormal activity, psychic possession, secret government

---

Stan Gordon's Bigfoot/UFO-themed *Silent Invasion*. Copyright: Stan Gordon (author), Michael Coe (cover design), and Keith Bastianini (cover illustration).

---

interest in Bigfoot, and prophetic visions of a dark and foreboding future, all come to the fore in a book that is guaranteed to make you think twice - probably far more than twice, actually - about the true nature of Bigfoot.

To his lasting credit, Stan does not just take the simplistic approach that Bigfoot is some sort of 'pet of the aliens', as some might very well assume. Instead, he logically, forthrightly and with supportive data in-hand, makes it abundantly clear that - even if we don't have all of the answers, and maybe even hardly any - addressing the Bigfoot controversy from a purely zoological perspective alone just simply does not work, at all.

He notes the problematic lack of a body (even just one would be nice), the meager evidence of Bigfoot's eating habits, and its uncanny ability to always avoid capture - not to mention that the beast appears to be nigh-on bullet-proof, too. And, I do mean that literally. Stan also hammers home, time and again, that when and where Bigfoot turns up, so - very often - do a host of other Fortean favorites. Something strange and diabolical was afoot in Pennsylvania between 1972 and 1974. Bigfoot, UFOs and a plethora of paranormal activity were all in evidence. Somewhere, somehow, there is a connection - even if it's one we're not fully able to understand or - in some cases - accept, just yet. Until we do, however, *Silent Invasion* will provide you with much to think about, to muse upon, and to ponder on. And it may just make you totally revise your views on North America's most famous ape-man. It's also a book that can be said to have a major bearing on Bigfoot in Britain too, since the hairy thing and UFOs are not exactly strangers in these quarters either.

A Man-Monkey-UFO Connection

Regardless of what people may personally feel or conclude about the Bigfoot-UFO connection - or, more correctly, the theoretical connection - none can deny that when we go looking for places in Britain where both enigmas have been seen and encountered, there's certainly no shortage of stories to address. As I have noted, a number of sightings of the Man-Monkey of the Shropshire Union Canal were made in the nearby village of Ranton. It so happens that, back in the 1950s, Ranton was the site of a famous - but now largely forgotten - UFO encounter.

Researcher Gavin Gibbons wrote in 1957 that one October evening in 1954, a Dutchman living in England named Tony Roestenberg returned home to find his wife, Jessie, 'in a terrified state'. According to Jessie: earlier that day nothing less than a flying saucer hovered over their isolated farmhouse in Ranton. In addition, Jessie could see peering down from the craft two very 'Nordic'-like men that could have stepped right out of the pages of the controversial Desmond Leslie-George Adamski tome, *Flying Saucers Have Landed*. Their foreheads were high, their hair was long and fair, and they seemed to have 'pitiful' looks on their faces.

The strange craft reportedly circled the family's home twice, before streaking away. Curiously, on the following Sunday, Tony Roestenberg had a 'hunch' that if he climbed on the roof of his house 'he would see something unusual', which he most certainly did. It was a high-flying, cigar-shaped object that vanished into the clouds.

Gavin Gibbons, who investigated the case personally, stated:

> 'When I visited the Roestenberg's house almost three weeks after the sighting...Jessie Roestenberg appeared. She seemed highly strained and nervous and her husband, coming in later, was also very strained. It was evident that something most unusual had occurred.'

A Castle Ring Connection

Castle Ring, Staffordshire - from where a number of significant Bigfoot-type reports have surfaced - also has longstanding link to UFO activity. Graham Allen, former head of the now-defunct Etchinghill, Rugeley-based Staffordshire UFO Group, and who had taken over the reins from the group's founder, Irene Bott, several years earlier, said in 2005:

'Castle Ring is the highest point on the [Cannock] Chase which makes it a good place for UFO spotting. There have been numerous incidents of UFOs, which could be because you are more likely to see something from a high point.'

Allen elaborated that with respect to unearthly encounters at Castle Ring:

'There have been reports of something landing there in the 1960s. From a research point of view there are a high number of reports around ancient sites. One argument could be that ancient sites have been located there because of the incidents of UFOs and natural phenomenon. There could be locations where there could be magnetic influences in the ground which have been attributed to earth lights.'

A Shug Monkey, a Wild Man and a Saucer

Then there is the Shug Monkey of Rendlesham Forest, Suffolk - which also happens to be the site of what is undeniably Britain's most famous UFO encounter: that of December 1980 and most vividly described in *Left at East Gate* by Larry Warren and Peter Robbins. And, to illustrate still further the UFO-hairy man connection, just down the road, so to speak, from Rendlesham Forest is the town of Orford - home to the legendary wild man caught in the seas off the coast of Orford all those centuries ago.

The MIB and Two Monsters

In 1968, Alistair Baxter - who had a lifelong interest in stories and folklore relative to Irish and Scottish lake monsters - travelled to Loch Ness and spent nine weeks armed with a camera and binoculars quietly and carefully monitoring the loch for any unusual activity of the long-necked and humped variety. Baxter never did see the elusive beast of Loch Ness, but he was able to speak with numerous people who had seen it. After being at the loch-side almost constantly for five weeks, however, an unusual event occurred. Baxter was awoken in the middle of the night by a curious humming sound that was emanating from a bright, small, ball of light about the size of a football that - at a height of around fifteen feet from the ground - was slowly and carefully making its way through the surrounding trees that enveloped Baxter's modestly sized tent.

Suddenly, and without warning, the ball of light shot into the sky to a height of several hundred feet and hovered in deathly silence over the still waters of Loch Ness. For reasons that Baxter was at a loss to explain, he felt an overwhelming urge to

Look out for the dreaded Men in Black. Copyright: Nick Redfern.

go back to sleep and the next thing he knew it was daybreak. But the strangeness had barely begun.

Shortly after breakfast three men in black suits appeared outside of Baxter's tent seemingly out of nowhere and proceeded to ask him if he had seen anything unusual during the night. He replied that he hadn't, at which point one of the three men turned to his two colleagues and made what Baxter said was 'a strange smile'. He turned to face Baxter. 'We might return,' said one of the mysterious men in black and all three departed by simply walking off into the woods.

They never did return.
Most interesting of all, and of deep relevance to the overall story this book tells, for the following three nights, Baxter had a recurring and frightening dream of a large and lumbering ape-man that would pace outside of his tent and that would then head down to the shores of the loch, whereupon, under a star-lit sky, it would tilt its head back, wail loudly and stand staring at the ink-black water. The dream would always end the same way: with an image of a huge and ominous atomic mushroom cloud exploding in the distance, and the beginning of the Third World War and the end of civilization.

Ape Men and Abductions
Baxter's story is made more thought-provoking for the following reason: I have numerous accounts in my own files from people who believe that they have undergone some form of 'alien abduction' and who, they maintain, have been shown images by 'the aliens' of a desolate and irradiated Earth of the near-future that had been ravaged by a world-wide nuclear war.

'This is a warning of what will happen if we don't change our ways,'

one of the abductees – Ann-Marie - said to me. Interestingly, she told of a frightening and futuristic scene that she believed showed a ruined and permanently cloud-covered city of London where the starving survivors were forced to do battle for food with strange, hairy ape men that would surface at night out of the rubble and remains of the flattened London Underground rail tunnels.

How do we explain such undeniably rogue events like those of Alistair Baxter and that of Ann-Marie? Well, right now, we don't, simply because we can't. All we can really say is that they offer yet further food for thought that the British Bigfoot is not all that it initially appears to be. Perhaps, until we do know more, it's apposite and wise to place such very hard to define cases in our definitive grey-basket and leave them there to languish. But before we move on to other avenues, there are the UFO-related words of a certain, well-known figure in Forteana to address…

Of Dimensions and Window Areas
Ronan Coghlan is the author of a number of acclaimed books, including *A Dictionary of Cryptozoology* and - with Gary Cunningham - *The Mystery Animals of Ireland*. In a 2012 interview with me, Ronan provided his views on the nature of the British Bigfoot, and what he believes may be evidence of a link between the phenomenon and that of UFOs.

'The idea that there is a viable, reproducing population of apes or humanoids in Britain is totally risible; it just couldn't be. So, alternative explanations for their presence are to be sought,'

Begins Ronan:

'A lot of the British reports seem to be quite authentic. So, there probably are actual beasts or humanoids out there. And the question is: How did they arrive there in the first place?'

Ronan answers his question with the following words of reply:

'It's now becoming acceptable in physics to say there are alternative universes.'

He continues on this controversial but thought-provoking path:

'The main pioneer of this is Professor Michio Kaku, of the City College of New York. He has suggested that not only are there alternate universes, but when ours is about to go out in a couple of billion years, we might have the science to migrate to a more congenial one that isn't going to go out. I think he expects science to keep improving for countless millennia, which is very optimistic of him, but whatever one thinks about that, the idea of alternative universes is now gaining an acceptance among physicists, and he's the name to cite in this area.'

The subject is far from one lacking in mysteries and questions, however, as Ronan acknowledges:

'Now, how do you get into, or out of, alternative universes? Well, the answer is quite simple: You have heard of worm-holes, I'm sure? No-one has ever seen a worm-hole, I hasten to add. They are hypothetical, but mainstream physicists say they could be there, and there's one particular type called the Lorentzian Traversable Wormhole. Physicists admit there is a possibility that this exists, and it would be like a short-cut, from one universe to another. Thus, for example, it's rather like a portal: Something from the other universe would come through it. Or, something from another planet could come through it.'

Turning his attentions towards the links between worm-holes and bizarre beasts, Ronan comments that:

'If there are any of these worm-holes on Earth, it would be quite easy for anything to come through, and it's quite possible any number of anomalous creatures could find their way through from time to time. You remember John Keel and his window-areas? That would tend to indicate there's a worm-hole in the vicinity; such as Point Pleasant, West Virginia, where the Mothman was seen.'

'I have the distinct suspicion we are dealing with window-areas that either contact some other planet, or they contact another universe. My money is on the other universe, rather than the other planet, to be honest with you. Either a short-cut through time, or a short-cut through space, is recognized as possible these days. This is kind of cutting-edge physics, as it were.

'Now, the other one isn't cutting-edge physics at all. It's my own little theory. I think, looking at a great many legends, folk-tales, and things of that nature, it is possible to vibrate at different rates. And if you vibrate at a different rate, you are not seen. You are not tangible. And, then, when your vibration changes, you are seen, and you are tangible; maybe that this has something to do with Bigfoot appearing and disappearing in a strange fashion.

'And, finally, on the question of UFOs: Quite a large number of Bigfoot-type creatures have been seen in the vicinity of UFOs. I'm not saying there's necessarily a connection between the two, but they do – quite often – turn up in the same areas. Now, if UFOs travel by worm-holes, and if Bigfoot does the same, that might allow for a connection between the two. They might not be mutually exclusive.'

Regardless of the extent to which certain aspects of the worm-hole theories may be wholly theoretical, possible, or literal reality, and whether or not there is some connection between UFOs and Bigfoot, Ronan, just like Jon Downes, Neil Arnold, Andy Roberts, and Richard Freeman, is absolutely certain of one thing:

'There's no possibility of a British, native, great-ape.'

Ronan Coghlan has deeply studied the Bigfoot/UFO angle. Copyright: Nick Redfern.

CHAPTER 35
BEAST OF THE MIND
'...He became more troublesome and bold.
In brief, he escaped my control...'

Alexandra David-Neel was born Louise Eugenie Alexandrine Marie David in France in October 1868, and was the first woman to gain the title of a Tibetan lama. A committed Buddhist who lived to the highly impressive age of one hundred years, she was a noted traveller, and someone who had a deep passion and love for Asia, and particularly so the Himalayas - home, interestingly enough, to the famous Abominable Snowman, or Yeti. David-Neel was also someone who brought to the Western world the phenomenon of the Tulpa, which may possibly help to answer the ever-vexing question of: what really is the British Bigfoot?

'A magically produced illusion or creation'

Essentially, a Tulpa is an enigmatic form of life that has its origins within the mysterious depths of the human mind; but which, when carefully focused upon by the creator, dutifully nurtured, and significantly empowered over an extensive period of time, can break free of its brain-based moorings and take on a degree of independent reality in the world at large. In simple terms, what we imagine internally - when we, quite literally, put our minds to it - can mutate into full-blown reality of an external nature. Walter Yeeling Evans-Wentz, a writer, anthropologist, and pioneer in the study of Tibetan Buddhism, said of the Tulpa concept:

> 'In as much as the mind creates the world of appearances, it can create any particular object desired. The process consists of giving palpable being to a visualization, in very much the same manner as an architect gives concrete expression in three dimensions to his abstract concepts after first having given them expression in the two-dimensions of his blue-print.'

He elaborated further:

> 'The Tibetans call the One Mind's concretized visualization the Khorva (Hkhorva), equivalent to the Sanskrit Sangsara; that of an incarnate deity, like the Dalai or Tashi Lama, they call a Tul-ku (Sprul-sku), and that of a magician a Tul-pa (Sprul-pa), meaning a magically produced illusion or creation. A master of yoga can dissolve a Tul-pa as readily as he can create it; and his own illusory human body, or Tul-ku, he can likewise dissolve, and thus outwit Death. Sometimes, by means of this magic, one human form can be amalgamated with another, as in the instance of the wife of Marpa, guru of Milarepa, who ended her life by incorporating herself in the body of Marpa.'

Monks, Monkeys, and Séances

Neel, who was never one to turn her nose up at a new experience, chose to attempt to
wn Tulpa after learning of, and becoming fascinated and slight awed by, the concept from
She duly focused her attentions on the image of a kindly Friar Tuck-type character from the
s of the somewhat Woodwose-like Robin Hood of Sherwood Forest, itself a locale noted for
ving-eyed Bigfoot, as we have seen.

After months of deep meditation, in which she visualised her creation gaining form, David-Neel provided it with a character, history and background, and the day finally came when the mind-monk cast away its chains of the brain and strode forth into the heart of the real world. At first, David-Neel could only see the figure in her peripheral vision, somewhat shadowy and ethereal, not unlike some of the British Bigfoot, it could be convincingly argued. That, however, soon changed, and not in a positive fashion either.

At first, all was good. In David-Neel's own words:

> 'He became a kind of guest, living in my apartment. I then broke my seclusion and started for a tour, with my servants and tents. The monk included himself in the party. Though I lived in the open riding on horseback for miles each day, the illusion persisted. It was not necessary for me to think of him to make him appear. The phantom performed various actions of the kind that are natural to travelers and that I had not commanded. For instance, he walked, stopped, looked around him. The illusion was mostly visual, but sometimes I felt as if a robe was lightly rubbing against me, and once a hand seemed to touch my shoulder.'

But, the friendly monk was not all that he appeared to be. Subtly, over time, he began to change, as David-Neel noted with regret later on. She reflected on the affair some years later, in the following fashion:

> 'The fat, chubby-cheeked fellow grew leaner, his face assumed a vaguely mocking, sly, malignant look. He became more troublesome and bold. In brief, he escaped my control.'

There was no choice: if David-Neel allowed her creation to continue living, it had the potential to pose a very real threat to each and every one of those with whom it crossed paths. So, there was only one option available to her: the Monk had to be reabsorbed into David-Neel's mind, and then banished into the depths of her subconscious, where it would ultimately, and eventually, fragment into nothingness, and its 'life' would be forever over.

According to David-Neel, it took more than half a year for the Monk to finally lose form, return to her control, and ultimately vanish from our 3-D existence, and back into her dreams and imagination. And,

Alexandra David-Neel, a major contributor to the Tulpa controversy. Copyright: Unknown, 1924.

eventually, and to David-Neel's great and lasting relief, it was gone from those realms, too, utterly and finally obliterated. But, the battle between David-Neel, who wished the creature dead and buried, and her creation, that was determined to cling on to its new-found existence no matter what, had proved to be a long and emotionally torturous one - thus demonstrating that creating a Tulpa is a matter that Should never, under any circumstances whatsoever, be entered into lightly or without the benefit of a high degree of careful forethought.

David-Neel was not the only one to attempt such a potentially dicey undertaking. A Polish medium born Teofil Modrzejewski, but who adopted the name of Franek Kluski, did very much likewise. He succeeded in summoning from the depths of his mind and imagination a wide range of beasts that have become absolute staple parts of cryptozoology: a mysterious ape, a giant, spectral bird, a huge cat, and a ghostly hound were just some of the Tulpas that put in appearances during Kluski's early-20th Century séances.

Might, then, the British Bigfoot be a Tulpa, something created and unleashed upon us Brits long ago, but which now deeply enjoys its existence in our world, and has no intention of returning - ever - to the domain of the human mind and, ultimately, the pits of complete and irreversible obliteration? Maybe. There is a fascinating story strongly suggesting that our old friend - the Man-Monkey of the Shropshire Union Canal - may not be the ghost of a deceased man or animal, or a circus escapee, after all, but could be nothing less than a British, and monstrous, equivalent of Alexandra David-Neel's sinister monk.

The Abomination of the Abbey

Psychic-questing books, like *The Green Stone* by Graham Phillips and Martin Keatman, and Andy Collins' books on the subject, such as *The Black Alchemist* and *The Second Coming*, have long fascinated me. But, it's Keatman and Phillips' sequel to *The Green Stone* - namely, *The Eye of Fire* - that we need to focus on here, and which contains a strange and intriguing reference to Ranton Abbey, which is situated only the very briefest of trips away from the infamous, haunted bridge where the Man-Monkey has for so long made its dark and diabolical dwelling.

Ranton Abbey - known more correctly as the Augustinian Priory - was founded by Robert Fitz-Noel during the reign of Henry Plantagenet, with the construction having been completed by 1150. In the early 19th Century, the property became part of the estate of the Ansons of Shugborough, latterly the Earls of Lichfield - who are, themselves, hardly what we would call strangers to the British Bigfoot, as we have seen. Today, the abbey is, unfortunately, in ruins, having been accidentally ravaged and destroyed by fire during the Second World War, while occupied by Dutch soldiers. And, with that said, on to the story.

While much of *The Eye of Fire* is far beyond the scope of this book, the relevant data relates to a July 1982 trip to the abbey that the team of investigators in the book embarked upon, as part of their quest to locate the Eye of Fire of the book's title. Basically, the relevant parts of Philips and Keatman's saga reveal how one of the characters in the book, named Mary Heath, created - back in the 19th Century - a monstrous 'Guardian' at the abbey, whose role was to protect an ancient artefact, one that plays a vital role in the story.

Interestingly, the 'Guardian' is described in the book's pages in highly ominous tones, and, variously, as:

> 'a complete blackness, seething within itself, shapeless but at the same time having substance'; as 'an abomination'; and as a heavy-breathing 'great beast.'

The 'Guardian', we quickly come to learn, is a horrendous, protector-style thought-form, brought into being, and roaming around an ancient abode in the heart of Ranton. But there's more. The vile Tulpa was reportedly created by Mary Heath in 1875. How intriguing that an ominous thought-form was created in Ranton in 1875, and then - only four years later - the Man-Monkey was seen rampaging around the nearby (in fact, the very nearby) Bridge 39 on the Shropshire Union Canal. Could it be that Mary Heath's monstrous offspring and the Man-Monkey were (and still are) one and the very same? Admittedly, this is a highly speculative and controversial question, but it is a question I simply cannot bring myself to dismiss out of hand. Rather, I suspect, it may offer us a most convincing explanation for at least some of the strange beasts that have passed, and that continue to pass, for the enigmatic phenomenon that has become known as the British Bigfoot.

Back to the Beast of Bolam

Some might very well say that what I am about to relate now is evidence that the story of the Beast of Bolam - as related earlier in these pages - should have been relegated to the section of this book on hoaxing. But upon careful, studious balance, I most certainly think not. Hopefully you'll see why, and you may even agree with me, bearing in mind what we have seen, so far, about the Tulpa phenomenon. One of the little-known, and seldom talked about, aspects of the Bolam affair is that in February 2003 - only one month after the amazing encounter with a one-dimensional Bigfoot-type creature reported by Jon Downes and members of the Twilight Worlds team occurred - a story appeared in the local press that suggested a very down to earth explanation for the presence of the creature. In an article titled Back to the Beast of Bolam: Hoaxers' Horror

The realm of the Bolam Beast. Copyright: Centre for Fortean Zoology.

of Bolam Beast, a journalist with the Newcastle-based *Evening Chronicle* - one Andy Lloyd - reported that:

> 'Young hoaxers today revealed how they created a monster myth only months before the real life Northumberland Bigfoot reared its head.'

The article told of how Harriet Warman and Alex Dordoy - then seventeen and eighteen, respectively - had hired a gorilla costume from a local shop, and duly roamed the pathways of Kielder Forest in the summer of 2002, as part of an arts project at school. And as Andy Lloyd noted: 'So the pals, both sixth formers at Gosforth High School in Newcastle, were spooked when they discovered Northumberland does have its own Yeti legend.' Harriet, who lived in Gosforth, told the *Evening Chronicle*:

> 'We were amazed - it was really weird when we saw the news about the Bigfoot, we followed it closely. We visited Kielder Forest with the idea of a photography project. The place was so atmospheric a Bigfoot myth seemed a great idea. We hired a gorilla costume from a fancy dress shop and took turns to dress up as Bigfoot and take pictures. We spent three days there. It was boiling hot inside the costume and the forest was full of midges.'

She continued:

> 'The idea was to recreate some of the famous Bigfoot photos from America with the animal walking away, as if a human and a monster had encountered each other and the person has grabbed their camera, snapped and hoped. We tried to capture that shaky, don't quite know what it is effect, but we also developed it as a story, from a police hunt for the beast to pictures of Bigfoot visiting a corner shop.'

Harriet added:

> 'No-one has taken a photo of this creature in Northumberland, but our photos show how easy it is to create a fake.'

Her final words, specifically on the matter of the Beast of Bolam encounter investigated by, and even witnessed by, Jon Downes, were:

> 'Lots of people in school are coming up and asking if we are behind this sighting, but I can say we weren't responsible for this one.'

And as the *Evening Chronicle's* Andy Lloyd noted in closing:

> 'Alex and Harriet were among dozens of young artists from the North East to devise arts projects through the Samling Visual Arts Foundation. Linda Russell, head of sixth form at Gosforth High School, said: "The project caused a real talking point in the school - the younger students loved it.'

So, you may wonder, where am I going with all of this? Well, let's look at the facts, such as they are. Most - but, granted, not all - of the reports of the Bolam beast did originate around the time that the kids from Gosforth High School were running around in an ape costume in the depths of Kielder Forest, which just so happens to be the largest man-made forest in all of England. The problem, however, is that the distance from Kielder Forest to Bolam Lake is more than forty miles, and the kids who took part in the arts project are adamant that all their activities occurred at the forest, and never, even on a solitary occasion, at the lake. But, Gosforth High School is situated only seven miles from the scene of all the action at Bolam Lake. In view of the close proximity between lake and school, maybe someone else - perhaps, even another student who took inspiration from the actions of Harriet Warman and Alex Dordoy - may have later, and secretly, hired the very same gorilla costume and decided to take part in some high jinks at the lake.

Such is not an impossible scenario. But, here's the important thing: regardless of what may have been behind the sightings at Bolam Lake - a real beast, a kid in a costume, or some odd combination of both, possibly, and incredibly, even at the very same time - the encounters most certainly instilled in the minds of many, including Jon Downes, other members of the Centre for Fortean Zoology, and the Twilight Worlds people, the idea that there really was a Beast of Bolam in the area.

Thus, with deep belief and firm expectation both brewing and expanding at near-exponential rates, is it feasible that - in a truly ironic and astonishing fashion - the one-dimensional monster that appeared before the startled eyes of Jon Downes and others was actually a thought-form, one unknowingly born out of that same belief and expectation, and which manifested before those present in all its shadow-like glory? Certainly, that particularly memorable encounter could not, under any circumstances whatsoever, be blamed upon the antics of a student of Gosforth High School - particularly so when one takes into consideration the utterly 'flat', shadow-style nature of the entity that appeared before the amazed and shocked throng.

Perhaps, then, we should give some very serious and deep thought to the idea that by sowing the seeds of a Bigfoot in the area, the antics of the kids of Gosforth High School caught the attention of numerous, seasoned monster-hunters who, all collectively hopeful that they just might be lucky enough to see the creature of Bolam Lake, inadvertently created a Tulpa equivalent of that very beast that, for a few brief moments - and right in front of Jon Downes, no less - had a tenuous grasp on external reality, before winking out and, perhaps, being reabsorbed into the minds of its unknowing creators: Jon, the CFZ and Twilight Worlds?

Neil on Tulpas

Neil Arnold is inclined to give a high degree of credence to the Tulpa theory, too. In January 2012 he told me that on the night of August 24 of the previous year, 2011, he was taking two women and their boyfriends on a private walk of Blue Bell Hill when amazing and unsettling events erupted, as Neil recalls:

> 'It was about 9:30 at night - pitch black - when we past the [Kits Coty House] stones and headed down into a dark corner of woodland. I was about to tell them about the man-beast sighting and had my back to the woods when they all screamed in tandem. It was funny seeing two grown men turn white as a ghost! They all stated that about twenty yards behind me in the wood, a tall, dark, muscular figure had run through the wood and vanished. I never saw this because as I said, my back was to the wood. They all frantically shone torches, but there was nothing.'

Of relevance to the Beast of Bolam issue, Neil makes a comment that strongly accords with my view on the controversy:

> 'I do have a belief, as in the case of the Bolam beast which was investigated by Jon [Downes], that some of these entities exist due to thought and be made unintentionally stronger when given attention, whether it's through newspaper reports, people talking about the creature, etc.'

On this same line of thinking Neil muses: 'I do not believe these things occur in the physical sense. I believe they exist on an astral level and are triggered. I believe the human mind and culture manifests these things and sometimes, especially in the case of alien abduction and UFOs, if we believe in them enough they are given strength, in a similar way to Tulpas. Some sporadic Tulpas have no real strength, hence the lack of sightings and any real depth to them.'

This latter point of Neil's - concerning the lack of depth of these creatures - does, without doubt, provoke memorable imagery of the one-dimensional Beast of Bolam encountered by Jon Downes, and members of the Twilight World, team at Bolam Lake, Northumberland in January 2003.

'For me,'

Neil comments further,

'UFOs, ghosts, dragons, fairies, are part of the same thing. They are forms we have unintentionally created over the centuries, and they change alongside our own cultures. It's all very in-depth, but not something that science seems to study in great depth. This doesn't mean that a U.K. wild man cannot leave a foot print; because, in my opinion, if a poltergeist can scratch a victim or throw a chair, then a spectral wild man can leave a print. However, unless in-depth scientific analysis is conducted, reports of U.K. wild men will only occasionally be investigated by amateur ghost hunters and cryptozoologists, who I believe, are approaching from the wrong angle entirely.'

Going around in circles. Copyright: Nick Redfern.

CHAPTER 36
MUTILATIONS AND ANOMALOUS ANIMALS
'...This was a sacrifice...'

I spent most of 2006 living back in England, and in the latter part of July of that year, I received a telephone call late one night from deep in the heart of the county of Wiltshire. It was my good friend Matthew Williams - one of just a handful of people in the world, thus far, that have been arrested, charged and duly convicted for making under cover of darkness a 'Pictogram'-style Crop Circle (in reality, the charge, as it usually is, was of causing damage to private property: a field).

Did I know, Matt asked me in somewhat excited tones, that a fairly complex Crop Circle design had appeared only days earlier next to Chartley Castle? No, I did not, I told him. But, given that this was where Mick Dodds and his wife encountered a British Bigfoot in 1986, I was most certainly determined to go and see for myself what was afoot at Chartley Castle...

The Evil Eye

I spent many a fun summer in the late 1980s and early 1990s driving around the county of Wiltshire in search of Crop Circles - and, on more than several occasions, with Matt himself. But as this specific design was relatively close to the home of my dad, Frank - who I was visiting at the time - I drove up there to check out the evidence for myself. Sure enough, there was the huge Crop Circle, sitting in a field practically right next door to Chartley Castle. Not only that: Lying strewn around the fringes of the Circle was a not inconsiderable pile of large and colourful peacock feathers.

While the presence of the peacock feathers at the site of the circle was interesting and odd, it wasn't necessarily connected. Or, maybe it was; according to one person, anyway. *The Dictionary of Phrase and Fable* recorded that:

> 'The peacock's tail is the emblem of an Evil Eye, or an ever-vigilant traitor. The tale is this: Argus was the chief Minister of Osiris, King of Egypt. When the king started on his Indian expedition, he left his queen, Isis, regent, and Argus was to be her chief adviser. Argus, with one hundred spies (called eyes), soon made himself so powerful and formidable that he shut up the queen-regent in a strong castle, and proclaimed himself king. Mercury marched against him, took him prisoner, and cut off his head; whereupon Juno metamorphosed Argus into a peacock, and set his eyes in its tale.'

And with that information now digested, I will acquaint you with the next player in the odd saga of the Chartley Castle ape-man. Jane Adams is a devotee of Wicca who I first met in a Wiltshire Crop Circle back in August 1997. She has an intriguing theory to account for the presence of those out of place feathers. She is of the opinion that the presence of the feathers at Chartley Castle is evidence that the people she believes are guilty of making the formations in the crops use the peacock's 'Evil Eye' in what she describes as 'black ceremonies'.

Adams further claims that these very same ceremonies have been conducted - under the camouflage of the hours of darkness and on a whole variety of occasions - within British-based crop circles, and ancient stone circles too. And, she adds that those responsible were endeavouring to create 'negativity' and invoke bizarre, life-threatening creatures from darkened realms that co-exist with ours, including some that would fit the image of the Chartley Castle beast encountered by Mick Dodds and his wife in September 1986. As for the reason why, Adams claims the goal is to harness the beasts and then make use of them in, as she describe it, 'psychic assassinations' of people who might be opposed to the activities of the group.

And there was more to come; much more, in fact. Adams also revealed to me that she possessed 'personal knowledge' - as she specifically described it - that these same people had engaged in sacrificing animals 'near a stone circle in Devon some time ago'. The purpose? To try to conjure up, from some ethereal netherworld, both 'a black cat' and a creature that would most certainly fit the description of the British Bigfoot and that would then duly perform the group's dark bidding. Adams' comments on this particular matter were of profound significance for one, prime reason: I knew very well that such attacks did occur in just such a fashion that she described, and in the precise locations to which she referred, too.

True or not, it is a fact that where the British Bigfoot has been seen, so strange and savage mutilations of animals - that appear to be ritualistic in nature - have, without doubt, occurred.

Terror at Tavistock

In October 2005, farmer Daniel Alford of Sampford Spiney, near Tavistock, Devon, made a shocking discovery on the wilds of Dartmoor, namely, six sheep, horrifically slaughtered, with their eyeballs removed and their necks viciously broken. More sinister, the corpses of the animals had been deliberately laid out in the form of what was undoubtedly a Pagan symbol, near a series of ancient standing-stones.

Alford was convinced that this was the dark and horrific work of occultists; primarily because this was not the first occasion upon which he had made such a gruesome find. In January 2005, Alford had stumbled upon five sheep, killed in a similar fashion and spread out in a circle, only half a mile away from the latest attack. Interestingly, on both occasions the animal attacks had occurred at the height of a full moon. I had to wonder if the presence of such a full moon was an indication that these same occultists were seeking to invoke werewolves as well as mysterious black cats.

Alford said at the time:

> 'This was a sacrifice - they had their necks broken. Initially, when you think of sacrifices you think sharp knives and slit throats. That wasn't the case here. If they had killed them and taken them, I would have accepted it more. Just to outright kill them and leave them is just a waste.'

Alford perceptively and rightly noted:

> 'You wouldn't just get kids catching sheep like that. Someone's got to know what they're on about.'

Alford was not wrong. Somebody most definitely did know what they were doing, and the attacks were only destined to continue.

In the following year, 2006, yet more unsettling sacrifices of sheep on Dartmoor occurred, again near Tavistock, and specifically on moorland at a location called Pork Hill. Once again, the necks of the animals had been broken, and their eyes had been removed, and taken. This time, however, there was another disturbing development; the tongues of the animals had also been removed.

RSPCA Inspector Becky Wadey commented:

> 'These sheep must have been rounded up on the open moor by whoever carried out this barbaric attack. That would have required a number of people and potentially been quite a spectacle. The bodies were found on open, exposed ground very close to the road, so somebody must have seen something, even if they did not realise at the time that it was suspicious.'

And, of relevance to the subject of this book, a very brief story tells of a large ape-like animal seen at Pork Hill in the 1970s. The witness, Brenda Randall, says:

> 'In 1974 and 1975 I had a boyfriend from Devon. I was living in Maidenhead when it happened, but John, that was my boyfriend, lived near Tavistock. And I fell in love with Dartmoor after we met, and we went around there nearly every weekend I got off work.
>
> We were up at Pork Hill – I couldn't tell you the date now, but it was the summer – and we thought for a minute we saw a big man – a tall man - running in the distance, like in a black tracksuit. Well, he got to about not more than a couple of hundred feet – he was running towards us first, so we could only see him from the front – and changed direction to the side, and then we could see how long his arms were when he was side-on. They were like a gorilla, and his legs were much shorter. We watched and watched, and he just kept running until he was gone. We told John's dad and he just laughed. So we didn't really say anymore about it. But, it was a funny thing – funny in it being weird, I mean, not funny-funny - and it made me feel a bit nervous about Dartmoor after that.'

Killings at Cannock

The killing of wild animals under unusual and suspicious circumstances in locations where the British Bigfoot has been seen is not limited to the county of Devon, however. Such incidents have also been sporadically reported on Cannock Chase. One such story came from Frank, who, while out walking his Labrador dog one day in 1998, found the remains of five fully-grown foxes laid out in a circle on a patch of grassy ground near the village of Brocton, with the remains of a large, thick candle lying about six or seven feet from the dead bodies.

Having no wish at all to get involved in what might very well have turned into a complicated and lengthy police investigation, Frank quickly grabbed his dog, walked away at a steady pace without once looking back, and opted not to report his macabre discovery at an official level.

Another account, of a somewhat similar nature at least, surfaced from a couple who had come across a dead deer on Cannock Chase on a Sunday morning in the latter part of the 1970s. It is a sad, harsh, and unfortunate fact of life that deer do get hit, and killed, by cars while racing across the roads of Cannock Chase. As I previously noted with respect to the theory that the British Bigfoot is a physical beast of flesh and blood origins, as of 2007 around 170 deer were being killed each year on the Chase, albeit almost exclusively as a result of traffic accidents. And it was certainly the first thought of the pair, when they stumbled across the body of the animal on land between Cannock Chase's German Cemetery and what is today called the Pye Green British Telecom Tower, that the deer had been hit by a fast-moving vehicle.

The deer, I was told, could have been hit by a car, and could perhaps have dragged itself into the woods before finally taking its last, dying breath - even though the animal had been found at least a couple of hundred yards from the side of the road. However, the most disturbing and curious part of the story was that someone, or something, had systematically removed the major organs from the animal and had carefully laid them out on the ground in what was most definitely a clear, delineated pattern.

Of equal interest to me: The pair added that it looked like both the internal organs and the body had remained completely untouched by the many other wild animals that live in the woods of Cannock Chase. It was this latter point that most puzzled the couple. Why would there be reluctance on the part of the numerous creatures of Cannock Chase to partake in what would most certainly be a considerable and hearty feast? I had no solid answers for the couple. That is, unless Jane Adams has been correct all along and that sacrificial rites designed to appease and invoke Bigfoot-like entities are indeed taking place all across the British Isles, for reasons as nefarious as they are nightmarish.

While it's important to note that this is one of the very few cases on record from Cannock Chase where the death of a deer has seemingly occurred under circumstances that do seem to be decidedly anomalous and suspicious, it's also equally important to note that, even in this one, the ritualistic element suggests a human aspect to the death of the deer, rather than anything prompted or provoked by a meat-eating Bigfoot of physical proportions.

CHAPTER 37
OF HAIRY MEN, BEASTLY BRIDGES, AND WATER-HORSES

'...He is also alleged to make his contacts with them at Montford Bridge...'

According to Scottish legend, the Kelpie - or the water-horse - is a wholly supernatural creature that haunts the rivers, bridges and lochs of ancient Scotland and that has the uncanny ability to shape-shift. The most common form that the Kelpie takes is that of a horse - hence the name. It stands by the water's edge, tempting any passing and weary traveller that might consider continuing on his or her journey to mount it. That, however, is always the fatal downfall of the traveller, as invariably the beast is then said to rear violently and charge head-long into the depths of the river or loch, and thus drowning its terrified rider in the process.

Very notably, the Kelpie was also said to be able to transform itself into both a beautiful maiden, or mermaid, and a *large, hairy man that would hide in the vegetation of Scottish waterways and leap out and attack the unwary* [Author's Note: Italics Mine], not unlike the Man-Monkey of the Shropshire Union Canal. And, let us also not forget the crazed actions of the Shuggy of Scotland's Tay Bridge, which have distinctly Kelpie-like aspects to them...

British Bigfoot Parallels
With the above said, the Kelpie may simply be a denizen of the world of folklore and nothing else at all. But the parallels between the Scottish legends and the events at Bridge 39 in January 1879, and at the Tay Bridge in December of that same year are truly - and undeniably - remarkable. The Kelpie could appear as a hair-covered hominid that would lurk within the lush greenery of Scotland's waters - just like England's Man-Monkey. The Kelpie would reportedly violently attacked passers-by. And, the Kelpie was said to be a much-feared killer of human beings, as the Man-Monkey may well have been, too.

On this very important, latter point, you will recall that the police in the vicinity of Bridge 39 had specifically associated the sightings of the Man-Monkey at Woodseaves in 1879 with the then recent death of a man who had unfortunately 'drowned in the cut'. The several parallels with the world of the Kelpie are, without doubt, truly uncanny. It goes without saying that none of this proves Kelpies exist - either in the world of the normal, or even, indeed, in the world of the paranormal. It does, however, strongly suggest a belief in, and an outright acceptance of, Kelpie-like entities in rural Shropshire and Staffordshire by elements of the British Police Force, no less, in the latter part of the 19th Century - which is, without doubt, a revelation of a pretty extraordinary magnitude.

It also suggests that if the latter day Man-Monkey reports are genuine (and I personally see no reason to dispute them or their attendant sources, having personally interviewed many of them), then far from being merely a harmless relic of centuries-old Scottish folklore, the Kelpie is still among us, still thriving, and still up to its infernal, and sometimes deadly, activities.

From a Beast of the Water to a Monster of the Woods

And another thought while we are discussing all-things of a Kelpie-like nature. Could it be that the large eel-like beast seen by fisherman Paul Bell in the hot summer of 1976 was in reality a Kelpie-style shape-shifter that, one week after his initial encounter, assumed for the same startled witness the form of the diabolical Man-Monkey? Given that ancient Scottish legend and folklore suggests the Kelpie can shape-shift from water-horse to hairy man-beast and vice-versa, ad infinitum, this would certainly seem to suggest such an incredible possibility. And, if that was the case, Bell can most definitely count his lucky stars that he did not pay for the encounter with both his soul and his life.

We should also recall that the Shropshire village of Child's Ercall has legends of a hairy wild man and a mermaid attached to it. And then there is Aqualate Mere, Staffordshire - which is very close to Woodseaves, the home of the Man-Monkey, no less - and also reputedly the lair of a beautiful mermaid. It must be said that sightings of predatory mermaids and magical maidens, as well as hairy monstrosities, are the veritable hallmark of the presence of a shape-shifting Kelpie, as well as being amongst its most preferred forms of appearance after that of the traditional water-horse.

The terror of the Kelpie. Copyright: Herbert James Draper, 1913.

And, still on this particular train of thought, it is very important to note that several stretches of canal and certain waterways within the British Isles have curious folk-tales attached to them that are inextricably linked with monkeys, apes, water, and bridges. In other words, the Shuggy of Scotland's Tay Bridge and the Man-Monkey of Bridge 39 on the Shropshire Union Canal are far from being alone...

'Then from the darkness came a huge, dark figure'

The August 2009 issue of *Phenomena* magazine included a then recent report that clearly linked the British Bigfoot with large bodies of water:

> 'Poachers in woods at Walkerwood Reservoir, Cheshire, heard noises brush in front of them, then their torches suddenly stopped working. Panic set in and they ran. They stopped several hundred yards away and could still hear the noises which seemed to be pursuing them. They opened fire, they heard no sound, and then the noises began again, as though something was moving towards them. Then from the darkness came a huge, dark figure. It was about seven feet tall and was completely black in colour. They could see no features, and the thing seemed to be absorbing the darkness, as if camouflaged in some way. The poachers fled.'

And, as we have seen, this is most certainly not the first time we have come across cases involving a British Bigfoot that has seemingly had an effect on powered equipment - in this case, torches. Jon Downes experienced something very similar at Bolam Woods in 2002, when recording equipment began to fail suspiciously.

Cider Strangeness

The village of Defford, Worcestershire, is home to a pub called the *Cider House*. One of the very few still-existing traditional cider houses in England, it has been in the same family for a century and a half, and visitors to the *Cider House* will find their drinks served to them in quaint pottery mugs, and amid a welcome atmosphere that harks back to a time long gone. More notable is the fact that for the locals that frequent the *Cider House*, it has a distinctly different moniker, namely, the *Monkey House*.

So the legend goes, many years ago, a regular customer charged breathlessly into the pub late one night, claiming to have fallen into dense bramble bushes, after being attacked by...a group of monkeys. Notably, the village of Defford is situated very close to Eckington, whose historic Eckington Bridge spans the River Avon and at which, late on a weekend night in 1957, a man named Albert Micklewright was witness to what was described as a 'big hairy thing from Tarzan'.

Locked in Mystery

Then there is the intriguingly named Monkey Marsh Lock. Situated on the Kennet and Avon Canal, it weaves its way through the Thames and the River Avon, links the city of London with the British Channel, and has been designated an ancient monument by English Heritage. It is also one of the only two remaining turf-sided locks in England of the type that were chiefly used in the early 1700s. Needless to say, the origins of the lock's admittedly eye-opening name remain shrouded in mystery and history.

An Island of 'Grotesque Monkeys'

And what of the so-called Monkey Island-Isleworth Canal Project of 1793? An ambitious plan first proposed in 1770 (but, ultimately, never brought to successful fruition) it was designed to link Maidenhead and Isleworth via a planned stretch of canal that would by-pass the River Thames. Monkey Island is a story in itself. The island is a small piece of land on the Thames that can be found near to the

Berkshire village of Bray. Its name is actually derived from the Old English term: Monks Eyot - meaning Monks' Island, and was specifically named after a group of monks that resided at Amerden Bank, which is situated near to Bray Lock on the Buckinghamshire banks of the river.

In the early 1720s, the island came into the possession of the third Duke of Marlborough, Charles Spencer, and who duly oversaw the construction of a fishing lodge and temple. Monkey Island Lodge (which today still stands - but as a pavilion) was built completely out of wood. Notably, the artist Andieu de Clermont was asked to provide the Lodge with his own unique brand of paintwork - and he most certainly did so; 'grotesque gentleman monkeys', engaged in scenes of fishing, boating and shooting adorned a small room in the Lodge, and can still be seen there to this day.

In 1738, Lady Hertford described Monkey Island Lodge thus:

> '[It] has a small house upon it, whose outside represents a farm - the inside what you please: for the parlour, which is the only room in it except the kitchen, is painted upon the ceiling in grotesque, with monkeys fishing, shooting, etc., and its sides are hung with paper. When a person sits in this room he cannot see the water though the island is not above a stone's cast over; nor is he prevented from this by shade; for, except for six or eight walnut trees and a few orange trees in tubs there is not a leaf upon the island; it arises entirely from the river running very much below its banks.'

Roughly a century later, the Lodge had become a river-side inn, accessible only by ferry; that is until 1956, when a foot-bridge was finally built. And although the island's curious name seems to have wholly down to earth origins, it is intriguing to note that, once again, here is yet another locale in the British Isles linked with canals, bridges and 'grotesque monkeys'.

Chaos at the Reservoir

Moving on, there is the encounter of Mike Atkins - an encounter that took place in 1996, but that Atkins steadfastly decided to keep firmly to himself until he read an *Express & Star* article penned by me in December 2002 on the exploits of the Man-Monkey of the Shropshire Union Canal. Not only that, Atkins' story eerily paralleled that of both Craig Blackmore - on Cannock Chase, late one night in early 2002 - and the man at Woodseaves in January 1879. Atkins' experience had not occurred at Woodseaves or on the Cannock Chase, however, but at the Blithfield Reservoir, Staffordshire.

According to Atkins, he was driving over the road-bridge that crosses the reservoir in the early hours of a particular morning in 1996 when a giant, hairy animal 'practically launched itself across the road at my car'. Fortunately, Mike was able to floor the accelerator, and thus both nimbly and skilfully avoided having to engage the wild animal in near hand-to-hand combat, as did the unfortunate victim at Bridge 39 back in 1879.

There was nothing more that Atkins wished to impart (although I did detect from his concise words that there was something more that he probably could have imparted). And so, after a brief yet cordial telephone conversation one evening in late December 2002, I quickly transferred my hastily scribbled pencil notes into a Word document on my computer, content in the fact that apparent encounters with beasts that sounded suspiciously like the Man-Monkey were still continuing to trickle in.

A Bridge too Weird

And what about the Kelpie's predilection for hanging out at bridges? Traditionally, and for centuries, within the folklore, mythology and legends of countless cultures, bridges have been associated with a wide array of paranormal phenomena, including strange animals, UFOs, and spectral entities. Without doubt, the most famous examples are the trolls of Scandinavia - whose actions and legends provoked the classic Norwegian fairy tale Three Billy Goats Gruff, which sees the trio of goats of the story confronted by a violent troll while trying to cross the bridge the creature calls its home. The big question is, why is there such an association between beasts and bridges? The answers are undeniably as strange as they are intriguing.

Nearly a century after the Man-Monkey reared its beastly head, weird and unearthly things were afoot at England's Montford Bridge, a village constructed in the early 1790s, and which - slightly confusingly - is home to a bridge of the very same name, and one that was designed, in the 1700s, by the acclaimed Thomas Telford, who also played a highly significant role in the creation of the Man-Monkey's haunt, the Shropshire Union Canal.

Declassified British Ministry of Defence files reveal that, in both 1964 and 1966, a young woman named Diane Foulkes underwent a series of traumatic UFO encounters at Montford Bridge - encounters that adversely affected the engine and headlights of her car, made her feel 'very ill' and 'extremely frightened', and gave every indication that alien entities were secretly lurking around the old bridge. Notably, one extract from the Ministry of Defence's official report on the affair says:

> 'Miss Foulkes further stated that she believed that the objects could be associated with a Mr. Griffin who lived in the area and who is reputed to have made contact with these objects and actually entered one and met one of the occupants. He is also alleged to make his contacts with them at Montford Bridge.'

Meanwhile, on the other side of the Atlantic...

Bridges and Beasts in the USA

There can be very few people who have not heard of Mothman - a creature that haunted the town of Point Pleasant, West Virginia, between November 1966 and December 1967. A definitive winged-thing, Mothman came hurtling out of nowhere. And, some say, its presence culminated in high tragedy. On December 15, 1967, Point Pleasant's Silver Bridge, that spanned the Ohio River and connected Point Pleasant to Gallipolis, Ohio, collapsed into the river, claiming forty-six lives.
After the disaster at the bridge, encounters with Mothman largely came to a halt. While a down to earth explanation for the bridge certainly circulated - that a flaw in a single eye-bar in a suspension chain was the culprit - many saw the cause of the disaster as being connected to the dark presence of Mothman.

Moving on to Texas, there is the tale of the diabolical Goat-Man that haunts the Old Alton Bridge in the town of Denton. One legend says that, many years ago, wannabe devil-worshippers in the area inadvertently opened up a portal to some hellish realm that allowed the vile beast access to our world. And now, today, and as a direct result of this reckless action, the Goat-Man has no intention of returning to the twilight zone from which he surfaced; hence his deep desire to forever haunt Denton's steel-and-wood bridge.

The Other Denton Bridge

Rather oddly, there is another U.S.-based bridge with a Denton connection that is also steeped in mystery. This one, however, is located in Michigan. It is one that the Centre for Fortean Zoology's

Michigan representative - Raven Meindel - paid a visit to in March 2009 with her daughter, Jessica. Raven takes up the story:

> 'Today Jessica and I took a ride out to the Canton area to do a pre-investigation study of the Denton Road bridge and the surrounding area. There is so much history that lies just beneath the surface of that entire area that we'll have to do many investigations to cover even a portion it. As we drove through where the bridge is located, an eerie ambiance fell over the van. It was like we had just slipped into another dimension of time. With the exception of the newly built condos that now dot the land heavily, and the occasional jogger or bicycle, there is a stillness to the place that can only be described as otherworldly.'

> 'We met a gentleman named Don who has lived there since 1963 and was not only able to give us a first-hand account of the folklore, but also had a wealth of knowledge regarding the development of the area as well. Don told us that the bridge was called "Knock Knock Bridge" by all the local children when he was growing up, because, as legend has it, if you knocked three times and waited, something spooky was bound to happen. From ghost lights to shadowy dark figures chasing cars, there have always been strange stories passed down from one generation to the next.'

Liminal Zones

So, what's going on? Is it merely down to chance and coincidence that bridges seem to play such integral roles in Fortean encounters, and particularly so cases that are linked so deeply to British Bigfoot reports? No, almost certainly not. It's at this point we have to turn our attentions to what have become known as Liminal Zones.

Big cat researcher and author Merrily Harpur has written of such mysterious locales and says that:

> 'These are the transitional zones between one area and another - the kind of no-man's-land traditionally regarded as magical.'

Merrily notes that such zones include streams, stiles, gates, churchyards and bridges. They are, she says,

> 'spots literally or symbolically at the point of transition over a boundary.'

And, perhaps, it is within such zones - particularly so streams and bridges - that the Kelpie lurks, sometimes in lake-monster form, occasionally as a mermaid, and, on a large number of times, as a British Bigfoot.

The Kelpie may well be a terrifying entity whose origins are based firmly in the past. But, as this chapter demonstrates, the malignant thing seems determined to maintain a strong foothold in the present. And, should we expect anything less of the future? Probably not, albeit unfortunately for those who may, one day, find themselves crossing its infernal, deadly path, whether in the guise of a terrible water-beast, an inviting maiden, or a giant, hairy, man-thing.

**OPPOSITE: Anomalies researcher and cryptozoologist, Raven Meindel.
Copyright: Raven Meindel**

Neanderthals in the UK. Copyright: Hermann Schaaffhausen, 1888.

CHAPTER 38
FROM NEOLITHIC TO NEANDERTAL
'...I began to wonder if people had seen, from a distance, some type of ghostly primitive man...'

When it comes to trying to ascertain the true nature of the British Bigfoot and wild man encounters - which is a deeply fraught and difficult task at the very best of times - as we have seen, the theories are as wide and varied as they are controversial and thought-provoking. But, without doubt, one of the most engaging of all scenarios to explain this undeniably nationwide, ancient conundrum comes from Neil Arnold, whose views on the matter I secured in a January 2012 interview...

'It was not "real" but gave off an air of malevolence'
Having extensively investigated such reports, Neil says:

'I've always wondered what type of manifestation these U.K. "wild men" could be. In the autumn of 2011 a psychic lady who I know as a friend and who I trust - I don't often have any interests in psychics - accompanied me to Blue Bell Hill, which is a very haunted village in Kent, a few miles short of the town of Maidstone. I knew of several obscure "man-beast" reports in the area which she knew nothing about. I took her to one particular spot, near some ancient stones, hoping she'd pick up a ghostly presence and she said she felt nothing whatsoever, but she did state quite categorically that a few years previous, around 2003 she'd had a bizarre encounter in the area one night.'

The story told to Neil goes like this:

> 'She had visited Kits Coty House - a set of stones - with a group of fellow psychics. Her friends were over on one side of the field which harbours the stones and she was in another area when she noticed someone walking towards her a few hundred yards away. The figure seemed to be striding rather aggressively and was coming from the direction of a thicket which runs alongside the field.'

This was no normal human of modern-day standards, however, as Neil's following words make acutely and abundantly clear:

> 'The woman, whose name is Corriene, stated that from a distance the figure appeared huge in build and covered in hair and she sensed it was not "real" but gave off an air of malevolence. The figure marched towards her and she could see it had long hair and a beard, covering most of its face. The hulking figure was taller than six feet and appeared to have a loin cloth around its waist and furred boots.

No-one else saw this figure, but I was intrigued as I knew that in the past several witnesses had come forward to say they'd seen similar figures in woods within miles of Blue Bell Hill.'

It was this encounter that set Neil on a decidedly intriguing train of thought:

'I began to wonder if people had seen, from a distance, some type of ghostly primitive man - long hair, bearded, muscular, animal fur around the waist - who, from several hundred yards away, or in ill light, may have looked as if he was covered in hair. Blue Bell Hill and much of Kent is steeped in history - so maybe people were seeing some type of Neolithic hunter. Corriene was intrigued by what I said and then, rather startled, mentioned that on another occasion whilst in the area of the stones she'd seen several of these people who she felt were not aggressive, and although armed with spears were simply guarding the area and stooping low in the bushes, curious as to what they were seeing.'

Significantly, this case did not stand alone, as Neil told me:

'In 1974 a woman named Maureen - who I became very close friends with after working with her ten years ago - was with her boyfriend in woods off a close named Sherwood Avenue, in Walderslade, which, as the crow flies, is only a couple of miles short of Blue Bell Hill. Her boyfriend was tending to the fire when Maureen felt as if she was being watched. She turned slowly and to her amazement saw a massive figure, standing over seven feet tall, seemingly covered in hair, just a few yards away. The figure had bright eyes which blinked. The figure seemed to crouch down behind the bushes very slowly, and Maureen asked her boyfriend if they could leave the area, and they did. Maureen never told her boyfriend what she'd seen. They eventually married and were together for many years. In fact, she never told anyone about what she'd seen until she realised what I was interested in.'

Neil concludes:

'I believe Maureen one hundred per cent, but I strongly believe this figure was some type of elemental [or] spirit. I also believe this figure could have been a Neolithic type of hunter.'

Recall, too, the words of paranormal authority Joshua P. Warren, who told me:

'Maybe Bigfoot is a "phantimal", perhaps even the ghost of a prehistoric creature, similar to the enormous extinct ape, Gigantopithecus, or maybe even the spirits of primitive humans' [Author's Note: Italics Mine].

Also remember that Jon Downes has uncovered a number of reports, similar to that of Maureen, of so-called "crouching" British wild men. And, I cannot ignore the delicious irony provoked by Maureen having lived in nothing less than Sherwood Avenue...

The Lustleigh Cleave Cave Men
Possibly of relevance to the theory and observations of Neil Arnold - and Maureen, too - is the story of a noted Devon folklorist and acclaimed writer, Theo Brown. The author of such titles as *Devon Ghosts* and *Family*

The British Bigfoot and ancient standing stones are curiously connected.
Copyright: Chris Eades.

Holidays Around Dartmoor, and someone who - as we have seen - had her very own experience with Devon's notorious Hairy Hands, Brown collected a number of deeply similar stories to those cited by Neil, including one chilling recollection by a friend of hers who had been walking alone at dusk near the Neolithic earthworks at the top of Lustleigh Cleave, which sits on the extreme east side of Dartmoor, in the Wrey Valley.

Lustleigh Cleave is an extraordinarily strange place at the best of times, and it appears to be one of those 'window areas' that Ronan Coghlan described earlier, and where an inordinate number of unexplained incidents and anomalous phenomena seem to take place on an amazingly regular basis. Moreover, the remains of prehistoric stone huts can be seen in the direct vicinity, and an ancient burial monument, Datuidoc's Stone - which is estimated to have originated at some point around 550 to 600 A.D. - still stands to this very day, pretty much as it did all those thousands of years ago.

Jon Downes says of the weirdness that dominates Lustleigh Cleave:

> 'I have got reports of sightings of a ghostly Tudor hunting party, of mysterious lights in the sky, and even the apparitions of a pair of Roman Centurions at Lustleigh Cleave.'

But, adds Jon, getting to the most important aspect of the story,

> 'Theo Brown`s friend saw, clearly, a family of "cave men," either naked and covered in hair or wrapped in the shaggy pelts of some wild animal, shambling around the stone circle at the top of the cleave.'

A Neanderthal in Coventry

The late Stan Gooch, the author of a number of books, including *Creatures from Inner Space* and *The Paranormal*, told of his encounter with nothing less than what seemed to be a Neanderthal man at a séance held at a house in the English city of Coventry in the 1950s! In Gooch's very own words, during the course of the séance, something both primitive and primeval materialised before the shocked attendees:

> 'This was a crouching ape-like shape, which became clearer as the moments passed. I guess it approximated to most people's idea of what an ancient cave man would look like. Yet one could not make out too much detail - the eyes were hidden, for example. It stood in half shadow, watching us, breathing heavily as if nervous. I must say, though, that I sensed rather than heard the breathing. I could not decide whether our visitor was wearing the skin of some animal, or whether it had a rough coat of hair of its own.'

All attempts to question the man-beast, and have it join the circle, were utterly fruitless, and, eventually, it melted away into nothingness. Nevertheless, Gooch never forgot the experience and later mused upon the notion that what he had seen on that fateful evening was a 'classic Neanderthal'.

Rather interestingly, Gooch, in later years penned a number of books, including *The Neanderthal Question and The Neanderthal Legacy*, which theorised that we, as *Homo sap*iens, are the result of a hybrid mix of Cro-Magnon man and Neanderthal man. And - once again - we should not forget that the 'crouching' appearance of the primitive man encountered by Gooch echoed certain cases that Janet Bord noted at Hangley Cleave, Somerset.

The Horrors of Hoy

Author W.E. Thorner was on the island of Hoy, off the north coast of Scotland, during the Second World War when he saw a group of wild men dancing on the top of a cliff at Thorness - a place named after the Norse God of the dwarfs - at the height of a tumultuous winter thunderstorm. In Thorner's own, captivating words:

> 'These creatures were small in stature, but they did not have long noses nor did they appear kindly in demeanour. They possessed round faces, sallow in complexion, with long, dark, bedraggled hair. As they danced about, seeming to throw themselves over the cliff edge, I felt that I was a witness to some ritual dance of a tribe of primitive men. It is difficult to describe in a few words my feelings at this juncture or my bewilderment. The whole sequence could have lasted about three minutes until I was able to leave the cliff edge.'

A Monstrous Vision

Beyond any shadow of a doubt whatsoever, the absolute strangest report I have on record of not just a British wild man of prehistoric proportions, but of an apparent whole tribe of them, is one which emanates from Staffordshire's Castle Ring, and which was first related to me many years ago by the

A Neanderthal nightmare at Castle Ring? Copyright: Nick Redfern

witness herself, a woman named Pauline Charlesworth. Pauline knows very well, I need to stress, that while I do take her story seriously, I most certainly do not take it literally - even in the slightest. Actually, and rather satisfactorily and refreshingly, neither does Pauline. It becomes very clear upon examining her extraordinary testimony that the experience she underwent occurred in some sort of highly altered state, possibly even one of a bizarre, visionary nature, or, maybe, a 'pisky led' condition similar to that described by Mike Johnson near Cannock Chase's German Cemetery in June of 2001. And, the distance from Castle Ring to the cemetery is barely ten minutes or so.

According to Pauline, it was a bright, summery day in July 1986 that her strange encounter occurred. As she worked on Saturdays, Pauline explained to me when we first met, she had a regular day off work during the week, and had chosen this particular day to prepare a picnic-basket, and take a trip up to Castle Ring.

On arriving, she prepared for herself a comfortable place to sit, stretched out a blanket on the ground, and opened up her picnic basket that contained drinks, fruit and sandwiches. For more than an hour she sat and read a book, but then something very curious happened. It was as if, Pauline explained, she was sitting within the confines of a vacuum and all of the surrounding noises, such as the birds whistling and the branches of the trees gently swaying, stopped - completely. Pauline also said that 'what was

/asn't quite right'. By that statement, she explained:

> 'The best way I can describe it is to say it was like I wasn't really on the Chase, but it was as if I was in someone's dream of what the Chase should look like; as if it was all a mirage, but a good one.'

That 'pisky-led' sensation, one might wisely conclude.

Then, out of the trees, came a horrific form running directly toward her. It was, said Pauline, a man. The man, however, was quite unlike any that she had ever seen before. He had long, filthy hair, a matted beard, and a 'dumpy' face that was far more prehistoric than modern in appearance. He was relatively short in height, perhaps no more than five feet two inches, and was clad in animal skins that extended from his waist to his knees, and with a long piece of animal skin that was draped over his right shoulder. In his right hand, the man held what were undoubtedly the large antlers of a deer that had been expertly fashioned into a dagger-like weapon that looked like it could inflict some very serious damage indeed, if needed. Pauline said that it was very difficult to ascertain who was more scared; her or the man. While she stared at him in stark terror, he eyed her curiously and in what Pauline described as a disturbing and sinister fashion. On several occasions he uttered what sounded like the words of an unknown language: 'It was like he was angry and firing questions at me,' she added. But that was not all.

In the distance, Pauline could hear other voices getting ever closer and closer and that, collectively and ultimately, grew into a literal crescendo. And then she found out the source of the noise. Through a break in the trees came perhaps thirty of forty more similarly clad people, mostly men, but others women, and all chanting in an unknown, and presumably ancient, tongue.

It was soon made clear to Pauline that some sort of significant ceremony was about to take place inside Castle Ring - and she, no less, was right in the heart of all the brewing action. The men and women proceeded to sit down at the edges of the Ring. One man, much taller than the rest and who she assumed was the 'leader of the group', marched over to her and said something wholly unintelligible; but that she understood by the curt wave of his arm meant that she should get out of the circle. This she quickly did and retreated with shaking legs to the tree-line. For more than fifteen minutes she sat, transfixed with overwhelming terror by the sight, as this curious band of people continued to chant and sway in rhythmic, hypnotic fashion.

Then, out of the sky, came the most horrific thing that Pauline had ever seen in her entire life. It was, she recalled, a creature about four feet in height, human in shape, with oily, greasy black skin, thin arms and legs and a pair of large, bat-like leathery wings. And, just for good measure, it had two hideous, red, glowing eyes, too. 'It was like the devil,' recalled Pauline, perhaps with a high degree of understandable justification.

The creature slowly dropped to the ground and prowled around the Ring for a minute, staring at one and all and emitting hideous, ear-splitting shrieks. Suddenly, seven or eight of the men pounced on the creature, wrestled it to the ground, and bound it firmly with powerful ropes. It writhed and fought to get loose and tore into the flesh of the men with its claws; but was finally subdued and dragged into the forest by the same tribe-members. The remainder of the party followed and Pauline said that the strange atmosphere began to lift and the area eventually returned to its original normality. For several minutes she stood her ground, too afraid to move, but then finally returned on still-unsteady legs to her blanket and quickly scooped up both it and her picnic basket and ran to her car.

I have left until last one factor that, in some fashion, simply has to be connected to the saga related above. The book that Pauline had taken with her to read at Castle Ring was Robert Holdstock's acclaimed fantasy novel, *Mythago Wood*. Ironically, the book is one of my all-time favourites, and one I read at least once a year. The story tells how, after the end of the Second World War, one Steve Huxley returns to England upon getting the news that his father has died. George Huxley had devoted his life to the exploration of the ancient Ryhope Wood that backed up against the family home and kept detailed records of his research into the mysterious area. But Ryhope Wood is unlike any other. It is inhabited by the 'mythagos' of the book's title. And what, exactly, might they be? They are creatures and characters from British folklore and mythology, such as Robin Hood and King Arthur, whose curious existence is directly tied to the imaginations and minds of those that believe in them and who, in unconscious, collective fashion, help bring them to some form of quasi-independent life, in the depths of the magical Ryhope Wood.

Of course, in view of the *Mythago Wood* connection, the sceptic would say that Pauline's unearthly experience was merely the result of a bizarre dream - or the absolute worst of all nightmares, perhaps. And, maybe, that really is all it was. More than a quarter of a century later, however, Pauline herself is still convinced that something very strange and diabolically evil occurred on that summer day in long-gone July 1986, and that she was provided with a unique glimpse into Staffordshire's very ancient past. Nine years down the line, something else of a somewhat similar nature occurred at this same, definitively paranormal, place. It, too, has a bearing on tales of the British wild man.

The Ancient Horseman

In October 1995, the *Cannock Mercury* newspaper reported on a series of very weird events that were then occurring in the midst of Beaudesert Old Park, which is situated very near to Castle Ring. Home to a camp for both scouts and guides, Beaudesert was the site of repeated, strange activity in the late summer and early autumn of 1995. Not only that, but a group of scouts was going to stake-out the area in a careful and dedicated bid to hopefully try and get to the bottom of the mystery, once and for all.
The Mercury noted:

> 'Wardens and assistants have reported strange noises, screams and eerie goings-on around the camp.'

Indeed, they had, including encounters with a dark-cloaked figure and a ghostly child roaming the woods and haunting the roads.

Steve Fricker, the assistant-leader of the 2nd Rugeley Hillsprings Scouts related at the time:

> 'It is said that the ancient horsemen of old are now seeking revenge for the disturbances they have had to face for several years from these excitable youths.'

The newspaper added:

> 'Scouts will be camping out to "confront" the spirits and attempt to restore peace. They will be staying awake from Saturday evening (October 28) until dawn on Sunday, entertained by wardens' tales of the hauntings.'

Ultimately, however, the 'horsemen of old' did not make a showing. But, maybe we have a precedent for such a prehistoric horse-rider, and one that may help explain at least some strange sightings of wild men in the British Isles.

Bronze Age Bizarreness on Bottlebush Down

The respected authority on prehistory, R.C.C. Clay, had just such an encounter while driving at Bottlebush Down, Dorset - an area strewn with old earthworks - during the winter of 1924. The story, however, did not surface until 1956, when Clay shared the details with an authority on all things ghostly and spectral, James Wentworth Day, an unlikeable, racist, homophobe with fascist leanings, who penned such titles as *Here are Ghosts and Witches*, *A Ghost Hunter's Game Book*, *In Search of Ghosts* and *They Walk the Wild Places*. The location of the extraordinary event that Clay related to a captivated and enthralled Day was the A3081 road, between the Dorset villages of Cranborne and Sixpenny Handley, on farmland known locally as Bottlebush Down. It was while Clay was driving home, after spending a day excavating in the area, and as the daylight was giving way to the magical, twilight hours, that he encountered something extraordinary. Maybe even beyond extraordinary.

At a point where the new road crossed with an old Roman road - perhaps one of Merrily Harpur's liminal zones, it might very well be reasoned - that a horseman, riding wildly and at high speed on the back of a huge and muscular stallion, seemingly appeared out of nowhere. But there was something wrong about this man, something terribly wrong.

In Clay's very own words to a captivated Wentworth Day:

> 'I could see that he was no ordinary horseman, for he had bare legs, and wore a long loose cloak. His horse had a long mane and tail, but I could see neither bridle nor stirrup. His face was turned towards me, but I could not see his features. He seemed to be threatening me with some implement, which he waved in his right hand above his head.'

It is deeply fortunate that the witness in this case was Clay - a man with an expert and profound knowledge of English history, folklore, and times and people long gone. There was no doubt in Clay's mind that, having kept the rider in careful sight for around three hundred feet, his clothing and weapon firmly identified him as nothing less than a denizen of the Bronze Age - which, incredibly, would have placed his origins at some point between 2100 and 750 B.C. Not surprisingly, with darkness falling fast, Clay floored the accelerator and headed for home, somewhat shakily but decidedly excited, too.

His interest most certainly piqued, Clay began to make careful and somewhat wary inquiries - of a somewhat understandably tentative and tactful nature - in the area, to determine if anyone else had ever seen the ancient hunter of the Downs. As it so transpired, they actually had. An old shepherd, who had worked in the fields his whole life, and answering Clay's questions, said: 'Do you mean the man on the horse who comes out of the opening in the pinewood?' When an amazed and excited Clay replied 'Yes!' and asked further questions, it became clear to him that he was not the only person to have seen the enigmatic old rider of the land. And, a couple of years later, while still investigating the strange affair, he learned of yet another encounter with the ghostly man and horse. In this case, the witnesses were two girls, cycling from Sixpenny Handley to a Friday night dance at Cranborne, who were plunged into a state of fear by the presence of what sounded like the very same character encountered by Clay back in 1924.

As Clay told Wentworth Day in 1956, he knew of no more recent encounters with the horseman, but theorised that what he had been fortunate enough to see was undoubtedly the spirit form of a Bronze Age hunter and his horse, both of who had probably died under violent circumstances on the Downs, and who - for a while, at least - roamed the very same old hunting grounds that they had called home during their clearly turbulent, physical lives.

Salisbury Plain and Stonehenge

Merrily Harpur has logged a fascinating account from one George Price, who had an undeniably bizarre experience on Salisbury Plain in September 2002, while then serving with the British Army. It was at the height of a military exercise, Harpur was told, and Price was a 'commander in the turret of our tank, and we were advancing to contact our warriors'. Suddenly, Price's attention was drawn to a 'large, ape-like figure' that 'looked scared because of the noise from the engines and tanks were moving at speed all around'.

Although the beast was not in sight for long - it raced for the safety of 'nearby prickly shrubs' - an amazed Price could see that 'its fur was similar to an orang-utan in colour...its height was impressive... [and] it seemed to run with its back low, i.e. bent over'.

Salisbury Plain is not just home to military manoeuvres, however. It is also home to one of the world's most famous ancient stone circles: Stonehenge. While most students of the legendary structure conclude it had its beginnings somewhere around 3,100 BC, evidence of human activity in the area has been found suggesting a presence as far back as 8,000 BC. And a degree of that same presence is indicative of ritualistic activity, even at that incredibly early age. But, regardless of when, precisely, large-scale construction of Stonehenge actually began, what can be said with certainty is that it is comprised of a ditch, a bank, and what are known as the Aubrey holes - round pits in the chalk that form a huge circle. And then, of course, there are those massive stone blocks.

Stonehenge, Salisbury Plain and the British Bigfoot: A connection. Copyright: Nick Redfern.

No less than eighty-two of Stonehenge's so-called bluestones, some of which weigh up to four-tons, are believed to have been transported from the Preseli Mountains in southwest Wales to the Wiltshire site, a distance of 240-miles. Although, the actual number of stones is in dispute since, today, barely more than forty remain. Certainly, such a mammoth operation to move such huge stones would be no easy feat in the modern era, never mind thousands of years ago. And yet, somehow, this incredible and mystifying task was successfully achieved.

Stonehenge's thirty giant Sarsen stones, meanwhile, were brought from the Marlborough Downs, a distance of around twenty-five miles. This might sound like a much easier task than having to haul the bluestones all the way from Wales. Hardly. As noted, the Welsh stones are in the order of four-tons. Some of the Sarsen stones from the downs, however, weigh in at twenty-five-tons, the heaviest around fifty. And people wonder why so much mystery and intrigue surrounds the creation of Stonehenge?

Is it possible that what George Price saw on Salisbury Plain was not actually a British Bigfoot, but, perhaps, one of Neil Arnold's ghostly Neolithic hunters, or possibly something akin to R.C.C. Clay's Bronze Age warrior, but one with a long-gone link to the nearby Stonehenge?

The Rollright Thing

Now we come to the Rollright Stones, which are situated near Long Compton, a centuries-old little village in the county of Oxfordshire. Collectively, they are comprised of a tomb, known as the Whispering Knights, a classic circle of stones called the King's Men, and a solitary stone referred to as the King's Stone. As for the time of the construction of the Rollright Stones, this appears to be a clear-cut issue: in the Neolithic and Bronze Age eras.

The Rollright Stones: Attracting monsters. Copyright: Unknown, 1919.

As with Stonehenge, legends and pet-theories abound as to the particular origin of the Rollright Stones. Certainly, the most engaging is that which surfaced in 1610 from a historian named William Camden. The story goes that the stones were not always stones. They originally represented an unnamed visiting king and his faithful knights who were turned to stone - in classic Gorgon-style, one might well suggest - by a legendary local witch, one Mother Shipton. The king, not surprisingly, became the King's Stone. The bulk of his men were turned into the King's Men. While a few who had initially avoided - but not for long, unfortunately - Mother Shipton's malevolent powers quickly and collectively became the Whispering Knights.

In 1977, author Paul Devereux established what became titled the Dragon Project; the purpose of which was to study claims that certain British prehistoric sites had unusual forces or energies attached to them, including magnetic, infrared and ultrasonic anomalies. While investigating none other than the Rollright Stones, Devereux reported that one of the team members - described as being a well-known archaeologist - was sitting in a van when an unidentified, hair-covered beast of considerable size walked by. An instant later, it utterly vanished, never to put in a re-appearance.

It's also worth noting that, with regard to the sighting of the large and lumbering beast that was seen near the Peak District-based Ladybower Reservoir in November 1991, less than one mile away, on Stanton Moor, stands a stone circle called the Nine Ladies. It was constructed during the Bronze Age era, and is a place at which, every year, druids and pagans alike celebrate the summer solstice. As the legend goes, the circle takes its name from nine women who were turned to stone as punishment for dancing on Sundays!

Perhaps, in light of the extraordinary data contained within this particular chapter, when it comes to British cases that seem to fall into definitive wild man territory, we should be focusing our attentions far less on what's going on in the relevant location of ancient stone circles right now, and far more on (A) the matter of what may have occurred there centuries or millennia ago, and (B) the issue of what - in some strange, ethereal, and wild form - may continue to linger and wander and, sometimes, terrorise the good folk of Britain, long after physical death claimed their lives in times past and largely forgotten.

Spirit Guardians

For the final word on the potential connection between unidentified, upright, hairy animals and places of specifically archaeological, spiritual, and historical nature, I refer you to the writings of one of the world's leading authorities on the phenomenon of werewolves, Linda Godfrey, the author of such fine pieces of essential reading as *The Michigan Dogman*, *Werewolves*, *Hunting the American Werewolf*, and *The Beast of Bray Road*.

Mother Shipton

The infamous crone, Mother Shipton. Copyright: Unknown.

Of the Native American phenomenon known as the Skinwalker - which Linda describes as 'entities created by magic ritual that look like animals but are really spirit doubles of the shaman that either go out from the physical body or envelope it like a supernatural costume' - she says they are 'related to the Tibetan ideas' of Tulpas.

Rather significantly, when one takes into account the various accounts cited in this chapter of British Bigfoot encounters that occurred in the vicinity of, or relatively close to, famous standing-stones, such as Stonehenge and the Rollright Stones, and ancient sites like Staffordshire's Castle Ring, the following words from Linda most assuredly stand out as being of keen relevance to such matters. She says, still on the subject of Skinwalkers:

> 'I can tell you that Native Americans from various locations have indicated to me
> that these things absolutely exist, as do zoomorphic (animal-shaped) spirit
> guardians made to watch over sacred grounds [Author's Note: Italics Mine].'

Linda also notes that in relation to ancient Native American burial mounds ('shaped like traditional "water panthers"') the mounds are 'located in almost exactly the same sites as manwolf posts'.

Perhaps, then, the American 'manwolf', or werewolf, was created, Tulpa-style, to watch over ancient American sites of deep significance, in much the same way that Bigfoot-like creatures seem to be doing precisely likewise at a multiplicity of standing-stones, and circles of stone, in the British Isles. One beast may exhibit ape-like characteristics and the other a far more wolfish appearance, but, at the end of the day, they may very well both be definitive supernatural 'guard-dogs', still faithfully patrolling the old sites they were created to protect all those centuries and millennia ago.

CHAPTER 39
PANIC ON THE MOUNTAINS
'...Some say the old Stone Men used to live up there...'

Since the majority of the data cited within this particular chapter is focused, to a great extent, on the phenomenon known as the Big Grey Man of Ben Macdhui - as well as the way in which the mystery may be explained - it is, once again, to the expertise of our old friend, colleague, and sinister cohort in matters paranormal, Andy Roberts, that we have to turn our attentions...

Following in the Footsteps of the BGM

'It has been suggested'

Andy begins,

'...that because witnesses to the BGM have heard "footsteps" as part of the experience these footsteps must have caused by something with a foot! In other words, another contention for the physical existence of a Big Grey Man. Affleck Gray, in his book on the BGM, devotes a whole chapter to this matter. BGM witnesses and others on Ben Macdhui have experienced phenomena which have been interpreted as being footsteps. These have been heard in winter conditions with snow underfoot and also in high summer, when the terrain is of bare rock with little or no vegetation.'

But, the matter of footsteps is not quite as clear cut as many might prefer it, as Andy knows only too well:

'A review of both the mountaineering and paranormal literature suggests that the sound of "footsteps" being heard with no evidence for their origin, are a relatively common phenomena. Dependent on the context they are often attributed to the unknown, usually in the form of "ghosts", or to natural phenomena such as unusual echoes. However in all these cases, as well as those concerning the BGM they have also been heard when the witnesses have been stationary and when no-one else seems to have been in the area.

Gray can find no fitting and comprehensive explanation for the footsteps. In the context of the BGM though nothing has ever been seen to make the sound of footsteps, no footprints have ever been discovered which could be connected

Pan and panic in the woods. Copyright: Mikhail Vrubel, 1899.

with the sounds. Walter Reid, in the Aberdeen Press & Journal the week after Collie's account was made public, is reported as having often experienced the "crunch-crunch" noise in the snow which Professor Collie described. He had got it when he was on the mountain-top alone and when there was perfect silence, but he attributed it to a weird echo effect.'

'It is possible,'

suggests Andy,

'...that some form of meteorological phenomenon similar to that which J.A. Rennie witnessed in Canada could be responsible. Echoes or other people in the same general area may also account for some of the footsteps heard, but it is impossible to isolate any consistent phenomena, natural or paranormal which causes them. As evidence for the physical existence of the BGM, though, the "footsteps" do not stand up to scrutiny, even though they remain largely unexplained.'

The Nature of the Experience

'In dealing with accounts of the Big Grey Man of Ben Macdhui all we really have are the accounts given by the people who have had the experience,' admits Andy, who stresses a very important point: '*No physical evidence exists* [Author's Note: Italics Mine].'

He adds to this a catalogue of other issues:

'The experiences appear to be random in location and time. They do not happen to everyone who visits Ben Macdhui, even those people who go to the exact spots where previous witnesses have had the experience. Nor do they appear to happen to the same people twice. The experiences appear to be non-physical in origin, spontaneous and transitory in nature. They seem to be as likely to happen to people who know nothing about the BGM legend as they do to hardened and knowledgeable mountaineers who scoff at the supernatural.

It would be easy to suggest, in the cold light of day, that the BGM legend appears to be little more than a few unusual experiences moulded by the media into a localised folktale. But a number of people have had unusual experiences on and in the vicinity of Ben Macdhui. They have been experiences which have caused rational and hard headed mountaineers to risk their lives in fleeing highly across dangerous ground. Something, physical or non-physical, must have caused those experiences.'

And that's where the whole subject begins to get very slippery, indeed!

When Terror Strikes!

On the matter of the seemingly illogical fear that seems to take a steely and strong grip of so many of those that have fallen under the spell of the BGM phenomenon, Andy says:

'Going back to the accounts, a close, analytical, reading reveals one underlying, constant motif. All the witnesses in the "good" accounts report some form of extreme, uncontrollable panic reaction, leading them to flee in blind terror, often for miles. Fair enough, you might say, anyone would panic if they saw the BGM. But some of the "panics" take place prior to any "sighting", and in the majority of cases the whole experience is solely a panic, the trimmings of BGM legend being tacked on later by writer or witness because of the geographical context of the experience.'

This has all led Andy to ask a most important and relevant question:

'So is there a genuine mystery, after all? Well, if this core phenomenon were isolated to the Cairngorms and the BGM legend, we could probably discount it as an artefact of the storytelling process. But accounts of being gripped by an uncontrollable panic, one which results in fleeing to the point of exhaustion or narrowly avoiding death by falling over cliffs intrigued me. In digging deep in both the paranormal and mountaineering literature I discovered that this core experience is relatively widespread in wild or mountainous areas, but has been either ignored or subsumed into the broader, and more "exciting", area of "ghost" stories. This is a mistake because, whether paranormal or psychological in origin, there appears to be a very real phenomenon at work.

With the specific evidence for a BGM being so sparse,'

Admits Andy,

'but the core phenomenon being so consistent and evidenced elsewhere, it would be a mistake to continue to see the BGM phenomenon in either isolation or terms of being caused by an encounter with a physical entity. The evidence I have gathered suggests that the BGM experience and others can be re-framed as mountain panics onto which local folklore is grafted. Bear with me while I take an excursion to the mountains of madness and speculate on what lives there.'

That excursion takes us back to May 1954, and a man named Clive Elliot. Intending to make use of the excellent weather on his day off, Elliott - who was a water company surveyor - elected to walk the hills from Kilmuir to Staffin, both situated on the Isle of Skye. Everything was fine and dandy until he reached a certain stream in Glen Sneosdale.

On jumping across, and in his, Elliot's, own words, he felt as if he had

'...stepped into another world, my mind just went to pieces. I cannot describe the feeling, one of total, absolute, blind terror. I didn't look round to see what was happening, I just went up the hill and I remember pulling myself against the grass and boosting myself as hard as I could. I've never felt anything like that in my life before and please god I never do again.'

'The feeling stopped after a few hundred yards and Elliot's day continued with no further problems,' adds Andy. As for me, I would add that, just maybe, we should give some degree of consideration to the notion that the process of jumping across the stream was akin to crossing one of Merrily Harpur's Liminal Zones that seem to play at least some sort of role in the affair of the British Bigfoot.

Andy has a further, few choice words of importance to make regarding the witness in this case from the Isle of Skye, who Andy, ultimately, had the very good fortune to personally interview:

'Clive Elliot's account is self-explanatory, a one-off experience totally out of character which has puzzled him intensely over the years. Had Elliot's experience taken place within the Ben Macdhui area, his account would surely have been part of the overall legend. The fact that he did not reveal his experience to anyone until 1996 and did not attempt to connect with any legendary creature suggests that we have got the data as "raw" as possible.'

And, perhaps, Andy has suggested, there just might be something about northern Skye that is somewhat weird, as a result of the fact that the following two accounts both originate from within a few miles of Clive Elliot's uncanny experience. Read on…

Encounters on the Island

Andy begins:

'On a visit to Skye in June 1971 veteran hill walker Brian Miller headed south from the Staffin-Uig road. After passing the top of Bioda Buidhe he began to feel distinctly uneasy, intimidated and depressed, as though something - some thing, perhaps - were watching him. He continued, becoming increasingly convinced that "something malignant was watching and waiting for a chance to spring". After another half mile he descended into a small hollow and, "...really felt fear, for all the world as if something was hiding behind the last rise and would spring if I took my eyes off the route I had taken".

Miller turned and retreated to his car in panic.

'Miller returned to Skye the following year and on one outing walked over the tops toward Baca Ruadh. "Before I'd gone more than three hundred yards I was assailed again by a feeling of unease," Miller told me. He pressed on, but, once again, "...the old feeling of being watched by something malignant became overpowering". The feeling of panic intensified and he, again, abandoned the walk.'

Intrigued by these distinctly out of character attacks of the panicky kind, Andy tells of how

'...Miller did some research and discovered Swire's book on the legends of Skye. In its pages he found the area round the Quaraing (about two miles from his first experience) described as having "an atmosphere which can never be captured. Perhaps it can best be summed up by saying that it is as if 'the terror that walketh in darkness' here walks by day."

Swire also recounts being told by two men that the "...Baca Ruadh....which they visited at different times, gives just this same feeling of terror and potent, living evil. All other Skye hills are friendly, but not the Baca Ruach."'

Andy sums up the curious and unsettling stories of Skye with a notable revelation:

'Both Elliot's and Miller's experiences took place in northern Skye, within a few miles of each other. Both experiences were reported to me independently and the witnesses do not know each other.'

The Legend of Jock o' Bennachie

'Another correspondent,'

Andy expands,

'Mr J. Craig, told me of an incident which took place on Bennachie near Aberdeen. He and his two friends were resting below the summit when, "...we all stopped talking and a most horrid feeling of unease and then absolute terror swept over us. As one person the three of us fled down through heather, boulders, with no thought except get away, get away.'

'They didn't stop running until they reached the foot of the mountain', adds Andy.

'There was no forewarning of this "terror" happening and, oddly, Craig, nor his companions, mentioned the experience to each other for years afterwards. Bennachie has a legend connected to a giant who protects the mountain, known as Jock o' Bennachie. Craig is convinced he and his friends experienced the power of Jock o'Bennachie.'

For the record, 'Jock' was said to make his bed between one tor and another situated on the north-eastern side of Craigshannoch, which has since become known as Little John's Length.

Townsend's Fright

Long-distance walker Chris Townsend, in his book *Walking the Munroes and Tops*, recalls a similar experience by the Allt Innis a'Mhuill in Glen Strathfarrar when he

'...suddenly had a strong feeling of a presence nearby, of something or someone waiting and watching...'

Townsend sensed a 'hint of hostility' in this presence and, 'for a second or two I felt frightened'.

Was Townsend's experience just the results of isolation and a hard day spent on the hill? Or was it caused by something primeval and brooding; something deeply indigenous to the landscape? Andy was determined to find out and contacted the author himself. He received an interesting reply:

'I never thought my brief experience would be noticed. I haven't really anything to add to the description but your email did set me thinking. I don't think isolation or a hard day were anything to do with it. I've walked thousands of miles alone in much remoter places than the Highlands and I often have long days. Much of that walking has been in Western North America where I would have put such a feeling down to there being a bear nearby - and felt much more frightened! Whether it was supernatural terror or not I don't know. Overall I tend towards the sceptical but I can't think of what could have made me feel like that.'

The Fear Spreads...

'Sensations of "presence"' and extreme panic are clearly not restricted to the confines of Ben Macdhui or even the broader area of the Cairngorms. They can occur in any mountainous or wild area. They do not fall into any easy category, which makes their reporting difficult,'

Andy is keen to stress. And there's a very good reason why witnesses may be reluctant to talk openly and publicly, and which Andy totally understands:

'After all, who wants to announce that they have been terrified to the point of flight by something they cannot see, hear or feel?'

The result of this, Andy suggests is that

'...these experiences are often ignored or go unreported until they are noticed as passing remarks in the literature or when they are specifically hunted out by researchers. When these experiences are reported they often become subsumed into local folklore, attached to ghost stories, hauntings and so on. The form that the experience is given by witness or commentator, i.e. giant, ghost, faerie, elemental or whatever supersedes the core phenomenon and becomes the motif for the experience. This makes for an interesting story but, I think, lays a false trail.'

Andy elaborates on his current train of thought:

'Ghost hunter and author Thurston Hopkins received a letter recounting an undated experience not dissimilar to many of the BGM and other panics discussed so far. The writer told of an experience which took place whilst visiting the hills above Rhossilly Bay in South Wales.'

'As he climbed higher he became aware of feeling uneasy, a sensation which increased until he "...sat still and waited-then looked from side to side. I was being WATCHED. Slowly, painfully, in an agony of horror I turned my head to see I knew not what...." He continued his climb, all the time aware of the sensation of being observed. "Then horror, violent sickening seized me. A huge menacing form enveloped rather than touched me. I prayed and shrieked aloud, and began to run - run madly down the steep to the sea." The following day he made enquiries locally to be told: "Many a one has been frightened badly up there. It's got an evil name. Some say the old Stone Men used to live up there..."'

Another account, this one dating from 1965, and also from south Wales, recounts how a local man was walking on the slopes of Foel Feddau, when:

'Suddenly, as though a curtain had fallen, all about him changed completely and he felt the raw edge of fear. He felt that he was in the presence of the unknown...He became aware that evil, invisible eyes were upon him, and he rushed away from that accursed spot.'

'I suddenly felt an intense feeling of my impending death'

The strange experiences keep on coming, such as the following provided to Andy:

'Experienced mountaineer Bill Steele wrote to me detailing an experience which took place on Mt. Giluwe on Papua New Guinea. Several kilometres above the tree-line, Steele and his German climbing partner, casting about for a suitable campsite topped at the mouth of a cave for lunch.'

le:

> 'As we finished we discussed whether to make a base camp there and push on to the peak with a light pack. At this time I suddenly felt an intense feeling of my impending death, there was a sense of being watched by something evil that seemed to be drawing near and about to pounce. Although there was nothing to be seen apart from the pleasant shelter and it was a bright dry day I knew I must get away immediately from that place.'

> 'When I called to Dieter to grab our stuff and run he thought I must have somehow lost all reason as he felt nothing unusual at all. I then panicked and said he could do what he liked but I was off! I threw the pack over my shoulder and ran as fast as I could down the track and only slowed down when I reached the treeline several kilometres away.'

Steele, offers Andy,

> '...also commented that he felt safer the further away he got from the cave mouth, echoing other accounts where witnesses have felt the feeling increase or decrease as they moved across the landscape.'

So, what is going on?

In an effort to try to rationalise the phenomenon of the Big Grey Man of Ben Macdhui, Andy commences with the following:

> 'There are many, many more similar accounts from across the world. All include isolated areas and mountain panics. Some, like those on Ben Macdhui and Bennachie, have become attached to and synonymous with entities said to cause the panic. Some appear to be in clusters, like those of Northern Skye, but remain as yet "unnamed".

> Others stand alone, as one-off, random experiences in space and time. All the witnesses were profoundly terrified by their encounters with this unknown terror. There is genuine mystery here. But once identified, even a possibly new genre of anomalous experience becomes just another "interesting" story for the Fortean equivalent of stamp collectors unless some attempt is made to untangle possible cause or to put the phenomena in context. As several of the experiences have taken place in the same general area it is tempting to suggest that the origin for the experiences are intimately connected to, and possibly caused by, the area.'

And, it's here that we began treading in decidedly choppy and mysterious waters...

Of Panic and Energy

> 'Earth Mysterians, nature mystics and fringe scientists have long suggested there are "energies" locked into the landscape,' says Andy. They are, he adds, 'energies which can be tapped into intentionally or accidentally and which are responsible for a wide variety of strange phenomena from fairies to ghosts to UFOs. It is also

claimed that these energies can cause illness, stress, unease and a range of psychological and physiological symptoms. This idea is echoed in the Chinese concept of feng-shui where landscapes or dwellings would be physically altered to aid the flow of an energy called ch'i, which in turn affected people's well-being. So could it be unspecified "energies" of this nature which are causing mountain panics?'

Well, let's see, shall we? Not surprisingly, it is still to Andy that we look for the answers on this particular aspect of the puzzle. He talks about something that we have covered earlier: suicide.

'Archaeologist and dowser Tom Lethbridge thought so and referred to these incidents as "ghouls". As a teenager he and his mother had experienced "a horrible feeling of gloom and depression" in some woods, which led them to hurry away. Later a suicide was found almost at the spot. When married, both Lethbridge and his wife experienced a similar ghoul independently at Ladram Bay in Devon. This seems to be one of the spots where the experience is replicable as they felt it again, together. His wife walked into it again at the top of a cliff and, moreover she had an odd feeling, as if someone - or something - was urging her to jump over. Shades of the fleeing panics detailed so far. Lethbridge attributed this phenomenon to a "place-field" caused by underground water producing changes in the earth's magnetic field and thus affecting the brain of anyone who happened to be in the right place at the right time.'

So-called 'Repeater Spots', like the Cairngorms, North Skye, and Ladram Bay may, if investigated further, suggests Andy,

'...yield positive evidence of "energies" which lead to panics and possibly suicides. The Christian church has certainly held this view and accident black-spots and regular suicide locations have been exorcised to rid them of the perceived demonic influence. Many of these locations are said to create effects which temporarily unbalance the human mind. As an example of how they include the type of "panic" I am discussing here, an earth mysteries journal printed the following letter from Michael Cook, in which he describes a car journey home along familiar, well travelled roads.'

The letter reads as follows: 'As I was driving around a not particularly sharp bend, and not too quickly, I suddenly felt seized by panic; I felt I was being dragged off the road and would not negotiate the bend. It took a considerable effort of willpower to keep to the road. In a short while the panic disappeared and my confidence returned.'

Cook, notes Andy,

'...had driven over that same stretch of road many times before and after his experience with nothing untoward happening. On the surface this seems to be exactly the same type of phenomena experienced by BGM witnesses and others who have encountered a random and meaningless "panic".'

Mothman Parallels

Andy's research into potentially paranormal panics has also touched upon another area of research, too:

> 'In his classic study of the fear which gripped West Virginia during 1966 John Keel describes his encounter with a panic zone. Whilst out driving alone after midnight in the "TNT area" Keel had, as he puts it: "one curious experience."'

Over to Keel, himself:

> 'As I passed a certain point on one of the isolated roads I was suddenly engulfed in fear. I stepped on the gas and after I went a few yards my fear vanished as quickly as it came.'

Andy adds that Keel:

> 'noted the exact spot and drove through it twice more, with exactly the same effect'.

Keel then stopped his car and walked back to the 'zone of fear', fully:

> 'alert for any rustle of bushes, measuring my own breathing and emotions. I was perfectly calm until I took one step too many and was back in the zone. I almost panicked and ran, but I forced myself to look around and proceed slowly'.

Keel, reveals Andy, determined that the zone was about fifteen feet across, and walked back through it to reach his car. Keel could only conclude that he was 'probably walking through a beam of ultrasonic waves.' Returning to the spot in the morning he found the 'zone' had gone, and there was nothing in the area to account for it.

From Budden to Devereux

> 'Researchers Albert Budden and Paul Devereux,'

Andy highlights,

> '...have both written extensively about "energies" which can have the type of effect we are discussing here. Devereux suggests consciousness-affecting energy can originate via natural radioactivity and electro-magnetic fields. His books list numerous examples of anomalous experiences he believes have occurred after an encounter with these energies. Budden contends that modern electro-magnetic pollution as well as natural electro-magnetism can have a radical and often deleterious effect on people.'

Andy feels, as do I, it is important to note that:

> 'None of this is completely proven, but between them Lethbridge, Devereux, Budden and others are building a persuasive case for the earth's natural energies playing a part as being at least the stimulus for "paranormal" experiences. Critics will have none of this. Even the kindest would say they are replacing old folk tales with new-age techno folklore, claiming that allegations of these "energies" are

rooted in unverifiable narrative and on science which is at best tenuous, at worst specious. But there is no doubt that the forces of natural radiation [and] electromagnetism exist and [it is] reasonable to speculate they can have an effect on consciousness. With or without the acceptance of "fringe" energies there are other ways of looking at the causation and interpretation of "panics."'

'They accommodate the gods of the ancients'

Quite possibly getting to the very core of the mysterious matter, Andy brings the following to the table:

'Being among mountains and other wild places is frequently an awe inspiring experience where the difference between the natural and supernatural is often only a matter of perception. Perhaps senses stretched by exertion, heightened by beauty and isolation create psychological phenomena which causes panic of the type outlined. Or perhaps the psychologists are wrong and there is another reason. In his book, Gulfs of Blue Air, Jim Crumley lists ten "More Reasons For Hills". Number six is because, "They accommodate the gods of the ancients". A clue?'

In answer to his own question, Andy offers these words:

'In the western world at the end of the 20th Century, it is our predilection as a society to interpret any unknown experience as psychological or paranormal in nature, as if that designation explains it. Frequently we use one unknown to "explain" another and explanations change with the times. The nature based cosmologies of our ancestors in these Isles would have no problem with the experiences I have recounted here. They believed every facet of the landscape had a presence, and was a personification of a god or spirit, the genius loci. Anomalous or visionary experiences would have been interpreted as belonging to that particular rock, valley, cliff etc and symbolised in a form relevant to local mythology or folklore.

Whether the experience was repeated or not the idea of the genius loci inhabiting that particular spot would become embedded in and handed down through the local tradition. My dictionary defines genius loci as the spirit dwelling in a particular spot or the characteristic atmosphere of a place. Does that sound familiar? So in a way the BGM and giant of Bennachie and so could be described as genius loci, still being experienced, irrespective of any pre-existing traditions concerning them.'

Now in full-throttle, Andy takes things a step further:

'So perhaps these mountain panics are the direct experience of a location's genius loci. But that's as un-provable a concept as the "earth energies"' theory or as pointless as a reductionist psychological viewpoint. Visionary experiences, mountain panics, earth "energies" can also be seen as metaphors for spontaneous psychic or psychological experiences, which in turn are metaphors themselves for any experience in which human consciousness comes up against the forces of nature. Not nature as described by the aesthetics of landscape appreciation via art or literature. Or nature as in the form of a scientific understanding via the various relevant ology's. All those are just temporary ways of describing. I mean what Cairngorm poet Nan Shepherd refers to as the "experience of nature in the raw, a primitive thing, and utterly, utterly baffling."'

The Beginnings of Panic

'To even begin to understand that,'

Admits Andy,

'we must go back to the description of experiences given by witnesses to all these phenomena and the core of that description seems to be one of "panic"'.

The word 'panic', which the witnesses to these strange experiences often use, derives, of course, from the Greek god Pan. According to one book on mythology:

'The feeling of solitude and lonesomeness which weighs upon travellers in wild mountain places....was ascribed to the presence of Pan.....And thus anxiety and alarm, arising from no visible or intelligible cause, came to be called 'panic fear', that is, such fear as is produced by the agitating presence of Pan.'

Another writer has it that:

'Pan is unlimited in movement or scope of action - in the original Greek he is literally "everywhere". The apparent form, again, is symbolic, rather than representational of any physical entity. The elemental archetype is more often sensed than seen.'

All descriptions of encounters with Pan, says Andy, speak of the same criteria and phenomena; lonely, often mountainous, or wilderness areas, the core phenomenon being randomly triggered, and frequently experienced, or later described in terms of a physical entity, which isn't really 'there.'

Pan Comes to Texas

The above makes me very mindful of the most notable resident monster of White Rock Lake, Dallas, Texas, USA, where I lived from 2004 to 2008: The legendary Goat Man. So the story went, on several occasions in the 1970s and 1980s a distinctly odd creature was seen flitting in and out of the trees after sunset, and that was described as being man-like in form, around seven feet in height, but with Goat-style protrusions sticking out of its head, and hooves instead of feet. The description of the animal was eerily like that of the fabled Satyrs of Greek and Roman legend. And it must be noted that numerous other cultures had an awareness that such strange creatures were lurking among them - and for millennia. There was, for example, the demon goat-man Azazel, the goat-beast of the mountains that was feared by the herdsmen of Parnassus, and, of course, the aforementioned god, Pan.

The deity of woods and fields and of flocks and shepherds, Pan dwelt in grottos, roamed both mountains and valleys, was a lover of music, and was universally feared. In ancient days, any form of overwhelming dread without a discernible cause was very often ascribed to the actions and presence of Pan, and became known as a Panic terror. Pan came to be considered a symbol of the universe and the personification of Nature, and was almost certainly the inspiration for the Latin divinities, Sylvanus and Faunus.

A fascinating account that is deserved on mention in this chapter was brought to my attention by Sandy

Weirdness at White Rock Lake, Dallas, Texas. Copyright: Nick Redfern.

Grace, who had seen the Goat Man up close and personal in August 2001 - right at White Rock Lake. Grace had been jogging around the lake on the nine-mile long trail when, at around 2.00 p.m., out of the trees, she told me, stepped the strangest looking thing she had ever seen.

Large, and covered in thin, coarse brown hair and with two large horn-like protrusions, the half-man-half-beast strode purposefully in her direction with a malevolent, sneering grin on its face. Bizarrely, when it got within about fifteen feet of the terror-stricken Grace, the animal crouched on its four limbs and vanished in a flash of light. She was sure that it had not been a hallucination, but was equally sure that such a thing could not live within the confines of White Rock Lake - or, indeed, anywhere on the face of the Earth.

Very interestingly, and of deep relevance to the words of Andy Roberts, Grace told me that less than a minute before the Goat Man appeared, she was overcome by an intense feeling of fear - albeit for no particular reason she could fathom, then or now. She had never suffered from panic attacks (before or since) but figured that this was probably the best way to describe how she felt. I thought to myself that it could also have been a classic description of an encounter with Pan, the God of the Woods, centuries or millennia ago.

~ss of Nature

ic-inducing monster of White Rock Lake now discussed and dissected, back to Andy who, ˄ably, given the sheer high-strangeness of what we have encountered thus far, asks:

'So, have all the witnesses to "panics" met Pan, and isn't that just another bonkers explanation anyway? The clue to it is to get away from notions of entities, nature spirits, energies and so on as being in any sense objectively real, and to look at "panics" and the Pan experience as yet another metaphor for the interpretation of "raw nature" when it overrides our normal waking consciousness.'

Perhaps the clearest synthesis of the panic experience and one with the most relevance here is that given by Jungian analyst James Hillman, who wrote:

'Panic, especially at night when the citadel darkens and the heroic ego sleeps, is a direct participation mystique in nature, a fundamental, even ontological experience of the world as alive and in dread. Objects become subjects; they move with life while one is oneself paralysed with fear. When existence is experienced through instinctual levels of fear, aggression, hunger or sexuality, images take on a compelling life of their own. The imaginal is never more vivid than when we are connected with it instinctually. The world alive is of course animism; that this living world is divine and imagined by different gods with attributes and characteristics is polytheistic pantheism. That fear, dread, horror are natural is wisdom. In Whitehead's term nature alive means Pan, and panic flings open a door into this reality.'

Andy notes that Hillman's words are, collectively,

'...an apt description of exactly what happens. In wild or mountainous country the solitude, exertion and oft overpowering awe of the surroundings together with realisation (consciously or otherwise) of being a fragile entity in an awesome and ultimately unknowable landscape could be said to overpower the "heroic", or rational, ego. The "objects", i.e. the environment and its contents become subjects - mist becomes BGM, areas of landscape become threatening, noises assume and infer preternatural origin, and then existence in all its forms is encountered directly. Human consciousness is not prepared for this and panic results, the witness fleeing until the spell is broken, often by contact with other human beings or a familiar sound or location.'

But, even Andy has to concede, questions still frustratingly linger:

'What triggers this? Well, as we've seen it could be any or all of the "energy" theories put forward for Devereux et al. Or just the age-old call of the wild. Recall how Tewnion's shooting of the BGM was, according to him, just a panic response to mist, or how Wendy Wood believed her terror could have started with a deer bark? Or how the Bleaklow informant could only see wisps of mist when the panic had subsided, the 'giant' long since receded into the imaginal realm.

Whilst they must remain a possibility for the trigger we need not even invoke mysterious energies as the cause of these panics as the following episode, from the Cairngorms near Ben Macdhui, illustrates: "I was coming home round about

1.00am along the Revoan road when my nerve suddenly gave way. It was a fine winter's night, fairly clear, and I was belting along it when it suddenly hit me. Exactly what triggered it off I don't know - maybe the call of a vixen or a wild cat, the hoot of an owl or the bark of a roe-buck. Anyhow, I trembled. I ran whiles and walked fast, looking over my shoulder till I got home in the small hours, soaked with perspiration...A doctor told me it could happen to any fit man and he could not account for it."'

That experience, reveals Andy,

'...occurred to a naturalist and forester with long experience in remote areas of the Cairngorms. Like many of the other witnesses he was a hardened hill man, knowledgeable about, yet sceptical of, local ghost lore and the like. In other areas of Fortean study, say ufology or ghost-hunting, these witnesses would have their experience as observers and scepticism used to support the objective reality of their experience. But that's the myth of the credible witness. We're all fallible and susceptible and like the doctor said, "it could happen to any fit man." And apparently does.'

A further, significantly important point is made by Andy:

'Irrespective of whether these experiences are caused by the mind suddenly glimpsing the immensity of nature in the raw, or whether they are caused by as yet unknown forces in nature, they amount to the same thing - the direct experience of the overpowering force of nature and existence, to be fled from, to be personified as the BGM, a giant, the devil, genius loci or whatever.'

Buchan's Comments

As another example of the random nature of these panics, and of how they can affect others, take careful note of author John Buchan's (writing as Lord Tweedsmuir) unscheduled meeting with Pan:

'We do not hear so much to-day of the goat-foot god.....But the experience which was the basis of the myth does not go unrecorded. In wild places or in wild weather, men are still awed by a sense of the immensity and pitilessness of Nature. There is a Natura rnaligna as well as the Wordsworthian Natura benigna...Sometimes, too, there come moments when one feels a kind of personal malevolence, the sense of a hostile will which almost takes bodily form, and which sets the nerves fluttering in despite of the reason. In such moments one sees- or at any rate feels-what the ancients meant by Pan.'

Buchan goes on to relate an experience from 1911 in the Bavarian Highlands. Returning from the summit of the Alpspitze he noticed his guide had:

'...fallen silent and, glancing at him, was amazed to see that his face was dead white, that sweat stood in beads on his forehead, and that his eyes were staring ahead as if he were in an agony of fear - as if terror were all around him so that he dared not look one way rather than another. Suddenly he began to run, and I ran too, some power not myself constraining me. Terror had seized me also, but I did not know what I dreaded. It was like the epidemic of giggling which overcomes children who have no wish to laugh. We ran-we ran like demented bacchanals, tearing down the glades, leaping rocks, bursting through thickets, colliding with trees, sometimes colliding with each other, and all the time we never uttered a sound. At last we fetched up beside the much-frequented high-way, where we lay for a time utterly exhausted. For the rest of the road home we did not speak; we did not even dare look at each other.'

Buchan could only offer questions and answers in the following fashion:

'What was the cause? I suppose it was panic. Sebastian had seen the goat-foot god or something of the kind...and he had made me feel his terror.'

Buchan's guide had experienced 'Pan' and therefore panic, which had been transmitted to him in the form of contagion.

'This experience,'

Andy observes perceptibly,

'is very like Craig's experience on Bennachie, even down to the fact of the percipients not discussing the event afterwards.'

Buchan, in passing, makes a very important point, namely that 'Pan' can be experienced as a terror or as its opposite; a benign force. And, once again, a trawl through the mountaineering literature reveals a plethora of experiences where people have experienced Wordsworthian raptures as an exact opposite to the malevolence personified by the BGM and the other nameless terrors that Andy has described.

So, now, it is finally time to allow Andy to summarise his views and ideas on what it is that provokes the Big Gray Man of Ben Macdhui and the accompanying feeling of overwhelming terror that strikes, very often out of the blue:

'All I can say for sure about this research is that the core experience appears very similar in all cases, and that there is no one single occurrence which triggers it. I am also wary about needlessly creating another Fortean pigeon-hole - that of mountain panic - for unexplained phenomena. But based on the evidence I have reviewed both new and old, I think this is a very real psychological or psychic phenomenon and one which may lie at the core of many so called "paranormal" experiences. Its triggers may be many but they all stem from the human instrument's perception of and relationship with the reality we live in. One commentator wrote to Affleck Gray: "The most mysterious thing to be found among mountains was the human brain."'

In the end, even Andy admits,

'...we can but speculate. It's entertaining and informative. But only the witnesses who have experienced these panics, witnessed the Fear Liath Mor and its brethren know for sure what it's like and what the experience means for them. There is a vast gulf between those who know and those of us who speculate. Huge Corrie's letter to Affleck Gray summed up both the experience and the difference well:,'

'Sometimes in dark days, in wild places, Skye in dense mist and rain, in desert, mountains and jungle, I have thought that I got a hint or two. From our fancied and narrow security, I know, having looked out upon the wilderness in turmoil where there could be no help and no witness of our undoing, where the gleams were fleeting, as though the daylight itself were riven and collapsing, that I saw the filmy shapes of those things which darken and affright the minds of primitives. While the sky is changeful and menacing, and there are storms at sea, when our fellows are absent, when shades take their hour of ease and voices whisper in wood and stone, and mischance and death are veiled, but here we shall have gods and ghosts. The sharp sighted collectors of old-train lumber, and similar curios may still keep busy, and tie-up their dry bundles of mythology and superstitions; but I myself - and any Scottish hillman could make plenty more.'

I know that feeling too.

A Personal Experience of the Panic

Ray Roberts Lake in Texas and its surrounding areas are notable: In times past they were the collective haunt of various Native American Indian tribes, including the Comanche, the Kiowa and the Tonkawa.

Lake Ray Roberts, Texas: A source of paranormal fear. Copyright: Nick Redfern.

And it was an area I visited in early 2008 with one Lance Armstrong, who runs DAPS: The Denton Area Paranormal Society. Lance had told me some months earlier that there had been a number of interesting UFO encounters in the vicinity. And in May 1990 strange roaring and screaming noises of a distinctly animalistic nature were heard in the woods. Notably, and in the same time frame, nothing less than an approximately eight foot tall hairy man-beast was seen late at night by several young men who were camped on the north side of the lake. Well, of course, with all of that going on, we just had to check the place out.

I followed Lance in my car as he drove to a small parking area - that was just about as close as a person could get by vehicle to where all the specific Bigfoot action had taken place eighteen years earlier. We were then faced with approximately a mile-long trek through the thick woods, up and down several very steep climbs, and across a couple of rocky sandbars, against which the lake's cool waters gently lapped. But, finally, we got to the location where all of the hair-raising – and hairy – action had occurred: A steep and wide hill that was packed from floor to ceiling with dense trees and rotting vegetation. In addition, there was a seeming distinct lack of animal life and noise. Deathly quiet would be a veritable understatement.

Even though the Bigfoot encounters had taken place many years before, experience has shown me time and again that one should never turn up the chance to conduct a deep investigation of such a mysterious locale - just in the event that something of profound interest might turn up. And it did.

Taking into consideration the fact that the hill was a large one, Lance and I decided that the wisest approach would be to split up and cover as much of the area as it was humanly possible to do so. It was a good idea, to say the least. As I have come to learn, in areas where Bigfoot has been seen on regular occasions, it is not uncommon to find what have become known in creature-seeking circles as 'Bigfoot Teepees' - very much like those found at Bolam Lake by Jon Downes, members of the CFZ, and the Twilight Worlds group in early 2003.

These curious structures are essentially comprised of thick branches that, in many cases, look like they have literally been wrenched off trees and placed into distinct pyramid-style formations. Some researchers have suggested they are made by the creatures as territorial markers, while others have suggested they might very well be connected to Bigfoot rituals of a mating nature.

A definitive answer to their construction still eludes us; however, I do not exaggerate when I say that the peak of the wooded hill was infested with such formations. To the left of us, to the right of us, in front of us, and behind us. They were everywhere. Of course, out came the cameras to preserve the astounding scene for posterity. But there was more. Curious stone structures were prevalent, including what looked like a miniature version of Stonehenge; and strange, almost cave-like, dwellings could be found in the undergrowth on the steep slopes of the hill.

But, it was while Lance was exploring elsewhere and I was wandering around these curious structures - of both a teepee and Stonehenge-like nature - that I began to feel uneasy, clammy, and short of breath. I was in the grip of the same fear that so easily and callously took over the minds and hearts of all those people on the Cairngorms years, decades, and maybe even centuries, earlier. It cannot be relegated to mere excitement, as I have been on numerous expeditions in search of strange beasts over the years, and on no other occasion - before or after - have I ever been affected in such an extreme manner. And although I am not, nor ever have been, prone to panic attacks, it took all of my strength to try and focus my breathing, relax, and banish from my mind the distinct feeling that invisible and hostile forms of a Bigfoot-type nature were watching me, and doing their very best to force me - mentally as opposed to physically - to leave the area.

Like those who found themselves so exposed to the Big Grey Man, I did not see any unusual creature. And, in my case, there were not even any crunching footsteps on the leaf-covered floor of the heavily wooded hill. In fact, I felt like I was in a vacuum. There was actually a distinct lack of sound, rather than the heavy, reverberating thuds of gigantic feet. There was just an overpowering sense of something to be greatly feared, and an equally overwhelming feeling of a malevolent presence. It stayed with me - in varying degrees that rose and feel for more than half an hour - until Lance and I returned to our respective vehicles, and we were on the road, homeward-bound and away from those unsettling woods. The panic, I know, is utterly real. And, in some fashion, it has played a significant role in the development of the Bigfoot puzzle in the British Isles (and particularly so with regard to the Big Grey Man of the Cairngorms, as the sterling work of Andy Roberts demonstrates), in the United States, and probably just about anywhere and everywhere in which the wild things are said to wander - whatever their ultimate point of origin, or origins, may be.

Richard Freeman, seeker of the truth behind the British wild man. Copyright: Nick Redfern.

CHAPTER 40
REBOOTING TO THE REALM
OF THE MONSTERS
'...something was playing around with my
cerebral cortex...'

F inally, we come to the truly fascinating theory of Jon Downes and Richard Freeman. It's one
that, to some degree, echoes the theories of Albert Budden and Paul Devereux. You will recall
the words of Andy Roberts in relation to the work of the latter pair:

> 'Researchers Albert Budden and Paul Devereux have both written extensively
> about "energies" which can have the type of effect we are discussing here.
> Devereux suggests consciousness-affecting energy can originate via natural
> radioactivity and electro-magnetic fields. His books list numerous examples of
> anomalous experiences he believes have occurred after an encounter with these
> energies. Budden contends that modern electro-magnetic pollution as well as
> natural electro-magnetism can have a radical and often deleterious effect on
> people. None of this is completely proven, but between them Lethbridge,
> Devereux, Budden and others are building a persuasive case for the earth's natural
> energies playing a part as being at least the stimulus for "paranormal"
> experiences.'

But here's the important question in relation to the above: why should so many of these experiences
result in the manifestation of creatures of a definitive cryptozoological nature? Jon and Richard have
more than a few ideas when it comes to answering that particular question, as Jon notes...

A 'Global Template'

> 'What I saw at Bolam in January 2003 was a very real phenomenon. But whether it
> had any objective reality outside of my own experience, I'm not sure. But, there
> were several of us who saw this thing at once; or, largely the same thing. I'm fairly
> convinced that what I saw was a para-psychological phenomenon, rather than a
> flesh and blood one,' says Jon. So, how does he explain the nature of the
> experience?'

Well, he does so in a fashion that may well get to the very crux of the puzzle:

> 'What I believe is a theory that Richard [Freeman] and I came up with years ago.

Actually, he came up with it first. Richard noticed that wherever he went on an expedition, the same types of mystery animal were being reported. As just one of many examples, he was in Thailand in 2000 and came back telling me that, as well as the Naga – this giant snake he was looking for, and which is analogous to the western dragon, and perhaps lake-monsters as well – there were sightings of a Bigfoot-type of hairy beast, a large and mysterious golden cat, and a large winged thing [Author's Note: the Garuda a bird man from Indo-Chinese legend that is akin to the Japanese Tengu], very much like the Owlman of Cornwall. Everywhere you go, there is what Richard calls a "global template" for monsters.'

And, me and Richard have looked into this very deeply, and you basically have got the same types of paranormal mystery animals reported all over the world, and in nearly each and every culture. There are the big, hairy, ape-like creatures. You have the little, hairy, ape-like creatures. You have phantom black dogs, phantom big cats, dragons and lake-monsters, and you have the large, flying things. So, we were looking for a unifying theory behind all this.'

And it's now that we come to the heart of that unifying theory:

'Richard and I have concluded that you have to go back to when the Human Race was a bunch of a couple of thousand, small, hairy creatures walking around on the plains of East Africa. And every man, woman and child on the planet is descended from these same, little, hairy creatures. And, at that time, there would have been a lot of things that would have scared the hell out of them, and which they would have been in mortal danger from, such as large, wild hunting dogs, and big cats of that era. They may even have been in dire danger from their own relatives, such as the smaller, stronger, hairy men, and the larger, and now-extinct, primitive, giant apes. They would have also been in danger from crocodiles and possibly very large birds, too, which the fossil record shows did exist – very large. All of these things would have provoked a "fight or flight" response in our ancestors. And all of these types of creature are present in today's world as mystery animals.

Richard and I believe the memories of these creatures, and our ancestors' experiences with them, and fear of them, have become hardwired into our subconscious as a kind of fossil memory. And when I say "our" I mean everyone. It's in all of us, whether we know it or not. And that, under certain circumstances, something can make your brain reboot to that primitive state, and perhaps create images of those primitive creatures our ancestors lived in fear of. This is, we believe, in much the same way as when your computer reboots it first goes back to its most primitive state, no matter how many programs you might be running when it crashes and needs to reboot. And, we think that when this happens to the human brain, you can experience one of those archetypal, primal fears, in the form of a dragon, a big cat, a black dog, and even the large hairy man-beast.'

A fascinating theory, certainly, but what might make the human brain reboot in the fashion that Jon describes? Once again, he has some specific theories and ideas with which Richard accords:

'The human brain is, basically, an incredibly sophisticated computer. And one of the things that make computers reboot from time to time is an electrical power surge. I think it's very interesting that in places where the British Bigfoot has been seen, such as at Bolam Lake, we had an enormous amount of electrical equipment fail on us. This was equipment that was tested in Devon before we left, and even on the day before I had my encounter, and it all worked perfectly – until we got to the lake. The idea of power-failures in Fortean situations goes back to John Keel, et al, and is very well known.'

We also found there were strange magnetic anomalies at the lake, too. And when we got back to Devon we found there were veins of magnetic iron-ore underneath that very part of the country. And we're wondering if these weird magnetic anomalies, caused by perfectly natural phenomena, can affect, or interfere with, the human brain, and cause it to reboot to that most primitive stage, and those very primitive, fossil memories – as me and Richard call them – of all these various types of archetypal creatures in Cryptozoology, and you can experience one of these great primal fears. In my case, at Bolam, it was in the form of a large ape-like animal.'

But, what of the so-called Bigfoot Teepees found at Bolam? Some might say that these are evidence of the presence of a tangible, living entity, rather than one that thundered out of the depths of some form of inherited memory. Jon feels that this issue is a definitive red-herring that actually has only served to muddy the waters:

'I've always found the whole "Bigfoot Teepee" thing dodgy as hell. I'll give you an example. Just recently, we bought a chainsaw, as there are places in the garden - the trees - that haven't been pruned in years. And there are bits and places where the branches have grown together in what look like quite a complicated way. This is in my little garden in Woolsery. You've got trees and branches doing odd things. And, it is things like this that mean I've never been impressed by the Bigfoot Teepees. I think they are purely natural phenomena and nothing to do with Bigfoot – in Britain or anywhere.'

Getting back to the issue of rebooting Bigfoot, Jon is careful to point out the following:

'Now, we admit it's not a theory that can explain everything, because some of the world's man-beasts, such as the Yeti and Orang-Pendek, are flesh and blood. Some of the Bigfoot sightings are; some aren't. But, for the ones in Britain, they aren't flesh and blood; so, both Richard and I feel that this theory is a very viable one to explain why people might see Bigfoot in Britain.'

And what I can also tell you is that what I saw at Bolam had a great effect on my cerebral cortex. Endorphins are the pleasure chemicals released during sex. There are two substances which mimic the production of endorphins. They are chocolate and opiates, both of which I have abused in my time. And I know the effect that drugs can have on the central nervous system. And, after whatever it was I saw in Bolam in 2003, my body was immediately flooded with endorphins. That is a sign, to me, that something was playing around with my cerebral cortex.'

As for the other people at Bolam who saw the same thing I saw, well, maybe, we can externalize these images – like a Tulpa. Or, quite possibly, the expectation of us all potentially seeing a British Bigfoot at Bolam made us all hardwire the very same image when we were all rebooted.'

A very similar theory has been postulated by North Carolina, USA-based researcher Micah Hanks, author of the groundbreaking book, *Magic, Mysticism and the Molecule.* His words, without interruption from me, follow:

'From time to time there are reports that fall under the "Bigfoot" category that are, to put it simply, present a lot of disturbing problems for eyewitnesses. While these "high strangeness" reports (an expression that had become innate to the study of odd occurrences tucked within the realms of Forteana) are in the seldom minority, they are often overlooked by the greater cryptozoology community for a number of reasons.'

Primarily, this has to do with the fact that the study of creatures like "Bigfoot," by virtue of the designated title cryptozoology (the study of hidden animals), approaches this mystery from the perspective that these entities, whatever they may really be, are in fact some form of biological entity that closely resembles humankind. To wit, if indeed the Sasquatch myth is anything more than a myth, the best avenue, and thus the most widely accepted approach to their study, seems to be afforded us in their treatment as flesh-and-blood entities. However, when peering a bit deeper into the mystery, these "beings" may boast a number of curious elements that beg further consideration...and may similarly warrant different modes of thought applied to understanding their overall meaning.

Chief among the kinds of "mysteries" I allude to here are the cases of "disappearing" Bigfoot creatures which, again, will most often tend to be dismissed by the serious Sasquatch researcher. Indeed, there are a small minority in the collected witness accounts that not only involve the appearance of creatures like Bigfoot, but also apparent metaphysical abilities some have ascribed to them in terms of being able to simply "vanish" into thin air.

On a personal note, I should mention here no less than two stories along these lines that I've been told over the years...while one seems like it may have been told to me under less-than-reliable circumstances, on at least one occasion while visiting a Bigfoot conference in Newcomerstown, Ohio, I was nonetheless told in strictest confidence by one of the presenters about his own encounter with "Chewbacca" on a dark country road in Pennsylvania back during the mid 1990s. It was right around dusk, and as he watched the animal strolling along the roadway between two corn fields at around dusk, illuminated in the headlights of his vehicle, the thing very suddenly vanished, leaving no trace of the creature he had observed! For rather obvious reasons, the presenter in question had felt it might be in good taste to omit this aspect of the story from his presentation.

This illustrates, again, the general treatment toward the high-strangeness angle associated with the annals of Sasquatchery. Indeed, while there may be a plethora of reports that seem to involve odd-goings-on ranging from the disappearances described above, to Bigfoot creatures seen wearing clothing—and even Sasquatch encounters that occur in conjunction with flying saucers—these things seem so outrageous within the cultural context we have ascribed to the Bigfoot beast (that of a relic hominid and possible missing link, or similar species that has evolved parallel to our own) that we simply cannot accept them.

But asking one of those really difficult questions, I think we must consider something else that is troubling about the mystery surrounding Bigfoot: while these "animals" appear to be quite physical and consisting of flesh and blood like you or I, they have a curious preponderance in terms of there elusiveness. That is, even if a small population of the creatures were all that existed worldwide, shouldn't we have just a bit more hard evidence supporting their existence?

To be fair, many would argue that such evidence does exist, in fact, and that the real problem involves the various avenues that are not being reached in terms of bringing compelling evidence to the forefront of the scientific mainstream. However, the apparent lack of what we might at least call a "smoking gun" could again point to the notion that there could be more to the elusiveness these creatures have such an apparent mastery of.

One working premise I've considered has to do with the possibility that Bigfoot creatures, while physical to some degree, may actually represent some aspect of humanity. This sounds very strange, and difficult to accept, no doubt. But bear with me for a moment: while they obviously aren't "human" like you or I, the thought has crossed my mind nonetheless that Bigfoot creatures could potentially by semi-physical entities, or representative of some kind of consciousness, but which for some reason are perceived in a variety of capacities by most humans which entails tapping into a sort of archetypal substructure within our own consciousness. In other words, certain strange phenomena witnessed at various times may appear as "monsters" similar to humans, simply because whatever the consciousness/intelligence behind those encounters may actually be exists beyond the realm of that which is entirely perceptible to humans, at least in a conventional sense.

While other alternatives exist in terms of the "disappearing" Bigfoot reports (such as active camouflaging abilities, etc), it is still worthy of consideration, when taking into account those serious high-strangeness reports, whether there could possibly be an ongoing interaction humanity is having with something, and that while Sasquatch may appear to us as one piece of that puzzle, they also seem to be, in this context at least, something which is only one aspect of a much larger mystery: an enigma spanning the various realms of human consciousness and perceptibility.'

CONCLUSIONS

And, now, our long and winding journey into the undeniably weird, abnormal, illogical, and mystery-filled world of the British Bigfoot is at its end. So, in light of numerous cases, witness testimony, reports, and theories that span a significant number of centuries and pretty much the entirety of the nation's very landscape itself, have we made any real sense concerning the real nature of the creature that lurks among us – sometimes within the ancient woods, forests and mountains of Britain, but also, on many occasions, right in the heart of modern day suburbia? I think, and certainly hope, we have!

Without doubt, I would like to believe that all but the most closed-minded of souls will now conclude that when we have carefully weeded out (A) the hoaxes, (B) the occasional escaped animal, (C) a very few cases of real people living wild (possibly including the Suffolk-based wild men of Sproughton and Orford, and the green children of Woolpit), (D) the occasional, tragic unfortunate, such as the wartime inmate of Starcross Hospital, Devon, and (E) the honest misidentifications, whatever is then left, and whatever still walks these fair isles and passes for Bigfoot, wild men or Woodwose, it most certainly is not an animal of physical properties, nor has it ever been. It is, by definition, something less than – or, quite possibly, something more than – a beast of mere mortal proportions.

Its seemingly never-ending association with old bridges, ancient stone circles, areas of archaeological significance, and bodies of water both large and small; its ability to apparently thrive very nicely with nary a morsel of food or living areas; those strange talents that permit it to significantly affect electrical equipment, and place people into a 'pisky led'-type state of confusion or a condition of sheer panic; the conundrum of its fragile 'here one minute and gone the next' existence; and its association to, and parallels with, countless other Fortean wonders, all lead me to conclude that the British Bigfoot is most definitely not what some may want it to be, believe it to be, or possibly – deep down, subconsciously, as a means to try and uphold their own beliefs on the matter – even need it to be.

Of the main, highly-informed body of researchers of the phenomenon of Bigfoot in Britain – whether it is Neil Arnold, Jon Downes, Richard Freeman, Andy Roberts, or Ronan Coghlan – not a single one of them adheres to the idea that a living ape-man dwells, or ever has dwelled, in these island parts. Not one of them. Yet, in their own unique ways, and by using their own experiences, case-studies, and theories as springboards into the dark domain of the unknown, they don't doubt the reality of a phenomenon of sorts. But, it's the nature of that phenomenon – internal, external, down to earth, or of a paranormal nature - that still keeps us, and them, guessing and pondering to a most significant degree.

Whether Tulpa-style guardians designed and created in centuries-gone to protect the nation's most sacred ancient sites from invading forces, the spirits of long-deceased animals, infernal beasts invoked as a result of the dastardly sacrifice of unfortunate animals, the by-products of poorly understood energies of the earth, murderous and shape-shifting Kelpies, worm-hole traversing nightmares of the type postulated by Ronan Coghlan, the human dead returned to this plane of existence in animalistic form – or, maybe, even a very weird and perplexing combination of each and every one of the above theories - of only one thing can we be really sure: the British Bigfoot most certainly lives. But, to shamelessly commandeer the title of Edward Verrall Lucas and George Morrow's satirical novel of 1911: *What a Life!*

ABOUT NICK REDFERN

Nick Redfern works full-time as an author, lecturer and journalist. He focuses upon a wide range of unsolved mysteries, including the increasingly tedious Roswell affair of 1947, the macabre Men in Black, Bigfoot, UFOs, the Loch Ness Monster, alien encounters, and government conspiracies. He writes for UFO Magazine; Mysterious Universe; Fate; Cryptomundo; and Fortean Times. He also has a regular, weekly, cryptozoology-themed column at Mania.com titled Lair of the Beasts.

His many previous books include *Space Girl Dead on Spaghetti Junction*; *The FBI Files*; *Man-Monkey*; *Monsters of Texas* (co-authored with Ken Gerhard); *Cosmic Crashes*; *Final Events*; *On the Trail of the Saucer Spies*; *Keep Out!*; *There's something in the Woods*; *Strange Secrets* (with Andy Roberts); *Memoirs of a Monster Hunter*; *Science Fiction Secrets*; *The NASA Conspiracies*; *A Covert Agenda*; *Celebrity Secrets*; and *The Real Men in Black*.

Nick has appeared on numerous television shows, including VH1's Legend Hunters; the BBC's Out of this World; Fox News; History Channel's Ancient Aliens, MonsterQuest, America's Book of Secrets; and UFO Hunters; National Geographic Channel's The Truth about UFOs and Paranatural; and SyFy Channel's Proof Positive – in which Nick and the Centre for Fortean Zoology's Jon Downes raced around Puerto Rico in a cool silver-coloured jeep in search of the blood-sucking nightmare known as the Chupacabra.

He lists his favourite 'things' as late 1970s punk-rock and new-wave music, black t-shirts and black jeans, Carlsberg Special Brew, Tennents Super, zombies, chocolate, Family Guy, The Walking Dead, Night of the Demon, Terrorvision, the works of Jack Kerouac, the novels of Carlos Ruiz Zafon, Rammstein, Motorhead, Abby from NCIS, Oasis, a nice cup of tea with lots of milk and sugar, and burned toast with mountains of margarine. His proudest achievement: he knows all the lyrics to each and every song recorded by the Macc Lads.

Nick can be contacted at http://nickredfernfortean.blogspot.com

BOOKS BY NICK REDFERN

Monsters of Texas (with Ken Gerhard)
Space Girl Dead on Spaghetti Junction
Man-Monkey
A Covert Agenda
The FBI Files
Cosmic Crashes

Strange Secrets (with Andy Roberts)
Three Men Seeking Monsters
Body Snatchers in the Desert
On the Trail of the Saucer Spies
Celebrity Secrets
Memoirs of a Monster Hunter
Science Fiction Secrets
There's something in the Woods
Contactees
The NASA Conspiracies
Final Events
The Real Men in Black
Keep Out!
The Pyramids and the Pentagon
Monster Diary
The World's Weirdest Places

ACKNOWLEDGEMENTS

I know that pretty much just about everyone who writes a book says it, but it still happens to be true all the same. This book could never, ever, have been written without the very generous help of a whole host of fine and varied characters, researchers, witnesses and friends.

First and foremost, I would like to thank good mate Neil Arnold, who truly went above and beyond the call of duty when it came to answering my many questions, supplying me with masses of data from his case-files and his own books, offering his theories and ideas, and providing me with a generous body of images to reproduce in this book – all on the controversial matter of hairy wild men in the British Isles. Then, there is Ronan Coghlan, for entertaining me with, and informing me of, his worm-hole-based theories pertaining to the Sasquatch of these shores – and, quite possibly, of many other shores, too; Andy Roberts, for giving me permission to descend, near-vulture-like, upon his paper on the Big Grey Man of Ben Macdhui, and tear through its contents for whatever I wanted, or needed, to reproduce; Kithra, without whose fine generosity the chapter of this book on Woodwose and Green Men could not have appeared; Richard Freeman, one of my closest friends, and a veritable mine of knowledge when it comes to addressing pretty much anything and everything relative to Bigfoot; Stan Gordon, for permission to reproduce the cover of his excellent book on the Bigfoot-UFO controversy, *Silent Invasion*; Jon Downes, for encouraging me to write *Wild Man!*, for being a good old mucker, and also for publishing the damned thing too!; Jon's dear wife, Corinna, for her excellent work aboard the good ship CFZ; Micah Hanks, for letting me present for you his paper on Bigfoot and high-strangeness; and, of course, each and every one of the many and varied witnesses that were willing to share with me their amazing, thought-provoking, and, at times, utterly chilling, accounts of – what else – the British Bigfoot.

BIBLIOGRAPHY

A History of the Book in Devon, www.devon.gov.uk.

Abbots Bromley Horn Dance, http://www.abbotsbromley.com/horn_dance, 2011.

Aberdeen Press & Journal, December 15, 1925.

Aberdeen Press & Journal, November 30, 1925.

Alexander, Marc, Phantom Britain, Muller, 1975.

Alexandra David-Neel, http://en.wikipedia.org/wiki/Alexandra_David-N%C3%A9el, 2012.

Ancients of Lustleigh Cleave, The, http://www.legendarydartmoor.co.uk/ancients_cleave.htm, November 22, 2007.

Apparitions Foretelling Death, http://www.oldandsold.com/articles31n/lore-19.shtml.

Arment, Chad, Cryptozoology: Science & Speculation, Coachwhip Publications, 2004.

Arnold, Neil, Monster! The A-Z of Zooform Phenomena, CFZ Press, 2007.

Arnold, Neil, Notes from Norfolk, http://forteanzoology.blogspot.com/2011/02/neil-arnold-notes-from-norfolk.html, February 22, 2011.

Arnold, Neil, Paranormal Kent, The History Press, 2011.

Arnold, Neil, Shadows in the Sky, The History Press, 2012.

Arnold, Neil, Stig of the Dump and its Crypto-Connections, http://forteanzoology.blogspot.com/2010/12/neil-arnold-stig-of-dump-and-its-crypto.html, December 21, 2010.

Arnold, Neil, The Mystery Animals of the British Isles: Kent, CFZ Press, 2009.

Arnold, Neil, The Mystery Animals of the British Isles: London, CFZ Press, 2011.

Arnold, Neil, The Phantom Ape-Man, http://forteanzoology.blogspot.com/2010/01/neil-arnold-phantom-ape-man.html, January 4, 2010.

Arnold, Neil, The Warrington Man-Beast! http://zooform.blogspot.com/2011/08/warrington-man-beast.html, August 19, 2011.

'"Baboon like" animal hunt', http://www.guardian.co.uk/uk/1999/jan/18/4, January 17, 1999.

Baly, E. C. C., Obituaries of the Fellows of the Royal Society, 1942.

'Barbaric' Attack on Moor Sheep, http://news.bbc.co.uk/2/hi/uk_news/england/devon/5129858.stm, June 29, 2006.

Barnes, Wally, Ghosts, Mysteries and Legends of Old Warrington, Owl Books, 1990.

'Bear sighting in Suffolk woods was "promotional" hoax staged by theatre group', http://www.dailymail.co.uk/news/article-1165868/Bear-sighting-Suffolk-woods-promotional-hoax-staged-theatre-group.html, Daily Mail, March 31, 2009.

Beast of Brassknocker Hill: (England), http://www.americanmonsters.com/site/2010/11/beast-of-brassknocker-hill-england/, November 28, 2010.

Beer, Trevor, Mystery Animals of Britain and Ireland, Robert Hale, Ltd., 1987.

'Ben Macdhui Spectre, The', The Cairngorm Club Journal, vol. 11, July 1926.

Benjamin, R.W., Beaman Monster, http://www.unknown-creatures.com/beaman-monster.html.

Bernheimer, Richard, Wild Men in the Middle Ages, Harvard University Press, 1952.

'Bigfoot Almost Made me Lose my Baby', Chase Post, March 23, 2006.

'Bigfoot or Big Cat – Frenzy Continues', Chase Post, February 22, 2006.

'Bigfoot Sighting on Cannock Chase', Sunday Mercury, September 2, 2008.

Bord, Janet & Colin, Alien Animals, Granada, 1980.

Bottlebush Down,
http://www.ghosts.org.uk/ghost/3255/haunted/road/bottlebush-down/cranborne.html, 2012.

Brandon, Jim, The Rebirth of Pan, Firebird Press, 1983.

Brewer, E. Cobham, The Dictionary of Phrase and Fable, Henry Altemus Publishers, 1898.

BRINDLEY, James (1716-1772), http://www.aim25.ac.uk/cgi-
bin/vcdf/detail?coll_id=18658&inst_id=118&nv1=browse&nv2=sub, 2008.

Brown, Theo, Devon Ghosts, Jarrold, 1982.

Brown, Theo. The Fate of the Dead, Folklore Society Mistletoe Series, 1979.

Brown, Theo & Dorothy, Family Holidays Around Dartmoor, Devonshire Association for the Advancement of Science, 1995.

Budden, Albert, Electric UFOs, Blandford, 1998.

Burne, Charlotte & Jackson, Georgina, F. Shropshire Folklore, F. Jackson, Trubner, 1883.

Campbell, Charlie, REDBRIDGE: 'Bigfoot' Spotted Again,
http://www.guardian-series.co.uk/news/rbnews/3854320.REDBRIDGE___Bigfoot__
spotted_again/?action=complain&cid=7356589 November 17, 2008.

Canning, John, Fifty Great Ghost Stories, Random House, 1988.

Cannock Chase German War Cemetery,
http://en.wikipedia.org/wiki/Cannock_Chase_German_war_cemetery, 2012.

Cannock Chase History, http://www.cannockchasehistory.org.uk/, 2012.

Cannock Chase Murders, http://en.wikipedia.org/wiki/Cannock_Chase_murders, 2012.

Carew Castle – Pembrokeshire, Wales,
http://www.medieval-castle.com/haunted_castles_wales/carew_castle.htm, 2011.

Castle Ring (Staffordshire), http://www.megalithic.co.uk/article.php?sid=4982, 2012.

Chartley Castle, http://www.castleuk.net/castle_lists_midlands/128/chartleycastle.htm, 2012.

Child's Ercall, http://en.wikipedia.org/wiki/Child%27s_Ercall, 2012.

Chippindale, Christopher, Stonehenge Complete, Thames & Hudson, 2004.

Chronicon Anglicanum, 1200.

Chorvinsky, Mark, et al, 'The Search for the Thunderbird Photo', Strange Magazine, no. 19, Spring 1998, p. 26-28.

Churston Woods, http://www.hiddenrealms.org.uk/churstonwoodsvigil.html, 2012.

Collie, J.N., "Dreams", Cairngorm Club Journal, vol. 15, p 214.

Cook, Michael. 'Road Story', Northern Earth, no. 74 (Summer 1998) p. 24.

Cooper, Rob, 'Where is the Wolfman? Hunt for wild man who has been hiding in a Welsh forest for FIVE YEARS', Daily Mail, February 10, 2012.

Cope, Tabitca, The Wodewose, the origin of Bigfoot?
http://cryptozoo-oscity.blogspot.com/2012/02/wodewose-origin-of-bigfoot.htmlFebruary 27, 2012.

Courtney, Margaret Ann, Cornish Feasts and Folklore, Beare & Son, 1890.

Crumley, Jim, Gulfs of Blue Air, Mainstream, 1997.

Crumley, Jim, The Heart of the Cairngorms, Colin Baxter Photography, 1997.

Cunningham, Gary & Coghlan, Ronan, The Mystery Animals of Ireland, CFZ Press, 2010.

Dahl, R., The Mildenhall Treasure, Jonathan Cape, 1999.

Dash, Mike, A British Bigfoot? http://blogs.forteana.org/node/65, February 11, 2009.

Dash, Mike, The Monster of Glamis, http://blogs.forteana.org/node/75, June 9, 2009.

Death Line, http://en.wikipedia.org/wiki/Death_Line, 2012.

Devereux, Paul, Places of Power, Blandford, 1990.

Downes, Jonathan, Man Beasts and Beast Men, Encounters, No. 3, 1996.

Downes, Jonathan, Monster Hunter, CFZ Press, 2004.

Downes, Jonathan, Return of the Shug Monkey,
   http://forteanzoology.blogspot.com/2009/03/return-of-Shug Monkey.html, March 30, 2009.

Downes, Jonathan, The Hunt for the 'Bolam Beast',
   http://www.cfz.org.uk/expeditions/03bolam/index.htm, January 2003.

Downes, Jonathan, The Owlman and Others, Jonathan Downes, CFZ Press, 2006.

Drummond, Allan, Wild Man of Orford, Jardine Press, 2002.

Dundonald Castle, http://www.dundonaldcastle.org.uk/, 2012.

Fraser, Mark, Dundonald Hill Beast,
   http://homepage.ntlworld.com/chris.mullins/DUNDONALD%20HILL%20BEAST.htm.

Edinburgh New Philosophical Journal, 1831.

'Face of the "Wolfman" of Pantyffynnon tips', South Wales Guardian, February 7, 2012.

Faire, The Phantom Horseman of Bottlebush Down,
   http://fairweatherlewis.wordpress.com/2010/05/18/the-phantom-horseman-of-bottlebrush-
   down/, May 18, 2010.

Fanthorpe, Lionel & Fanthorpe, Patricia, The Big Book of Mysteries, Dundurn Group, 2010.

Fiskerton Phantom, http://en.wikipedia.org/wiki/Fiskerton_Phantom, 2011.

Folklore, Myths and Legends of Britain, The Reader's Digest Association, Ltd, 1973.

Franek Kluski, http://en.wikipedia.org/wiki/Franek_Kluski, 2012.

Freeman, Richard, Orang-Pendek: Sumatra's Forgotten Ape, CFZ Press, 2011.

Gable, Andrew D., A trip to Lock 49, http://masksofmesingw.blogspot.com/2009/11/trip-to-lock-
   49.html, November 13, 2009.

Gerhard, Ken & Redfern, Nick, Monsters of Texas, CFZ Press, 2010.

Ghostly Guide, http://www.waterscape.com/canals-and-rivers/shropshire-union-canal/ghostly-
   guide, 2012.

Gibbons, Gavin, They Rode in Space Ships, Citadel Press, 1957.

Gifford, T. 'The Unseen Hands', Daily Mail, October 17, 1921.

Ginger Beast of Beckermet,
   http://www.mysteriousbritain.co.uk/england/cumbria/cryptozoology/ginger-beast-of-
   beckermet.html.

Glacial Boulder, Cannock Chase, http://www.geograph.org.uk/photo/57546, 2012.

Glamis Castle, http://www.glamis-castle.co.uk/, 2012.

Godfrey, Linda S., Hunting the American Werewolf, Trails Media Group, 2006.

Godfrey, Linda S. Real Wolfmen, Tarcher, 2012.

Godfrey, Linda S., The Beast of Bray Road, Prairie Oak Press, 2003.

Godfrey, Linda S., The Michigan Dogman, Unexplained Publishing Research LLC, 2010.

Godfrey, Linda S., Werewolves: Mysteries, Legends, and Unexplained Phenomena, Checkmark
   Books, 2008.

Gooch, Stan, Creatures from Inner Space, Rider & Co., 1984.

Gooch, Stan, The Dream Culture of the Neanderthals, Inner Traditions, 2006.

Gooch, Stan, The Neanderthal Legacy, Inner Traditions, 2008.

Gordon, Seton, Highways and Byways of the Central Highlands, MacMillan, 1949.

Gordon, Stan: Silent Invasion: The Pennsylvania UFO-Bigfoot Casebook, Stan Gordon
   Productions, 2010.

Gorilla: Food and Foraging, http://en.wikipedia.org/wiki/Gorilla#Food_and_foraging, 2012.

Grant, Joan, Far Memory, Corgi, 1975.

Graves, Tom, Needles Of Stone Revisited, Gothic Image, 1986.

Grisales, Carolina Manosca, Men and Apes,
    http://www.forteantimes.com/strangedays/ghostwatch/5710/men_and_apes.html.
'Group's Spooky Findings', Birmingham Post, February 15, 2006.
Guide to the W. Y. (Walter Yeeling) Evans-Wentz Papers , 1894-1961,
    http://www.oac.cdlib.org/findaid/ark:/13030/tf900006xp/, 2009.
Hall, George, 'Leaves From a Rambler's Diary', Cairngorm Club Journal, Vol. X. No. 56,
    January 1921, p.86.
Hallowell, Mike, Cleadon BHM, http://forteanzoology.blogspot.com/2009/12/mike-hallowell-
    cleadon-bhm.html, December 10, 2009.
Hallowell, Mike, 'Is there a hairy humanoid in the hills?' Jarrow & Hebburn Gazette,
    http://www.jarrowandhebburngazette.com/community/columnists/wraithscape/is-there-a-
    hairy-humanoid-in-the-hills-1-4326022, March 8, 2012.
Hanks, Micah, Bigfoot is an Archetype: Sasquatch Reigns Supreme among 'Folk Devils',
    http://gralienreport.com/cryptozoology/bigfoot-is-an-archetype-sasquatch-reigns-supreme-
    among-folk-devils/, March 8, 2012.
Hanks, Micah, Magic, Mysticism and the Molecule: The Search for Sentient Intelligence From
    Other Worlds , CreateSpace, 2010.
Harpur, Merrily, Mystery Big Cats, Heart of Albion Press, 2006.
Harpur, Merrily, 'The ABC X-Files', Fortean Times, No. 278, October 2011.
Harris, Paul, 'The Green Children of Woolpit', Fortean Studies, No.4, John Brown Publishing,
    1998.
Hastie, Jack, 'Big Grey Man - The Evidence', Scottish Mountaineering Club Journal, 1998, p.
    507-513.
Hillman, James, Pan and the Nightmare, Spring Publications, 2007.
Hippisley Coxe, A.D., The Cannibals of Clovelly, Bideford Community College, 1982.
Holdstock, Robert, Lavondyss, Victor Gollancz, Ltd., 1988.
Holdstock, Robert, Mythago Wood, Grafton Books, 1986.
Holland, Richard, Wild Men of the Woods, http://www.uncannyuk.com/235/wild-men-of-the-
    woods/, May 9, 2008.
Holiday, F.W., The Dragon and the Disc, Sidgwick & Jackson, 1973.
Holiday, F.W, The Goblin Universe, Llewellyn Publications, 1986.
Holiday, F.W., The Great Orm of Loch Ness, Faber, 1968.
Honey Island Swamp Monster, http://en.wikipedia.org/wiki/Honey_Island_Swamp_monster,
    2012.
Hope, Robert Charles. The Legendary Lore of the Holy Wells of England, Including Rivers,
    Lakes, Fountains and Springs, Elliot Stock Books, 1893.
Hopkins, R. Thurston, Adventures With Phantoms, Quality Press, 1946.
'Hunt for Dark Forces at Chase Monument', Chase Post, June 8, 2005.
Hypochromic anaemia, http://en.wikipedia.org/wiki/Hypochromic_anemia, 2012
Imperial Gazetteer of England and Wales,
    http://en.wikipedia.org/wiki/Imperial_Gazetteer_of_England_and_Wales, 2012.
Jeffrey, Martin, 'The Big Hairy Encounter', Mystery Magazine,
    http://homepage.ntlworld.com/chris.mullins/DERBYSHIRE%20BHM.htm, February 1998.
Jones, Richard, Haunted Castles of Britain and Ireland, Barnes & Noble Books, 2003.
Keel, John. The Mothman Prophecies, Tor Books, 2001.
Keel, John, Visitors from Space, Panther, 1976.
Kelpie, http://www.mysteriousbritain.co.uk/scotland/folklore/kelpie.html.
Kelpies and water-horses,
    http://www.educationscotland.gov.uk/scotlandsculture/lochness/kelpies/introduction.asp.

King, Clive, Stig of the Dump, Penguin Books Ltd., 2010.

Kithra, The Woodwose and the Green Man, http://www.kithra.com/woodwosegreenman.html, September 2011.

Konungs skuggsja, http://en.wikipedia.org/wiki/Konungs_skuggsj%C3%A1, 2012.

Lanugo, http://en.wikipedia.org/wiki/Lanugo, 2012.

Lewis, Oll, The big hairy man of Nant Gwynant, http://forteanzoology.blogspot.com/2009/05/oll-lewis-big-hairy-man-of-nant-gwynant.html, May 16, 2009.

'Little Known History of the Hill,' Lichfield Post, January 15, 2010.

Lloyd, Andy, 'Hoaxers' horror at Bolam beast', Newcastle Evening Chronicle, February 3, 2003.

London Underground Ghosts – British Museum Station, http://www.ghost-story.co.uk/stories/londonundergoundghostsbritishmuseumstation.html, 2010.

Lowe, Keith, Tunnel Vision, MTV Books, 2001.

Lucas, Edward Verrall & Morrow, George, What a Life! Methuen & Co., 1911.

MacManus, Dermot, Middle Kingdom, Colin Smythe, 1980.

Maidstone Zoo (Sir Garrard Tyrwhitt-Drake) in United Kingdom, http://www.elephant.se/location2.php?location_id=1031, 2012.

Marchioness Townshend of Raynham & Ffoulkes, Maude, True Ghost Stories, Konecky & Konecky, 2009.

Marrs, Jim, PSI Spies, New Page Books, 2007.

Martin, Tom, The Tay Bridge Disaster, http://taybridgedisaster.co.uk/.

Mastin, Luke, The Enigma of the Green Man, http://www.greenmanenigma.com/index.html, 2011.

Matthews, Marcus, Big Cats Loose in Britain, CFZ Press, 2007.

McCaskill's Myths, http://news.bbc.co.uk/2/shared/spl/hi/programmes/morning_show/html/myths.stm, 2012.

McGowan, Rennie, Magic Mountains, Mainstream, 1996.

Meindel, Raven, 'Knock, Knock' Bridge, http://moonshadowinvestigations.blogspot.com/2009/03/knock-knock-bridge.html, March 17, 2009.

Mirrors bought to cut deer deaths, http://news.bbc.co.uk/2/hi/uk_news/england/staffordshire/6917597.stm, July 26, 2007.

Monkey Business at a road junction, the origin of 'Monkey's Jump', http://darkdorset.blogspot.com/1997/04/monkey-buisness-at-road-junction-origin.html, April 30, 1997.

Monkey Business Jokers, The, http://www.expressandstar.com/latest/2007/05/10/the-monkey-business-jokers/, May 10, 2007.

Monkey Hanger, http://en.wikipedia.org/wiki/Monkey_hanger, 2012.

Monkey Island, http://monkeyisland.co.uk/live/history, 2012.

Monkey Island, Bray, http://en.wikipedia.org/wiki/Monkey_Island,_Bray, 2011.

Monkton Combe, http://en.wikipedia.org/wiki/Monkton_Combe, 2011.

Monster of Glamis, http://en.wikipedia.org/wiki/Monster_of_Glamis, 2012.

Moor Sheep Killed by Occultists, http://news.bbc.co.uk/2/hi/uk_news/england/devon/4357188.stm, October 19, 2005.

'Mountain Climbers and the "ghost" of Ben Macdhui', Aberdeen Press & Journal, December 12, 1925.

Murray, Alexander S., Who's Who in Mythology, Studio Editions, 1992.

Murray, W.H., Mountaineering in Scotland, Dent, 1947.

Nine Ladies, http://en.wikipedia.org/wiki/Nine_Ladies, 2012.

North, Mark & Newland, Robert, Dark Dorset, Oakmagic Publications, 2002.

O'Donnell, Elliott, Animal Ghosts: Or Animal Hauntings and the Hereafter, Kessinger Publishing, 2003.

O'Donnell, Elliott, Scottish Ghost Stories, Nabu Press, 2010.

O'Donnell, Elliott, Werewolves, Kessinger Publishing, 2003.

Owen, Elias, Welsh Folk-lore, Benedicition Classics, 2011.

Paul Devereux speaking at the Rollright Stones: Part 1, The Dragon Project, http://www.megalithic.co.uk/mm/book/devereux1trans.htm, 2011.

'Paranormal Team Report UFO Activity', Chase Post, September 21, 2005.

Phenomena, August 2009.

Phillips, Graham & Keatman, Martin, The Eye of Fire, C.W. Daniel, 1986.

Police get caught up in spot of monkey business, http://www.heraldscotland.com/sport/spl/aberdeen/police-get-caught-up-in-spot-of-monkey-business-1.309867, January 18, 1999.

Ranton Abbey, http://en.wikipedia.org/wiki/Ranton_Abbey, 2012.

Redfern, Nick, About Those Sasquatch Structures, http://www.cryptomundo.com/cryptotourism/sasquatch-structures/, April 13, 2012.

Redfern, Nick, An Interview with Mark North on 'Dark Dorset', http://monsterusa.blogspot.com/2007/08/interview-with-mark-north-on-dark.html, August 1, 2007.

Redfern, Nick, 'In Search of the British Bigfoot', Fate, July 2005.

Redfern, Nick, Man-Monkey, CFZ Press, 2007.

Redfern, Nick, Memoirs of a Monster Hunter, New Page Books, 2007.

Redfern, Nick, Monster Diary, Anomalist Books, 2012.

Redfern, Nick, On the Trail of the Saucer Spies, Anomalist Books, 2006.

Redfern, Nick, The Beast of Brassknocker Hill, http://manbeastuk.blogspot.com/2008/04/beast-of-brassknocker-hill.html, April 17, 2008.

Redfern, Nick, 'The Cryptozoological Aspects of the George Edalji Affair', The CFZ Yearbook, 2011, CFZ Press, 2011.

Redfern, Nick, The Doctor's Menagerie, http://www.mania.com/doctors-menagerie_article_115352.html, May 30, 2009.

Redfern, Nick, There's something in the Woods, Anomalist Books, 2008.

Redfern, Nick & Bott, Irene, Man-Monkeys and Big Cats, Chase Post, August 31, 2000.

Rennie, J.A., Romantic Strathspey, Robert Hale, 1956.

Rhodes, Peter, Night Terror with a British Bigfoot, Express & Star, January 11, 2003.

Roberts, Andy, Cat Flaps! Northern Mystery Cats, CFZ Press, 2007.

Roberts, Andy, 'The Big Grey Man of Ben Macdhui and Other Mountain Panics,' Strangely Strange but Oddly Normal, CFZ Press, 2010.

Roberts, John, Exploring Cannock Chase, self-published, 2003.

Rollright Stones, The, http://www.rollrightstones.co.uk/index.php/stones/, 2011.

Ross, Dr. Helen, Behaviour and Perception in Strange Environments, George Allen & Unwin, 1974.

Royal Western Counties Hospital Starcross, http://www.nationalarchives.gov.uk/A2A/records.aspx?cat=027-5916f&cid=-1#-1, 2012.

Ryan, V., The Tay Bridge Disaster, http://www.technologystudent.com/struct1/taybrd1.htm, 2009.

Salisbury Plain, http://www.mod.uk/DefenceInternet/AboutDefence/WhatWeDo/Defence EstateandEnvironment/AccessRecreation/SouthWest/SalisburyPlain.htm, 2011.

Salisbury Plain Training Area, The, http://www.eng-h.gov.uk/archrev/rev95_6/salisbry.htm, 2011.

Salkeld, Luke, 'Lost middle class tribe's "secret" eco-village spotted in aerial photograph taken by plane', Daily Mail, September 17, 2008.

Sheldrake's Aldershot & Sandhurst Military Gazette, December 8, 1878.

Shepherd, Nan, The Living Mountain, Aberdeen University Press, 1981.

Shugborough History, http://www.shugborough.org.uk/theshugboroughestate/EstateHistory.aspx, 2012.

Shuker, Karl, A Devil of a Mystery from Smethwick, http://karlshuker.blogspot.com/2010/09/devil-of-mystery-from-smethwick.html, September 4, 2010.

Shuker, Karl, Karl Shuker's Alien Zoo, CFZ Press, 2010.

Sikes, Wirt, British Goblins, Charles River Books, 1976.

Squire, Charles, Celtic Myth and Legend, Newcastle Publishing Co. Inc., 1975.

Slitting Mill, http://en.wikipedia.org/wiki/Slitting_Mill, 2011.

'Some Thing in the Woods', Nottingham Evening Post, November 28, 2002.

Staff Reporter, Where Did All the Doctor's Pets Go?, Chase Post, May 3, 2006.

Strangest Pubs in Britain: Seeing is Believing, The, written and published by Strangest Books, 2002.

Swire, Otta F., Skye: The Island and its Legends, Blackie, 1961.

Tewnion, Alex, 'A Shot in the Mist', The Scots Magazine, 1958, p 227.

Torness Trows – An Eyewitness Account, The, http://www.orkneyjar.com/folklore/trows/hoytrow.htm, 2012.

Torphins BHM, Hominid: Scottish Bigfoot Encounter, http://homepage.ntlworld.com/chris.mullins/SCOTTISH%20BHM.htm, 2004.

Townsend, Chris, Walking the Munros and Tops, Mainstream, Edinburgh, 1997.

Trubshaw, Bob (Editor), Explore Phantom Black Dogs, Heart of Albion Press, 2005.

Tweedsmuir, Rt. Hon. Lord, 'Pan', Scottish Mountaineering Club Journal, vol. 22, April 1939, no. 127. p. 41-43.

Vinci, Leo, Pan: Great God of Nature, Neptune Press, 1993.

Warren, Joshua P., Pet Ghosts, New Page Books, 2006.

Warren, Larry & Robbins, Peter, Left at East Gate, Marlowe & Company, 1997.

Watson, Adam, The Cairngorms, Scottish Mountaineering Trust, 1992.

Weller, Philip, The Hound of the Baskervilles – Hunting the Dartmoor Legend, Devon Books,, 2001.

Wild Man of Orford, The, http://www.orfordmuseum.org.uk/panel4.html, 2012.

Wilkes, David, 'Police launch hunt for "Wolfman behind mini crimewave who lives on rabbits and berries in woods', Daily Mail, April 29, 2009.

Williams, Michael, Supernatural Dartmoor, Bossiney Books, 2003.

Willis, Ronald J. 'Ben Macdhui - the Haunted Mountain', Info Journal, no. 15, May, 1975, p. 5.

Wolfman, http://www.southwalesguardian.co.uk/search/?search=wolfman&topic_id=2078.

'Wolfman of Pantyffynnon can't be living here', This is South Wales, May 4, 2012.

Worthington, Andy, Stonehenge: Celebration and Subversion, Alternative Albion, 2004.

THE WORLD'S WEIRDEST PUBLISHING COMPANY

HOW TO START A PUBLISHING EMPIRE

Unlike most mainstream publishers, we have a non-commercial remit, and our mission statement claims that "we publish books because they deserve to be published, not because we think that we can make money out of them". Our motto is the Latin Tag *Pro bona causa facimus* (we do it for good reason), a slogan taken from a children's book *The Case of the Silver Egg* by the late Desmond Skirrow.

WIKIPEDIA: "The first book published was in 1988. *Take this Brother may it Serve you Well* was a guide to *Beatles* bootlegs by Jonathan Downes. It sold quite well, but was hampered by very poor production values, being photocopied, and held together by a plastic clip binder. In 1988 A5 clip binders were hard to get hold of, so the publishers took A4 binders and cut them in half with a hacksaw. It now reaches surprisingly high prices second hand.

The production quality improved slightly over the years, and after 1999 all the books produced were ringbound with laminated colour covers. In 2004, however, they signed an agreement with Lightning Source, and all books are now produced perfect bound, with full colour covers."

Until 2010 all our books, the majority of which are/were on the subject of mystery animals and allied disciplines, were published by `CFZ Press`, the publishing arm of the Centre for Fortean Zoology (CFZ), and we urged our readers and followers to draw a discreet veil over the books that we published that were completely off topic to the CFZ.

However, in 2010 we decided that enough was enough and launched a second imprint, `Fortean Words` which aims to cover a wide range of non animal-related esoteric subjects. Other imprints will be launched as and when we feel like it, however the basic ethos of the company remains the same: Our job is to publish books and magazines that we feel are worth publishing, whether or not they are going to sell. Money is, after all - as my dear old Mama once told me - a rather vulgar subject, and she would be rolling in her grave if she thought that her eldest son was somehow in `trade`.

Luckily, so far our tastes have turned out not to be that rarified after all, and we have sold far more books than anyone ever thought that we would, so there is a moral in there somewhere...

Jon Downes,
Woolsery, North Devon
July 2010

CFZ PRESS

Other Books in Print

Sea Serpent Carcasses - Scotland from the Stronsa Monster to Loch Ness by Glen Vaudrey
CFZ Yearbook 2012 edited by Jon and Corinna Downes
ORANG PENDEK: Sumatra's Forgotten Ape by Richard Freeman
THE MYSTERY ANIMALS OF THE BRITISH ISLES: London by Neil Arnold
CFZ EXPEDITION REPORT: India 2010 by Richard Freeman *et al*
The Cryptid Creatures of Florida by Scott Marlow
Dead of Night by Lee Walker
The Mystery Animals of the British Isles: The Northern Isles by Glen Vaudrey
THE MYSTERY ANIMALS OF THE BRTISH ISLES: Gloucestershire and Worcestershire
by Paul Williams
When Bigfoot Attacks by Michael Newton
Weird Waters – The Mystery Animals of Scandinavia: Lake and Sea Monsters by Lars Thomas
The Inhumanoids by Barton Nunnelly
Monstrum! A Wizard's Tale by Tony "Doc" Shiels
CFZ Yearbook 2011 edited by Jonathan Downes
Karl Shuker's Alien Zoo by Shuker, Dr Karl P.N
Tetrapod Zoology Book One by Naish, Dr Darren
The Mystery Animals of Ireland by Gary Cunningham and Ronan Coghlan
Monsters of Texas by Gerhard, Ken
The Great Yokai Encyclopaedia by Freeman, Richard
NEW HORIZONS: Animals & Men issues 16-20 Collected Editions Vol. 4 by Downes, Jonathan
A Daintree Diary -
Tales from Travels to the Daintree Rainforest in tropical north Queensland, Australia by Portman, Carl
Strangely Strange but Oddly Normal by Roberts, Andy
Centre for Fortean Zoology Yearbook 2010 by Downes, Jonathan
Predator Deathmatch by Molloy, Nick
Star Steeds and other Dreams by Shuker, Karl
CHINA: A Yellow Peril? by Muirhead, Richard
Mystery Animals of the British Isles: The Western Isles by Vaudrey, Glen
Giant Snakes - Unravelling the coils of mystery by Newton, Michael
Mystery Animals of the British Isles: Kent by Arnold, Neil
Centre for Fortean Zoology Yearbook 2009 by Downes, Jonathan

CFZ EXPEDITION REPORT: Russia 2008 by Richard Freeman *et al*, Shuker, Karl (fwd)

Dinosaurs and other Prehistoric Animals on Stamps - A Worldwide catalogue by Shuker, Karl P. N

Dr Shuker's Casebook by Shuker, Karl P.N

The Island of Paradise - chupacabra UFO crash retrievals,
and accelerated evolution on the island of Puerto Rico by Downes, Jonathan

The Mystery Animals of the British Isles: Northumberland and Tyneside by Hallowell, Michael J

Centre for Fortean Zoology Yearbook 1997 by Downes, Jonathan (Ed)

Centre for Fortean Zoology Yearbook 2002 by Downes, Jonathan (Ed)

Centre for Fortean Zoology Yearbook 2000/1 by Downes, Jonathan (Ed)

Centre for Fortean Zoology Yearbook 1998 by Downes, Jonathan (Ed)

Centre for Fortean Zoology Yearbook 2003 by Downes, Jonathan (Ed)

In the wake of Bernard Heuvelmans by Woodley, Michael A

CFZ EXPEDITION REPORT: Guyana 2007 by Richard Freeman *et al*, Shuker, Karl (fwd)

Centre for Fortean Zoology Yearbook 1999 by Downes, Jonathan (Ed)

Big Cats in Britain Yearbook 2008 by Fraser, Mark (Ed)

Centre for Fortean Zoology Yearbook 1996 by Downes, Jonathan (Ed)

THE CALL OF THE WILD - Animals & Men issues 11-15

Collected Editions Vol. 3 by Downes, Jonathan (ed)

Ethna's Journal by Downes, C N

Centre for Fortean Zoology Yearbook 2008 by Downes, J (Ed)

DARK DORSET -Calendar Custome by Newland, Robert J

Extraordinary Animals Revisited by Shuker, Karl

MAN-MONKEY - In Search of the British Bigfoot by Redfern, Nick

Dark Dorset Tales of Mystery, Wonder and Terror by Newland, Robert J and Mark North

Big Cats Loose in Britain by Matthews, Marcus

MONSTER! - The A-Z of Zooform Phenomena by Arnold, Neil

The Centre for Fortean Zoology 2004 Yearbook by Downes, Jonathan (Ed)

The Centre for Fortean Zoology 2007 Yearbook by Downes, Jonathan (Ed)

CAT FLAPS! Northern Mystery Cats by Roberts, Andy

Big Cats in Britain Yearbook 2007 by Fraser, Mark (Ed)

BIG BIRD! - Modern sightings of Flying Monsters by Gerhard, Ken

THE NUMBER OF THE BEAST - Animals & Men issues 6-10

Collected Editions Vol. 1 by Downes, Jonathan (Ed)

IN THE BEGINNING - Animals & Men issues 1-5 Collected Editions Vol. 1 by Downes, Jonathan

STRENGTH THROUGH KOI - They saved Hitler's Koi and other stories by Downes, Jonathan

The Smaller Mystery Carnivores of the Westcountry by Downes, Jonathan

CFZ EXPEDITION REPORT: Gambia 2006 by Richard Freeman *et al*, Shuker, Karl (fwd)

The Owlman and Others by Jonathan Downes

The Blackdown Mystery by Downes, Jonathan

Big Cats in Britain Yearbook 2006 by Fraser, Mark (Ed)

Fragrant Harbours - Distant Rivers by Downes, John T

Only Fools and Goatsuckers by Downes, Jonathan

Monster of the Mere by Jonathan Downes

Dragons:More than a Myth by Freeman, Richard Alan

Granfer's Bible Stories by Downes, John Tweddell

Monster Hunter by Downes, Jonathan

CFZ Classics is a new venture for us. There are many seminal works that are either unavailable today, or not available with the production values which we would like to see. So, following the old adage that if you want to get something done do it yourself, this is exactly what we have done.

Desiderius Erasmus Roterodamus (b. October 18th 1466, d. July 2nd 1536) said: "When I have a little money, I buy books; and if I have any left, I buy food and clothes," and we are much the same. Only, we are in the lucky position of being able to share our books with the wider world. CFZ Classics is a conduit through which we cannot just re-issue titles which we feel still have much to offer the cryptozoological and Fortean research communities of the 21st Century, but we are adding footnotes, supplementary essays, and other material where we deem it appropriate.

Headhunters of The Amazon by Fritz W Up de Graff (1902)

Fortean Words

The Centre for Fortean Zoology has for several years led the field in Fortean publishing. CFZ Press is the only publishing company specialising in books on monsters and mystery animals. CFZ Press has published more books on this subject than any other company in history and has attracted such well known authors as Andy Roberts, Nick Redfern, Michael Newton, Dr Karl Shuker, Neil Arnold, Dr Darren Naish, Jon Downes, Ken Gerhard and Richard Freeman.

Now CFZ Press are launching a new imprint. Fortean Words is a new line of books dealing with Fortean subjects other than cryptozoology, which is - after all - the subject the CFZ are best known for. Fortean Words is being launched with a spectacular multi-volume series called *Haunted Skies* which covers British UFO sightings between 1940 and 2010. Former policeman John Hanson and his long-suffering partner Dawn Holloway have compiled a peerless library of sighting reports, many that have not been made public before.

Other forthcoming books include a look at the Berwyn Mountains UFO case by renowned Fortean Andy Roberts and a series of books by transatlantic researcher Nick Redfern.

CFZ Press are dedicated to maintaining the fine quality of their works with Fortean Words. New authors tackling new subjects will always be encouraged, and we hope that our books will continue to be as ground breaking and popular as ever.

Haunted Skies Volume One 1940-1959 by John Hanson and Dawn Holloway
Haunted Skies Volume Two 1960-1965 by John Hanson and Dawn Holloway
Haunted Skies Volume Three 1965-1967 by John Hanson and Dawn Holloway
Haunted Skies Volume Four 1968-1971 by John Hanson and Dawn Holloway
Haunted Skies Volume Five 1972-1974 by John Hanson and Dawn Holloway
Haunted Skies Volume Six 1975-1977 by John Hanson and Dawn Holloway
Grave Concerns by Kai Roberts

Police and the Paranormal by Andy Owens
Dead of Night by Lee Walker
Space Girl Dead on Spaghetti Junction - an anthology by Nick Redfern
I Fort the Lore - an anthology by Paul Screeton
UFO Down - the Berwyn Mountains UFO Crash by Andy Roberts
The Grail by Ronan Coghlan
UFO Warminster - Cradle of Contract by Kevin Goodman
Quest for the Hexham Heads by Paul Screeton

Fortean Fiction

Just before Christmas 2011, we launched our third imprint, this time dedicated to - let's see if you guessed it from the title - fictional books with a Fortean or cryptozoological theme. We have published a few fictional books in the past, but now think that because of our rising reputation as publishers of quality Forteana, that a dedicated fiction imprint was the order of the day.

We launched with four titles:

Green Unpleasant Land by Richard Freeman
Left Behind by Harriet Wadham
Dark Ness by Tabitca Cope
Snap by Steven Bredice
Death on Dartmoor by Di Francis
Dark Wear by Tabitca Cope

Ingram Content Group UK Ltd.
Milton Keynes UK
UKHW051120220523
422140UK00008B/332